Trading Options For Dummies®

FOR DUMMIES®
A Wiley Brand

2nd Edition

by Dr. Joe Duarte

FOR DUMMIES®
A Wiley Brand

Trading Options For Dummies®, 2nd Edition

Published by: **John Wiley & Sons, Inc.,** 111 River Street, Hoboken, NJ 07030-5774, www.wiley.com

Published simultaneously in Canada

Library of Congress Control Number: 2014954665

ISBN 978-1-118-98263-1 (pbk); ISBN 978-1-118-98264-8 (ePub); ISBN 978-1-118-98265-5 (PDF)

Manufactured in the United States of America

10 9 8 7 6

Contents at a Glance

Table of Contents

Introduction

Welcome to *Trading Options For Dummies,* 2nd Edition!

This book is about introducing you to option strategies for managing risk and navigating a variety of market conditions. It's geared to managing risk first, with the knowledge that profits will follow. With that in mind, the approaches described focus on reducing potential losses from traditional stock positions and building an option strategy repertoire that allows you to maximize your chances of making sound trades whether the markets are moving up, down, or sideways. To incorporate the comprehensive steps required when trading, it also provides discussions on market and sector analysis, as well as things to look for when trying out a new strategy.

An option contract is a unique security that comes with contract rights and obligations. When used correctly, an option contract strikes a balance between risk of loss, the amount of money you put at risk, and reward, providing you with leverage while still allowing you to reduce overall trade risk. Of course, there's another side to that leverage, increased risk, which will be managed, which is the main reason you should take the time to read through this book carefully. You need to understand the risks and characteristics associated with these contracts.

When applying for options trading with your broker, the broker will send you the reference guide *Characteristics and Risks of Standardized Options.* This publication, written by the Options Clearing Corporation (OCC), must be distributed by brokers to their clients prior to allowing them to trade options. It describes option contract specifications, mechanics, and the risks associated with the security. Together, that publication and the one you're reading right now help you to understand your risks and use options effectively.

About This Book

There are hundreds of trading titles out there, including those focusing on option strategies. This book focuses primarily on approaches aimed at managing risk — the consistent theme throughout. By setting it up this way, you can read about different topics while keeping that key objective in mind. So go ahead, jump around to areas that interest you most.

This book can be read from cover to cover or used as a reference guide. Each strategy provided identifies risks and rewards associated with the position. It also identifies alternative strategies to consider for risk management, when applicable. There are a million ways to successfully trade the markets, but certain challenges are universal to all of them. Tools and techniques focused on addressing these challenges are also provided throughout.

To make reading and understanding the world of options trading a bit easier, we've used some conventions to help you along the way:

- *Italics:* We provide newly defined terms in italics in all parts and chapters.
- **Acronyms:** We try to spell out acronyms quite a bit so you don't have to flip around a bunch to find out what VIS (very important strategy) stands for — we hate when we have to do that, too.
- **Glossary:** You'll find an online glossary of option trading terms at `www.dummies.com/extras/tradingoptions` so you can find the definitions that you need fast.
- **Websites**: You'll find references to websites that may provide additional information or make a task easier (like the one in the preceding bullet). And if you ever see a website split from one line to the next, rest assured that we've added no extra hyphens, so type the site in your browser just as it appears. If you're reading the e-book, just tap the link to go to that website.

Foolish Assumptions

Here's what we assume about you:

- **You have some experience.** We are all dummies, but we are not all beginners. If you've chosen this book, you doubtless have some familiarity with the stock market and the risks and rewards it presents to you. As a self-directed investor, you seek ways to manage those risks and rewards. However, if you're not familiar at all with options or you've just had a little exposure to them, don't worry — option fundamentals and mechanics are covered here and may be a great way to improve your knowledge base. Even if you have traded these instruments before, you can consider this a review if you're looking for one.

- **You've read investing books before and you will read this section carefully at some point in order to avoid pitfalls and misunderstandings as you go through this book**. We assume that you know that this book won't have all the answers to your trading needs but you also know that it was written in a careful and thoughtful way, including technical reviews and careful editing. You also know that as a second edition, the editing team has taken previous material and scrupulously revised it in order to both update and improve the content as needed.
- **You hold longer-term investments.** Regardless of whether or not you choose to actively trade options, we assume you hold longer-term investments such as stocks and mutual funds. For that reason, core strategies aimed at managing risk associated with longer-term holdings are included. The small amount of time needed to implement them may be well worth it.
- **You've already decided how to allocate your investment and trading dollars.** Although we distinguish investment assets from trading assets, we don't address how to allocate those dollars because everyone's financial situation is different. We do assume this is something you've already completed, because plans should strike a balance between the two (long term and short term) to grow assets.
- **You have computer and Internet access.** We can't imagine trading or investing without a computer and reliable access to the Internet . . . so we assume you have both.
- **You use a broker.** We assume you contact a broker to further manage your risk when needed, and we assume you also have a comfort level with your broker's web platform. It may serve as a resource for some of the ideas covered in this book.

Icons Used in This Book

To supplement the topics discussed in *Trading Options For Dummies,* 2nd Edition, we've also added icons to highlight different core ideas and give you some hard-earned trading insight. We use the following icons to point out these insights:

When encountering this icon, you'll find slightly more detail-oriented tools and considerations for the topic at hand, but the information included with icons isn't necessary to your understanding of the topic at hand.

This icon is used to give you experienced insight to the current discussion. Consider these to be asides that any trader might mention to you along the way.

Some topics previously discussed or assumed to be part of your base knowledge are identified by the Remember icon. If you hesitate for a moment when reading the core content, check for one of these to keep you progressing smoothly.

Concepts that reiterate ways to manage potential risks appear with this icon. It highlights important things to watch out for if you want avoid trouble.

Beyond the Book

In addition to the material in the print or e-book you're reading right now, this product also comes with some access-anywhere goodies on the Web. Check out the free Cheat Sheet at `www.dummies.com/cheatsheet/tradingoptions` for helpful summaries of trading order types, charts for tracking investments, how financial indexes are constructed, and ways in which changing stock affects indexes.

This book also includes some free articles — which are kind of "extra" mini-chapters. Go to `www.dummies.com/extras/tradingoptions` if you want to check these out.

Where to Go from Here

Whether you're seeking to improve longer-term investing or shorter-term trading results, you will find strategies aimed at both goals in this book. By using the techniques in the book and viewing yourself as a risk manager, your losses should decrease allowing you to move forward to increased profits.

You may decide to pick up this reference while evaluating your investments on a quarterly basis or keep it handy at your desk for weekly trading assessments. During your regular review routine, you may also find that current market conditions that once kept you on the sidelines are now ideal for strategies you reviewed here.

Ready to go? You have lots of options ahead. (Get it?)

If you've recently been perplexed with action in the markets, you may want to start with Chapter 5. It identifies different things happening in the options markets that may clarify stock market activity.

Those new to trading options or who feel you can benefit from a refresher, should consider perusing Part I. Because the markets are ever-evolving, Chapter 3 gets you up to speed on current conditions.

If you have a basic handle on option contracts and want to quickly access unique ways to capitalize on different stock movement, consider jumping to Part IV. This part includes a variety of approaches you just can't match with stocks.

Chapter 18 provides my thoughts on what it takes to be a successful option trader. Because trading options comes with many of the same challenges encountered when trading any security, you may want to make it the first thing you read to help you succeed with your current trading.

Part I
Getting Started

getting started with

Trading Options

web extras

Visit www.dummies.com for Great Dummies content online.

In this part . . .

- An overview of options contracts
- Rights and obligations of buyers and sellers
- Trading securities on the exchanges
- Risks and rewards of contracts

Chapter 1

Options Trading and the Individual Investor

In This Chapter

- Getting to appreciate options
- Analyzing options with any market in mind
- Making the markets work for you

Whatever your level of experience, your general tendency to trade or hold positions for a long time, and your risk profile, as an individual investor you can add options on individual stocks, indexes, and exchange traded mutual funds (ETFs) to your investment war chest. You should do so with two goals in mind: risk management and growing your assets. And because there are so many ways to use options, just about anyone can use them — as long as you take the time to learn the associated risks and rewards and become familiar with the particular strategies that suit your purposes.

There is a difference between trading and investing, especially in terms of time frames. *Investing* is all about using the power of time and the benefits of compounding to build wealth over long periods. The traditional *buy and hold* strategy for stocks is a perfect example, as is the owning of rental properties for long periods to generate income.

Trading is by design a shorter-term proposition, where you may hold a position for minutes, hours, days, or weeks. Options can be used for both trading over the short term and the protection of longer-term investments, especially during times when the value of the longer-term holdings declines. No matter your time frame — whether you hold positions for short or long periods — your goal is essentially the same. You want to have more money at some point in the future than what you have now and increase your wealth using opportunities provided by the markets. This chapter is all about giving you the big picture on options and setting the stage for the more detailed chapters that follow.

Taking Your Own Financial and Strategic Pulse

Before you start any kind of trading or investing program, it's a good idea to know three things:

- Your risk profile
- Your financial situation
- Your time commitment possibilities

Any time you add a new trading strategy, only one thing is certain: the early stages will be challenging and will require a fair amount of your attention, or you will lose money, often in a hurry.

As you prepare to become an options trader, here are some simple steps to consider in order giving yourself a good start. Even if you are experienced in other forms of investing, or have experience with options, you should still stop and consider the following:

- **Check your financial balance sheet.** Before you start trading, go over your living expenses, review your life and health insurances, and put together a financial net worth statement. Make sure it's healthy before you take extraordinary risks.
- **Set realistic goals.** Don't trade beyond your experience levels, and don't risk too much money in any one trade.
- **Know your willingness to take risks.** If you are a cautious person who thinks that mutual funds are risky, you may not be a good options trader. But you shouldn't count yourself out either. There are many options strategies that could suit you, especially once you understand the built-in safety nets that make some of them really decrease your risk. Just make sure you read through the book and find the ones that make you comfortable before you jump in. The chapters in Part IV have excellent information on this topic.
- **Become a good analyst.** If you like to roll the dice without doing your homework, you could get in trouble with options pretty rapidly. In order to maximize your chances of trading options successfully, place a high priority on improving your technical and fundamental analysis skills. You should do this both for the entire market and for the underlying securities that are the basis for your options.
- **Don't be afraid to test your strategies before deploying them.** Doing some paper trading on options strategies before you take real-life risks is a good idea. Chapter 7 guides you through this process.

- **Never trade with money that you aren't willing to lose**. Even though options are risk-management vehicles, you can still lose money trading them. And as you progress to more sophisticated and riskier strategies, your losses could be significant. Bottom line: Don't trade options with your car payment or your rent money.

Understanding Options

Options are financial instruments that are priced based on the value of another underlying asset or financial measure. In this book, the focus is mainly on options with value based on stocks and stock market indexes, although there is also a very useful section on options based on exchange traded mutual funds (ETFs).

There are two kinds of options — *calls* and *puts*. When you add them to your current investing and trading tools and strategies, you can participate in both *bullish* (rising markets) and *bearish* (falling markets) moves in either underlying you select. You can use options to limit your total portfolio risk or to protect an individual existing position, such as a stock or ETF.

In the options market, it's acceptable to call the security that an option is based on the *underlying*. You will see that terminology used in this chapter and throughout the book. If you're going to trade options, you have to get used to the lingo.

To fully understand and use stock and index options to limit risk or as a standalone trading strategy, you must also have a thorough understanding of the asset on which they're based. This understanding is likely to require another layer of analysis beyond your current approach. Because volatility is a key component of option prices, for example, you will have to look at the underlying's volatility more carefully as part of your analysis in order to pick the best possible option for your particular strategy.

This book will help you by focusing on techniques that compare options to their underlying security or other securities. Chapter 9 goes into detail on several approaches that you can apply toward this goal when you analyze stocks and index options.

Contrary to what many in the mainstream may believe, your primary focus for trading any security is not to learn about how to profit from its use, but to understand the risks associated with its use, including all of the following:

- Knowing what conditions, both in the markets and in the individual security, to consider when analyzing a trade
- Using proper trade mechanics when creating a position

- Recognizing, understanding, and following trading rules and requirements for the security
- Understanding what individual variables make any position gain and lose value

The sections that follow address these key components of options trading to give you a good platform for creating rewarding positions and cutting any losses before they become catastrophic.

Knowing option essentials

A *listed* stock option is a contractual agreement between two parties with standard terms. All listed options contracts are governed by the same rules. When you create a new position, one of two things is triggered:

- By buying an option, you are buying a specific set of rights
- By selling an option, you are acquiring a specific set of obligations

These rights and obligations are standard and are guaranteed by the Option Clearing Corporation (OCC), so you never have to worry about who's on the other end of the agreement. Chapter 3 provides more information and detail on the Options Clearing Corporation and its central role in options trading.

Time means everything to option traders. The one particular wrinkle in options, and the primary risk involved, is *time risk*, because options contracts have a limited lifespan. The price of a call option rises when its underlying stock goes up. But if the move in the stock is too late, because it happens too close to the expiration date, the call can expire worthless. You can literally buy yourself more time, though — some options have expiration periods as late as 9 months to 2 1/2 years.

When you own call options, your rights allow you to

- Buy a specific quantity of the underlying stock (exercise).
- Buy the stock by a certain date (expiration).
- Buy the specific quantity of stock at a specified price (known as the *strike price*).

In other words, the price of the call option rises when the stock price goes up because the price of the rights you bought through the option is fixed while the stock itself is increasing in value.

Conversely, a put option gains value when its underlying stock moves down in price, while the timing issue is the same. The move in price still has to occur before the option contract expires or your option will expire worthless. Your put contract rights include selling a specific quantity of stock by a certain date at a specified price. If you own the rights to sell a stock at $60, but events such as bad news about the company pushes the stock price below $60, those rights become more valuable.

A significant part of your skill as an options trader is your ability to select options with expiration dates that allow time for the anticipated moves to occur. This may sound too challenging at the moment, but as you learn more, it will make perfect sense because it's all about giving yourself time and giving the option time to deliver on your expectations. Of course, there are some basic trading rules of thumb that help, including the development of proper trade-management techniques, such as planning your exit from a position before you trade. Planning your exit is a simple but required part of any trade, and it is one good habit that will save you money and heartache if a position moves against you.

All stocks with derived options available for trading have multiple expiration dates and strike prices. There are two important pricing factors to keep in mind:

- Options with more time until the expiration date are more expensive.
- Options with more attractive strike prices are more expensive.

Information about options and your available choices are widely available on the Internet, especially from your broker. It takes time and practice to get to a point where you can pick the best options based on current market conditions and your outlook for the underlying asset. But as you read the different sections in this book, you will start to get a good feeling for how to go about this. Even more important is how you manage your emotions and how you gain trading discipline. This is best achieved by developing a maximally effective trading plan with easy-to-follow rules that includes planning for different scenarios. For more on this, see Chapter 8.

Trying different strategies before deploying them in real time

Options are different from stocks both in terms of what they represent — leverage, rights, and obligations instead of partial ownership of a company — and how they're created, by demand. These important distinctions result in the need for additional trading and decision-making beyond the basic buy or sell considerations. Part of the learning process, as you transition from direct stock trading to options trading, is developing a new and complementary way of thinking. That includes not just evaluating the price of a stock or an index, but also how the price of the underlying asset along with other factors, such as supply and demand for the option and overall market conditions involved in options prices all come together. Your final decision, as the trade develops, may be to exercise your rights under the contract or simply exit the position in the market. Fortunately, market prices will help you with those decisions, and so will some thoughts from Chapters 9 and 18.

If you haven't traded options in the past, your best approach (as we already mentioned) is to try out some trading strategies on paper and see how things work out. Your goal here is simple: You want to get to the point where you think of your option trades based not just on the option but on the underlying security.

Before you invest real money, you should be able to do the following:

- Gain a comfortable feel for the activity and characteristics of underlying stocks or indexes on which you are looking to trade options and understand their relationship both to the market and to the options related to them.
- To be able to mix and match sound strategies to particular market situations while keeping the preceding principles in mind.

Are these extra complications worth it? For many people, the answer is yes — especially when you consider the combined risk reduction and profit potential those options trading offers. And even though making the transition may sound difficult, the actual differences in stock and option mechanics are pretty straightforward and manageable. At the end of the day, the big advantage to options is the way they provide you with leverage while giving you a mechanism to control the rights to the stock rather than the stock itself.

An important aspect of this mental reshaping exercise involves paying special attention to how the real market action affects the value of options over time. Once you get this part of the puzzle locked in, the rest will fall into place more easily, and your paper trading will be more satisfying. Along with paper trading, you can also backtest options trading. And don't worry about how long this learning process may take. Any time spent on decreasing your risk of big losses in the future is well spent.

TIP: Widely available options trading and technical analysis programs let you backtest your strategies. Some brokerage houses offer sophisticated analytical packages to their active traders for low prices or for free. *Backtesting* means that you review how a set of strategies has worked in the past.

Paper trading and backtesting an options-based trading approach may take a little more time than a stock approach. The advantage is that it could save you a lot of money. Consider paper trading as part of your trading plan. And even though it may slow down your pace, and possibly delay your getting started in real-time trading, this type of studious approach will let you address different option trading nuances in advance, and will get you in the habit of being a disciplined trader.

Noodling out where options will work for your trading

There is a time and a place for everything. And options are used best when deployed optimally — meaning when the risk reward ratio offers you the best mix of both profit potential as well as risk reduction.

When you buy an option contract, you have two choices: You can exercise your rights, or you can trade your rights away based on current market conditions and your trading objectives. You can do either one based on what is happening in the markets or to any individual position at the particular time and by executing the best strategy for what the situation calls for. The most important thing is that you know what your choices are before making the trade because you have planned for either situation.

You can use options to reduce your risk by hedging a particular position or by hedging your whole portfolio. If your analysis of the situation makes you so bearish that you are looking to capitalize from a falling market, options are a much less expensive and uncomplicated way of selling individual stocks short. Chapter 10 is all about portfolio protection.

Options also let you leverage your positions. Because options cost less than stocks, you can participate in a market for less than if you owned the actual shares. This is an excellent way to reduce risk, as you are spending less capital but potentially getting a similar rate of return to what you might receive if you owned the actual underlying stock, depending on your position size. You can apply this leverage even more astutely if you are speculating and are willing to cap your profits.

Differentiating Between Option Styles

This book is mostly about options on individual stocks. But index options are also an important part of the market, which may be of interest and use to you at some point in your trading life. The most important fact at this point is to understand the major differences between options on indexes and individual stocks. Here are some important general facts:

- You can trade stocks but you can't trade indexes.
- The dates for exercise (of your option rights) and the last trading date for the option are the same for individual stocks, meaning that they fall on the same date. These two important dates can be variable for index stocks, meaning that you may be able to trade the option on a different day than the exercise date.
- There are two types of options: American and European style. Each has its own particular set of characteristics that will affect your ability to make decisions about exercise. Always know which style option you are using and the particular factors associated with it before you trade. Chapter 9 is all about option styles.

Using options to limit your risk

Getting the details of option risk profiles is important and will be useful. But actually devising and using strategies in trading is even better. You start by evaluating the many options that are available for asset protection. And although, you may not think that is sexy, spending the time up front to figure out what options work better than others in different situations isn't only a good step in your learning process, it's also practical. When using options to limit your risk:

- You can reduce risk for an existing position partially or fully and adjust the hedging process gradually based on changing market conditions. See Chapter 10.
- You can reduce risk for a new position to a very small amount by using a combination of options or by using single long-term options. See Chapter 12.

You will need a margin account for these strategies, and you can get one by filling out and signing the margin account agreement that you obtain from your broker. These are complex strategies that you can work toward as you gain experience. Some of these more complex strategies include

- Vertical debit spreads
- Vertical credit spreads
- Calendar spreads
- Diagonal spreads

The most influential factor on when to use these spreads will be market conditions. And this book will help you make those decisions.

Applying options to sector investing

One of the best recent advances in the financial markets has been the creation and proliferation of ETFs. Through these vehicles, you can make sector bets without having to drop down to the individual stock level of decision-making or research beyond some basic steps. ETFs are great trading vehicles because

- **You can trade them like stocks.** That means you can buy and sell shares in them at any time during the trading day instead of waiting until the market closes, as with non-exchange traded traditional mutual funds.
- **ETFs offer listed options.** That means you can apply all option strategies to sectors of the stock market by trading options on the underlying ETF. This often lets you make index bets without using index options with expiration and last day of trading may cause you some extra steps.
- **There are ETFs based on commodity indexes.** These let you participate in commodity markets without trading futures. When you add the extra dimension of options being available, you have a nice array of different strategies available.

ETFs are an excellent trading vehicle category, for all those reasons and more. You can design entire diversified portfolios with ETFs and then use options to hedge individual positions or the entire portfolio. Chapter 13 gives you all the details.

Using Options In Challenging Markets

You can participate in rising or falling markets through stocks and ETFs, assuming that you are comfortable with both owning these securities and selling them short. But what do you do in a sideways market, except maybe sitting it out or collecting a few dividends? You can craft option strategies for sideways markets whether you have any underlying positions or not. Chapter 16 tells you all about this great set of strategies.

Reducing your directional bias and making money in flat markets

Directional bias refers to the connection of profits to the direction of prices. To make money when you are long, you need prices to rise. And to make money when you're short, you need falling prices. When you use option combination strategies, you design trades that let you make money when the underlying stock moves up or down. Consider this:

- You can set up strategies that let you profit if the underlying rises or falls, depending on your trade setup. Chapters 14 and 15 tell you all about these trades.
- Options let you set up strategies that can make money in sideways markets.

Controlling your emotions

Perhaps the most difficult part of trading any market is the emotional responses that can be triggered by price movements in things you own, or wish you owned. Let's face it, we are all emotional. It's part of being human. The problem is that emotional trading is usually the path to big losses. That's why we have rules and why you design an anticipatory trading plan, in order to control the emotion that goes along with trading.

A good trading plan has these key characteristics:

- **Access to the proper equipment:** Make sure you have all the technology you need: computers, mobile devices, and backup systems along with a quiet place to work.
- **Knowledge of time commitment:** Think about whether you will day trade or be a longer time position trader. If you can't devote a couple or three hours at a time to monitor a position, day trading is not for you.
- **Access to good information:** Put together a good list of websites and a reliable real-time quote-charting service.
- **Flawless trade execution:** Pick an online broker that has some scale and can execute your trades in a timely fashion without leaving you in the cold.
- **An excellent educational component:** Work on your analytical skills, technical and fundamental, every day. You need to be a crack chartist and hone your decision-making skills.

Each chapter is this book reveals new information that is intended to make it easier to appreciate and execute the end game, the successful trading of options. Chapter 2 is all about the different types of options.

Chapter 2

Introducing Options

In This Chapter

- Making sense of an option contract
- Discovering an option's value
- Getting reliable option data
- Starting out in options trading

There are many forms of options, but this book spends most of its time on listed stock options and listed index options, both of which trade on exchanges. These two distinct types of options function in two ways. First, they can be used to manage your risk by limiting your losses. And they offer you the opportunity for profits when used with the right strategy.

As silly as it may sound, to make the most out of options trading, it's imperative that you really understand what options are and know the risks and potential rewards associated with them. That's why this chapter details the information on the individual components of an option and how to recognize them in the market.

Understanding Option Contracts

By learning the basics of options contracts and then being able to compare them to other derivatives, you will be able to get a good working understanding of these securities and how to best use them both for risk reduction and for speculative gains. The next few sections are all about the basic concepts that will get you to a comfortable point in trading options and then lead to a good understanding of the risks and rewards associated with options trading.

Grasping option basics

A *financial option* is a contractual agreement between two parties. Although some option contracts are *over the counter*, meaning they are between two parties without going through an exchange, this book is about standardized contracts known as *listed options* that trade on exchanges. Option contracts give the owner rights and the seller obligations. Here are the key definitions and details:

- **Call option:** A call option gives the owner (seller) the right (obligation) to buy (sell) a specific number of shares of the underlying stock at a specific price by a predetermined date. A call option gives you the opportunity to profit from price gains in the underlying stock at a fraction of the cost of owning the stock.
- **Put option:** Put options give the owner (seller) the right (obligation) to sell (buy) a specific number of shares of the underlying stock at a specific price by a specific date. If you own put options on a stock that you own, and the price of the stock is falling, the put option is gaining in value, thus offsetting the losses on the stock and giving you an opportunity to make decisions about your stock ownership without panicking.
- **Rights of the owner of an options contract:** A call option gives the owner the right to buy a specific number of shares of stock at a predetermined price. A put option gives its owner the right to sell a specific number of shares of stock at a predetermined price.
- **Obligations of an options seller:** Sellers of call options have the obligation to sell a specific number of shares of the underlying stock at a predetermined price. Sellers of put options have the obligation to buy a specific amount of stock at a predetermined price.

In order to maximize your use of options, for both risk management and trading profits, make sure you understand the concepts put forth in each section fully before moving on. Focus on the option, consider how you might use it, and gauge the risk and reward associated with the option and the strategy. If you keep these factors in mind as you study each section, the concepts will be much easier to use as you move on to real time trading.

Use stock options for the following objectives:

- To benefit from upside moves for less money
- To profit from downside moves in stocks without the risk of short selling
- To protect an individual stock position or an entire portfolio during periods of falling prices and market downturns

Always be aware of the risks of trading options. Here are two key concepts:

- **Option contracts have a limited life.** Each contract has an expiration date. That means if the move you anticipate is close to the expiration date, you will lose our entire initial investment. You can figure out how these things happen by paper trading before you do it in real time. You can read more about paper trading in Chapter 7. Paper trading lets you try different options for the underlying stock, accomplishing two things. One is that you can see what happens in real time. Seeing what happens, in turn, lets you figure out how to pick the best option and how to manage the position.
- **The wrong strategy can lead to disastrous results.** If you take more risk than necessary, you will limit your rewards and expose yourself to unlimited losses. This is the same thing that would happen if you sold stocks short, which would defeat the purpose of trading options. Options and specific option strategies let you accomplish the same thing as selling stocks short (profiting from a decrease in prices of the underlying asset) at a fraction of the cost. Chapters 9–11 give you details on how you can profit from falling markets through options.

Comparing options to other securities

Options are a form of *derivative*, a type of security that *derives* its value from an underlying security. Stock options derive their value from the underlying stock. In order to better understand option valuations, it makes sense to know more about other derivatives and exchange traded mutual funds (ETFs), which are quasi-derivatives:

- **Commodities and futures contracts:** Like options, commodity and futures contracts are agreements between two parties. The major difference between a commodity or futures contract and an options contract is that the former obligates you, whereas an options contract gives you rights as an owner. This is because commodities and futures contacts set the price for a predetermined quantity of a physical item to be delivered to a particular location on a predetermined date. Options have no delivery date. On the other hand, commodities and futures contracts are similar to options in that they lock in the price and quantity of an asset. However, in both cases, you can trade away your rights and obligations if you exit the contract before expiration.
- **Indexes:** Think of *indexes* as collections of assets whose value is pooled together to measure the price of the group. Stocks, commodities, and futures are all index components. Chapter 9 covers index options in

detail. Here is the important difference: Indexes are not securities. That means you can't buy an index directly. Instead, you buy securities that track the value of the index, such as mutual funds that own the stocks in a particular index — for example, Standard & Poor's 500 Index.

- **Exchange traded funds (ETFs):** ETFs are mutual funds that trade like stocks on an exchange. Most ETFs are designed to track an index or an underlying sector of a particular market. ETFs can be considered quasi-derivatives because they don't always hold the exact same securities of the index that they track. For example, some *leveraged* ETFs use more exotic securities known as swaps to mimic the action of the underlying index while adding leverage. Two of the most popular ETFs are the S & P 500 SPDR (SPY) and the Powershares QQQ Trust (QQQ), which tracks the Nasdaq 100 index. These two popular ETFs let you trade their underlying indexes, directly or through options.
- **Stocks and bonds:** Stock ownership gives you part of a company, whereas bond ownership makes you a debt holder. Each dynamic has its own set of risks and rewards. Comparison of the three assets, stocks, bonds, and options, yields a fairly straightforward picture. All three asset classes can lead investors to total loss of their investment. And though stocks give you a piece of the company, and bonds offer you income, options offer you no ownership of any tangible assets. Stocks offer indefinite holding periods, and bonds have a maturity date and options have a limited life.

A *swap* is an insurance contract whose terms are privately agreed upon by the participants. They can be thought of as non-exchange traded options and they can be used to bet on the direction of just about anything that the two parties agree upon. By design, swaps are very sophisticated securities that are not available to individual investors because of the financial requirements and the specific agreements required to be signed before you trade them. When you own shares in a leveraged ETF, check the prospectus carefully to see if this is what you are buying. We're not suggesting that you don't consider leveraged ETFs if they make sense for your portfolio. We use them often in our personal trading. It's important for you to always know what you are investing in, even if it's an indirect investment such as an ETF.

When swaps get out of control, the markets can suffer. This is what happened in 2008 as lots of big money players bet (correctly) that subprime mortgage holders would not be able to make their monthly mortgage payments. They were right, and the rest, as they say, is history.

Valuing Options

Part of knowing your risks and rewards results from understanding how an investment derives its value and what affects the rise and fall in its price. In order to value an option, you must know the following:

- The type of option (put or call)
- The market value of the underlying security
- The characteristics of the past trading pattern of the underlying security calm or volatile
- The time remaining until the option expires

Knowing your rights and obligations as an options trader

There are two types of options: calls and puts. By owning a call you have the right to buy a certain stock at a pre-specified price by a certain date. Owning a put give you the right to sell a certain stock at a specific price by a certain date. Put option prices go up when the price of the underlying security falls. Call option prices rise when the underlying security's price rises. When you own options, you can assert your rights at your own discretion. So, between the time you buy an option and its expiration date, you can

- Sell the option for a profit.
- Sell it for a loss.
- Exercise it.
- Let it expire with no value (for a loss).

As an option seller, you are obligated to complete a specific set of requirements. In fact, selling options gives you fewer choices, and the actionable choices are heavily influenced by the action in the markets. As the expiration date nears, you can

- Buy the option back for a profit.
- Buy it back for a loss.
- Let the option expire with no value (for a profit).

An easy memory trick to help you keep your rights and obligations in the correct framework is to think about buying the stock as *calling* it back while selling the option as *putting* the stock to someone.

Terms of endearment and importance

Here are key terms you have to nail down in order to make good option trading decisions:

- **Underlying security:** The stock that you buy or sell and that determines the value of the option.
- **Strike price:** The price you would pay if you decided to exercise your rights as an option buyer.
- **Expiration date:** The date the option and your rights disappear.
- **Option package:** The number of shares and the name of the underlying security that you can call away or put to someone.
- **Market quote:** The most current price of a security that is being bid on by buyers and offered by sellers of options.
- **Multiplier:** The number used to determine the value of the option and how much money you pay when you call away or put options to someone.
- **Premium:** The total value of the option you buy or sell. The premium is based on the market quote for the option and its multiplier.

Option rights don't last forever, so it's important to keep track of how much time you've got left in a position before it expires. To figure out how much time you've got until the expiration date, identify the expiration date and determine the number of days or months away that date is.

Making Sense of Options Mechanics

Good decisions are only as good as the information you have and how well you understand it. So, whether you trade options without ever considering owning the underlying stock or otherwise, you will need the best data possible in order to assess their value and develop your strategies. Just as important is knowing the basic structure of how options quotes work and how the expiration cycle operates. This section is about deciphering the information you will require to understand your rights and obligations when trading options.

You can gather option market information online, often free of charge, if you are willing to deal with delayed data — typically lagging by 15–20 minutes. A good premium charting service, or your broker's online trading platform, will usually have excellent real-time data at your finger tips as well. Yahoo! Finance (`www.finance.yahoo.com`) is a good free site for all kinds of quotes and financial information. You can also find excellent options information at Optionetics (`www.optionetics.com`).

Identifying options

Although not all stocks have options, those that do feature multiple strike prices and expiration dates. The list of options for a stock is also known as the *option chain*. When you look through a stock's option chain you see all the calls and puts available, along with specific data for each listing, including the following:

- **Open interest:** The number of existing contracts for this option
- **Market quotes:** May be delayed or in real time, depending on your data source
- **Recent trading levels:** Current or delayed

Option symbols have been standardized and radically changed since the first edition of this book. The old "root" nomenclature methodology that made it difficult to sometimes identify options for Nasdaq listed stocks with four letter symbols was replaced by the new Options Clearing Corporation (OCC) system. The new symbol system is much easier to decipher and has several components:

- The underlying stock or ETF's symbol
- The expiration date, expressed in six digits using the *mmddyy* format
- The option type, P for put, C for call
- The strike price × 1000

Mini options are a different type of option. These options are based on smaller amounts of the underlying. They afford you rights and obligations for 10 shares of stock instead of the standard 100 shares feature the number 7 at the end of the symbol to distinguish them from standard listed options. Mini options are aimed at investors who have smaller positions but who want to reduce their risks based on the smaller number of shares in their possession.

Here is an example of the symbol for an Apple Inc. (Nasdaq: AAPL) 76.43 call option that expires on June 13, 2014:

AAPL061314C00076.430

For a mini option of the same underlying stock, expiration date, and striking price, the symbol would be:

AAPL7061314C00076.430

Turning with the expiration cycle

There are three expiration cycles, as listed in Table 2-1. All options feature at least four expiration dates throughout the year based on one of these cycles. Some listed options, such as those linked to important index tracking ETFs, have expiration dates every month. Long-term options (Long-term Equity Anticipation securities, or LEAPs) also have monthly expiration dates.

Expiration dates are important because as time passes and expiration nears, options lose value. So, in order to manage positions in the best fashion, knowledge of the expiration dates is central.

All options have at least four monthly expiration dates available at all times. Each option features at least the current month and the following month expiration dates. For example, an option that runs with the January cycle also has a February expiration date while the next expiration will be in April, its normal cycle month. This option would also have July available, making four months of expiration dates available for trading. When January expires, February is the near month, so March options become available, along with April and July options. When February expires, October options then come online making four months of expiration dates and rounding out the cycle. The cycle repeats as the near month expires.

Table 2-1 Option Expirations by Cycle

Cycle	*Months*
I	January, April, July, October
II	February, May, August, November
III	March, June, September, December

When you add LEAPs and mini options to the mix, the number of expiration dates can become confusing. Before you trade, make sure you are very clear on what you are trading and how much time the option has before it expires. Also pay attention to whether you have the type of option, call or put, that you suits your trading objective.

Option strike prices are generally available in increments of 0.50, $1, $2.50, and can be as high as $10, depending on the price of the underlying stock. There are exceptions to this general tendency, which becomes especially noticeable after pricey stocks split. That was the case with Apple in June 2014, which is why the strike price in the earlier example was peculiar. Most of the time, this is not the case.

Options expiration is decision time

If you have an open option position, you should have a good idea about what you will do with it well before it expires. Here are your choices:

- **Taking advantage of your rights as a contract holder:** This means you are exercising the option. It requires contacting your broker and submitting the exercise instructions. Chapter 9 covers this in detail.
- **Trading out of the option:** This means submitting to your broker the instructions required to exit the position.

Option expiration dates fall on Saturday. Because there is no trading on Saturday, you must deliver your instructions or exit the position on the last trading day before expiration, usually a Friday. This is weird and can cost you money. But rejoice. As of February 2015, a transition to Friday expirations begins.

Here are some key details about expiration dates and how to handle them:

- **Know your last trading day:** There is no stock market trading on Saturday, which has been the traditional last trading day. This won't as be meaningful for options expirations after February 2015, though, when Saturday expirations begin to phase out. Some options, depending on their own particular properties and issue dates, retain the Saturday last trading day date. But over time, they expire, and eventually all options have last trading days on Friday.
- **Keep up with your last exercise day:** The last trading day and the last day to exercise usually fall on the same day. In most cases, you have one hour after the market closes to submit your instructions to your broker. But some brokers may have different rules, thus it's important to check and know this well before you make any trading or exercise plans.

Detailing your rights

When you buy a call option, you are buying the right, but not the obligation, to buy a specified amount of stock at a certain price (strike price) at any time (just about) before the expiration date. This right lets you either exercise your right or trade out of the position.

When you buy a put option, you are buying the right, but not the obligation, to sell a specific amount of stock at a specific price (strike price) at any point in time (just about) up to the option's expiration date. During this defined period of time, you can exercise your rights as an option holder or decide to trade out of the position.

It is quite possible that you may never actually exercise an option, as the option position may be part of an overall trading strategy you have devised. That's the beauty of options, you have rights which give you the choice to act in the way that makes the most sense based on your strategy and market conditions. However, if you decide to exercise an option, here are some advantages:

- **Exercising a call option:** When you exercise a call option, you may benefit from the shareholder rights of the underlying stock. This could mean that you receive cash or a dividend or that you participate in the benefits of other corporate actions such as mergers, acquisitions, and spinoffs.
- **Exercising a put option:** Exercising a put option lets you exit a stock position. This could come in very handy when a company releases bad news after the close of regular trading in the stock market.
- **Exercising either a call or a put option:** This practice may be of help in minimizing commission costs. By selling the option and then buying or selling the stock in the open market, you generate an added commission.

Even though the last bullet sounds confusing, there are times when selling the rights inherent in an option, to buy a stock in the open market, makes sense from a profit and commission savings standpoint. Chapter 9 covers this strategy in detail.

Birthing Option Contracts

There is an important difference between what it takes to issue new shares of stock and how options contracts come to exist. The number of shares available to trade in a particular stock is called the *float*. If there is a need for more stock to be issued, shareholders vote on whether it is sensible or not to do so, and the company goes through a process of registration before the new shares are offered to the public.

It's different with options, where the potential number of contracts possible is limitless because options contracts are offered based on demand. The actual number of existing contracts for any option is known as the *open interest*.

Opening and closing positions

When you enter your order to buy an option, there may or may not be a contract available. But you won't know that since your demand will create a contract if one isn't already available. The important factor is how you enter and exit positions. The type of order you enter will lead to the execution of the trade. Attention to detail is very important, so you need to pay close attention to how you enter your order, and that means specifying whether you are opening a new position or closing an existing one. To buy a call option, you would enter the following order:

Buy to Open, 1 XYZ June 21 35.00 strike call option

To exit the position, you would enter the following order:

Sell to Close, 1 XYZ June 21, 35.00 strike call option

The same type of order format applies to opening a position in an option that you don't own. The important factor is the correct use of language and the specificity of the option you are selling. Use the following to sell an option you don't own:

Sell to Open, 1 XYZ June 27 42.00 strike call option

Buy to Close, 1 XYZ June 27 42.00 strike call option

When you enter your orders correctly, it allows the exchange and the clearing company to keep accurate track of the number of open contracts, which is also known as the *open interest*, and to keep tabs on the number of contracts traded on any given day. The open interest number displayed on options contract quotes has a one-day delay, meaning that today's number is accurate up to the prior day's action.

TIP: If you make a mistake when entering an order, contact your broker immediately. The error should be readily fixable both in your account and at the exchanges.

Selling an option you don't own

When you sell an option as an opening transaction, you are obligated to sell a stock at the strike price at any time until the option expires. During that period, if a call option holder decides to exercise their rights, you may have to meet your obligation. When this happens, it's called *being assigned* the option, and your broker will contact you to inform you about it. When you are assigned on a call option contract, you must weigh two possibilities:

- If you own shares of the underlying stock, you must sell the shares and close the stock position.
- If you don't own the shares of the underlying, and you don't sell the shares, you have created a short position in your account.

The easy part of selling an option that you don't own is putting in your order. The more important part is understanding the risk of the trade. If you own shares when you sell a call option, it is known as a *covered* transaction, because the shares *cover* the short call position. If you don't own the shares when you sell the call, it's called a *naked call*. What makes this strategy most dangerous is that it has the same risk as a stock short position. In other words, *your risk of loss is unlimited*, given the potential of a stock to continue to rise indefinitely.

When you sell a put option as an opening transaction, you are obligated to buy a specified amount of stock at the predetermined strike price at any point until the option expires. You own this obligation from the time you open the transaction until the expiration weekend and you are require to satisfy the obligation if a put option holder decides to exercise their right. Getting assigned on a short put usually happens when the underlying stock has declined. If assigned you will be buying stock at a higher price than the current market value. Your short put transaction can also be covered or naked.

When you sell a put short, you are under obligation to buy shares, so you cover the position with a short stock position in the underlying. Buying the shares closes the short stock position. If you sold a naked put and you are assigned, you will have a new long position in your account.

Selling puts is a tricky transaction, so it takes a little time to figure it out. Here is why:

- When you take on the obligation associated with this transaction, you are no longer making active decisions with regard to the transactions involving the underlying stock.
- The risks associated with the short option transactions are very different, depending on whether you have a covered or naked transaction.

I cover the risk reward ratio of transactions more fully in Chapter 4.

Keeping Some Tips in Mind

You not only want to get off on the right foot when you begin trading options, but you also want to keep both feet firmly grounded throughout the process. The following tips should help:

- **Get approval.** When you want to start trading options, you need to get approval from your broker . . . the Securities & Exchange Commission (SEC) requires it. They need to make sure that trading these securities is appropriate for your financial situation and goals. It's part of the process and means you typically get approved for basic option strategies if you haven't traded them in the past.
- **Be disciplined.** When you enter a trade for a specific reason, such as an earnings announcement, pending economic report or a particular value for an indicator you use, you must exit the trade when conditions change or your original reason for purchasing the security no longer exists. Don't let a stock or option position you intended to hold for three weeks become part of your long-term portfolio. Being disciplined and following your rules is a must for all traders.
- **Keep track of the expiration date.** Many option chains include the actual expiration date for each month along with the option quote data. The expiration date may also be included with your account position information. Knowing when the option expires is critical to managing the position.
- **Practice.** Always remember that you can paper trade a security that is new to you. Although the emotions you experience trading this way don't exactly mimic having real money on the line, it helps you get familiar with new types of securities.

Chapter 3

Trading Places: Where the Action Happens

In This Chapter

- Finding your way around the option markets
- Leveraging your investment while managing risk
- Valuing options with the Greeks
- Looking at the past to gauge the future

Your trading career probably started with the stock market. Because there are plenty of similarities between stocks and options, comparing the two takes advantage of your base knowledge to expand firmly into a new trading environment, so we do that where possible in this book.

Covering options from a trader's standpoint, this chapter provides information about the option exchanges you encounter, the different market participants impacting your transactions, and the market conditions that affect your trades. All these things have some influence on your trading success. The biggest key to success though, is really getting a handle on the factors that come into play when valuing options. With that in mind, we introduce formal option pricing components, known as the *Greeks*.

The U.S. Options Exchanges

There are six option exchanges in the United States, which is pretty amazing for a security that just started trading in the 1970s. Two of these were launched since 2000, and all six offer some form of electronic execution:

- **American Stock Exchange (AMEX):** www.amex.com
- **Boston Options Exchange (BOX):** www.bostonoptions.com

- **Chicago Board Options Exchange (CBOE):** www.cboe.com
- **International Stock Exchange (ISE):** www.ise.com
- **New York Stock Exchange (NYSE/ARCA):** www.nyse.com
- **Philadelphia Stock Exchange (PHLX):** www.phlx.com

TIP

There is common information on the different option exchange Internet sites, along with information specific to the exchange's listings. Each also seems to have a unique strength. We recommend periodically checking these sites for new tools and insights.

Navigating the Markets

This section covers how to navigate the options market, including executing trades, understanding key players in the options game, and recognizing some of the more unique characteristics of options trading.

Trade execution

Entering an order through the Internet on your broker's system triggers an extremely fast series of events:

- The order is routed to one of six exchanges where it gets executed if it satisfies the current market quote or is reflected in the market if it improves the accuracy of the current quote.
- If your order is routed to an exchange with a less favorable market quote, that exchange can either improve its price or send it to the exchange with the best quote because the exchanges are linked electronically.
- If and when your order is executed, a report is sent back to your broker with the trade details. This information appears almost immediately in your account when received by your broker.
- Orders that improve the best market quote are posted quickly on the exchange where it was routed. The order is reflected across all exchanges as the best bid when buying or the best offer (ask) when selling. It remains there until it is executed or a better bid or offer replaces it.

So much of the order process is completed electronically that you can have an execution report in seconds — unless there is a problem, such as an electronic glitch or a problem with the liquidity of the option. Always check the trading volume of your underlying stock and its related options. Generally, less liquid stocks and out-of-the-money (OTM) options have less trading volume than in the money options and high-volume stocks. And your order fill could be potentially slower, although this is a rare phenomenon.

If you are experiencing regular delays, you need to consider what role your Internet connection plays in that problem.

Option market participants

The option market includes market participants similar to the stock market:

- **Brokers:** A broker with a specialized license must approve your account for option trading. Not only does the firm need to protect you, it also needs to protect itself because unlimited risk option positions, such as short naked calls, could expose you both to high losses. Be patient with the approval process and only use trading strategies in which you fully understand the risks associated with a worst-case scenario. If you want to trade options, you need to complete an additional application for each brokerage account you want to include. There are different approval levels for option trading that reflect an increasing amount of risk for the strategies approved. Typically, you can receive approval for basic strategies when starting out.
- Brokers must follow minimum rules and regulations, but can also operate under ones that are stricter. Communicate with your broker to understand key trading items such as margin and maintenance rules, minimum balances for option trading, cutoff times for submitting exercise instructions, and similar issues.
- **Market makers and specialists:** Market makers and specialists are responsible for providing a market for your orders — meaning they're required to take the other side of your trade at the quoted level. You may not always agree with their quotes, but they are key to the exchanges by providing liquidity and assuming risk. They also keep the markets orderly so your orders are handled by price and time priority, even when chaos erupts during buying frenzies and selling panics.
- When trading options, you want to lean toward those contracts that are more actively traded. Doing so allows you to get into and (much more importantly) *out of* the position more easily. You can find the most active options for each exchange on its website.

- **Options Clearing Corporation:** We don't know about you, but when we enter into a financial contract, we want to know a little something about the person on the other side of the agreement. So, if you are a little concerned about who's protecting your option rights, pay attention. The Options Clearing Corporation (OCC) is the clearing firm that guarantees option sellers will meet their obligations. This means when you buy an option contract on an exchange, you don't have to seek out the seller when it's time to exit the position. When you buy an option that trades on multiple exchanges, it has the same terms regardless of whether you bought it on the CBOE, ISE, or any of the six exchanges listed. All of these exchanges clear through the OCC (`www.optionsclearing.com`).
- **Options Industry Council:** The OCC and six option exchanges all participate in an investor education partnership known as the Options Industry Council (OIC). The mission for this organization is to educate the investing public about listed stock options. The OIC website is `www.optionscentral.com` and should definitely be on your list of ones to check out.

Transactions unique to options

Because option contracts are created as needed, there is a unique way to enter option orders. You identify whether you are creating a new position or closing an existing position by including the following with your order:

- Buy to Open
- Sell to Open
- Sell to Close
- Buy to Close

In addition, exercising contract rights create a buy or sell transaction in the underlying stock that goes through the OCC.

The exercise process

You exercise your option contract by submitting exercise instructions to your brokerage by its cutoff time. Check with your brokerage for this information. It usually takes one day for the option exercise and associated stock transaction to appear in your account.

When you exercise a put and do not own the underlying stock in your account, you are creating a short stock position. Be sure you understand all the risks and rewards associated with submitting exercise instructions.

The assignment process

When you sell an option, you are creating a short position on a stock option contract. Thus you are at risk of assignment from the time you create the position through expiration of the contract. The only way you can alleviate yourself of the obligation is to exit the position by entering a Buy to Close order for the option. Basically, when *assigned* you are on the receiving end of the transactional flow:

- When holding a short put, the assigned option is removed from your account, and a Buy transaction occurs for the underlying stock.
- When holding a short call, the assigned option is removed from your account, and a Sell transaction occurs for the underlying stock.

Contact your broker to find out the method the firm uses to assign short options. Almost all use a random selection process.

Trading rules you should know

Whenever you begin trading a new market, you'll likely get some butterflies until the first few trades go off without a hitch. It's always nice when everything unfolds as you expected. That actually requires some advance work on your end. The following short list of trading rules hopefully helps your comfort level with initial executions, as well as considerations down the road:

- **Contract pricing:** Options in general trade in $0.05 and $0.10 increments rather than $0.01 increments as with stocks. The exchanges began trading a pilot group of stocks and ETFs at $0.01 increments in 2007. Additional securities have been added to the program in a trend that will likely continue.
- **Transaction premium:** The premium value that you pay for an option is obtained by multiplying the option price quoted in the market by the option's multiplier. The multiplier value is usually 100 for stock options. So, when you purchase an option quoted at $2.80, you are actually paying $280 for the option, plus commissions.
- **Market conditions:** There are different market conditions that impact both the stock and options markets. These include the following:
    - **Trading halts for a security or entire market:** If you hold options for a halted stock, the options are also halted. You still have the ability to exercise your contract rights when this occurs before expiration. Generally, a trading halt will not restrict your right to exercise at all.

- **Fast trading conditions for a security or securities:** When this happens, you can expect to see quotes that are changing quickly, and you'll likely experience significant delays in order execution and reporting. Unless you must exit a position for risk reasons, we strongly advise against using market orders for options in fast markets.
- **Booked order:** A *booked order* is one that improves the current market quote and updates it. The market maker isn't necessarily willing to take the trade at the quoted level, but another trader is. You may encounter problems with such orders because the size can be as small as one contract. If you enter a ten-contract order that matches the booked order price, you may only be filled on one contract. The rest of your order may or may not be filled.

- **Best-execution:** *Execution quality* is a general term used to describe a broker's ability to provide trade completions at, or better than, the current market for the security. This means that when you place an order to buy an option with an asking quote of $2.00, your order is filled in a timely manner at $2.00 or better. Execution quality reports use the National Best Bid and Offer (NBBO) for all exchanges trading the security. Option exchanges are required to send a daily report to your broker whenever a trade is executed at a price other than the NBBO, referred to as *traded-through*. They must also provide an exception reason for the trade-through. Even with the reporting, you may feel you're not getting the best possible executions on your option trades.

  If you are not satisfied with the execution you receive on a specific order, or if you have an order that was marketable and is still open, contact your broker immediately. The broker can check the status of the order (it may be executed but the trade report is delayed) and market condition details that are more difficult to track as time passes. More often than not, your broker really wants to get you the best execution possible.

SEC execution quality rules

In 2001, the Securities and Exchange Commission (SEC) adopted rules requiring market centers, including brokerage firms, to report on the execution quality and handling of its brokerage operations retail order flow (order flow from you and me). SEC Rule 11ac1-5 and Rule 11ac1-6 are the two primary rules that set the standards for reporting to the public. Option trades were originally excluded from this reporting, but exchanges do need to report any trades not executed at the National Best Bid or Offer (NBBO).

SEC 11ac1-5 provides a monthly report on a variety of speed and execution measurements for all orders (collectively) covered by the rule, which includes covers retail orders for market and marketable limit orders that are received during regular trading hours, and specifically excludes orders with special handling requirements. SEC 11ac1-6 is a quarterly reporting identifying where the brokerage firm sent its covered order flow, along with any material relationships the firm has with that market venue (that is, any payment it receives from an exchange for its orders).

Execution quality reporting focuses on two key elements: how close to the NBBO your order was executed and how long it took. The NBBO measurement is calculated using the *effective to quoted spread* (E/Q%), which is equal to 1.00 or 100% when your order is executed at the midpoint of the NBBO spread. An E/Q% of 98% indicates a trade that was executed at a price better than the NBBO (price improvement), whereas an E/Q% of 105% indicates a trade that was executed at a price that was worse than the NBBO (price disimprovement).

The time for order completion begins when the market center receives your order (the trading department acting as market maker or specialist if your brokerage firm completes that portion of the transaction). The time measurement ends when the order is executed in the marketplace, not when you receive the trade report back via the web or your broker.

The SEC requirements are specific, but there are enough vagaries for firms to highlight their strengths and down play their weaknesses. You may find firms using best-ex reporting (referring to *best exchange*) as part of their marketing campaigns. Because order flow routing information provides summary information rather than specific order details, the results you experience on your order execution may seem vastly different from what you see reported from 1-5, 1-6, or marketing literature.

WARNING!

Because an option eventually expires, you really need to understand option valuations so you don't pay too much for the time remaining. You can manage this time risk by exiting a long option at least 30 days before it expires. Within 30 days, the option's time value erodes at an accelerated pace.

Weighing Option Costs and Benefits

There are benefits to using options, but you don't get those for free. The biggest risk associated with an option is its limited life because an option can expire worthless. You could lose your entire investment. Clearly this is a risk that needs to be addressed, which, of course, we do throughout the book. Two other option cost factors to be considered:

- Costs associated with the trading process
- Cost of future movement for the stock

By understanding the basic cost structure for an option (discussed in the following sections), you can see how options provide leverage at a reduced risk. The extent to which options do this is very powerful.

Option prices are partially based on probabilities. For stock options, you want to consider the likelihood a particular option will be in-the-money at expiration given the type of price movements the underlying stock has experienced in the past.

Identifying costs unique to options

Because options are a little different than other securities, it's important to recognize that they have certain characteristics that make them more expensive than trading more commonly held securities such as stocks. The main costs to consider include the following:

- **Liquidity:** The ease with which you can enter and exit a trade without impacting its price, varies by option. Low liquidity securities are more expensive.
- **Time:** The more time you are purchasing, the greater the cost of the option.
- **Volatility:** Stocks with greater price movement in the past are expected to continue such movement in the future. The more volatile the stock, the more expensive the option.

This section covers the ways each of these items impact your trading costs.

Paying for less liquidity

Although many option contracts are actively traded with high open interest, the sheer number of contracts available to trade means there will also be those that have limited daily volume and open interest levels. This results in a wider spread, which translates to higher costs for you.

The *spread* is the difference between the market bid and the ask. When liquidity is low, the spread widens. *Slippage* is the trading term associated with money lost due to the spread. The best way to think about this cost is if you were to buy on the ask and then immediately turn around and sell the option on the bid, you would have a loss — called slippage.

Lean toward higher open interest contracts with higher volumes when trading options to reduce the impact of slippage costs. These liquid contracts can be more easily entered and exited without widening the spread and increasing your costs.

Compensating for time

All option contracts have a time value associated with them. The more time until the contract expires, the more the option costs. The only problem is, every day you own the contract, time to expiration is decreasing, and so is the option's value associated with it. *Theta* is the measure that provides you with the estimated value lost on a daily basis. The section "Grasping Key Option Pricing Factors" later in this chapter covers theta.

When first reviewing option chains, be sure to compare options that have the same strike price but different expiration months to note the cost of time.

Paying for time means you need to consider options that reasonably reflect potential movement for the underlying. Given the wide range of strike prices and expiration months available to you, this is certainly possible.

Shelling out money for high flyers

Some stocks are more volatile and regularly swing a few percentage points each month, while other, quieter stocks take a few months for those kinds of moves. Generally, the cost of time for an option increases if the stock has proven to be more volatile in the past.

Valuing options benefits

By keeping the rights associated with a particular option type straight, you can often quickly estimate an option's value from the option's strike price and the market price of the stock. Here are the three primary factors for valuing any stock option:

- The type of option, call, or put
- The option strike price
- The price of the underlying stock

Understanding these basic structural valuation features allows you to appreciate the limited risk and unlimited reward potential that options possess. Although we often reiterate the fact that you can lose your entire option investment, you have to compare that to the losses accumulated when owning the underlying stock. By substantially limiting the investment amount through the options market, you also substantially limit risk.

Stock values and option premiums

You need to consider two things when valuing an option:

- The value of the option rights given the current price of the stock
- The potential for stock movement between now and expiration

Option prices are broken into two kinds of value:

- **Intrinsic value:** The value of the contract rights if the contract is exercised and the resulting position is then exited in the market. With a call option, this value is the profits realized if you were to exercise the call and then immediately sell the stock. When these two transactions result in a gain, that gain is the option's intrinsic value. When there's a loss, intrinsic value of the option equals zero. Intrinsic value is calculated differently for calls and puts:
  - Intrinsic Value (Call) = Market price of stock – Option strike price
  - Intrinsic Value (Put) = Option strike price – Market price of stock
- **Extrinsic value:** The remaining value, which is attributable to time, is also known as *time value* because it adds potential value for the option based on future moves for the stock. The extrinsic value is what remains after you account for intrinsic value. To determine the time value for an option contract, subtract the intrinsic value from the option price:
  - Extrinsic Value = Option Price – Intrinsic Value

An option's intrinsic value cannot be less than zero. Whenever the calculation used to determine intrinsic value falls below zero, intrinsic value equals zero.

Option moneyness

Options are said to have a certain *moneyness,* which describes relative information about the intrinsic value of a contract. The calculation for intrinsic value can lead to three different results in terms of moneyness:

- In-the-money (ITM) when Intrinsic Value > 0
- At-the-money (ATM) when Intrinsic Value = 0
- Out-of-the-money (OTM) when Intrinsic Value < 0

These three terms are used regardless of whether an option is a call or a put. Whenever an option is OTM, its market price reflects only time value.

Options that are OTM have only extrinsic value. This is also referred to as time value.

Leverage with reduced risk

The greatest benefit of trading individual options is the type of leverage you access. First, consider leverage with the stock market — when buying on margin, you borrow from your broker to buy stock which gives you the opportunity to own more shares. As you probably know, using leverage this way is a double-edged sword:

- When using leverage to buy stock you reap additional rewards when the stock moves in your favor, *but*
- You also reap additional losses when the stock goes down.

Just because brokers help finance stock transactions doesn't mean they share in the losses — those are all yours. On top of that, you still have to pay the broker's financing fees in the form of margin interest — whether you have a profit or loss.

When you access leverage with an option, you gain control of a certain number of shares of stock through your rights at a cost that is much, much lower than purchasing (or selling) those shares outright. This significantly amplifies gains and losses resulting from the position.

REMEMBER

When using margin to leverage a stock position, both your gains and losses accelerate. Gains must outpace financing costs in the form of margin interest.

An example of leverage with reduced risk

The best way to get a feel for how to leverage with reduced risk is through an example. Using stock ABC trading at $43, assume you purchase 100 shares at this price with a 50% margin position, and the stock moves up to $47 in one month. The value of a $40 strike call option is $4. After the move to $47, the call will be at least $7 because this represents its intrinsic value.

- Option rights (purchase rights) = $40
- Market value (sale price) = $47
- Call intrinsic value: $\$47 - 40 = \$7$

Calculating the returns for the stock using a 50% margin purchase:

- Initial investment: $\$43 \times 100 \times 0.50 = \$2,150$
- Gains: $(\$47 - 43) \times 100 = \$400$
- Gain as percent of initial investment: $\$400 \div 2,150 = 18.6\%$

Calculating the returns for the option:

- Initial investment: $4 × 100 = $400
- Gains: ($7 – 4) × 100 = $300
- Gain as percent of initial investment: $300 ÷ 400 = 75%

Both the stock and option position provide you with leverage. What if the stock dropped $4 instead of moving upward and the option lost all its value? Instead of gains, there would be losses of 18.6% and 100%, respectively.

The real power for the leveraged option position is its limited loss nature. Assume a third scenario: Really bad news is released for the stock and it drops $13 instead.

Calculating the losses for the stock using a 50% margin purchase:

- Initial investment: $43 × 100 × 0.50 = $2,150
- Losses: ($43 – 30) × 100 = ($1,300)
- Loss as percent of initial investment: ($1,300) ÷ 2,150 = (60%)

Calculating the losses for the option:

- Initial investment: $4 × 100 = $400
- Losses: ($4 – 0) × 100 = ($400)
- Loss as percent of initial investment: ($400) ÷ 400 = (100%)

Although the loss percent is higher for the option, it is capped. The losses can continue with the stock position and can even generate margin calls requiring you to deposit additional funds to hold the position.

Grasping Key Option Pricing Factors

Option prices are determined by the type of option (call or put), its strike price, the price of the underlying stock, and the time remaining to expiration. Prices are also determined by the volatility of that underlying stock. It turns out this last pricing component plays a pretty big role in options analysis and strategy selection.

There are option valuation measures available to you that help you determine whether an option price quoted in the market represents a reasonable value or not. The measures provide you with a feel for how decreasing time or changes in the stock's price or volatility impact the option's price. These measures are available for each individual option and are referred to as the option *Greeks,* because most of their names are derived from Greek letters.

Introducing option Greeks

An option's Greeks are individual variables that combine to provide you with the value of expected changes in the option, given changes in the underlying stock. They are derived from one of several option valuation models and are available to you from various sources, such as an option calculator. Most option exchange websites and charting services provide this tool.

Using an option calculator, you enter the price of the underlying stock, the option strike price, time to expiration, and the option quote. The calculator then provides each of the Greek values listed. The insight you gain from the Greeks include the following:

- **Delta:** Represents the expected change in the option value for each $1 change in the price of the underlying stock.
- **Gamma:** Represents the expected change in delta for each $1 change in the price of the underlying stock.
- **Theta:** Represents the option's expected daily decline due to time.
- **Vega:** Represents the expected change in the option value due to changes in volatility expectations for the underlying stock.
- **Rho:** Estimates changes in the option value due to changes in the risk-free interest rate (usually T-bills). Option price changes attributable to interest rates are much smaller, so this last measure receives less coverage.

TIP

Option valuation models can be used to determine whether a particular option is relatively expensive or cheap. A model is best applied when you understand its assumptions and recognize that the Greeks provide expected values that by no means guarantee the future.

Delta

Delta is probably the most important Greek value for you to initially understand because it connects changes in the underlying stock's value directly to changes in the option value. Delta values range from:

- Calls: 0 and 1.00 or 0 and 100
- Puts: 0 and –1.00 or 0 and –100

Gamma

Gamma provides you with the expected change in delta for each $1 change in the price of the underlying stock. By understanding and checking gamma, there's less of a chance that delta values will get away from you.

TIP

The delta for an ATM option is approximately +/–0.50 regardless of the stock's past volatility. Option valuations assume that there's a 50% chance the stock will move up and a 50% chance it will move down.

Assuming ABC is trading at $20 and moves to $21, Table 3-1 provides option data before and after the move for a 20 strike call and put.

Connecting past movement to the future

Past movement in the underlying stock is used to determine the probability that a certain minimum or maximum price will be reached. As you know, past movement doesn't provide you with a map of what's going to happen during the next month, next week, or even next day. But that doesn't mean you can't look at past movement to evaluate the potential for certain price targets to be reached. This section takes a look at two key measures that relate past movement in a stock to movement that is expected in the future.

Table 3-1 Option Values for ABC Call and Put

Type	*Moneyness*	*Value*	*Delta*	*Gamma*
Stock at $20: Call	ATM	$1.10	+0.50	0.1962
Stock at $20: Put	ATM	$1.00	–0.50	0.1931
Stock at $21: Call	ITM	$1.60	+0.70	0.1438
Stock at $21: Put	OTM	$0.50	–0.30	0.1467

Historical volatility

Historical volatility (HV) is a measure of past movement in a stock. It is also referred to as *statistical volatility* (SV). To calculate HV, you must do the following:

1. Calculate the daily price change over a set number of days.
2. Calculate the average value for price change over that period.
3. Determine how each daily price change compares to that average value by taking the standard deviation for the price changes in the set.
4. Divide the value in step 3 by 0.0630 to approximate an annualized standard deviation.

Sorry, but it's next to impossible to avoid statistical lingo when discussing option valuations. Don't get hung up on the math — HV is calculated in this manner so you can make an apples-to-apples comparison of a stock's most recent movement versus its past movement. HV also allows you to compare two different stocks.

Standard deviation measures how dispersed data is from its average value. When applying this measure to stocks, those with a higher HV are expected to make bigger daily moves that are less predictable than those with a smaller HV. Lower HV stocks have daily changes that stay close to the average daily change.

Past stock movement is used as a basis for future expectations. Expected values don't use just this information, though. Each day, news is released that impacts expectations going forward. This is where implied volatility (IV) enters the picture.

Implied volatility

Implied volatility (IV) is one component of an option's price and is related to the time remaining until expiration. On a given day, you can identify as follows:

- Current price for a given stock
- Nature of past movement for the stock
- The type and strike price for a particular option
- The number of days until that option expires

What you don't know, of course, is what the stock is going to do between now and expiration. Don't let anyone kid you. No one knows this. However, what everyone in the market does know, including you, are the previous four things listed.

IV is based on HV, but there is more to it than just that. IV also incorporates supply and demand pricing pressures for the individual option. IV is part of the extrinsic value and provides you information about what market participants expect to see happen in the underlying stock.

The biggest distinction between HV and IV is that there is a specific formula for HV — it uses past data for the stock. IV is based on this calculation but is more abstract and reflects new information about the market. There's also a psychological component to IV. A large one-day move in a stock has some impact on its 100-day HV calculation, but the impact on the option's IV will likely be much more pronounced because of the uncertainty this one-day event brings.

REMEMBER

IV is the volatility implied by the current market price for the option.

Modeling option values

An option pricing model uses stock and option data to provide you with a theoretical value for the option. A few similar models exist, such as the one available on the OIC's website (`www.optionscentral.com`), and you can access them via an options calculator. By comparing an option's theoretical value to its market price, you get a feel for whether the option is relatively expensive or cheap.

The difference between the option's model value and actual value reflects the difference between historical and implied volatility. An option model incorporates HV, while the market value reflects IV. You may be able to identify a good reason for an option to be expensive or cheap — expensive isn't always bad and cheap isn't always good.

TIP

Different HV values are available using a variety of time frames and typically include 10-day, 20-day, and 100-day. IV is an option-specific value based on its current price. Both HV and IV values are available to you from a variety of sources, including option analysis software.

There are two ways you can use an option calculator:

- Using HV to get the option's theoretical value
- Using the current market price of the option to get IV

TECHNICAL STUFF

The first option pricing model was developed by Fisher Black and Myron Scholes, earning them a shared Nobel Prize in Economics.

An option calculator that uses HV in the volatility field will provide you with the following when you click Calculate:

- The theoretical value for both the call and put at that strike price
- The theoretical Greeks for both the call and put

Nice, eh? This is good information, and you can compare the theoretical price to the actual price in the market. When first starting out, change-up the inputs to see how they impact option prices.

Now you have a sense of appropriate option prices, assuming the stock moves the way it did in the past. At those prices, you can use the Greeks to estimate option prices changes based on changes in the underlying or changes in interest rates.

Something that will actually provide you with better information in terms of the Greeks, though, is to calculate the IV using this feature on the OIC calculate. Now when you click Calculate, you obtain the IV for the call or put which can be used to get the Greeks expected when you buy or sell the call and put.

Theoretical option values are based on HV, versus actual option market prices which are based on IV. These values are compared to artfully determine if future expectations reasonably reflect what's happened in the past for the stock. Even when actual prices exceed model prices, the option may still represent a trading opportunity.

Chapter 4

Option Risks and Rewards

In This Chapter

- Recognizing your true stock and option risk
- Maximizing stock and option rewards
- Visualizing stock and option risk and reward
- Introducing combination positions

Risk is a part of life, and options and stock trading have more than their share of it. Traditionally, successful, professional, and experienced traders at any level decide when they are going to exit a position before they open the trade. And though that is an excellent idea, how the strategy is carried out is even more important. That's because even though you may enter an advanced order, or you may choose to execute the exit manually, stocks may *gap down* (that is, open for trading significantly below the previous day's closing price) below your pre-decided exit level and lead you to greater losses than you planned for. If you are planning a manual exit, the hit to your position may be even greater.

The bottom line is that the maximum risk from a stock trade is your entire initial investment. If you use margin, you can lose more than what you started with. That means that in order to avoid catastrophic losses, you need to accept the fact that you could lose large amounts of money, and you need to be aware of how this could happen in order to reduce the odds of it happening to you.

This chapter takes a good look at risks and rewards and discusses how to manage them so you can trade another day.

Understanding Your Trading Risks

Risk and reward are related but aren't necessarily equal. For example, not all risk-reward profiles are equal, even in trades that may, at face value, seem similar. The fact is that given two different trades, you can face a lot more risk in one trade compared to the other — even if both trades share similar reward potential. The final outcome depends on the risk characteristics of the security you trade. To understand your risk, you need to know the following:

- The maximum amount of loss possible
- The conditions that create this maximum loss

If you want to hang around as a trader, you'll spend a lot of time mapping out your potential risks. Appreciating your risk should come before worrying about your reward potential. More important: Managing your risk should be at the top of your list, way above daydreaming about what you can do with your gains.

TIP

Risk comes in two basic varieties: the potential for losses and the lack of gains. In the latter instance, investments that don't keep up with rising costs of living (inflation) may be depleted or significantly reduced.

Risking money with stocks

A well-known trader once wrote that he looks at himself in the mirror every morning before he makes any trades and calls himself a loser. That may sound harsh and depressing, but the truth is that every time you trade stocks, you could lose all of your initial investment, even if you use sell stops to reduce your risk.

Long stock

There are two ways to establish a long stock position:

- Purchasing the stock with 100% cash
- Purchasing the stock on margin with 50% cash

Although you can limit the amount of margin used to some number below 50%, this one half of the amount is the maximum amount allowed for an initial position and a good place to start.

As the old timers on Wall Street used to say: "Prices will fluctuate." So, when you buy stock ABC at a price of 32, the price can move up, down, or just drift sideways. Worst of all, if prices fall, losses accrue with continued downward moves. Usually stocks vacillate up and down, but it is possible that you may buy in on a really bad day when ABC starts on a prolonged down trend. An even worse scenario is that ABC stops trading, preventing you from exiting at any level.

So, keep this in mind. Although you will likely exit at some point, the fact remains that when you buy a stock with 100% cash, the stock can move downward to zero, resulting in a complete loss of your investment. So the maximum risk you have when buying a stock is:

# of Shares × Price of Stock = Risk

Margin has pluses and minuses. Purchasing a stock on margin provides you with leverage, allowing you to own more stock for a set initial investment. This magnifies both gains and losses and is often referred to as a *double-edged sword*. (For more on margin, see Chapter 8.)

Assuming you purchased ABC on margin rather than using 100% cash, your risk increases by 1 divided by the initial margin percentage, or 1 / 0.50 = 2. Welcome to leverage.

To calculate your maximum risk when buying stock on margin, you can start by multiplying the initial investment by 1 divided by the initial margin percentage. You need to also add the cost of using margin, which is the margin interest rate for the stock holding period.

The maximum risk you have when buying a stock using 50% margin is:

Risk = (# of Shares × Price of Stock) × (1 ÷ Initial Margin %)

Use of margin to purchase stocks must consider the downside for the strategy.

Short stock

When you short a stock, you reverse the order of the typical stock transaction. Rather than buying first and selling later, you sell first and buy the stock later. You still want to buy low and sell high, but a bearish outlook for a particular stock means you have to sell first to capitalize on this view.

To sell a stock you don't own, you need to borrow the shares from your broker. If the stock is a popular one to short, shares may or may not be available to you. You need to check your broker's short sale list or contact them directly to determine this. Traders using brokers that specialize in active trading accounts will likely find it to be less of a problem for them.

When completing brokerage account paperwork you may be providing them with authorization to lend out shares in your account which are then made available to short sellers.

You can only hold a short stock position in a margin account — short selling stock is not allowed in retirement accounts such as Individual Retirement Arrangements (IRAs). Although a credit is received for the sale of stock, a 150% margin is required to establish the position. This basically translates to a 50% margin after deducting the initial credit you receive for the sale.

Where does that put you in terms of risk? Selling stocks short puts you in a very risky situation. Because there is no limit to how high a stock can move upward, shorting a stock is an unlimited risk strategy. Granted, you can buy back a stock before it goes to infinity and beyond, but in the same way a stock can gap down, it can gap up. Consider how many short positions feel pain after an intra-meeting Federal Reserve rate cut occurs or if the earnings report is better than estimates and the outlook for future earnings is positive.

Long stock represents a limited, but high-risk position. It is limited because a stock can only move down to zero; it can't trade below that. The risk remains high because a stock can do just that — move to zero. This risk increases when margin is used and creates a situation where you can lose more than your initial investment.

Calculating option risks

Both call and put options have risk that is limited to the initial investment. This initial investment can vary in size, but is less than the investment required to control the same number of shares of the underlying stock. Although the risk is relatively smaller in terms of dollars, it's important to recognize that the likelihood that an option will go to zero is much higher than the underlying stock going to zero.

The chance that an option will go to zero is 100% because an option is a limited life security that eventually expires. At expiration, the option value goes to zero unless the option, put, or call is in-the-money.

Call option

A call option gives the buyer the rights to purchase the underlying stock at the contract's strike price by its expiration date. When the strike price for the call option is below the price for the underlying stock, it will lose time value as expiration nears. Assuming the stock remains at the same price level, this time decay can result in losses for the trader. The losses will be limited because the option retains its intrinsic value.

However, when the stock is trading below the strike price, the option's value is all time value. Assuming the stock remains at the same price level, time value diminishes as you get closer to expiration. Continuing in this manner will result in a total loss of the initial investment.

Most of the time a stock doesn't stand still — it does that vacillation thing. That means that although there's a chance the underlying stock will increase in value by rising above a call strike price, the stock may also decline in value and fall below the strike price. Once again that puts you in a situation where you can lose your entire investment as expiration nears.

Put option

A put option provides the buyer with rights to sell the underlying stock at the contract's strike price by its expiration date. The option will lose time value as expiration nears, which can result in losses for the trader when the stock is trading above the option strike price. When trading below the strike price, the losses will be limited because the option retains intrinsic value.

However, when the stock is trading above the strike price, the option's value is all time value. Assuming the stock remains at the same price level, time value diminishes as you get closer to expiration. Continuing in this manner will result in a total loss of the initial investment.

Because the stock has the same chance of rising as falling, there's a chance the underlying stock will increase in value rising above a put strike price. As a result, as is also the case with call options, you can lose your entire investment as expiration nears.

Reaping Your Rewards

So, with all this stock and option risk, why bother? Because the interest you receive on a regular money market account can often be below the rate of inflation, the only way for your savings to keep up or outpace your expenses in the future is by assuming this risk. And if you're willing to take higher risks, you should expect rewards that are better than a money market rate, which was near zero in the years after the subprime mortgage crisis. Both stocks and options provide this potential.

Benefiting from stocks

As a stock holder, you can benefit by receiving dividends and/or gains in the price of the stock. This often results when a company's sales or profits increase, when new products or technologies are introduced, and other countless reasons. There are also approaches that allow you to benefit from downward moves in the stock.

Long stock

A long stock position is created by purchasing shares of stock in the market. Because stock can continue to exist indefinitely, it can continue to rise without limit. What ultimately happens is a function of the company prospects and general market conditions. So your potential reward with stock is unlimited, especially over very long periods of time.

REMEMBER

Not all companies distribute profits in the form of dividends to stock holders. Many growth stocks retain profits to fuel continued growth. This trend can vary over time. Generally, when interest rates are very low, more companies tend to pay dividends, although this is not a hard-and-fast rule, and other variables may also influence dividend trends.

Short stock

You create a short stock position by reversing the standard stock transaction (long stock); you sell first with the expectations that the price of the stock will go down. In this situation you profit when you buy the shares back. You complete such transactions in a brokerage account that allows margin trading.

The rewards you reap for a short stock position are high, but limited. A stock can continue to decline, but only until it reaches zero. This is the downside limit that caps your rewards.

REMEMBER

Call options increase in value when the underlying stock rises, whereas put options increase in value when the underlying stock falls.

Breaking even with options

A call option provides you with profits similar to long stock, whereas a put option provides you with profits similar to short stock. This makes sense given your rights as an option holder, which allow you to buy or sell stock at a set level. There is one slight difference between stock rewards and option rewards: Options require an initial premium payment that you must consider when identifying potential gains.

There are three key value points for option trades: break even, in the money (ITM), and out of the money (OTM). So, calculating potential option rewards requires you to add option premiums to call strike prices and subtract option premiums from put strike prices to come up with a price known as the position's *breakeven* level. A stock's price must

- Rise above the breakeven for call option profits to kick in.
- Fall below the breakeven for put option profits to kick in.

In each case, this results in profits that are slightly less than your stock profits.

TIP

A stock's breakeven point is your purchase price when buying stock or your sell price when shorting a stock. As soon as the stock moves away from this price, you have gains or losses.

Call option

Purchasing a call option gives you rights to buy stock at a certain level. As a result, the option increases in value when the stock moves upward. After a stock moves above your call option's strike price, the option has intrinsic value which increases as the stock continues to rise. Calls with strike prices below the price of the stock are referred to as ITM.

For a call position you own to be profitable at expiration, it must remain above the strike price plus your initial investment. At this level, option premiums will minimally equal your cost when you bought the call.

The breakeven for a call option is:

Call Breakeven = Call Strike Price + Call Purchase Premium

After a stock's price is at the option's breakeven level, it can continue to rise indefinitely. Your call option can similarly rise indefinitely until expiration. As a result, call option profits are considered to be unlimited, just like stock.

REMEMBER

An option's moneyness is determined by the option type and the price of the underlying stock relative to the option strike price. Call options with a strike price that is below the stock price are OTM, and their premium is all time value. After the stock moves above the strike price, it is referred to as ITM and has intrinsic value along with the time value.

Put option

Purchasing a put option gives you rights to sell stock at a certain level. As a result, the option increases in value when the stock's price moves downward. When a stock moves below your put option's strike price, the option has intrinsic value, which increases as the stock continues to fall. Puts with strike prices above the price of the stock are referred to as ITM.

For a put position you own to be profitable at expiration, it must remain below the strike price minus your initial investment. At this level, option premiums will minimally equal your cost when you bought the put.

The breakeven for a put option is:

Put Breakeven = Put Strike Price – Put Purchase Premium

When a stock is at the option's breakeven level, it can continue to fall until it reaches zero. Your put option can continue to increase in value until this level is reached, all the way to its expiration. As a result, put option profits are considered to be high, but limited, just like a short stock.

Call options have risks and rewards similar to long stock, whereas put options have rewards that are similar to short stock. Put option risk is limited to the initial investment. The reason your rewards are similar rather than the same is because you need to account for the premium amount when you purchased the option.

Profiling Risk and Reward

Profiling risk and reward means you're using a visual aid to get a feel for potential gains and losses for a trade. By doing this, you can quickly assess strategies you already use as well as new ones. *Risk graphs* or *risk profiles* are graphical views of potential risks and rewards in option trading. You can create a generic graph that excludes prices to identify the risks and rewards for any asset type. You can also create a more specific risk graph that includes stock price levels, with breakeven levels, profits, and losses for a particular position.

Profiling stock trades with risk graphs

Although risk graphs are more commonly used in option trading, it's important for you to get a good working understanding of stock risk graphs. Such basic profiles simply look at maximum potential risks and maximum potential rewards.

Long stock

The maximum potential risk for a long stock trade is high, but limited to the downside. This is because a stock can only decline to zero. The maximum potential rewards for a stock position is unlimited because a stock can technically rise without limit.

The long stock risk graph displayed in Figure 4-1 reflects this risk-reward profile.

By profiling the risks and rewards this way for long stock, you quickly see that losses (which are limited to the initial investment amount) accumulate as the stock price declines, while profits continue to rise as the stock price rises.

Short stock

Because selling stocks short is the opposite of being long, the maximum potential risk for a short stock trade is unlimited. That's because a stock can technically rise in price without limit. The maximum potential reward for a short stock position is high, but limited to the downside. This is because a stock can only decline to zero.

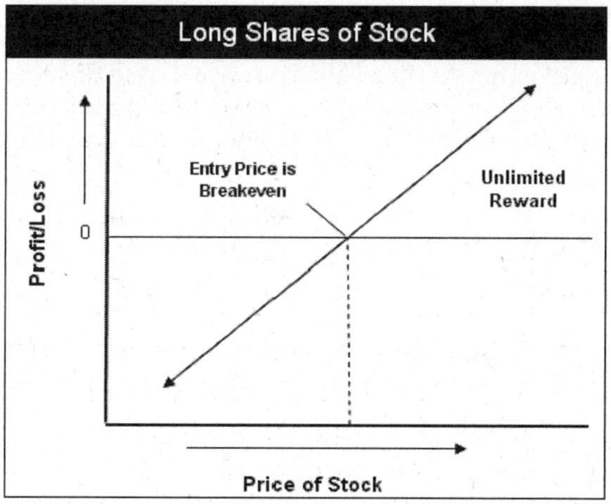

Figure 4-1: Risk graph for a long stock position.

Image by Optionetics

The short stock risk graph displayed in Figure 4-2 reflects this risk-reward profile.

The short stock risk graph displays the rapid rate of losses that rise without limit as the stock rises and profits that are high but limited, because the stock can only fall to zero.

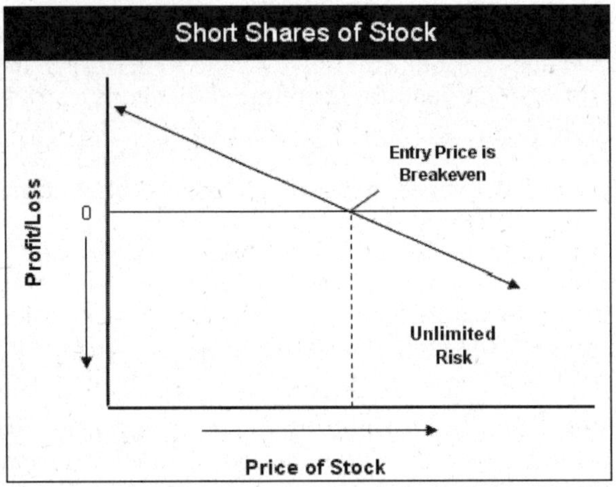

Figure 4-2: Risk graph for a short stock position.

Image by Optionetics

Profiling option trades with risk graphs

Basic call and put option risk graphs are slightly different than stock risk graphs because they incorporate the risk and reward for the security, along with the breakeven level. Position-specific profiles will include stock prices on the x-axis and profits/losses on the y-axis. The profile also identifies the following:

- The option strike price
- The position breakeven

Although it's less obvious when you're viewing generic risk profiles, the main benefit of using options to limit losses can be viewed in these risk graphs.

Call option

A basic call option risk graph is similar to a long stock risk graph, with two important distinctions:

- You need to account for the call option premium in the breakeven level.
- Your losses are capped to the downside before a stock declines to zero.

The potential risk for a call option is limited, whereas the potential rewards are unlimited. This is displayed in the generic call option risk graph displayed in Figure 4-3.

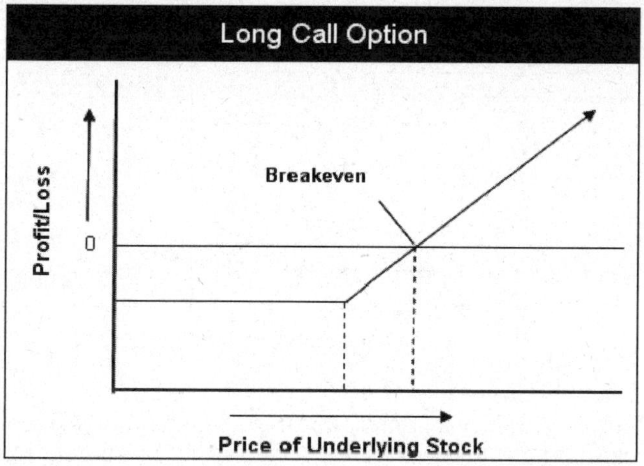

Figure 4-3: Risk graph for a call option position.

Image by Optionetics

The call option risk graph provides a picture of losses that are limited to the initial investment as the stock declines. This amount is much smaller than those for a long stock position. A call option allows unlimited profits that are similar to a long stock position, but must also account for the call option breakeven level.

Put option

A basic put option risk graph is similar to a short stock risk graph, with a couple of distinctions. The second one is extremely valuable if you're bearish on a stock and things go against you:

- You need to account for the put option premium in the breakeven level.
- Your losses are capped to the upside and are therefore limited.

The potential risk for a put option is limited while the potential rewards are limited, but high. This is displayed by a generic put option risk graph displayed in Figure 4-4.

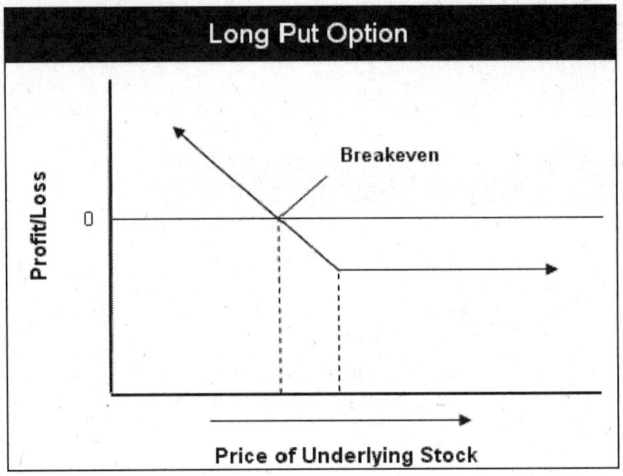

Image by Optionetics

Figure 4-4: Risk graph for a put option position.

The put option risk graph provides a picture of losses that are limited to the initial investment as the stock rises. As a trader, you have to prefer this graph to the short stock profile, simply because your risk, although high, is limited. It also provides profits that are similar to a short stock position. The put risk graph also accounts for the put option breakeven level.

REMEMBER

When you buy a put option, the most you can lose is your initial investment. Although that's not your intention, you need to remember that this initial investment is much smaller than a short stock position which is also used when you have a bearish outlook for the stock.

Combining option positions

Chapter 2 introduced a combination position for options. Many investors use put options as a form of insurance for existing stock positions. You can buy puts for stocks you own, as well as for those you don't own because holding the underlying asset is not a requirement in the listed option markets.

A *combined position* can be structured in two distinct ways:

- Stock and options for a single underlying stock
- Multiple options for a single underlying stock

In addition to creating a risk graph for a single stock or option position, you can also create ones for combined positions. This comes in handy, giving you easy access to the reward profile for the position and, more importantly, its risk profile.

Trading options with stock

Three basic combination positions for long stock and options include the following:

- A married put position
- A covered call position
- A collar position

In each case, long stock is paired with a long put, a short call, or both to improve the risk and/or reward potential. Similar combination positions can be applied to a short stock position.

You can hold a stock position and purchase options on that same stock to change the risk or reward profile for the stock, or you can hold option positions without holding a position in the underlying.

Trading options with options

You can construct multiple combination positions by using multiple options to capitalize on certain market conditions or to improve the risk and/or reward potential. Different market conditions include the following:

- High relative volatility
- Low relative volatility
- Sideways stock movement
- Directional stock movement (up or down)

After you formulate an outlook or identify a market trend, you can combine different strike prices and options to vary risk and reward.

Profiling a combined position

You can design risk graphs for combination positions by first drawing the risk graph for each individual position and then overlaying them. You then check to see if the risks or rewards for any one position provide a cap for the unlimited or limited-but-high risks or rewards for the other position.

This is better understood through example. Figure 4-5 displays the risk graph for a married put position, one that combines long stock and a long put for the same stock.

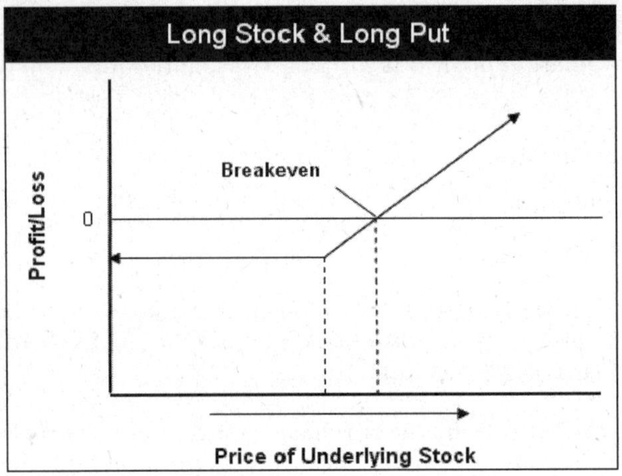

Image by Optionetics

Figure 4-5: Risk graph for a married put position.

This trade creates a risk-reward profile that is similar to a long call, once you account for the put premium in the breakeven price. By adding the put, you minimize losses for the stock. At the same time, your potential rewards remain unlimited after accounting for the new breakeven point.

Considering the worst-case scenario

Considering the worst-case scenario is likely the most important concept in options, and essentially all trading, although inexperienced, eager traders may be tempted to ignore it (at their peril). Before looking at your potential gains, you must look at the downside if you want to continue trading for any extended period of time. By managing your risk, you stay in the game long enough to master different strategies that are appropriate for changing market conditions. That's why considering the worst-case scenario is so hugely important — these worst-case scenarios can and will happen during your trading career. And being unprepared will cost you money.

WARNING!

Avoid the temptations of ego and fear. The market is a very nasty place. All new traders assume they'll do the right thing when the time comes — exit a position when their predetermined exit level is reached. But after you've been trading a while, you know how hard this seemingly simple action can be. Never assume you will completely control the emotions you experience when trading. The best traders know that all they can do is manage them.

Start with single position risk graphs

Looking at the worst-case scenario means looking at the lower portion of the risk graph, the one that profiles your losses. After you have a certain stock or market outlook, you can select the position or strategy (that is, long stock or long call option) that has the most desirable risk graph.

Look to trade strategies that do the following two things:

- Limit losses
- Allow unlimited profits

Chapter 10 discusses more specific position risk graphs that will make this more intuitive and easy to incorporate in your trading strategies.

Improve existing risk graphs

There's a lot more to cover before exploring advanced strategies using combination positions with just options. Throughout the strategy review process, consider adding options that improve the risk profile first. This can be done by

- Capping losses that are limited but high and even better.
- Capping losses that are unlimited.

REMEMBER

If your first goal is risk management, you get the opportunity to realize gains.

Part II

Evaluating Markets, Sectors, and Strategies

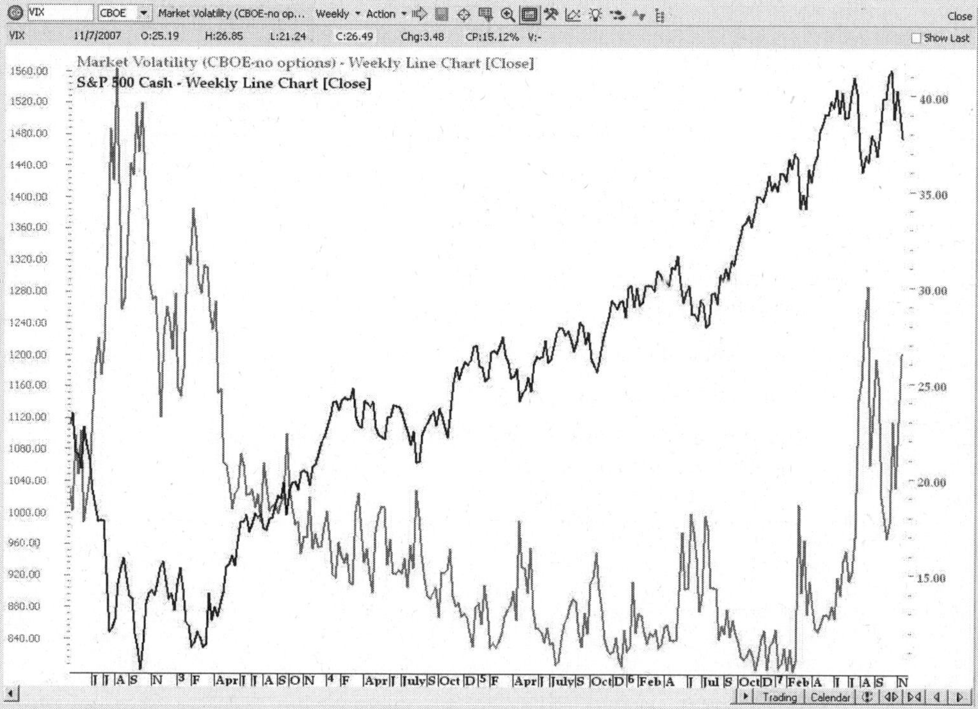

Find out more about making good trading decisions in a free online article at www.dummies.com/extras/tradingoptions.

In this part . . .

- Market assessment methods using breadth and sentiment analysis
- Technical analysis of sectors
- Evaluation of new strategies
- The unique characteristics of options, such as trading costs and order placement methods

Chapter 5

Analyzing Mood Swings in the Market

In This Chapter

- Digging deeper into market results
- Using option activity to determine market mood
- Assessing indicator levels

When trading stocks, you gauge whether a market has sustainable momentum or whether some kind of reversal is more likely by using *breadth tools* and *sentiment analysis,* such as the New York Stock Exchange advance decline line and the TRIN index, to measure market breadth or put/call ratios to measure market sentiment. Both are described later in this chapter. More specifically, by carefully examining key statistics such as volume and the number of advancing versus declining stocks, you get a better understanding as to why markets are behaving in certain ways and whether gains or losses were due to just a handful of stocks or if a large number of them fueled the advance or decline. Generally speaking, market advances tend to last longer and have a better overall "health" when more stocks are advancing than declining. The opposite is true for falling markets.

It so happens that the options market can also be used to gauge the health of a stock market move. Monitoring option activity gives you a sense of the degree of fear or greed associated with an advance or decline. It helps you decide whether the trend has more room to go or may be stalled in the near future.

And although there are no certainties, the hallmark of success with market sentiment analysis is to be aware of when each specific indicator is delivering extreme readings. Using past data to identify atypical readings, you can often identify levels associated with unsustainable advances or declines. In this chapter, we'll have a thorough look at the different ways you can monitor the market to help make better trading decisions.

A Few Words About Select Macro Factors

Before we jump into the markets themselves, it's a good idea to consider that there are three major macro factors to consider:

- **Interest rates:** Generally, low or falling interest rates are bullish for stocks, and rising interest rates are eventually negative. This may seem like needless information, but if history is any guide, the general trend of interest rates can affect the price of underlying stocks, which will affect the price of your options. It makes sense to keep your eye on interest rates all over the world. In the past, the U.S. Federal Reserve was the only central bank in the world with enough power to influence global markets. Presently, because all markets are linked, other central banks, specifically the People's Bank of China, and the European Central Bank's actions can also be market movers. It is important to understand that the U.S. Federal Reserve is still the most influential.
- **Central banks:** Central banks set interest rates. Think of central banks as think tanks with power to move markets. In the 21st century, it's even easier to follow what central banks are thinking because they use much plainer language than ever with regard to their intentions. And if their statements are a little vague, they now hold post-interest-rate-setting-meeting press conferences. What central bankers say at these moments can have significant effect on stocks, and, yes, that means your options will be affected.
- **Global economic trends:** Because the global economy is mostly synchronized now, what happens in one country — especially China, as well as Europe and the United States — can affect not just the local economy, but also the globalized economic landscape. Eventually, economic activity leads to some kind of action by central banks, which eventually will have an effect on stocks and options.

Thus, while much of this book will be geared toward technical analysis, it is useful to keep an eye on these very important external factors.

Assessing the Market's Bias

It is often said by market old-timers (like us) that the market's main job is to make as many of us look as foolish as possible as often as possible. In other words, the stock market has a mind of its own, and it pays to remember that — especially when you think you have the next move figured out. For example, you might expect a decline when weak economic numbers are released only to be surprised by the rally that follows. Or you are certain that you will see a boring day after a profitable earnings report is released by a widely held company, and then your jaw drops with the ensuing decline that's attributed to this news. And although you can't ever be 100% certain about any market event or response, you can be better prepared by following market breadth and sentiment data. When you become well versed in using these types of indicators, you are more likely to get a sense of the market's mood before these seemingly crazy swings as they alert you to pending changes.

Judging the strength of a move

All market advances and declines are not the same. Advances can occur at a moderate pace with lots of sectors rising together, in a frenzied manner with some stocks and sectors strongly outperforming others, or any variation in between. For that reason, it's a waste to time to try to predict what a market will do at any one time. Instead, you want to gear your analysis toward assessing the odds of the direction of a trend continuing.

It's no different for either advances or declines. As a trader, you want to keep the odds in your favor by trading in the direction of the dominant trend, whether it is up or down. And even though it's hard to create new positions when you feel you may have already missed the move, by looking at market breadth, you will often be able to decide with a high degree of certainty whether conditions in an advance are improving or if there's more room on the downside as a market shows signs of deterioration.

REMEMBER

Keep the odds in your favor by using a variety of tools to confirm your market assessments and then use strategies consistent with such assessments.

TIP

Large profits are often the product of vigilance. If you can spot a potential change in the trend early, you can plan for it and gain from following a new trend for a longer period of time.

Defining market breadth

Market breadth gives you an in-depth look at the nature of the internal components of market rises and declines. When you keep track the number of advancing versus declining stocks for a specific index, you can gauge the health of the move for that index. During rising markets, you want to see the gains spread out among the largest variety of companies possible. On declines, you look for signs that there's so much participation the bear exhausts itself.

Breadth indicators use statistics based on the following:

- Number and volume for advancing and declining issues
- Number of issues reaching new highs or lows
- Up and down volume
- Issues trading above or below moving average lines

An advancing market with declining stocks outnumbering advancing stocks in both number and volume is bearish. It suggests that a select group of stocks may be doing well, but overall the market is not healthy. This is known, in technical analysis terms, as a *bearish divergence*. On the other hand, market advances where there are stocks in a variety of sectors trading above their 200-day moving average (the line that divides bull and bear markets) is more bullish, suggesting a healthy rise that will likely continue.

The advance-decline line breadth indicator

A commonly used breadth indicator is the *advance-decline* (Adv-Dec, or A-D line) line, used in combination with the New York Stock Exchange (NYSE) Composite Index (NYA). You won't be looking for a specific bullish or bearish number for this indicator — you use it more as a confirming or diverging tool via visual inspection. In fact, the most important aspect of the A-D line is the picture of the line itself and whether it is trending up, down, or sideways, especially in respect to the direction of the market or the index that you are tracking. You construct the line by keeping a daily cumulative total of the following:

Adv-Dec Line = # of Advancing Issues – # of Declining Issues

TIP

You can save time by visiting the A-D line graphic, which is updated daily at Stockcharts.com (`www.stockcharts.com`) under the Market Breadth Indicators heading. Use the Gallery View option in order to see the indicator appropriately.

You may note an index is rising even when the Adv-Dec Line is falling. This happens when:

- Component stocks with more influence on the index increase even if a majority of the component stocks decrease
- A smaller number of stocks advance, but the value of gains from advancing stocks is greater than the value of losses from decliners.
- The number of unchanged issues are excluded from this indicator. When using the tool, focus on the visual trends, rising or falling, rather than absolute values (numerals) for this tool. Figure 5-1 displays the daily Adv-Dec Line with the NYSE Composite Index (NYA).

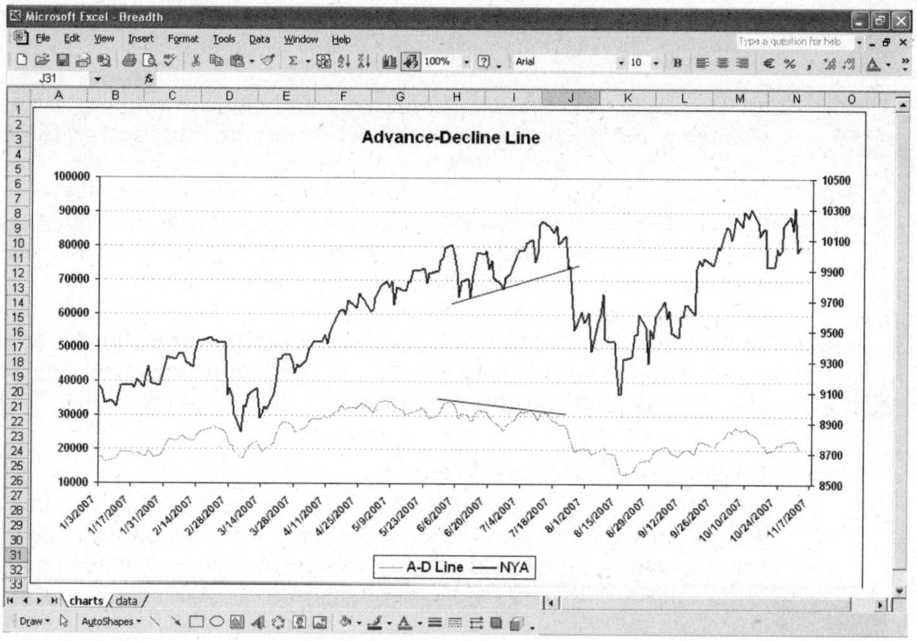

Figure 5-1: Daily Adv-Dec line with nd NYA overlay.

This is a fantastic illustration of the usefulness of this indicator because it pictures a classic warning sign from the A-D line prior to a major decline in the markets. From June to mid-July in 2007, NYA was rising, but this move was not confirmed by a large number of advancing issues. Note the rising line under the index and the declining line above the A-D line. In this case, the Adv-Dec Line was diverging from the NYA — a significant warning sign that correctly predicted some serious declines.

TIP

Any significant decline since 1987 has been preceded by a negative divergence in the NYSE Advance-Decline line.

Calculating the advance-decline line as a ratio

You can also calculate the A-D line as a ratio rather than a cumulative value (Adv/Dec). This method results in an oscillating indicator with the following characteristics:

- Oscillates around the value one.
- When there are more advancers, the ratio is greater than one (more common).
- When there are more decliners, the ratio moves between zero and one.

You monitor oscillator crosses of the center line, divergent movement, or movement into extreme ranges for potential turns.

Adv-Dec indicators can be calculated on any index that provides daily advancing and declining statistics. When monitoring the Adv-Dec line, look for advancers to outpace decliners in rising markets and decliners to outpace advancers in falling markets to confirm index changes. When the indicator diverges from index action, the current trend may be in trouble. You can find reliable Adv-Decline numbers for several key indexes on the home page of Investing.com (`www.investing.com`).

Recognize that *contrarian strategies* are those that are counter to existing market trends. These represent higher risk trades because they anticipate a change in momentum and direction.

Adding volume as a key tool

Volume is a measure of trader commitment to a trend, and is thus a key tool used in market analysis — it provides fuel for upside moves and animates fear as declines pick up steam. Increasing volume confirms the current trend. Without it, the move becomes very suspect.

Splitting volume by movement type (advancing or declining) allows you to incorporate it into breadth analysis. For example, during a bullish move, you see whether a handful of advancers are leading the way with strong participation or if interest in even these popular shares is tapering off. When used in this fashion, volume lets you know if the trend is in good shape or if you should start looking for other signs of weakness.

When markets are moving downward, the volume for declining issues is like a panic meter. You can practically see traders scrambling to hit the Enter button for sell orders. But then a funny thing happens . . . the decline continues, but there is a shift in these two volume components. Advancing volume starts to pick up, particularly for the favored stocks of the day.

Viewing advancing and declining volume separately provides one picture of market strength, but these two variables can also be combined as ratios with the number of advancing and declining issues to display overall market breadth. The result is an interesting battle between the bulls and the bears. A breadth indicator using all this information is the Trader's Short-Term Index (TRIN), also known as the Arms Index, described next.

If you have easy access to index component quote lists, you can create advance-decline indicators for the index.

Measuring breadth with the Arms Index

The Arms Index, also known as the Trader's Short-Term Index (TRIN), is a widely used breadth indicator developed by Richard Arms, Jr. Incorporating volume provides additional insight about the strength of a market move. Calculating the Arms Index is pretty straightforward:

> [# of Advancing Issues ÷ # of Declining Issues] ÷ (Advancing Volume ÷ Declining Volume]

Once again, the NYSE Composite Index is used; however, readings for the Nasdaq Composite Index and AMEX Composite Index are also available. A daily close of 1.0 is neutral, although daily readings between 0.70 and 1.30 could be classified as neutral.

TIP: The Arms Index is primarily used for short-term alerts and trend indications, but it can also be used to assess the market. This is definitely one of those indicators that you should look at past data to help in understanding its movement. Be sure to include an overlay chart of the index to get the most out of the review. You can find end-of-the-day closing numbers for any given week at Barron's magazine (`www.barrons.com`) in the Market Lab section.

Checking out an Arms chart

Arms noted that adding moving averages (MAs) to the indicator helped with market assessments. By also highlighting key levels with horizontal lines showing neutral areas and extremes, your analysis is more complete. It makes for a busy chart at first, but speeds up things in the long run. For more information on chart scaling and MA techniques used here, see Chapter 6. For now, keep in mind that moving averages are used to smooth out the peaks and valleys in daily data.

Figure 5-2 provides a daily chart for the Arms Index (light, thin line) with NYA (dark, thick line) as an overlay. The Arms Index (TRIN) is shown as an inverted, log chart. Inverting it allows extremely high readings (bearish) to spike downward as the NYA sells off. A log scale displays relative readings more clearly. The chart also includes a 21-day EMA (lighter) and 55-day EMA (darker), as well as the following horizontal lines displaying key levels:

- 1.0 (dark, solid line) designates a neutral area for the index.
- 0.70 designates an extreme daily reading that generally indicates a lower opening the next day (values less than 0.70 which are above the line).
- 1.30 designates an extreme daily reading that generally indicates a higher opening the next day (values more than 1.30 which are below the line).
- 2.85 designates an extremely bearish day.
- 1.10 designates oversold conditions for the EMAs.

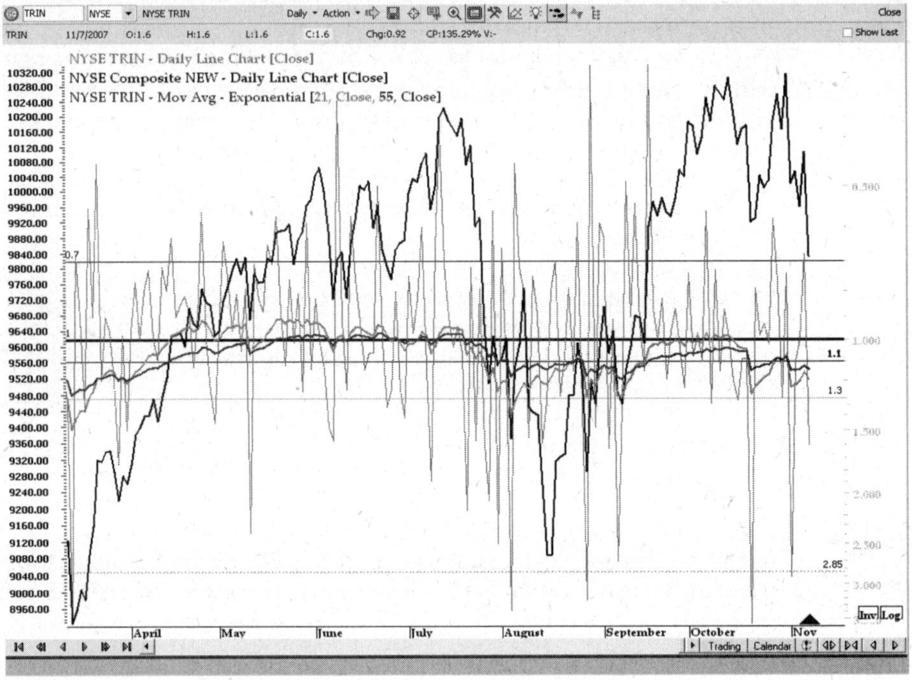

Figure 5-2: Daily TRIN with NYA overlay and EMA trend lines.

The TRIN chart displayed in Figure 5-2 coincided with a strong decline in the fall of 2007. Note the movement of the MAs.

Taking a long-term look back

When viewing past conditions to gain insight on the here and now, it's good to keep in mind that the Arms (TRIN) index is a very short-term–oriented indicator. It also pays to look further back at periods resembling the current one. As of late 2007, a long-term bull market was in place, but in November 2007, the market, as measured by the S & P 500 Index, had topped out. By 2008, the subprime mortgage–related financial crisis was in full swing. The chart shows the start of the decline in late October, early November 2007, which proved to be the absolute top in the market until March of 2009. So, even though the Arms Index is often seen as a short-term indicator, it proved correct in predicting a significant decline in this case. Nevertheless, the more data you have the better off you will be, so it pays to compare any current situation to two types of trends and one major bottom:

- One was associated with continued bullish conditions (late 1998).
- One was signaling a major trend change (early 2000).
- A third was associated with the major bottom that launched the bull market that began on March 9, 2009 and that was still unfolding in December of 2014.

Regardless of the different scenarios you consider, focus on managing risk for existing conditions rather than betting on an anticipated move. Generally, though, breadth indicators are extremely useful in identifying bottoms because market declines occur much faster. Still, there are no guarantees for a reversal.

TIP

The TRIN index is useful but not perfect. Use it as part of an analytical method that uses multiple indicators and compare what it's telling you to your other indicators. Never look to just one factor. Instead look for consensus and confirmation among multiple indicators.

(Psycho)-analyzing the market

Some people would rather be correct in knowing why markets do what they do. Yet, over the long haul, it's much better to make money and leave the answering of why things happen to someone else.

Embracing the idea that the market has a mind of its own is easier when you consider that human behavior drives it. Some argue the market is efficient because people respond rationally to all available news about stocks, the economy, and prospects for both. That sounds great, but all you have to do is watch the way an index moves after big reports are released and you get the feeling that something very irrational is going on. Another way to look at it is that markets act on information that they have at any one time and respond whether it's the right or wrong response, based on the opinion of the majority of players. The point is that it doesn't really matter why markets do what they do. Instead of wondering why something happens, you want to be on the right side of the equation as often as possible.

There are many rules-based approaches allowing you to make money in the markets, but that doesn't mean the market moves in a predictable way. Human nature is about self-preservation and self-interest. And because buying and selling securities translates to making or losing money, you have to figure that market participants bring a good amount of irrationality, influenced by self-preservation, to the game. Multiply one irrational person by many irrational people, whose goal is not to lose money, and you have a crowd moving prices up or down, quickly or slowly, depending on the day.

Crowds can behave in very strange ways when feeding on each other's greed or fear. There are ways to monitor market conditions and crowd behavior to better understand why the market reacts the way it does. One helpful step in this process is identifying which human emotion is in command at the time: greed or fear. That's where market sentiment analysis comes in handy.

Defining sentiment

Sentiment broadly describes the overriding bias for the market, be it bullish or bearish. Greed (with a touch of fear) generally drives the former while it's all about fear when markets decline. Month after month, year after year, and decade after decade, these greed-fear patterns repeat regardless of economic changes that occur along the way. Think of the market as an ocean full of waves, and the undulation of the waves as reflecting sentiment. The only variation from cycle to cycle, as with any wave in an ocean, is in the length of time that each emotion rules the roost and the underlying dynamics that lead to the unfolding of any particular wave.

Sentiment tools use stock and options statistics to provide you with information about crowd activity during advances and declines. Most of this data is available from exchange websites or charting packages. It's a matter of identifying which tools to monitor along the way.

When employing sentiment analysis, you try to identify periods when greed has gotten unsustainable or fear is just about exhausted. Think of it as a weird game of musical chairs . . . at some point the music stops, and everyone is scrambling for a spot so they can participate in the next round or move. You just want to be prepared so that you can respond quickly when a change in direction eventually take place. Focusing on market sentiment is a helpful tool that can help you to do just that.

TIP

Trading is a balancing act. Always remind yourself of what *is* happening in the market versus what you anticipate happening next.

Measuring investor actions

Sentiment analysis makes you a Doubting Thomas, because it attempts to measure bullish and bearish actions versus what's being said about the market or even its current direction. Watch for whether different factors that are related act in ways that make sense or not, such as the following:

- Bullish commentary contradicted by unusually high put volume.
- A mild economic report that produces a wild swing in the market.
- A major change in interest rate policy from the Federal Reserve that brings an unexpected reaction. For example, if the Federal Reserve were to raise interest rates after multiple years of zero interest rates, as in the 2008–2014 period, and the market rallies 3% in a day.

The options market gives you quick indications about trader sentiment:

- Are traders bullish (buying calls/selling puts)?
- Are they bearish (buying puts/selling calls)?

TIP

Here is the take-home message: Option data primarily provides insight to fear. Historical volatility and volume measures give you a feel for how much emotion was involved with moves in the past. Implied volatility levels let you know what's anticipated for the road ahead.

Watching Call and Put Activity

Investors, especially professional traders, are generally optimistic people. That makes their market outlook bullish. If they weren't generally positive people, they couldn't do what they do for a living. You can see that reflected in the fact that the markets spend more time going up rather than down. Wait a minute . . . does that mean we think investors are rational? Not necessarily. It just means that market trends generally reflect the overall positive disposition of the people who drive them: investors and traders. No matter how you feel about this type of thing, know this: The reason it pays to note market bullishness is because typically call volume exceeds put volume, reflecting the tendency for the market to advance. It provides you with an option activity baseline.

When people start getting nervous, as they will eventually do, put volume increases. Monitoring the put-to-call relationship, you can identify extreme levels corresponding with market reversals. Indicators may use call and put volume, or put volume alone, to measure fear or complacency in the market.

TIP

Consider using extreme sentiment readings to reduce positions in the direction of the trend and slowly establish counter-trend positions.

Understanding put-to-call ratios

The late Martin Zweig is credited with creating put-to-call (P:C) ratios, deriving them by simply dividing put contract volume by call contract volume. Zweig predicted the 1987 stock market crash on national television on the Friday before "Black Monday" and made money by being short the market. A wide variety of such ratios are now available to you. And although alert levels have changed over the years, the emotion they signal remains the same: fear.

A P:C ratio focuses on bullish and bearish action taken by various market participants. Many are also contrarian measures, meaning the implications for the indicator are opposite of market sentiment. When everyone is excessively bearish, conditions are right for an upside reversal — a rally. And when everyone is exuberant about market prospects, the odds of a significant decline are higher. You interpret P:C ratio readings the following way:

- Extremely low readings are bearish.
- Extremely high readings are bullish.

Now for the good stuff. A select list of ratios using call and put volume follows, with information about the indicator construction and readings:

- **CBOE equity put/call ratio:** Total volume for all stock options trading on the CBOE. Readings from the former option volume leader are now less comprehensive given significant gains from the International Securities Exchange (ISE). In the past, readings above 0.90 suggested increased fear in the market and oversold conditions. More recently, readings above 0.80 reflect growing fear.
- **CBOE index only put/call ratio:** Total volume for all index options trading on the CBOE. This measure includes SPX and OEX index volume, which remain important market barometers. A distinct aspect of this indicator is the type of trader it reflects — the index options trader is considered more sophisticated and on target with market moves. As a result, high readings reflect pending bearishness for the market. Readings above 2.4 reflect approximately three standard deviations (SD) above the mean and have occurred immediately before short-term and intermediate term tops.

  REMEMBER: Drops in the market typically happen faster than rallies.
- **ISE Sentiment Index (ISEE):** This tool is actually a call:put ratio, with two other important distinctions noted by the ISE:
  - It focuses on new buys only, versus total volume, which reflects short sellers too.
  - It excludes market maker and other professional trader activities, leaving customer activity only (money managers and retail).
  - Because this index is an inverse of the typical ratios, low readings coincide with extreme bearishness and thus are interpreted as predictive of market advances on a contrarian basis. Since 2002, readings less than 85 are 2SD below the average and have coincided with short-term and intermediate-term bottoms. You can find the ISE indicator, updated every 20 minutes during the trading day, at www.ise.com/market-data/isee-index/.

- **ISE index and ETF put/call ratio:** Total volume for all index and ETF options trading on the ISE. Consider augmenting the CBOE index-only ratio with this tool to round out your assessment of broad hedging activity.

Three keys to getting the most from all these sentiment tools are

- Knowing basic indicator construction information
- Understanding the historical extremes and implications for the tool
- Recognizing significant market changes and impact on indicator data

If you're zeroing in on the sentiment for individual security, be sure to capture the data from all exchanges that trade options for that underlying. Rather than a specific reading, identify atypical readings for the data by calculating the average value and standard deviations, and then add lines to identify extreme levels.

REMEMBER

Many widely followed ETFs and their options trade until 4:15 p.m. Eastern time — be sure to track the correct closing time and price.

Figure 5-3 provides a daily chart for the S&P 500 exchange-traded fund (SPY) and its put/call ratio with a five-day moving average and a +1SD line.

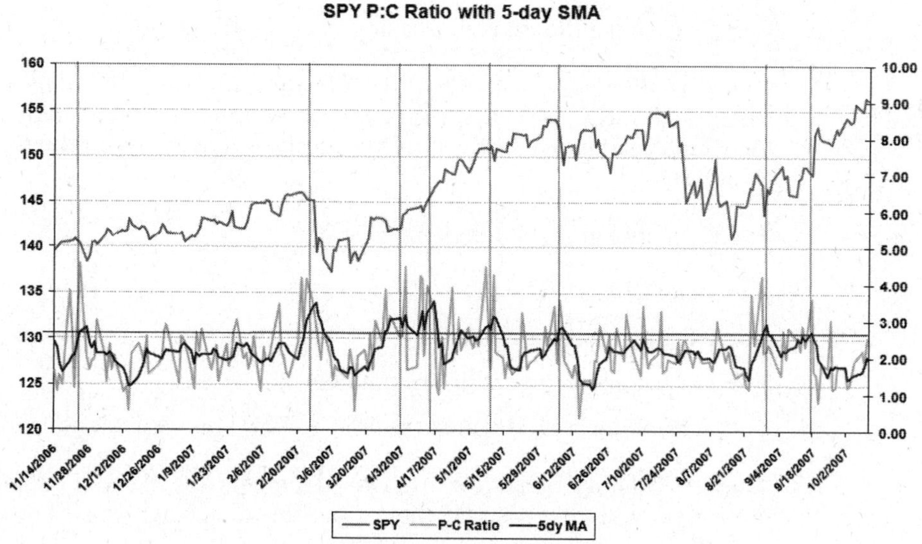

Figure 5-3: Daily SPY chart with P/C ratio.

When the 5-day simple MA for the SPY put/scall ratio reached more than +1SD, a near-term bottom was signaled six of eight times.

TIP

Indicators may behave differently during bull and bear markets and even during different stages of bull or bear markets (early, mid, late). When using a new indicator, check its performance during similar periods in the past.

You can also use these SD lines when identifying extremes for exchange data, particularly when market changes impact volume.

Using the put volume indicator

The *put volume indicator* (PVI) is a sentiment tool created by John Bollinger that measures relative put activity levels. It's similar to a P:C ratio, with extreme readings used to identify periods of excessive fear or complacency. PVI can also be applied to individual stocks, indexes, or an entire exchange.

The PVI is calculated using daily put option volume data, which is available from a number of sources, including the OCC and options analysis software. It's calculated by dividing daily put volume by the 10-day simple moving average (SMA) of that volume. A rising ratio indicates the following:

- Put volume is increasing
- Bearish sentiment is increasing

Figure 5-4 displays a daily chart of PVI values for the S&P 500 Index (SPX) with an overlay of SPY, the exchange-traded fund (ETF) based on the index. Very high readings identify extreme pessimism, which sets the tone for a reversal.

The chart includes the following:

- Daily price data for SPY
- PVI line across the bottom
- Central mean line at approximately 1.0
- +2SD line above the mean at 1.80 & –1SD line below it at 0.60

The vertical lines help view bearish extremes. Four of six of these extremes coincided with, or occurred shortly before, an acceleration of the selling and a subsequent bottom reversal in the market. These readings should not necessarily be interpreted in contrarian fashion, immediately, but as signs that the bears are gaining the upper hand, at least in the short term, and that an acceleration of the down trend may be near. So, when you see these high

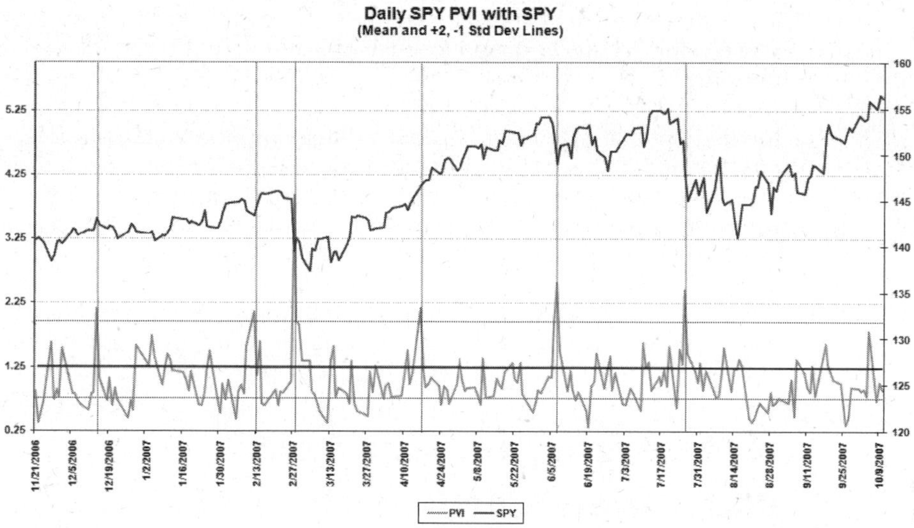

Figure 5-4: Put volume indicator.

readings, it's a time to pay even closer attention to the action in the market, especially because down trends tend to be shorter in duration than up trends and that, because there is an extreme in sentiment, a big move to the down side is increasingly likely, but also that a reversal may be close at hand.

TIP

If you have data to create a put to call ratio, you can also create the PVI.

Using Volatility to Measure Fear

Although it's hard to believe, fear is a stronger emotion that greed. Thus, panic is more dramatic. It makes market participants generally head for the exit much faster than what you see when they are committing new money to stock positions. The result is that markets generally fall much faster than they rise. This can be seen with increased volatility as daily and weekly price swings move in a larger range. Using volatility sentiment measures helps you recognize declines that are nearing exhaustion.

Measuring volatility

Volatility really just gives you information about the price range for a particular security. You can use a variety of trading periods to calculate an annualized value allowing you to compare movement for different securities. Historical volatility (HV) can be plotted on a chart, enabling you to view trends and gain a sense of how current HV stacks up to periods.

Implied volatility (IV) is an option pricing component that is referred to as a *plug figure*. It's the volatility level that accounts for the current option price after all other, more tangible pricing factors (that is, price, time, and interest rates) are valued. IV incorporates HV because it's reasonable to expect the stock to move in a similar manner to the past, but not necessarily the same.

IV can also be plotted on a chart, allowing you to view trends and relative levels. Such charts highlight strong seasonal tendencies for certain stocks.

Recognizing impact from changing volatility

You want to understand IV so you can make the best decisions when buying and selling options. It can be advantageous to buy options when IV is relatively low and sell them when it's relatively high, but there are no guarantees that seemingly low or high conditions won't persist.

Clearly there's always a chance of being wrong about the direction of an index or stock (two out of three really), but generally:

- When IV is relatively low and increases quickly, it adds value to both calls and puts.
- When IV is relatively high and decreases quickly, it decreases value for both calls and puts.

Pending news and reports, along with unexpected events, can spike IV. After the news or event is in the past, and an initial reaction occurs in the stock, IV declines as quickly as it spiked. Changes in IV that are more gradual may also occur, in either direction.

Spelling fear the Wall Street way: V-I-X

VIX stands for *volatility index*. It is a blended implied volatility value calculated using specific S&P 500 Index option contracts and is used as a sentiment indicator. You may have heard references to the VIX by market analysts commenting on conditions. The CBOE publishes the VIX closing values daily. Because VIX is an optionable index, trading programs graph the values in real time.

Because statistical volatility usually climbs when securities decline, you should expect IV to increase too. By viewing the VIX and SPX on the same chart, you can see just how often it does. The following holds for VIX readings:

- A climbing VIX reflects bearish conditions in SPX and typically the market as a whole.
- A declining VIX reflects neutral to bullish conditions in SPX and typically the market as a whole.

Overly bearish sentiment is reflected by high VIX levels. Eventually the bearish fear is exhausted, a reversal in stocks occur, and the VIX declines

The VIX was previously calculated using the S&P 100 (OEX) Index. This former VIX measure can be accessed using its new symbol: VXO.

Figure 5-5 displays a weekly chart for VIX with an SPX overlay.

The relationship between the two indexes appears pretty strong when viewed together. The two are negatively correlated, so when SPX goes down, VIX goes up, and vice versa. Look for VIX reversals to confirm market bottoms.

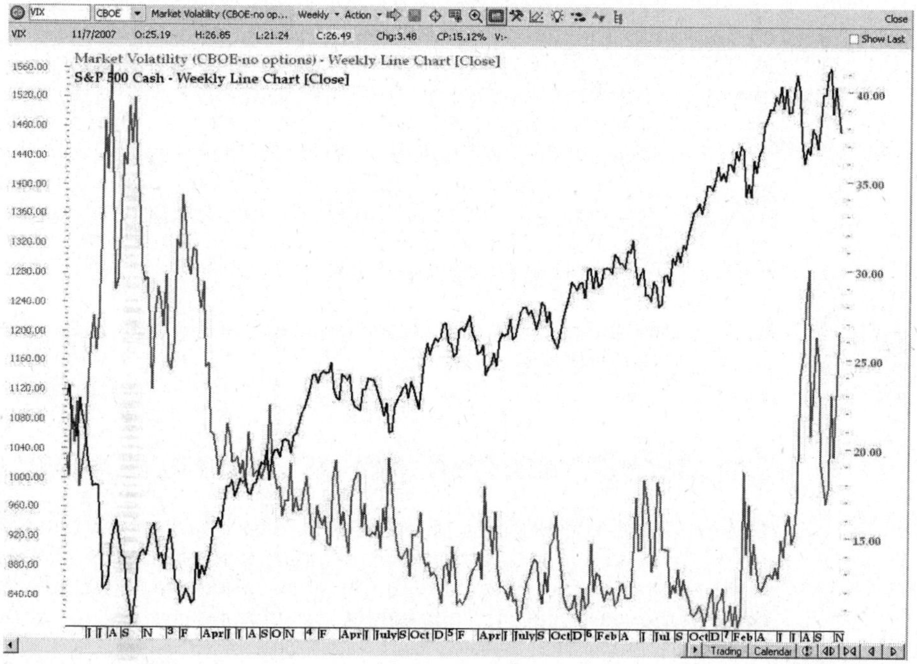

Figure 5-5: Weekly VIX chart with SPX overlay.

Two other stock indexes with implied volatility data to watch include the Nasdaq Composite Index (COMPQ) and the OEX. The corresponding volatility indexes are VXN and VXO, respectively.

When viewing a chart for the VIX, readings prior to the revised SPX methodology are constructed using historic data.

Applying Breadth and Sentiment Tools

Most breadth and sentiment indicators make use of the same logic:

- Weakness in the reading is a bearish sign.
- When the reading is extremely bearish, it becomes bullish.

And thus goes the behavior of the crowd. The only notable exception is the CBOE index-only P/C ratio. Because exchanges, trading platforms, and market products can potentially change over time, the nature of extremes for different indicators can also potentially change over time. Rather than using set-in-stone values for any one of them, you may want to combine a qualitative and quantitative assessment of them periodically.

When evaluating different breadth and sentiment tools, be sure to consider which indicators provide you with new information. It makes sense to include two or three option sentiment tools, but probably not five or six if that's the only type of sentiment indicator you're using. By becoming familiar with a few tools, you will avoid indicator burnout. One way to avoid overkill is to backtest different combinations of indicators and figure out which ones work best for you. The one constant should be that you try to use tools that provide different or complementary information, in order to maximize your time efficiency and the usefulness of the indicator.

To calculate the standard deviation for a column of data in Excel, use the cell formula: '=stdev(data)'[CC10].

Locating neutral areas for indicators

The Arms Index (TRIN) chart includes a neutral range between 0.70 and 1.30 — in this region there is no bias for the next day's open. When TRIN readings stay in that area, you simply have to look to other indicators to confirm moves or gain insight on potential changes.

Although it might seem that 1.0 would be a neutral reading for a put/call ratio, it doesn't work that way. Under normal conditions the ratio will be less than 1.0 because markets typically move upward, reflecting a bullish bias.

One method used throughout this chapter to identify both neutral areas and extremes for different indicators is an average +/– standard deviation approach. Here are some things to keep in mind when applying this:

- The calculations require a data set from some series — the data selected must be representative of the series.
- When you move forward in time by a significant amount, you run the risk of applying outdated conditions to current conditions.
- Consider calculating values for clearly defined bullish and bearish periods to see if the indicator behaves differently in each.

This is where qualitative judgment comes in — you don't necessarily want to include all possible data points in your assessment because conditions change over time. But they don't change often, so you need to include enough data so you're capturing information that is truly representative.

Stock and index price data is not normally distributed, so commonly used statistical rules for this data won't apply. You need to use returns.

By calculating an average value (mean) and standard deviation value, you're able to create bands around the central value to identify a region where most of the data is found. Points outside that area are atypical — when focusing on these areas, you're pinpointing times when emotions are running high and decisions are far from cool and calm.

Identifying indicator extremes

When analyzing data sets, you can complete different statistical tests directly on the data, including the following:

- Mean and median calculations for information about central tendencies
- Standard deviation calculations to identify extreme levels

Most often you'll use mean levels, but if one or two very extreme data points skew the results, you may opt to use a median value. When outliers are present, the mean value and median value will not be very close together.

In addition to applying these calculations directly to the data, you can apply them to smoothed segments of the data — namely moving averages. When doing this, you want to keep the moving average period pretty short so that you don't overly smooth the values. Remember, you want to view extreme behavior, not smooth it over to the point where you miss important turning points.

TECHNICAL STUFF

An *outlier* is a data point that is a good distance away from the other data points in the set and can't be dismissed.

A last look at advancing and declining breadth data is completed here using the advance-decline ratio, which oscillates around 1.0. This value is reached when the number of advancers on the NYA equals the number of decliners.

Figure 5-6 displays daily Adv-Dec ratio values along with the NYA. Two horizontal lines appear with the data: a darker average line, a +1SD line, and a –1SD line near the very bottom of the chart.

Compared to the P:C ratios, the extreme high values for the A/D ratio lag a bit. That's to be expected because put buying reflects pending doom and gloom while improvement in breadth occurs with a broad market rally. After that, things settle back to normal. The upward spikes don't exactly identify bottoms. Two light vertical lines are drawn to help you view this lag.

REMEMBER

When an indicator diverges from the index or stock you're evaluating, it may be an early warning of trend trouble.

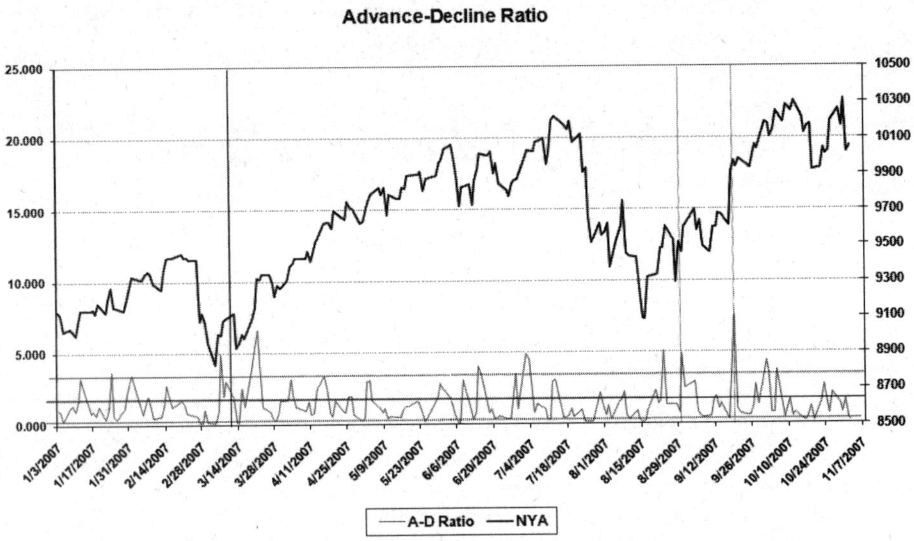

Figure 5-6: Daily Advance-Decline ratios along with the NYA.

The darker vertical line toward the beginning of the chart captures strong fear and coincides with the short-term market low. Although the number of extreme values is limited in both directions, the low extremes provide more timely information. The upward spikes confirm the reversal after the fact.

When applying SD lines, consider using multiples of 1, 2, and 3 to see what extremes are highlighted. It may be necessary to use one multiple for spikes on the high end and a different multiple for those on the low end, depending on how fast the values used in the indicator respond to market changes.

Chapter 6

Sector Analysis: Technical and Fundamental

In This Chapter

- Understanding chart advantages
- Selecting sectors with strength
- Projecting price movement

In a market that is functioning optimally, there are broad advances that include most market sectors. That means that when the broad averages move strongly up, so do most stocks and sectors. Thus, it follows that in a true down trend, the opposite is true, meaning that most stocks and sectors follow the down trend evident in the broad averages and market indexes.

But that is not always the case. In some situations, sectors don't move in exact tandem with indexes. This is because in some instances economic conditions favor one group or another for a period of time, and then as conditions change, so do the sectors displaying strength or weakness.

Focusing on strong or weak sectors allows you to apply strategies that are best suited for current market conditions. First, of course, you have to know how to find them. *Technical analysis* provides you with tools for analyzing sectors, including those geared toward identifying relative strength and weakness. In this chapter, we give you the technical analysis basics you need to accomplish this so that you can build your sector trading strategies.

Getting Technical with Charts

Chart analysis is the aspect of technical analysis that focuses on visual analysis to ferret out price and volume data that will let you discover the dominant trends in the market. There are a variety of chart types and data displays, providing you with an extremely large list of tools for analysis. By focusing here on a handful of technical tools and techniques geared toward sector and option trading, traders new to chart analysis should get up to speed quickly while those more familiar with it will get a bit of review.

Chart basics

Charts are pictures that are built by plotting price data to provide you with a view of trading activity during a given period. A short list of common chart types include the following:

- **Line chart:** Documents price movement versus time. A single price data point for each period is connected using a line. Line charts typically plot closing values, which are generally considered the most important value for the period (day, week, and so on). Line charts provide great "big picture" information for price movement and trends by filtering out noise from more minor moves during the period.

  Disadvantages to line charts include the fact that they provide no information about the strength of trading during the day or whether price gaps occurred from one period to the next. A *price gap* is created when trading for one period is completely above or below trading for the previous period. This happens when significant news impacting the company comes out when the markets are closed. Doesn't that seem like good information for you to have when you're trading?

- **Open-high-low-close (OHLC) bar chart:** Pictures price versus time. The period's trading range (low to high) is displayed as a vertical line with opening prices displayed as a horizontal tab on the left side of the range bar and closing prices as a horizontal tab on the right side of the range bar. A total of four price points are used to construct each bar.

  OHLC charts are more complete and useful over different periods of time because they provide information about both trading period strength and price gaps. Using a daily chart as a point of reference, a relatively long vertical bar tells you the price range was pretty big for the day. Another way to look at it is to say the stock was volatile that day — good information for option traders. It also hints at strength in the stock when the stock closes near the high of the day and weakness when it closes near the low for the day.

- **Candlestick chart:** These are the most commonly used charts by professional traders. They also plot price versus time and are similar to an OHLC chart with the price range between the open and the close for the period highlighted by a thickened bar. Patterns unique to this chart can enhance daily analysis.

  Candlestick charts have distinct pattern interpretations describing the battle between bulls and bears. These are best applied to a daily chart. Candlesticks also display price ranges and gaps.

View charts using both:

- Longer-term line charts noting price trends
- OHLC or candlestick charts for better understanding of price action during the period, including security strength and volatility

TIP

Many technical charting packages are available as independent software programs or web-based applications. The cost ranges from free to thousands of dollars, depending on the package features. When first using technical analysis, consider starting with a free web-based package and then identify your specific needs and expand from there. Your online broker will often have a "home" charting program available. Sometimes these packages are available at some cost, whereas at other times, they may be free of charge, especially if you are an active trader. It's a good idea to research this aspect of your broker's services.

Adjusting your time horizon for the best view

Before focusing on one specific chart interval, consider your investment or trading horizon, also known as your *timeframe*. Think about your objective. What you want to view when evaluating your 401(k) investment is different than your focus for active trading.

Technical analysis places different emphasis on timeframes. Longer-term trends are considered stronger than shorter-term ones. To get the best view of trends, it's extremely helpful to carefully and systematically evaluate charts that depict price action over multiple intervals of time. The typical chart default is a daily chart, but others exist as well.

When completing a market analysis to locate strong sectors, an ideal progression includes evaluating the following:

- Long-term major trends using monthly charts on indexes and sectors
- Intermediate-term major and minor trends using weekly charts on broad market indexes and sectors
- Short-term minor trends using daily charts on sectors

By first recognizing major and intermediate trends, you're less likely to get caught up in the emotion associated with shorter-term moves.

TECHNICAL STUFF

A horizontal support line can be drawn after price moves down to touch a price level twice. The line is confirmed when a third touch of that price level successfully holds and buying demand returns to the security, sending the price up.

Visualizing supply and demand

Charts can be thought of as a visual display of supply and demand:

- Buying demand pushes prices upward.
- Supply creates selling pressure that drives prices downward.
- Volume displays the magnitude of supply or demand.

Markets don't just move straight up and down — price variations are a direct result of the constant and dynamic battle between the bulls (demand) and the bears (supply).

TECHNICAL STUFF

A horizontal resistance line can be drawn once; price moves up to touch a price level twice. The line is confirmed when a third touch of that price level successfully holds and selling demand returns to the security sending the price down.

Areas of support and resistance

Price support and resistance halt the trend that is in place:

- Support represents a transition from declining prices driven by supply to climbing prices when renewed demand kicks in at that price level.
- Resistance represents a transition from climbing prices driven by strong demand to declining prices when selling pressure comes in at that price.

When trading, notice that these transitions line up over time, sometimes creating sideways trading channels as price moves between the two. As with all price trends, the longer the price serves as support or resistance, the stronger it's considered.

Support and resistance levels are not just chart points to look at; they are areas where you can take action. For example, support and resistance levels are useful for identifying trading position entry and exit points. Consider also using them in price projections to identify stop-loss and profit-taking exits, as well as calculating risk-reward ratios.

TIP

Price areas that previously served as support often serve as resistance areas in the future and vice versa. When prices rise above resistance or fall below support, it's a signal that a new price trend may be on the way.

Trend analysis

We use the concept of trend quite a bit before reaching this formal definition. That's because we're pretty sure you have a sense of what an upward trend and a downward trend is for any asset — painfully so if you were holding on to that asset in the latter trend. More formally, trend identifies price direction:

- **Upward trend:** Prices climb and pull back in such a way that a rising line can be drawn under the pullbacks which display higher lows. Higher highs are also characteristic of uptrends.
- **Downward trend:** Prices fall and retrace in such a way that a declining line can be drawn above the top of retracement peaks that display lower highs. Lower lows are also characteristic of downtrends.

Create a trend line by connecting two higher lows (uptrend) or two lower highs (downtrend). When price successfully tests the line a third time, the trend is confirmed. You can use these lines as entry and exit points similarly to the trading technique used at support and resistance levels.

TIP

Consider drawing two trend lines using a longer-term chart, such as a monthly chart, to highlight an area of resistance versus a subjective single trend line. One may use closing data while the other uses market lows. If you do this, you will highlight a *trading channel*, which gives you a nice visual record of the trading activity and lets you plan entry and exit points as well as monitor the situation in an open position.

Moving averages

Moving averages are lines constructed on a chart using an average value of closing prices during a certain number of days. These lines are considered *lagging* indicators because the historical data follows price action. Here are the two main types of moving averages:

- Simple moving averages (SMA) use a basic average calculation.
- Exponential moving averages (EMA) incorporate all available price data, providing greater weight to more recent data.

Simple moving averages equally weigh all closes for the time period selected, while exponential moving averages are calculated in such a way that more recent data carries greater weight in the line.

Both SMAs and EMAs can be constructed using a variety of settings and chart intervals. So you can view a five-day SMA on a daily chart or a ten-week EMA on a weekly chart. Moving average lines are considered unbiased trend indicators because the lines are derived from objective calculations.

The three most common settings for either moving average include the following:

- 20-day moving average displaying short-term trends
- 50-day moving average displaying intermediate-term trends
- 200-day moving average displaying long-term trends

You may have heard financial media reporting that *price is approaching the 200-day moving average*. That's because a break of this line is considered significant and may confirm a trend reversal. Other popular averages include the 10- and 100-day moving averages. The concepts are the same, with the only real difference in their use being trader preference based on their own time frames and experience.

Exponential moving averages incorporate all available price data for the underlying security, with more recent data having a greater weight on the EMA value for the period. As a result, they are more responsive to price changes and can be considered more sensitive when making trading decisions.

Identifying Relatively Strong Sectors

Major market moves up or down generally result in gains or losses for most sectors and securities too. However, during more moderate trending, certain sectors and securities perform better than the market while others perform worse. A sector or security can also move in the opposite direction during these periods. Your objective as a trader is to find those relatively strong and weak groups so you can apply profitable sector strategies.

Relative ratios

You construct a relative ratio line by dividing one security into another. This allows you to objectively compare the performance of one security relative to the other, because the line rises when the primary security is outperforming the second one and falls when it is underperforming. Adding an overlay chart to a relative ratio allows you to view both securities on one chart. Log scales typically provide a better view for the movement of each.

Trend lines drawn on a log chart will appear differently when you switch to an arithmetic scale.

Figure 6-1 displays a weekly log chart for XLF (dark solid line), an exchange-traded fund (ETF) comprised of S&P 500 financial companies. It also displays an overlay of SPY (light, thinner line), which is the S&P 500 Index ETF. The 10-week and 40-week EMAs (two dashed lines) are also included for XLF, displaying intermediate- and long-term trends, respectively. Finally, the bottom portion shows the relative ratio line for XLF/SPY.

Shorter moving averages measure a shorter time period and move more closely with price, and thus are used to smooth out shorter-term trends. You can distinguish these lines on a chart because they are somewhat jagged.

When including relative ratios on a chart, you have a clearer view of the performance for two securities. In Figure 6-1, at plain sight, it appears that the two indexes moved pretty similarly until the latter part of the time period charted. But a look at the relative ratio line tells another story. Throughout a good portion of the three-year period pictured, SPY outperformed XLF, very significantly from June 2007 through October 2007, a period that preceded the first down leg of the U.S. market in relationship to the subprime mortgage crisis. Thus, this type of analysis was good for both evaluation of XLF, but also hinted that financial stocks were starting to weaken.

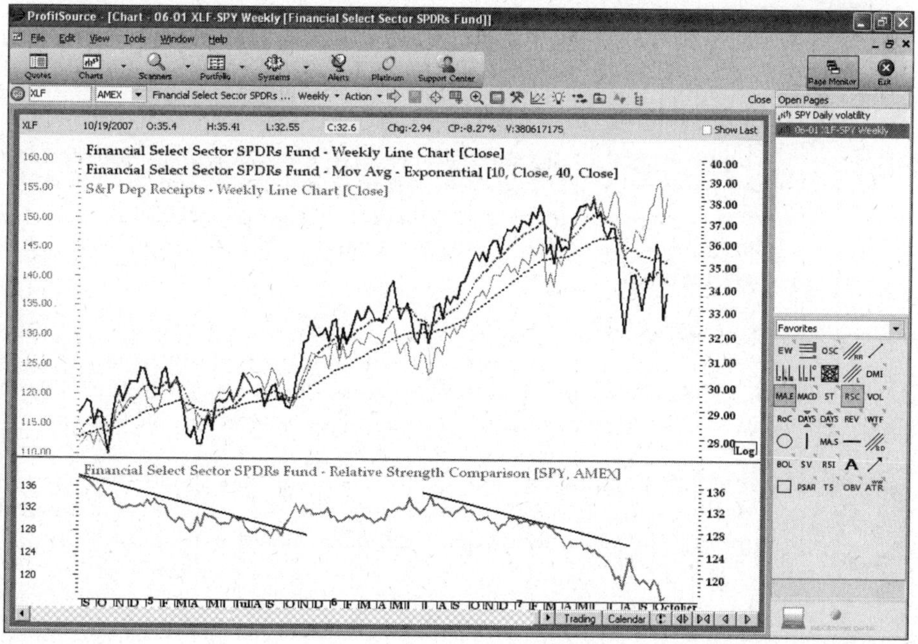

Figure 6-1: Weekly chart for XLF with EMAs and performance relative to SPY.

Image by Optionetics

TIP

Relative ratio lines are commonly referred to as *relative strength comparisons*.

The chart also shows that the indicator was timely, because within a month after the deterioration in the relative ratio line, XLF dropped below its 200-day EMA and shortly after the 50-day EMA followed. Although not labeled, the shorter EMA is identified by noting which one moves more closely with the price. When downward-trending conditions are ideal, prices and MAs line up with price data appearing lowest on the chart followed by the shorter EMA, and then the higher EMA — just as Figure 6-1 is showing.

Some traders use moving average crosses as trading system signals. This approach has its place in trading, but note where price was when the cross occurred — almost at its lowest point. Remember, moving averages lag price data. Moving average crossovers are better used as trend confirmation, but not necessarily as timing tools. Thus, relative strength lines can be used as leading indicators and moving averages as confirmation. Once that negative cross occurs, it makes sense to favor bearish strategies.

Before moving away from this particular chart, note that trend lines can be applied to relative ratios. The same rules apply:

- Draw uptrends using the low points in the trend.
- Draw downtrends using the high points in the trend.

Also, previous areas of support can become resistant and vice versa.

TIP

When using overlay capabilities on a chart, indicators added to the chart are based on the primary security.

When using relative ratios, it's good to identify a group of related indexes or sectors to monitor. Cash flows from one outperforming market or sector to another as economic conditions and market perceptions change. Portfolio allocations should favor outperforming markets and underweigh underperforming ones.

The wide range of ETFs that track different assets (for example, the U.S. dollar or oil) allow you to employ an asset allocation plan across markets using a single security type. Add the existence of options for many ETFs, and you have reduced risk access to the commodity and foreign exchange markets.

TIP

Trend lines can be used on relative strength comparison lines to better identify changing conditions and areas of support and resistance. Similarly, support that has been broken will often serve as resistance in the future.

Especially in the beginning, it helps to simplify your methods. A good way to do this is by focusing on sectors. By selecting one optionable ETF fund family sector group, you will be able to quickly evaluate and compare multiple sector trends and their relative performance to each other and to the overall market. As an example, the Select Sector S&P Depository Receipts (SPDR) include ten ETFs based on the S&P 500 Index:

- SPY tracks the entire S&P 500 Index.
- Nine ETFs track each of the nine major sectors that make up the index.

Collectively, the nine sector ETFs make up the SPY ETF. By analyzing ten charts, you can complete a broad market and sector assessment, which can serve as a basis for comprehensive sector investing or trading. Thus, seeking an ETF fund family that is liquid and optionable is crucial and should be your first objective — then you follow up by confirming liquidity in the ETF options.

A relative ratio line only compares performance of two securities — it does not indicate the trend for either security. A rising line can indicate the primary security is trending upward at a faster rate than the second security or that it is trending downward at a slower rate.

Rate of change indicator

Relative ratios provide you with a good visual approach for assessing sectors. A rate of change (ROC) approach allows you to also quantify and rank performance for those sectors. The ROC for a security is the speed in which it moves — when calculating security returns, you are using one type of ROC. There is also an ROC indicator that can be drawn on charts for analyzing, trading, or ranking securities.

To calculate a ten-day ROC, you use the following formula:

(Today's Price ÷ Price 10 (Trading) Days Ago) × 100

Using the nine sector ETFs, you can rank the sectors by strength using a 14-day ROC value for each, as shown in Table 6-1. When calculating the formula, keep in mind that there are ten trading days in a two-week (14-day) trading period. In this chapter, the 14-day period refers to the ten trading sessions that took place during that time period. Just to keep it simple, if you are keeping this record by hand, unless you are calculating this ratio on a daily basis, it makes sense to use Friday closing values as your starting point whenever possible, but to keep in mind that holidays may break up your usual cadence of numbers.

Table 6-1 14-day ROC Sector Rankings on 7-11-2014

ETF	*Sector*	*10-Day ROC*	*Rank*
XLE	Energy	101.64	1
XLP	Consumer Staples	101.34	2
XLV	Healthcare	100.90	3
XLI	Industrials	-100.40	4
XLF	Financials	99.60	5
XLB	Materials	99.67	6
XLY	Consumer Cyclicals	99.07	7
XLK	Technology	98.50	8
XLU	Utilities	98.21	9
SPY	Entire Index	-99.60	--

XLE, XLP, XLI, and XLV are considered relatively strong, whereas XLY, XLY, and XLK relatively weak compared to price 14 days ago. Does this mean XLE is trending upward or XLU trending downward? Not at all — it's simply a way for you to compare the performance of a group of securities using specific criteria. This kind of analysis becomes extremely useful in a market that is in a possible trend transition period, such as how the market was acting in July of 2014 after the Federal Reserve announced that it would stop its Quantitative Easing program in October of 2014. Because utilities are the most interest-sensitive sector in the market, it makes sense that they were the weakest group during this period, as traders were beginning to consider that interest rates could rise in the not-too-distant future.

TIP

As an alternative approach to sector trading, you can expand the list to include industry groups, investment styles (small or large cap, value or growth), or countries, among others. The main goal is to develop a group of ETFs that experience related capital inflows and outflows.

When using ROC trends, you really want to capture money flows from one market or sector to another. Consider checking out different periods, such as weekly or monthly ROCs, and see how the rankings change each week. Relative-strength trading approaches seek to establish bullish positions in relatively strong performers and bearish position in relatively weak performers. This works best when the periods used result in rankings that persist more than a week or two, so that you remain in a strong position.

When trading, the ROC is used with a simple moving average (SMA) as a trade alert. When the ROC rises above its SMA, it is a bullish alert, and crosses of the ROC below its SMA are a bearish alert. An example of this is shown in the next section.

The term *normalize* refers to the process of expressing data so that it is independent of the absolute value of the underlying. This allows comparison to other securities.

Using Sector Volatility Tools

Technical analysis displays volatility in a variety of ways, including basic range bars and historical volatility (HV) plots. Objective technical indicators available in many charting packages and covered in this section include the following:

- Statistical volatility
- Average true range
- Bollinger bands
- Bollinger %b

These tools provide you with different volatility views and allow you to scan the markets for securities that may be gearing up for a change. Although volatility can remain high or low for extended periods of time, these measures may provide you with the following:

- A buy alert when declining
- A sell alert with jumps higher
- A tool to help identify appropriate strategies
- Detection of seasonal movement

The value used for technical indicators is referred to as the *setting*. Commonly used settings are referred to as *default values*.

Displaying volatility with indicators

Statistical volatility and the average true range are two different displays of price movement. Here's how they differ:

- **Statistical volatility (SV):** SV, another term for historical volatility, uses closing values to plot an annualized standard deviation line that represents the degree of price movement in the security. Because various time periods can be used on a chart, SV reflects the chart period, not necessarily a daily calculation as you see on option HV or SV charts.
- **Average true range (ATR):** The ATR uses a true range (TR) value to define price movement and was developed by Welles Wilder. TR incorporates extreme movement such as gaps, so it better reflects volatility. TR uses the previous close and current high and low values to calculate three different ranges. The biggest range for the three is the TR for the period. Therefore, it's an excellent indicator to use along with more traditional momentum indicators to confirm important market turning points.

REMEMBER

A rate of return calculation is one measure of rate of change. It allows comparisons for securities with different prices by creating a value that is independent of price.

Figure 6-2 provides the three TR range calculations and a bar chart example of each.

ATR is an exponential moving average that smoothes TR. A strong move in the ATR incorporates price gaps and provides traders with important information about price volatility that can be missed by other smoothed indicators. Because ATR uses historical prices and a smoothing process, it's a lagging indicator and does not predict volatility. However, a sharp move upward in a security's ATR is often accompanied by an increase in IV for its options.

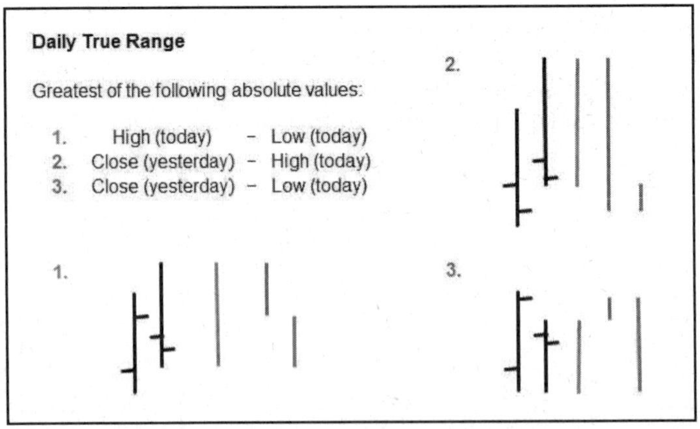

Figure 6-2: Daily true range calculations and display.

Image by Optionetics

WARNING!

When using rankers to identify stocks with narrowing bandwidth, be sure to check the chart to see what's happening with the stock. Price may have flattened due to a pending corporate action such as a stock buyout and is less likely to move from that point.

Figure 6-3 displays a daily OHLC bar chart for SPY, the S&P 500 Index ETF with the 14-day ATR and 14-day SV.

Figure 6-3 is an example of how you can use volatility indicators to

- Spot potentially meaningful changes in the market's trend.
- Use the information as a wake-up call in a market where you may have been standing aside.
- Consider implementing low-risk and high potential-return trading strategies.

In the late July through early August period, the volatility for SPY increased, as seen by range bars increasing in length. In this particular decline, SV peaked approximately five days before SPY bottomed, which was followed by a peak in the ATR one day later.

All nine sector ETFs bottomed on the same day, with each ATR peaking within one day of this bottom. The SV profile for the ETFs varied more, but most also peaked a few days prior to the bottom. When reviewing the charts, note the following about XLI (Figure 6-4):

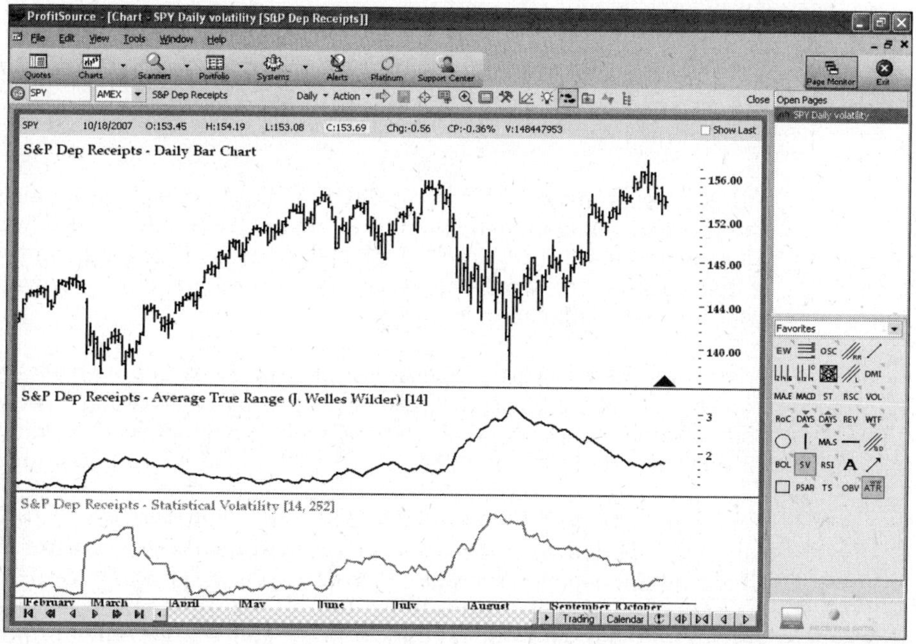

Figure 6-3: SPY daily OHLC bar chart with ATR and SV.

Image by Optionetics

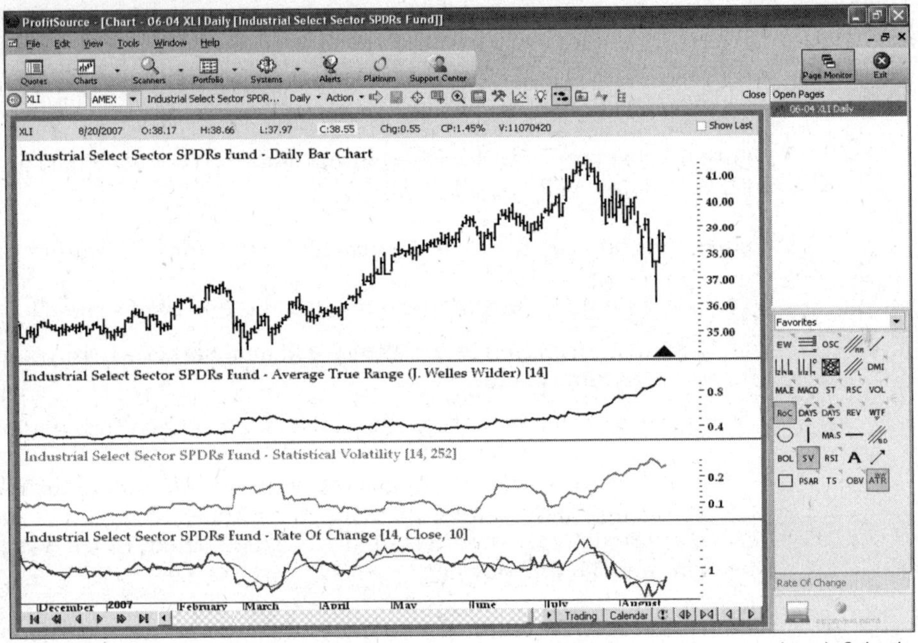

Figure 6-4: XLI daily OHLC bar chart with ATR, SV, and ROC.

Image by Optionetics

- Price moved in a very wide range, closing the day at its high with a slight net gain.
- SV was pulling back from a peak two days prior.
- ATR was still moving upward.
- The SMA for the 14-day ROC was flattening, suggesting a possible end to the decline.

Although XLI ranked fifth on a 14-day ROC basis, closing at its high for the day was extremely bullish given the range of trading for that day. The situation merited monitoring to confirm a reversal. By following conditions for a couple of days, you would have seen the directional change toward higher prices in XLI displayed in Figure 6-4.

Price continued upward while ATR appeared to be pulling back and SV conditions remained elevated. ROC crossed up above its ten-day SMA, which was a bullish signal. The only strategy briefly discussed so far that suits these conditions (bullish, high volatility) is a long stock, short call position.

Buying the ETF near the close at $38.55 and selling the Sep 39 strike price call for $0.80, you've created a moderately reduced risk position. Rather than $3,855 on the line, you've reduced your exposure to $3,775 or by 2%. There are actually better strategies to capitalize on this situation — ones that allow you to limit your risk much more — but this one is suitable for now.

You can establish a short-term covered call strategy with the goal of being called out of the position. That's the case here, so you want XLI to be trading above 39 at September expiration. This is exactly what happened. On expiration Friday, XLI closed at 40.63 and you would have been assigned. This means you bought the position for $3,775 and sold it for $3,900.

Analyzing volatility with Bollinger bands

Bollinger bands provide you with another nice visual of relative volatility levels. This technical tool uses a simple moving average (SMA) surrounded by upper and lower bands, both derived from a standard deviation calculation. John Bollinger, the tool's developer, uses the following as default settings:

- 20-period SMA
- Upper band (SMA + two standard deviations)
- Lower band (SMA – two standard deviations)

The bands contract and expand as price volatility contracts and expands. Two additional Bollinger band tools include the following:

- **Bandwidth (BW)** measures the distance between the two bands using the calculation: BW = (Upper BB – Lower BB) ÷ Moving Average.

  According to Bollinger, when BW is at its lowest level in six months, a squeeze candidate is identified. That's a security that is consolidating before a potentially strong breakout higher or lower. It is not uncommon for a false move to occur, so straddle strategies — where you make both long and short bets simultaneously in order to be prepared for which way the stock breaks (see Chapter 14) — can provide a way to play this situation.
- **%b** identifies where the price is relative to the BW, calculated using a variation of George Lane's Stochastic indicator, with values ranging from
  - 0 to 100 when price is at or between the bands.
  - Less than 0 when below the lower band (bearish).
  - Greater than 100 when above the upper band (bullish).

TIP

Look for confirmation from more than one indicator and compare the action in the price charts to what the indicators are predicting. Also review the news to see if known meaningful developments are affecting prices. In a world where conflicts are numerous and escalating on a regular basis, external events could easily affect market as well as individual security prices at any time.

A value of 75 reflects price that is within the bands and one quarter below the lower band from a total bandwidth standpoint. %b normalizes price relative to bandwidth size and allows you to make an apples-to-apples comparison of different stocks for ranking purposes.

Different sectors experience bullish and bearish trends at different times. Although strong rallies and declines in the broad markets often move all securities in the same direction, the strength and duration of the moves for these different securities can vary greatly. In general, the following principles apply:

- Securities and sectors with very high values for %b are bullish when confirmed by other technical tools and the activity on the price charts.
- Securities and sectors with very low values for %b are bearish when confirmed by other technical tools and the activity on the price charts.

Bollinger noted that rather than prices being extended when near a Bollinger band, the condition actually reflects strength and a breakout that can continue. Look for pullbacks toward the moving average line to establish new positions in the direction of the trend after such a breakout.

Projecting Prices for Trading

Because there are no guarantees in the markets, it is important to give yourself room when you set up trades. Options with low implied volatility levels can remain low, stocks in a downtrend can continue dropping, and options with a 75% chance of being in the money at expiration according to the models can expire worthless. That's why risk management is your first order of business as a trader. Using support and resistance areas and trend lines is a straightforward way to manage your risk.

Price projections can include those identifying exits for a loss or a profit. Both are important. Sometimes you focus so much on managing risk that you forget to also be on the alert for profit-taking. By identifying areas above and below the current price prior to establishing a position, you simplify trade management. Consider using objective techniques such as price channels, retracements, and extensions for identifying exit levels.

The following sections give you both sides of the coin: methods for projecting price moves (magnitude and time) and risk-management tools — just what's needed for option traders.

Support and resistance

Support and resistance provide you with subjective tools that identify

- Concrete exit levels for a loss.
- Potential exit levels for a profit.

Although support and resistance lines are subjective, because prices can become volatile near them, they do represent a reasonable approach to managing your risk because they identify a maximum loss or an area where you can take a reasonable profit. As your skills develop, applying such tools and exit points will improve.

The reason we use the term *potential exit* related to taking profits is because changing conditions may warrant an early exit for partial profits or they may allow you to extend gains, depending on the change. Suppose you hold a bullish position. If your indicators become bearish, you may receive an alert prompting an earlier-than-anticipated exit from the position. On the other hand, you may have already taken a portion of your profits when the stock reaches your original projection price. If the chart remains bullish, you can revise your price target for additional profits.

WARNING!

You have to follow your rules or you will lose more money than you can imagine. Extending the exit only applies to profit-taking; exit points for a loss have to be written in stone. You can exit the position early, but you absolutely cannot revise the exit level in a way that extends losses. It's critical for you to identify a maximum loss price for the position and execute it if it's reached, period.

REMEMBER

Because trend lines are drawn by the analyst, a degree of bias may be introduced. Consider allowing a little bit of leeway when using these price areas for entries and exits to help minimize the impact of bias.

Figure 6-5 shows an example of how to use support and resistance levels to plan a trade and to manage risk. Using a moving average crossover system, you decide to enter a long position in XLF (financials ETF) the day after the 20-day EMA crosses up over the 50-day EMA. One exit signal includes a cross of the 20-day EMA down below the 50-day EMA. Because this exit doesn't identify a specific exit for a loss, you add a support line below the current price to manage your risk.

In the previous uptrend, $36.58 served as support, but this area was broken when XLF declined a couple months ago. The market has since reversed and the same $36.58 level served as resistance when XLF started moving upward. The ETF recently broke above this level, making it a reasonable stop-loss support area going forward. Because the ETF is trading around $37.10, it represents a 1.4% loss, which is well within your risk parameters.

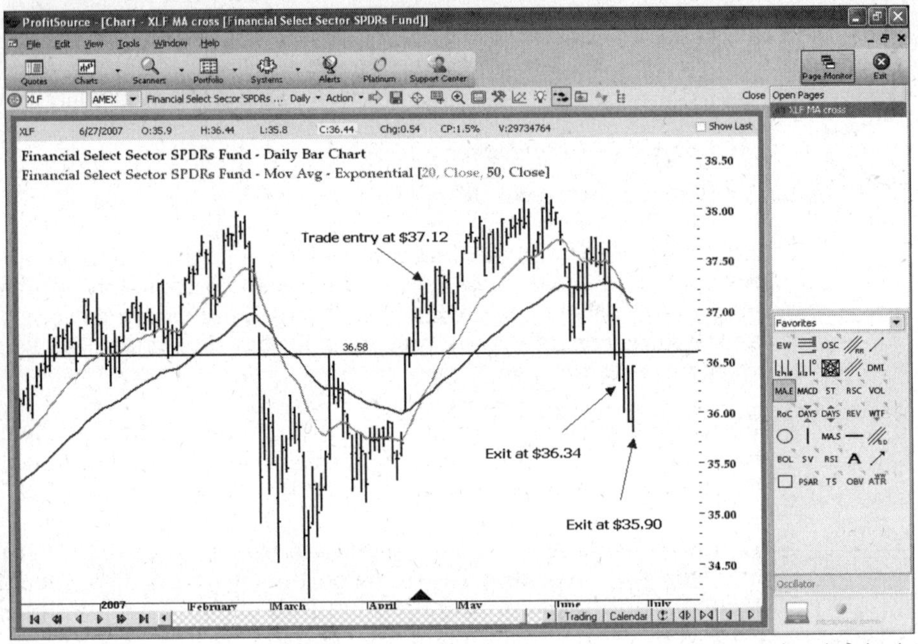

Figure 6-5: XLF daily OHLC bar chart with support line and 20- and 50-day EMAs.

Image by Optionetics

TIP

To view a 200-day moving average on a weekly chart, you must use a setting of 40 because there are five trading days in a week. That's why it is also known as the 40-week moving average.

Figure 6-5 displays the daily OHLC bar chart for XLF with 20-day and 50-day EMAs, and a horizontal support line drawn at $36.58. The entire trade period is shown, including trade entry, which was established at $37.12. Both exit signals that resulted are also identified.

Price moved upward for a little more than a month and then dropped, but remained above the support line. Another weaker advance failed, and now price dropped below support. The trade was exited at the next open for $36.34. Assuming 100 shares were purchased, the position loss was $78, which represented 2.1% of the initial position. Unless a physical stop loss order is in place (see Chapter 8), actual losses will be greater than those calculated using the support price. Regardless, this exit did prevent an additional $44 (1.2%) loss had you waited for the EMA crossover.

When viewing the chart, you may notice that price reached an approximate double top at $38.00, and then declined. An approach that took partial profits at this previous resistance level would have yielded more gains than losses.

Longer moving averages (that is, high setting) are considered slower and less responsive to price changes. You can distinguish these lines on a chart because they are smoother. Calculating a moving average is referred to as a *smoothing process.*

Trends

Trend lines are upward and downward moving lines drawn across higher lows (uptrend) or lower highs (downtrend). These lines can similarly be used for price-projection purposes. The actual price level you use with these lines is estimated because the lines are trending rather than horizontal.

Many technical analysis packages include a crosshair tool, allowing you to identify the price and date for different areas on the chart. Using the same EMA crossover entry technique for XLF, a trend line exit can be identified with the crosshair tool.

Many trend-following systems have a larger number of small losses and fewer large profitable trades. These systems rely on using the system exit rather than physical stop-loss exit levels. To properly manage risk while allowing the system to perform as it should, incorporate percentage loss exits into your backtesting to determine whether the system is viable when a stop-loss is included.

Figure 6-6 incorporates a successfully tested trend line on a daily chart for XLF. The crosshair level one day after the trade entry date is included. Although this method uses an estimate for the stop, it represents a stop that is dynamic because it increases over time as the trend remains intact.

Using the trend line approach on the example resulted in profits, but don't jump to the conclusion that it's a superior approach — it just worked out better in this case. The main point is that it's possible for you to use basic tools when identifying reasonable price levels for downside protection. Exiting a bullish trade when an upward trending line is broken makes a lot of sense.

Options come with an expiration date, so the time it takes for a stock to reach a projected price is as important as the projection itself.

There are many technical tools that generate entry and exit signals, but not price projections. When identifying a maximum loss exit point, remember to consider basic techniques for managing risk.

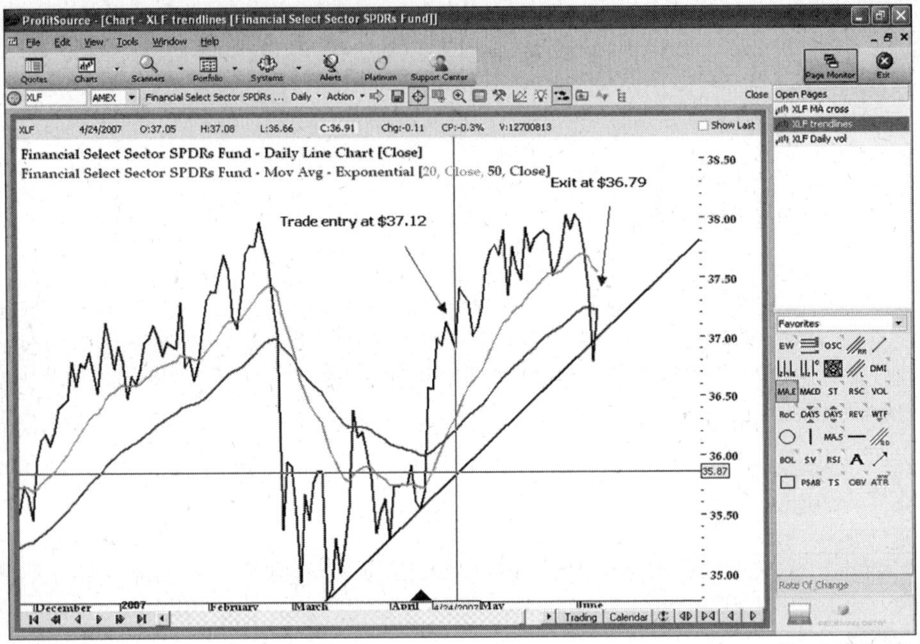

Figure 6-6: XLF daily line chart with trend line and 20- and 50-day EMAs.

Image by Optionetics

Channels

Price channels include those drawn using two different trend lines and those constructed using a regression line — here we display the latter to focus on objective tools. A regression channel

- Uses a specific number of past prices to create the channel.
- Includes a middle regression line that represents the expected value for future prices (no guarantees).
- Fixes the data period and then extends the channel lines forward in time.

A regression line is *fixed*, meaning it's constructed using data that has a start and end date rather than adding and dropping data the way a moving average does. Price is expected to revert the mean with these channels.

TIP

A regression line is also referred to as *a line of best fit*. It's the line that represents the shortest distance between the line and each data point.

When creating a regression channel, you use an existing trend that is expected to remain intact. Price contained by the channel confirms the trend, and price moving outside of the channel suggests a change in trend may be developing.

There are a variety of ways you can construct a channel. Here we focus on a basic linear regression approach. After identifying the trend period, the regression line is drawn and the boundary lines are created as follows:

- Upper boundary line uses the distance between the regression line and the point furthest above the line.
- Lower boundary line uses the distance between the regression line and the point furthest below the line.

Very wide channels reflect volatile trends, whereas narrow channels reflect more quiet trends. Oftentimes price will remain in the upper or lower region of the channel for periods of time while it is trending. If price breaks out of the channel and then returns to it without moving to the middle regression line, a change in trend may be developing.

Suppose you constructed the regression channel in Figure 6-7 using a weekly OHLC bar chart for XLB. The data range for the channel is shown above it, and a long trade entry point is identified by the arrow.

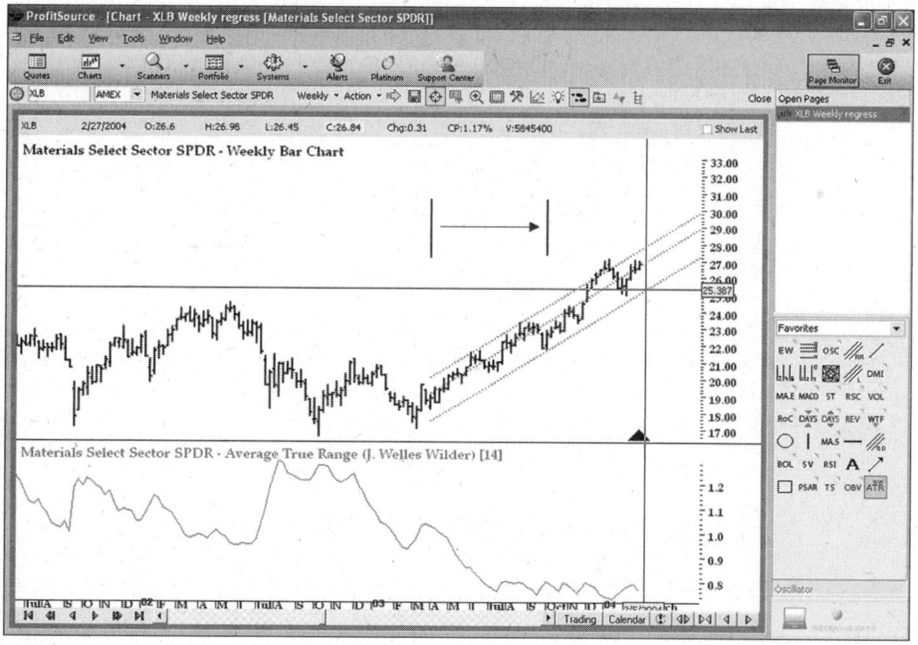

Figure 6-7: XLB weekly OHLC chart with regression channel.

Image by Optionetics

As the trend progresses upward, you can identify a rising exit point using the lower channel boundaries and regression line. Your exit rules may include the following:

- Exit the position on the Monday after price closes outside of the lower channel line on the weekly chart (projected at 25.36).
- Take profits if price moves above the upper channel line and then returns to the channel.
- Take partial profits at the middle regression line if price fails to move to the upper channel line.

Check out the chart package Help links to obtain information about indicator construction and applications.

Using the crosshairs tool allows you to identify realistic price projections that correspond to future points in time.

Consider creating regression channels on monthly and weekly charts. Then move down in time to weekly and daily charts, respectively, to apply stronger trends to the relatively shorter time period.

Although difficult to see in Figure 6-7, the crosshair tool also identifies March 12 as the corresponding date for movement to the lower boundary line — that is, assuming price continues to behave as it has in the past.

You may be thinking that's a pretty big assumption, but it's the one made any time you enter a position in the direction of the trend. This approach to a time projection is subjective, but it does provide you with a nice reality check when considering potential moves.

Trends are not considered predictive. They exist in the market, but they do not predict price because they can either continue or fail. Technical tools like fundamental analysis are good to have and provide guidelines for risk management and profit-taking, not guarantees.

Price retracements and extensions

Retracement tools make use of existing trends to identify potential areas of price support and resistance. The fact is that market trends and conditions are largely associated with two primary human emotions: greed and fear. Technical analysis acknowledges the impact of such crowd-driven behavior and uses visual and quantitative tools that attempt to provide an actionable snapshot of the current situation whenever possible. One such application includes the use of Fibonacci ratios for retracement purposes. These ratios are derived from a numeric series of the same name, originally defined by Italian mathematician Leonardo Fibonacci.

Examples of the series and ratios are found throughout nature — in diverse areas such as the distribution and arrangements of rose petals and tree branches — and are used by many traders in various applications. Because different market participants will be taking action when certain Fibonacci price levels are reached, you should be aware of these levels. A basic understanding will likely help you assess market action.

W. D. Gann was a successful commodities trader who also developed a series of ratios and retracement and extension tools that are widely used. Gann's ratios include 0.125, 0.25, 0.50, and 1.00, among others.

Fibonacci series and ratios

The Fibonacci integer series is generated starting with 0 and 1, and adding the two previous integers in the series to obtain the next integer:

0, 1, 1 (0 + 1), **2** (1 + 1), **3** (1 + 2), **5** (2 + 3), **8** (3 + 5), **13** (5 + 8), . . .

The *Fibonacci ratios* are values reached when dividing an integer in the series by specific previous or subsequent integers in the series. The primary Fibonacci ratios used in technical analysis are as follows:

0.382, 0.500, 0.618, 1.00, 1.618 and 2.618

Because prices do not move straight up or down, retracements develop which are counter-trend moves. A retracement includes

- A pullback in price during an uptrend.
- A rise in price during a downtrend.

Fibonacci ratios are often used to define and predict potential retracement areas. Extensions use the same ratio process to identify projections beyond the starting point for the base trend.

Fibonacci numbers can be used for indicator settings when making adjustments to the default setting.

Figure 6-8 displays Fibonacci retracements (thinner lines occurring during the trend) and extensions (thicker lines occurring beyond the trend) for XLI.

Time extensions

A second method uses Fibonacci numbers or ratios to identify future dates for potential turning points. Projections are determined using

- A ratio based on the time taken to create the original trend.
- A count using Fibonacci integers moving forward.

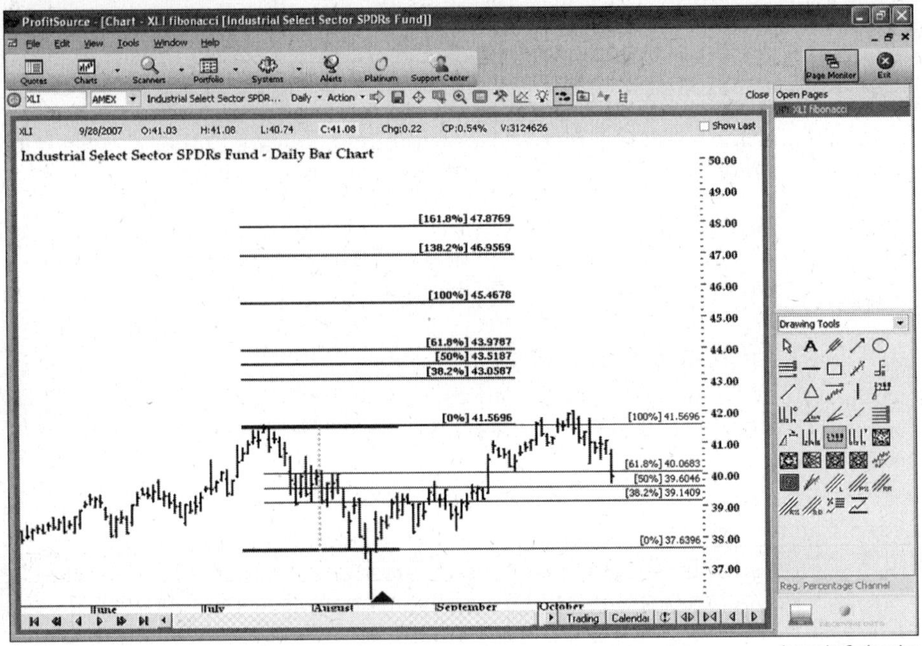

Figure 6-8: XLI daily chart with Fibonacci retracements and extensions.

Image by Optionetics

Another commonly applied approach to time objectives is the use of market cycles. Similar to the economic business cycle, the stock market undergoes bullish and bearish cycles that are measured from low point to low point. Cycle analysis can be imprecise and variable, whereas Fibonacci analysis is more reliable.

Projections and probabilities

By lining up different high probability factors, you create a situation where you put the odds in your favor for a particular strategy or trade. By managing your risk, you limit losses and realize larger gains. The process partly involves science (supported by rules) and partly involves art (supported by experience). The key is to let both art and science balance each other and to take hope, emotion, and ego out of the picture.

Weighing possibility versus probability

Even though basic tools can be subjective, at least trust what you see and develop reliable rules for those times when what you see isn't totally clear. For example, a valid trend line helps you more easily identify intact trends and provides a reasonable exit point when the line is broken. Such a break is a clear signal that the original reason for entering the trade is no longer valid. However, you can still encounter problems when that time comes.

What if the trend line you drew was on a weekly chart, and during the week the trend line was broken? Technically, you don't have a weekly close below the trend line, but that doesn't mean you should continue to simply watch price erode. Technical methods rely on confirming indicators to help line up probabilities.

Identifying a stop exit point before entering a position helps reduce your emotion during the trade.

Here are some things to look for: During an uptrend, if volume increases as price moves down towards the trend line, it's a bearish alert. A break of the line with increasing volume is more bearish evidence. Such action on a daily chart supports exiting a position established using weekly data.

Referring back to Figure 6-4, a covered call position in XLI was created based on a bullish price reversal and high implied volatility. Table 6-2 presents conditions in place to assess probabilities for the strategy. The indicators narrowly favor a bullish resolution.

Table 6-2 Lining Up Probabilities

Indicator	*Action*	*Bias*
Price	Higher close for two days	Bullish
Price	Returns to bearish channel	Bearish
ATR	Declining after peak	Bullish
ROC	Crossing above SMA	Bullish
SV	Diminishing	Neutral — Bullish
IV	Recent peak	—
Volume	Bottoming pattern possible	Neutral — Bullish
Weekly Trend	Long-term uptrend intact	Bullish
20-day EMA	Downward sloped	Bearish
50-day EMA	Downward sloped	Bearish
200-day EMA	Flat	Neutral

There are no guarantees that a trend will remain intact.

Waiting for every tool to turn bullish will typically result in no trades taken at all. Or those that are signaled will be created toward the end of a move. Much of your decision-making process when your indicators are mixed will be based on the action in the overall market, as well as what the indicators are saying. Try to assess market conditions and use your experience to put the odds in your favor. Although XLI moved upward and the trade realized gains, the same conditions on a different day could result in continued bearish movement. The bottom line is that when trading in the face of some uncertainty, which is a common occurrence, managing risk is the key to success. If you lose a little money 60% of the time but you are able to make good money the rest of the time, you are more likely to come out ahead. The big problems in trading are the ones caused by frequent heavy losses.

Reacting to versus anticipating a move

The only thing that is certain in the markets is that price action will be predictably unpredictable. Anything can happen in the markets the next week or trading day . . . even by the time the market closes. Trends can continue, reverse, or simply stall. The further out in time, the more uncertain things become, so it's always good to remind yourself that you simply don't know what will happen tomorrow.

The best you can do is identify rules for managing risk and keep the odds in your favor. When conditions change, take the necessary action and move on.

Practice disciplined trading through these methods to gain the experience needed to hone your skills over varying market conditions:

- **Sector analysis:** When completing an analysis, use tools that provide objective information about current conditions for different timeframes, including moving averages and Bollinger bands. This keeps you tuned in to "what is" happening versus what may happen next. Consider broad market movement and how the sector moves in relation to the market.
- After assessing current trending and volatility conditions, incorporate other tools that provide you with insight about the strength of those conditions and potential changes. Then develop your strategy accordingly.

Only take on new positions if you can effectively manage all your open trades and avoid using too many indicators, because indicator overkill can be confusing and paralyzing.

- **Trade evaluation:** When evaluating potential trades, use tools that provide reasonable projections to assess reward:risk ratios. Only consider those positions with risk levels that are within your guidelines. Identify an absolute exit price for a loss, as well as tools used for taking profits.
- **Trade management:** When managing a position be sure to monitor conditions — don't walk away from a trade that requires your attention. Use order types that automatically execute a stop loss exit when possible (see Chapter 8).

Try to put the odds in your favor by emphasizing risk management.

Chapter 7

Practicing Before You Swing

In This Chapter

- Understanding option price changes
- Practicing by paper trading
- Testing an approach
- Gaining strategy mastery

Baseball players take a few practice swings before they step up to the plate. What's at stake for them might be a base hit, but when you trade, your game is all about money. So, it makes sense to try some practice trading (called *paper trading*) before you put real money on the line. Thus, even if you're excited about trying new trading strategies, be careful before pulling the real money trigger. Before you trade in real terms, be prepared.

Here are three critical steps to take before using a new strategy in the market:

- Understand the security's risks and rewards
- Practice strategies
- Analyze a trade

This chapter is different than previous ones because it takes the leap from "learning" and "analyzing" to trading, even though it's about paper trading. You are transitioning from concept to action.

There are two important steps. First, by monitoring different option pricing components and paper trading, you simulate live conditions. This gives you a better intuitive feel for price changes and helps you avoid costly mistakes. Next, by developing your backtesting skills, you implement only the best approaches, allowing you to stay in the game long enough to gain valuable experience. Through practice and experience, you eventually reach strategy mastery.

Monitoring Option Greek Changes

Understanding basic option strategies is a much quicker learning curve than recognizing the proper pricing for options used in those strategies. Theoretical models and conditions impacting option premiums are discussed in Chapters 3, 14, and 15. But one of the best ways to really grasp the value of these securities is by monitoring price and Greek changes under actual conditions. (See Chapter 3 for more on the Greeks.)

Tracking premium measures

Developing your skills with any option strategy means really understanding how option premiums are impacted by changes in both of the following:

- The price of the underlying
- Time to expiration

It's time to get active, and a great way to get a better intuitive feel for the impact from both of these factors is by formally tracking changes in all the different components of options prices on a day-to-day basis. All you need in order to do this is access to market prices, an option calculator, and a spreadsheet program. By monitoring a few different options, you should be able to learn a lot about how changing conditions impact prices in general. By including Greeks in the process, you also understand which factors play more significant roles at different times.

Ideally you'll end up reviewing the markets and tracking prices during a period when prices are moving around a bit. This helps highlight delta, gamma, and theta impacts on price. Prior to putting your trading dollars on the line, set up a spreadsheet to track the following:

- Price of the underlying
- Prices for in-the-money (ITM), at-the-money (ATM), and out-of-the-money (OTM) calls and puts with varying days to expiration
- Days to expiration
- Option intrinsic value, delta, gamma, and theta

By tracking these values, you can identify which measures have the biggest impact on option strategies.

REMEMBER

Delta may be displayed based on values from –1 to +1 or –100 to +100.

Figure 7-1 displays a spreadsheet for a Microsoft (MSFT) call-and put. Although only a portion of the month is displayed, monitoring these values over an extended period helps you view varying market conditions. Note that option prices don't change by the exact amounts projected by the Greeks.

Also note the effect of time and the price of the underlying on the price of both the put and call options. The call options decline in price as the number of days to expiration decreases and the price of the underlying falls. The put holds its value better because the price of the underlying is falling, but it too loses time value.

Tracking Price & Time

Date	MSFT	Change	Days to Expiration		Price	Intrinsic Value	Delta	Gamma	Call Theta	Strike	Put Theta	Gamma	Delta	Intrinsic Value	Price
1-Aug-07	29.30	0.31	77		**1.10**	0.00	45.64	0.118	-0.0097	30.00	-0.0065	0.124	-54.49	0.70	**1.61**
2-Aug-07	29.52	0.22	76		**1.14**	0.00	47.88	0.124	-0.0096	30.00	-0.0064	0.128	-52.01	0.48	**1.44**
3-Aug-07	28.96	-0.56	75		**0.90**	0.00	41.04	0.122	-0.0093	30.00	-0.0064	0.123	-58.75	1.04	**1.80**
6-Aug-07	**29.54**	**0.58**	**74**		**1.09**	**0.00**	**47.77**	**0.129**	**-0.0097**	**30.00**	**-0.0065**	**0.133**	**-52.13**	**0.46**	**1.38**
7-Aug-07	29.55	0.01	73		**1.06**	0.00	47.70	0.133	-0.0096	30.00	-0.0064	0.136	-52.16	0.45	**1.35**
...	...	...	...		**...**	...	...	...	...	...	...	...	...	...	**...**
28-Aug-07	27.93	0.66	52		**0.35**	0.00	23.76	0.123	0.0004	30.00	0.0045	0.120	-70.20	2.07	**2.25**
29-Aug-07	28.59	0.66	51		**0.45**	0.00	30.57	0.149	-0.0090	30.00	-0.0056	0.159	-71.27	1.41	**1.71**
30-Aug-07	28.45	-0.14	50		**0.43**	0.00	28.95	0.143	-0.0091	30.00	-0.0056	0.153	-73.29	1.55	**1.82**
31-Aug-07	28.73	0.28	49		**0.45**	0.00	31.74	0.158	-0.0090	30.00	-0.0057	0.169	-70.01	1.27	**1.57**

Image by Optionetics

Figure 7-1: Tracking price and time changes for option premiums.

Changing volatility and option prices

The volatility impact on option prices is a little tough to get a handle on at times because implied volatility (IV) includes pricing factors that vary during the life of the option. IV incorporates the following:

- Past volatility (historical)
- Volatility expected in the future (implied)
- Contract demand

It's easy to get confused when it comes to volatility terminology. So here's a good way to keep things straight: Historical (past) volatility is a measure of the underlying stock. Implied (future) volatility is a measure of the option.

Past volatility

Crowd behavior can drive up option prices when demand for specific contracts increases as news on a company hits the wires. Figure 7-2 displays a similar spreadsheet for the MSFT call and put options, tracking price, and volatility changes.

Figure 7-2: Tracking price and volatility changes for option premiums.

Tracking Price & Volatility

								Call		Put			
Date	MSFT	Change	Days to Expiration		Price	Intrinsic Value	IV	Vega	Strike	Vega	IV	Intrinsic Value	Price
1-Aug-07	29.30	0.31	77		**1.10**	0.00	24.671	0.054	30.00	0.054	23.441	0.70	**1.61**
2-Aug-07	29.52	0.22	76		**1.14**	0.00	23.571	0.054	30.00	0.054	22.799	0.48	**1.44**
3-Aug-07	28.96	-0.56	75		**0.90**	0.00	23.905	0.052	30.00	0.052	23.709	1.04	**1.80**
6-Aug-07	**29.54**	**0.58**	**74**		**1.09**	**0.00**	**23.129**	**0.053**	**30.00**	**0.053**	**22.395**	**0.46**	**1.38**
7-Aug-07	29.55	0.01	73		**1.06**	0.00	22.639	0.052	30.00	0.052	22.057	0.45	**1.35**
...	...	...	...		**...**	...	...	...	...	...	...	...	**...**
28-Aug-07	27.93	-0.56	52		**0.35**	0.00	23.878	0.033	30.00	0.030	20.999	2.07	**2.25**
29-Aug-07	28.59	0.66	51		**0.45**	0.00	21.998	0.037	30.00	0.036	19.963	1.41	**1.71**
30-Aug-07	28.45	-0.14	50		**0.43**	0.00	22.690	0.036	30.00	0.034	20.338	1.55	**1.82**
31-Aug-07	28.73	0.28	49		**0.45**	0.00	21.427	0.037	30.00	0.036	19.463	1.27	**1.57**

Image by Optionetics

Implied volatility (IV)

Implied volatility (IV) is the volatility implied by the option's price. Because IV is a pretty important option pricing factor, it's probably good to expand on that definition a bit.

In terms of trading and IV:

- It's better to buy options when IV is relatively low.
- It's better to sell options when IV is relatively high.

TIP

A volatility of 30% for a stock priced at $100 means that you should expect the price of the stock to trade between $70 and $130 over the next year.

The problem with these rules of thumb is that you can't always follow them. When holding a long-term stock position you want to protect, should you just throw caution to the wind because put IV is high? Definitely not, especially when you consider that increasing IV often translates to increasing fear in the market. When faced with buying options in a high-volatility environment, you may need to evaluate a broader range of expiration months and strike prices.

TECHNICAL STUFF

When implied volatility (IV) is relatively high and then drops significantly, it's referred to as an *IV crush.* This type of occurrence is usually event driven and is a response to news such as earnings reports or product launches. When the event becomes a reality, it is no longer an uncertainty, which reduces its effect on the options price.

Remember that IV can vary:

- **By time to expiration:** This contributes more uncertainty to the option's value.
- **By strike price:** Usually at-the-money (ATM) IV is the lowest, but it doesn't always work out that way. Skew charts (discussed in Chapter 15) provide IV by strike price and can speed up the option-selection process when you need to purchase contracts while IV is relatively high. An option price can be broken into two components: intrinsic and extrinsic value. The intrinsic value is completely determined by the option moneyness, but IV does not play a role in this value. The deeper in-the-money (ITM) the option is, the less impact IV will have on the total option premium.

REMEMBER

When using short option strategies, time decay works in your favor. Selling options with 30 to 45 days to expiration accelerates this decay for you.

Paper Trading a Trading Strategy

Continually seeking and implementing new strategies naturally develops your trading skills. By paper trading, you make risk-free progress on the new strategy learning curve.

TIP

When paper trading, be sure to incorporate trading costs associated with the position to get the best value for strategy profitability.

Trading on paper: Pluses and minuses

Masters of any craft practice constantly, and options traders are no different. Paper trading may seem boring, but it is an excellent way to work out a method of analysis, record keeping, and responding to the market. The goal is to train yourself to learn how to minimize losses as you develop new strategy mechanics and you make changes to your trading routine. Watching a long out-of-the-money (OTM) option deflate in value as implied volatility drops is much less painful when it's on paper. To be sure, it doesn't really prepare you for the battle of greed and fear from within, but it forces you to address the situation prior to having money on the line. Some pluses and minuses for paper trading appear in Table 7-1.

Table 7-1 Advantages and Disadvantages to Paper Trading

Advantages	*Disadvantages*
Provides feedback via profits/losses	Does not prepare you emotionally for losses
Allows you to incorporate all trade costs	There are no assignments
Identifies issues you may not have considered	Typically does not address potential margin problems
Avoids account losses	Does not help trade execution understanding

Implementing electronic paper trades

Paper trading can be done on a spreadsheet, an electronic platform, or . . . you got it, paper. Do whatever works best for you. If you plan on setting up your own log, incorporate option Greeks, too.

Many financial websites allow you to enter different positions in a portfolio tracker that updates at the end of the day or intra-day on a delayed basis. Unfortunately, not all of them accept option symbols. A basic tracker will provide position information that includes price changes with profits and losses. A more advanced platform can include risk chart displays and other trade-management tools. Figure 7-3 displays the free Optionetics.com portfolio tracker with shares of Microsoft (MSFT), as well as the MSFT Jan 30 call and Jan 30 put.

Using Trading Systems

A *trading system* is an approach with specific rules for entry and exit. Even if you currently use a systematic approach to a strategy — such as only purchasing a call when implied volatility is relatively low — a trading system is more rigidly defined. When using a system, you should do the following:

- Establish a position for all buy signals generated by the rules.
- Exit each position when the exit signal is generated.

TIP

Getting used to following your new trading system rules can lead to more frequent trading, especially during volatile markets. Make sure you allow for this type of situation with regard to time commitment and other potential changes in your daily routine.

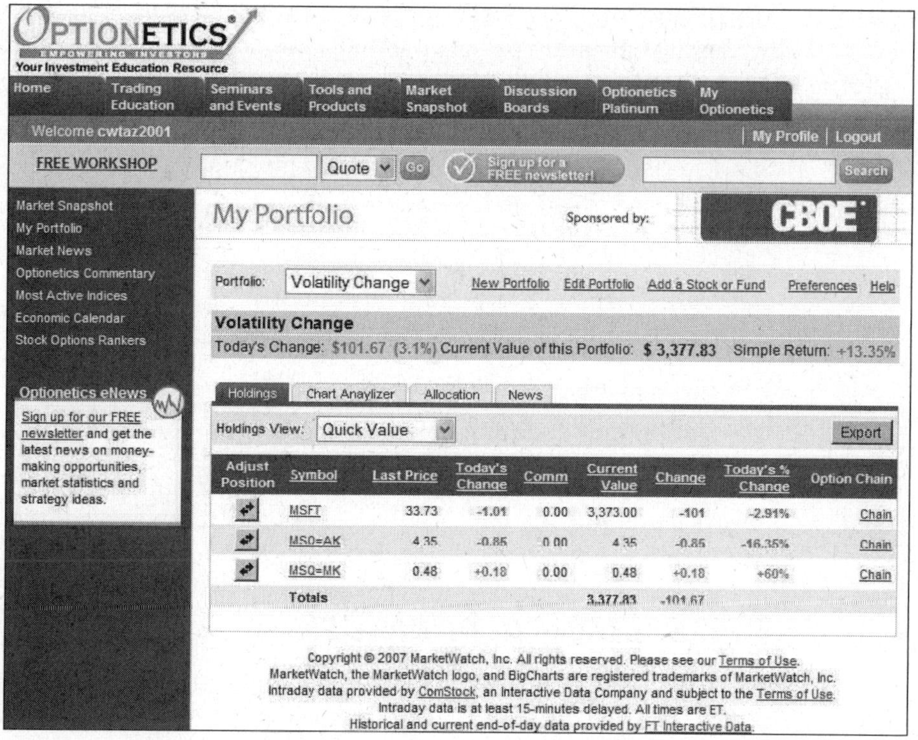

Figure 7-3: Electronic platform for portfolio tracking.

Image by Optionetics

Knowing what you're getting

Trading systems are mechanical. That means there is no decision-making when implementing the system — you never think about whether or not to accept an entry or exit signal. If the system is frequently producing losses or something seems amiss, you completely stop the system. The two best things about a formal system are that

- It minimizes your trade emotions.
- It allows for backtesting to get a sense of expected performance.

If you start using discretion by deciding which trades to take, both of these advantages disappear. Emotions creep in, and your results can vary significantly from test results. As with any trading approach, an important key to system trading is working with systems that are suitable to your trading style and account size.

Although the rules for a system are rigid, building in flexibility is common, by varying indicator speeds or adding filters. A *filter* is an extra rule for trade entry or exit. Indicators and similar system components are defined as system *parameters.*

Characteristics of a good trading system include the following:

- Profitability across a variety of markets, securities, and market conditions
- Outperforming a buy-and-hold approach
- Stability with manageable drawdowns (trading losses)
- Diversifying your trading tools
- Suiting your style and time availability

WARNING!

Be extremely careful about creating a system and putting it on autopilot. Always monitor trades.

Performing a backtest

A backtest uses past data to determine whether a system generates stable profits. You can complete backtesting using data downloads or by tracking trades mechanically, but the most efficient way of doing it is via a software application intended for backtesting. You just have to be sure that you're testing what you think you're testing.

When performing backtesting for a system, include periods of time that are long enough to capture bullish, bearish, and sideways moving markets. This way you generate results under worst-case conditions and experience (in a test environment) realistic drawdowns. *Drawdown* is the term used to define cumulative account losses from consecutive losing trades. Evaluating drawdown is just another way to manage your risk.

TIP

A robust trading system can work for a variety of markets (commodities, stocks, and so forth) under a variety of conditions (bull/bear markets). At the same time, it's important to backtest the system in each individual environment before using it.

When reviewing backtest results, you're looking for both profitability and stability. *Stability* refers to the consistency of results — you want to know if just a few trades are generating all the profits or if they are spread over a variety of trades. A stable system

- Has winning trades with average profits that exceed the average losses of losing trades.
- Has an average system profit that is close to the median system profit (low standard deviation).
- Sustains manageable drawdowns.
- Does not rely on a handful of trades for profitability.

Note that a system doesn't have to have more winning trades than losing trades. Many trending systems rely on letting profits run for a smaller number of trades while cutting losses quickly on the losing trades. The bottom line is that you're looking for consistency. You don't want to fool yourself into thinking that your system is good when in fact all you're doing is getting lucky in a big way once in a while.

After creating a system that performs reasonably in backtests, you complete forward testing by running the rules on a shorter period of time. Generally you start the test at the latest backtest date and run it to some point in time before implementation. Expect diminishing returns during forward testing. System trading is not a secret key that unlocks profits. It is a way you can minimize harmful trading emotions and deliver more consistent results. Consider it an approach that merits your attention if you're willing to roll up your sleeves and do some exploring.

Following the right steps

Here are the steps you should take when backtesting a system:

1. **Identify basis of strategy (for example, capture trending conditions).**
2. **Identify trade entry and exit rules.**
3. **Identify market traded and period backtest.**
4. **Identify account assumptions (system and trade allocations).**
5. **Test system, evaluate results.**
6. **Identify reasonable filters to minimize losing trades (number and/or size of such trades).**
7. **Add filter based on conclusions from Step 6, test system, and then evaluate results.**
8. **Add risk-management component.**
9. **Test system, evaluate results.**

Although each step is not illustrated with a figure, you will see figures in this chapter that highlight some of these steps to give you a feel for what you'll be doing when you perform your own backtest.

Check the average value of losing trades, as well as maximum and consecutive losses to determine if a system is suitable.

A long-only, rate of change (ROC) momentum system was tested using a simple moving average (SMA) crossover to signal trade entry [ROC: 34, SMA: 13] and exit [ROC: 21, SMA: 8]. Because a faster signal was used for trade exit, a second parameter had to be added to trade entry requiring the 21-day ROC to be higher than its 13-day SMA. Otherwise, the appropriate trade exit may never be signaled. This is a trending system that seeks to capitalize on a longer-term momentum push upward. To limit losses and profit erosion, a faster momentum signal is used to exit the position.

The backtest was performed over a six-year period that included bullish and bearish periods on a group of six semiconductor stocks including SMH, an ETF for the sector. $20,000 was used for the system with 50% of the cash available used for each trade. A $10 per trade commission was added to the costs. No stops were part of the initial system test.

Figure 7-4 displays side-by-side charts for a trade generated by the system.

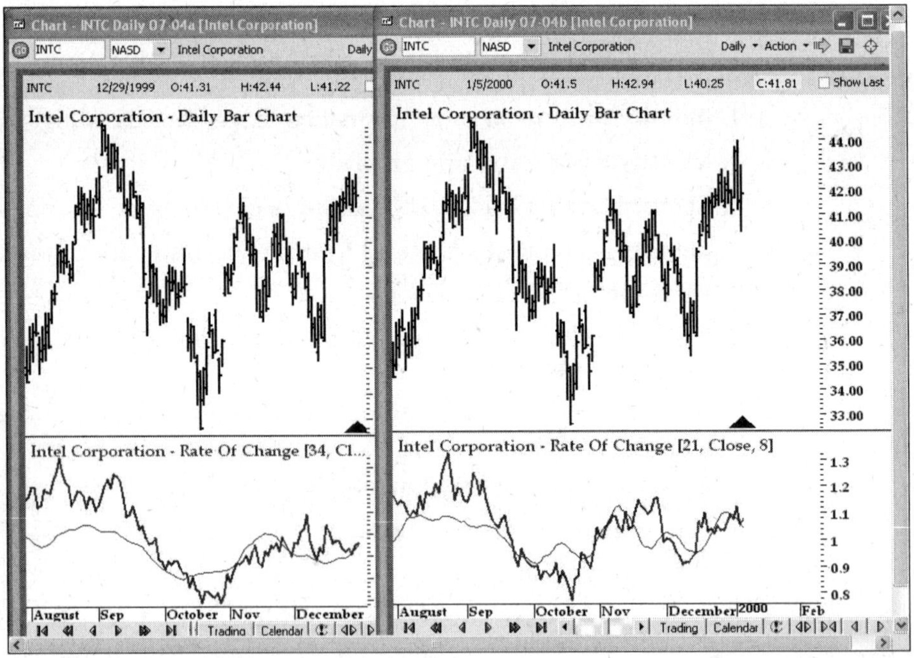

Figure 7-4: ROC trending system sample trade (INTC 12/30/1999–1/5/2000).

Image by Optionetics

The image provides two charts for Intel Corporation (INTC) showing trade entry and trade exit conditions. The position was entered on 12/29 and exited six calendar days later for a gain of 3%.

TIP

A system does not have to be robust or complex to be effective. Because volatility and trending characteristics vary for different securities, some are better suited to certain types of systems. Generally, less-volatile stocks are better suited to less-complicated systems geared more toward trend analysis rather than more frequent trading.

Reviewing system results

It's better when designing or reviewing a system to work backward. Because managing risk is a main theme throughout this book, evaluating a system with no stops may seem counter-intuitive. When you think about it though, stop levels are pretty arbitrary — the market doesn't really care if you entered a position at $45. It may or may not have support 5% or 10% below that amount. Allow the system to identify a viable stop-loss point when backtesting it and then decide if it represents suitable risk for you.

System results were very favorable on a variety of measures for the initial run, so no filter was added. The Max Adverse Excursion % was reviewed to determine if a reasonable stop level could be added. A 15% stop was included, and the system test was run once again. Results were only slightly less favorable, so the stop was incorporated.

TECHNICAL STUFF

Charting packages may use different calculations for the same indicator. If changing systems, be sure to compare indicator values that provide signals so you're trading the same system tested. Always consider re-testing the system on the new platform.

Two forward tests were also run, with and without the stop. A two-year period was used for each, and the system remained viable, with much lower profitability. Expect this to happen with forward tests and actual system performance. This is due to changing conditions and inefficiencies that get worked out of the markets. That's one of the reasons why you need to periodically review system performance and incorporate reasonable stops whenever possible.

Table 7-2 provides system results for the four different runs.

A lower percentage stop can be considered to bring the average and median return closer, but because average gains are outpacing average losses (letting profits run), you want to first compare the average and median for winning trades and losing trades separately.

Table 7-2 ROC System Review

System Run	*Average Return*	*Median Return*	*Gain:Loss (number)*	*Average Gain*	*Average Loss*	*Max Loss*
Test1	4.7	3.0	1.96	10.1	5.8	35%
Test2	4.6	3.0	1.91	10.0	5.9	16%
FTest1	1.6	1.0	1.56	4.0	2.3	10%
FTest2	1.6	1.0	1.56	4.1	2.3	10%

You can use a standard deviation calculation to assess the stability of profits for any market approach.

Adding risk management to a backtest

All trade approaches need to take risk management into account. Focus on the largest adverse moves for a strategy when trying to identify stops that still allow the strategy to work. If adding this stop maintains profitability and stability of the system *and* is consistent with your risk tolerance, you can consider implementing the strategy or system.

Cutting losses

An approach that is systematic, but not mechanical, can still be backtested. Regardless of how you go about performing that backtest, you should keep an eye on large adverse moves that occurred for the trades generated. This allows you to identify reasonable, systematic filters and stops geared toward minimizing losses.

A stop-loss order can result in a larger percentage loss by the time a trade is executed. A worst-case scenario occurs when a signal is generated at the close of trading one day and the security has a price gap at the open the next day.

Taking profits

Identifying stop-loss points that manage risk is probably secondhand to you by now. On the other end of the spectrum, have you ever been in a profitable trade that starts moving the wrong way? Right around that point you realize you don't have a specific exit plan for taking profits. Sometimes you focus so much on risk that you forget to identify favorable price targets. Or maybe you do identify a profitable exit point, but conditions start to deteriorate before that price level is reached.

Here is how to take care of that problem: In addition to identifying a stop-loss level, identify a trailing stop percentage or dollar amount to minimize the number of profitable trades that turn into losses. The trailing stop should be incorporated into your system or strategy and tested. If you want the system to generate the trailing amount, evaluate trades with large favorable moves that yielded significantly less in the way of profits (or turned into losses). After completing your review, you may do as follows:

- Add a filter that accelerates your exits.
- Generate a trailing percentage using max favorable excursion % data.

Letting profits run

An effective trading approach doesn't necessarily have to have more winning trades than losing trades. It just needs profits to outpace declines. That's actually the case for many trend-oriented systems. You end up with more losing trades, but the average value of the loss is much smaller than the average value of gaining trades. And so goes the mantra: *Be sure to cut your losses while letting profits run.*

TIP

Sorting trades by greatest lost to greatest profit allows you to more easily review statistics for both.

Although you need to identify a method for taking profits, you also have to avoid cutting profit levels in such a way that they no longer outpace losses. Trading successfully requires quite a bit of pre-work. You'll see your trading evolve by focusing on the following:

1. **Cutting losses.**
2. **Preventing profits from turning into losses.**
3. **Letting profits run. . . .**

Shifting from Knowledge to Mastery

Strategy mastery doesn't mean that every trade you place for a given strategy is profitable — it means that the appropriate conditions were in place when placing a particular trade, putting the odds in your favor for a profitable trade. Managing the position correctly is another component that highlights discipline by exiting a trade if conditions change. It sounds pretty easy, but strategy mastery can take years to evolve. Your goal is to stay in the trading game long enough to achieve this mastery.

The best trades are the ones that often take the longest to find. As you analyze the markets and individual stocks, it's best to look for the right setup, or set of conditions, than it is to trade as often as possible just to eventually find the right trade. That means that sometimes it may take several hours or several days before you find the right opportunity. Indeed, trading, like many other professions, can be described as one made up of hours of boredom combined with minutes of sheer panic or pleasure.

TIP

By focusing first on basic concepts and mechanics, you create a strong foundation that allows you to grasp advanced techniques more quickly. You implement new strategies via paper trading to avoid the most costly mistakes. When you're ready to take the new strategy live, you can further minimize the cost of mistakes by reducing your position size and remembering to take profits. This approach keeps you in the markets longer, allowing you to find and develop strategies that are best suited to your style.

Setting the right pace

There are a ton of great option strategies in this book, and some probably pique your interest more than others. Start out by paper trading a couple of the more straightforward approaches and then transition to live trading with them. After that, check out the strategy that has the most appeal to you, again by paper trading. There's no guarantee that market conditions will be conducive to that strategy, so you may prolong your paper trading days until the market changes or you're ready to explore a new strategy. But . . . it's really important to keep this in mind: You want to focus on strategies that make sense to you and suit your style. That's how you'll ultimately develop mastery.

Starting with a few strategies

Learning new strategies is, hopefully, something you enjoy. It's amazing to find out about all the different ways you can make money in the markets. But not all strategies work in all market conditions. More importantly, they won't all suit your style. If you're new to option trading, stick with one or two basic strategies to develop a really good understanding of premium changes and mechanics.

REMEMBER

A variety of strategies are available to you that allow you to make money in the markets. Just like your preferred method of analysis, you'll find that you develop a preferred list of strategies that work for you.

Experienced option traders should identify current market conditions and then explore one, maybe two strategies that excel given those conditions. Start by paper trading and progress from there. If there's a specific strategy that really intrigues or speaks to you, but conditions aren't quite right, just paper trade it. In the long run, it's better to focus on market approaches that make sense to you.

Adding strategies as market conditions change

The markets are a lifelong pursuit because conditions are always changing. And although there's a continuous cycle of bullish and bearish phases, the market is never exactly the same. You probably already recognize that since you purchased this book in the first place.

TIP

Do a strategy checkup if things aren't following the norm. When strategies that typically work well for you start weakening, take some time over the weekend to complete a comprehensive market assessment. You may detect early signs of a change in conditions.

Option trading allows you to implement strategies that can be profitable regardless of market conditions. Here's a sampling:

- Bullish, low volatility (basic long call, married puts)
- Bullish, high volatility (covered calls, credit spreads — Chapter 11)
- Bearish, low volatility (basic long put, debit spreads — Chapter 11)
- Bearish, high volatility (collars, credit spreads — Chapter 11)
- Range-bound, low volatility (butterfly, condor — Chapter 16)

The combination of stock with options or options with options really provides you with great choices. That can be good and bad news because each approach requires some time to master. Be thorough when checking out a strategy. Consider the circumstances of the current market and the type of security you used in the strategy before discarding it because "it doesn't work."

Chances are you won't be trading every strategy available. Most traders try different ones along the way and then master a smaller number of them. The experience gained allows them to maximize profits on their favored strategies (knowing when to hold them), while minimizing their losses (knowing when to fold them).

Deciding which option strategies to use is just like market analysis — there are a variety of ways to approach it, none of which represent the one "right" way. The best approach for you is the one that intuitively makes the most sense, so that when conditions change and things get tougher (and they will), you have the confidence to stick to your plan.

Achieving mastery through longevity

Longevity is all about developing patience and staying power and showing up to work every day. In order to do that, you have to stay on top of your game and develop a consistent routine that allows for the inevitable changes in volatility and market trends. Bull markets can run for years, and volatility conditions can remain stable, but things can change in a hurry. To prevent burnout and heartburn, expect to incur additional losses when markets transition or when implementing a new strategy. Managing risk by using limited-loss, unlimited-gain strategies whenever possible sets a foundation for longevity.

Paper trading provides a technique to minimize learning curve losses. A second method is through proper position sizing. By starting out with smaller initial positions, potential losses are manageable. Adding rules that include profit-taking is the icing on the cake.

Successful trading does not happen overnight. Be prepared to spend time making low-cost mistakes, observing different market conditions, experiencing varying levels of emotion, and developing your trading skills.

Determining appropriate trade sizes

There are different techniques available to identify proper trade sizes. Many are beyond the scope of this book simply due to space constraints. Two easily incorporated ones include the following:

- Identifying a maximum dollar amount allocated per trade
- Identifying a maximum percentage amount allocated per trade

The latter may make sense because it automatically changes as your account size changes. On the other hand, there are some markets that may be best traded using the former approach. It's always a good idea to keep your options open, especially if you're having a difficult spell when your strategies are not working as well as they have in the past.

Because options represent a leveraged position (see Chapter 3), you don't need to allocate the same amount of money to option positions as you do for stocks. In fact, it's probably not a good idea to do that at all. Using your stock allocation plan as a base, you can estimate an initial allocation amount by identifying an option position that controls the same amount of stock. This serves as a starting point that should be tested and reviewed.

Establish trade allocation amounts prior to analyzing a specific trade. You need to know in advance the maximum amount available for an individual trade so that you minimize your account risk.

When trying a new strategy (after paper trading), further reduce trade sizes so mistakes are more forgiving. If that means trading in one-option contract sizes, so be it. Remember, you're not out there to impress Wall Street with your trade sizes — you're out there to make money in the markets.

As your skills develop, increase position sizes to those tested allocations. This will improve profits because option trading costs are often higher than stock trading costs from a percentage standpoint. If you've properly prepared and continue to manage your risk, increasing position sizes shouldn't be a problem. In fact, it should improve results because you'll realize economies of scale with trading costs.

Emphasizing profit-taking

Throughout this book there's an emphasis on managing risk. In this chapter, though, there's an additional emphasis: profit-taking. It's not enough to simply have a high number of profitable trades. Your profits must:

- Exceed trading costs.
- Exceed conservative investment approaches.
- Exceed your losses.

This doesn't just happen out of the blue. You have to have a plan that includes reviewing strategy and trade results to put the best profit-taking rules in place. Such rules should minimize the number of profitable trades that turn into losses and allow profits to run. Developing these skills means you're evolving as a trader.

REMEMBER

There are a lot of different price points that can invoke an emotional response while in a trade. Be sure to identify exit points for a loss as well as exit points for profits.

Chapter 8

Designing A Killer Trading Plan

In This Chapter

- Identifying business costs
- Minimizing learning curve costs
- Understanding order execution

Trading is a business, and developing as a trader means evolving as a business manager. Understanding the costs associated with the business helps you budget accordingly. Initially certain costs will be higher, and others will be lower. You'll likely be paying more for education and your learning curve (a.k.a. losses) when you start out. As your trading evolves, those costs will go down, while subscriptions to analysis platforms and data services will go up.

Always keep in mind that losses are part of operating expenses. Minimizing them by managing risk is your goal — not eliminating them. This is done by determining proper trade allocation amounts and maximum loss per trade. Effectively executing trades is another step toward minimizing losses. We cover all these topics in this chapter.

Managing Your Costs

There are a variety of costs to consider with your trading — some are higher when you first start and many continue throughout your career. You need to think of trading as a business and manage these expenses so you can minimize them and their effect on how much money you actually earn as a trader as your business matures. The expense categories included in the following list will all continue throughout your trading career, but some will begin higher than others:

- **Education:** Education expenses include materials, courses, and learning curve costs for new markets and strategies. These costs will decrease as time progresses, but will remain ongoing as you stay current with market conditions (books, periodicals) and continue to develop new strategies.
- One of the largest education costs is your learning curve. This tends to decline as you figure out how to do the following:
  - Trade under best conditions for the strategy.
  - Use options with the appropriate liquidity.
  - Develop paper-trading skills.
  - Allocate the appropriate amount to the trade.
  - Effectively enter orders for the best exit.
  - Take profits.
- **Analysis costs:** As your skills progress and your trading generates regular profits, you may add analytical tools to your business costs. Talking to fellow traders that use such tools and finding out which ones you may be able to take for a spin using free trials are good ways to start. Such costs represent one of the few that may increase over time. Be sure to only subscribe to a limited number of services and get to know them well so you can make the most out of them.
- **Trading costs:** You have to not only account for commission but also for slippage. *Slippage* is the cost associated with the market spread — the difference between the bid and the ask. A good exercise is to calculate commission and slippage percentages for different size option positions (for example, 1, 5, 10 contracts) established at different price points ($1, $5, $10).
- Taxes are another consideration, so you need to identify what types of trading will be completed in your different account types. If you do the limited options trading allowed in retirement accounts, you will defer those taxes. Otherwise, you'll pay taxes on your profits in all non-retirement accounts. You can get the full information on what type of options trading is allowed in retirement accounts from the Internal Revenue Service (IRS) (`www.irs.gov`).
- In addition, when establishing certain option positions when you already hold a position in the underlying, you may trigger a tax event. Be sure to contact your account about option-trading tax considerations. The bottom line for these cumulative costs is that that in the long term, they must outpace a buy-and-hold approach.

- If you borrow from your broker via trading on margin, you need to add monthly margin interest charges to your trading costs as well. Short option positions have margin requirements that can get complicated. The main consideration for this margin is whether the option is covered or naked. If you decide to move forward with strategies requiring margin, be sure to contact your broker so you fully understand all of the calculations and account requirements. Then add these costs to your expenses.

Losses are another trading cost that should be considered part of doing business. They will likely be higher at first, but reduced with time and experience. Following these trading plan guidelines should help keep these initial costs to a minimum:

- **Determining the trading allocations:** As part of an overall trading plan, you should identify both your total trading assets and your maximum allocations for different assets and strategies. Stock and ETF trading will require larger allocations than option positions. You may even want to break this down further to include a maximum allocation amount for new strategies based on paper-trading results.

- **Calculating trade size:** You must also determine guidelines for maximum position size prior to entering any trade. Once these are set, identifying the maximum number of contracts you can allocate to a position is pretty straightforward. Divide the option price by an allocation amount below your maximum and you're all set. Don't anticipate using the max allocation.

- **Identifying maximum acceptable loss on trades:** Your maximum acceptable loss can be defined as a dollar value or a percentage. You may prefer the latter because a fixed dollar amount can be significant with smaller trades or if your trading assets decrease. Periodically perform an analysis on your trade results to determine if your losses remain at reasonable and sustainable levels. The bottom line should be how much money is left in your account and whether it makes sense to continue your current approach.

- **Focusing on entry and exit rules:** Option entries are often driven by trending and volatility conditions but may also be time oriented with positions created prior to specific scheduled event. Option exits can also be time driven (post-event or pre-expiration) or may be triggered by movement in the underlying security. Regardless, these methods must be focused on supporting your risk management and maximum allowable loss.

Exiting with technical indicators typically does not provide you with a price for use with risk calculations. A maximum loss price should also be identified.

Optimizing Order Execution

Successfully trading options means gaining proficiency with order execution. A variety of factors come into the mix here:

- Understanding order placement rules unique to options
- Knowing how different order types work
- Learning how to use combination orders for multi-leg positions
- Gaining skill while using the underlying to identify option exits
- Recognizing your broker's role in execution quality

There is also a learning curve for executing option trades, but for the most part these are mechanical steps that can be easily mastered with some practice. You can get a leg up on this with your paper trading, but it's never the same as the real-time action. This will go a long way toward successful strategy implementation.

The *ask,* or best price available from sellers, is also referred to as the *offer.*

Understanding option orders

Options are not limited to a certain number of contracts the way stock is constrained by its float. Contracts are created by the marketplace, so they have some unique considerations when placing orders for them. An option is created when two traders create a new position, or *open* a trade. This increases open interest for that specific option. Open interest decreases when traders close existing positions.

Float is the term used to describe the number of shares outstanding and available to trade for a stock.

Open interest doesn't get updated on a trade-by-trade basis. It's more an end-of-day reconciliation through the Options Clearing Corporation (OCC). That explains why option orders are placed in a specific manner — the OCC needs to keep the accounting straight. It also means you'll be communicating a little more information when placing option orders.

Knowing basic option order rules

Buying or selling options can be done in any order. Choosing whether you want to be long (buy) or short (sell) a contract depends on your strategy and the option approval level for your account. You can't jump out of the gate creating unlimited-risk, short-option positions until your broker approves you for it — after checking your temperature of course.

The current bid and ask price for a security is referred to as its *current market.*

Because contracts are created and retired based on market demand, you need to enter orders in a way that supports this end-of-day reconciliation by the options markets. You need to identify

- A new position you're creating as an *opening order.*
- An existing position you're exiting as a *closing order.*

Using a call option as an example, Table 8-1 provides you with the transactions required to enter and exit a long call or short call position.

Table 8-1 Option Order Entry Process

Position	*Entry*	*Also*	*Exit*	*Also*
Long Call	Buy Call to Open	BCO	Sell Call to Close	SCC
Short Call	Sell Call to Open	SCO	Buy Call to Close	BCC

When exercising or getting assigned on an option contract, there is no closing transaction. The same holds true for options expiring worthless. In each case, the appropriate amount of contracts are removed from your account after the transaction completes or expiration weekend comes to an end.

Reviewing order types

You have a variety of different order types available to you, some guarantee executions (such as market order) whereas others guarantee price (such as limit orders). Although there are unique considerations for option orders, this execution-versus-price distinction remains the same. Effectively managing order execution means knowing when it's more important to get the order executed versus the price where it's executed. When in doubt, consider what limits your risk.

Table 8-2 takes a quick glance at popular order types and which guarantee execution or price.

Table 8-2 Order Types by Guarantee

Order	*Guarantees*
Market order	Execution
Limit order	Price
Stop order or stop-loss order	Execution
Stop-limit order	Price

Generally, limit orders are good for entering a position, so you only establish those that are within your trading allocations. If you need to guarantee an exit, only a market order accomplishes that for you.

A stop order is your risk-management tool for trading with discipline. The stop level triggers a market order if the option trades or moves to that level. The stop represents a price less favorable than the current market and is typically used to minimize losses for an existing position when emotions run high. Placing a stop order is similar to monitoring a security and placing a market order when certain market conditions are met.

Stops are superior to stop-limit orders for managing risk because they guarantee an execution if the stop condition is met.

In terms of duration, the two primary periods of time your order will be in place are as follows:

- The current trading session or following session if the market is closed
- Until the order is cancelled by you or the broker clears the order (possibly in 60 days — check with your broker)

Order duration is identified by adding day or good 'til canceled (GTC). Market orders guarantee execution, so they are good for the day only.

If you want to cancel an active order, you do so by submitting a Cancel Order. After the instructions are completed, you receive a report back notifying you that the order was successfully canceled. It is possible for the order to already have been executed, in which case you receive a report back indicating too late to cancel, filled with the execution details. Needless to say, you can't cancel a market order.

Changing an order is a little different than canceling one because you can change an order one of two ways:

- Cancel the original order, wait for the report confirming the cancellation, and then enter a new order.
- Submit a Cancel/Change or Replace Order which replaces the existing order with the revised qualifiers unless the original order was already executed. If that happens, the replacement order is canceled.

Even though the order process is incredibly fast, when replacing an order it's better to use the Change/Cancel approach. Otherwise, you must wait for the cancellation confirmation to avoid duplicating an executed order.

There are other, less widely used order types available. Check with your broker if you need additional information about them or if you need help placing a new order type. For the most part, they'd much rather be on the phone helping you place an order than explaining to you why the trade wasn't executed as you expected.

It is absolutely, positively your responsibility to understand order types and how they are executed (or not) in the market.

Identifying option stop order challenges

Just in case your eyes haven't glazed over yet, there are a few additional considerations specific to option stop orders. There are many of them, but here is what you need to know about the major ones. An option stop order can be triggered in two ways:

- If a trade is executed at the stop price
- If the bid or ask moves to the stop price

There are some significant differences between stock and options trading mechanics and dynamics. Because option contract volume is much lower than stocks, the quote frequently is the trigger for a stop order. Otherwise, it's possible for hours to pass before an actual trade triggers the stop. At that point, who knows where the underlying would be trading and what the quote would be when your market order got triggered.

Because of the volume involved and the derivative nature of the options market, when placing an order, you must be ready to experience a certain amount of uncertainty and to factor that into your overall strategy. Typically, when placing a stop order on an option, you use a maximum risk amount to target an exit price for the option. It's an estimated amount because the order may be triggered by the option quote and you won't know in advance the spread amount when it's triggered.

The worst-case scenario for this type of order is to have the underlying security gap up or down (against you) at the open, causing the order to be triggered well below your risk target. But it could be worse — you could have no order in place and be left with a position that keeps declining.

Some systems allow you to have two standing orders for the same underlying. They include a stop-loss order (risk management) and a limit order (profit-taking). If your platform allows a "one cancels other" trade type, then enter such orders using that feature. If not, be extremely careful about entering two orders — they both may be filled.

A *one cancels other order* allows you to enter two different orders that are active in the market. If and when one of those orders is executed, the system automatically cancels the other order. If this order setup is not available to you, having two live orders for the same position is pretty dangerous. A strong swing in the position can result in both orders being executed, possibly leaving you with an unlimited risk position. Still, if you use this type of strategy, it pays to pay attention to your order. Too often casual traders who are used to trading stocks fail to pay attention to options trades and pay the price, literally, for not paying attention to detail and not being vigilant. To be sure, someone reading this book may not qualify for this painful description, but it's still worth a mention.

TIP

The best markets for bidding and asking (offering) prices are referred to as the National Best Bid-Offer (NBBO). The NBBO represents composite information from the various option exchanges.

A sell-stop order gets triggered when the option trades at or below your stop price *or* if the ask reaches your stop. A buy-stop order gets triggered when the option trades at or above your stop *or* the bid reaches your stop. Because you sell on the bid and buy on the ask, you need to account for the bid-ask spread when determining an option stop level.

A second issue with option stop orders is duration. The option contract you're trading may only allow day-stop orders. If this is the case, you'll need to enter a new stop order each evening after the market closes.

REMEMBER

If you're used to trading stock, don't assume option orders work the same exact way. Be sure you know the implications of all orders you place.

Entering a new position

Ready to enter an option order? Just a few more points ahead. Option positions can include the following:

- Single option contracts
- Options contracts and stock
- Multiple option contracts

A quick review of single contract order entry is provided, followed by combination orders.

Creating a single option position

A single contract option order entry requires information about the following:

- The transaction type (buy or sell)
- Position information (open or close)
- Contract specifics (underlying, month, strike price, and option type)
- Order type (market, limit . . .)
- Order duration (day, good 'til canceled . . .)

REMEMBER

When you have multiple potential orders for different strategies, some of the orders may be filled, but others may not be filled because the bid and ask may move from your stop.

After entering your order, it goes from the broker's system to one of 13 option exchanges. The exchanges are linked, so your order can be executed on the exchange receiving the order or it can be forwarded to the exchange with the best market. Technology makes the process seamless and speedy. Some brokers also allow you to direct the order to the exchange of your choice. This latter approach may or may not offer you the best price, though.

Creating a combination position

Combination positions can be entered as a single combined order or individual orders for each portion of it (also called *legging in*). An advantage to combining the order is that you have a better chance of having the trade executed between the bid-ask spread. This applies to both option-stock combinations as well as option-option combinations.

Assume ABC is trading at 33.12 by 33.14 and the ABC Jan 30 put is trading at 1.00 by 1.05. You want to place a limit order for a married put position that is good for the current market day. The combination is entered as follows:

- Buy 100 shares of ABC
- Simultaneously Buy to Open 1 ABC Jan 30 put
- For a limit (net debit) of $34.17, good for the day

All legs for a combination order will either be executed or not executed.

The qualifiers for a combination order are the same for each leg, and you can only get filled on both portions of the order. Chapter 11 introduces spread trades, including a bull call spread, which is a debit position that combines two calls. A long call is purchased at the same time a less expensive call expiring the same month is sold.

Using ABC, you create a bull call spread by purchasing a $30 call and selling a $35 call. The quotes for the two options follow:

- Mar 30.00 Call: Bid $3.10 by Ask $3.30
- Mar 35.00 Call: Bid $1.00 by Ask $1.05

Because you're buying the 30 strike call (Ask $3.30) and selling the 35 strike call (Bid $1.00), the net debit at the quote is $2.30. You can identify this net debit as a limit amount for the spread order or you can try to reduce the cost by reducing the debit slightly. Entering an order slightly lower than the market is accomplished as follows:

- Buy to Open 1 ABC Mar 30 call and
- Simultaneously Sell to Open 1 ABC Mar 35 call
- For a limit (net debit) of $2.25, good for the day

Again, the qualifiers for a combination order are the same for each leg, and you can only get filled on both portions of the order.

Fill is another term for order execution.

Exchange traders agree to make a market on the list of securities they handle, which subjects them to risk that they must manage constantly. They do this for single option orders by buying and selling the underlying stock or other options to hedge the risk (see Chapter 12).

Spread trades are different — they represent a naturally hedged position and are appealing to the trader regardless of whether it creates a debit or credit in their account. When trading spreads you should

- Moderately reduce the limit below the market on a spread debit order.
- Moderately increase the limit above the market on a spread credit order.

Spreads have high appeal on the trading floor; try to shave a little off the market price for these orders.

Spread orders have higher risk due to execution mechanics. This type of trade is less automated on the exchanges, which means it can take a little more time to receive an execution report. With that in mind, expect the process of replacing an order to really take some time if you've shaved too much off the price. If executing the spread is more important than shaving some money from the current quote, stay closer to the current market. Prices can move significantly in the time it takes you to receive a confirmed cancellation report for an unexecuted order.

Executing a quality trade

Execution quality describes a broker's ability to provide speedy order executions at or better than the current market for the security. This means if you have an order to buy a security with a bid of $22.95 and an ask of $22.98, your order will be filled in a timely manner at $22.98 or better. When considering brokers, good execution quality is as important as reasonable commission costs.

Not all brokers are the same. Trading platforms are so fast these days, and a lot of orders never even touch an exchange trader's hands — it's all about the technology. If you're having significant option-execution problems, it's possible your broker does not handle many option-trading accounts, and you should consider using a different broker for the option-trading portion of your assets.

A variety of factors can impact your execution quality and are generally good for you to know about when trading. We discuss a few of these in the sections that follow.

Fast markets

A security is in a *fast market* when a very large volume of orders is flowing to the market and it's difficult for the market maker or specialist to maintain an orderly market for the security. Volume is high, and quotes and execution reports are delayed. Although technology has reduced the number of securities placed in fast markets by the exchange, traders must be aware that standard rules for execution are waived at this time. That means that the prices at which your orders are filled may not be close to your expectations and that you could have some unexpected losses. This is yet another reason to be close to your trading station when you have open option orders.

REMEMBER

When a stock goes into a fast market, so do the options derived from it.

If you place a market order when fast markets are declared, the trade may end up getting executed minutes after the order is placed when the price is significantly different. The trade could cost you much more than anticipated.

If you must exit a position, you may have no choice but to trade under these conditions, but consider entering a marketable limit order that provides you with a cushion, because it's not uncommon for movements to occur quickly in both directions. And although some of these potential events may seem daunting to those who may not be familiar with higher-risk forms of trading, these are just the chances that you take when you trade. That's why, over and over in this book, we continue to note that no matter what, managing your risk comes first.

Trader-driven conditions

Consider your trading platform and connectivity when identifying factors that impact order execution. If the time it takes to get a quote and submit an order is lengthy, the delay in obtaining an order execution may be on your end and not the broker's or exchange's. Given the amount of bandwidth required for trading platforms, a slow computer or connection could put you behind the trading curve. Execution delays may not be a broker or exchange issue — it may be your system.

If you're trading this way and can't upgrade, keep the real short-term trading to a minimum and consider using marketable limit orders instead of a market order any time you enter a new position so you can control your costs.

Booked order

When an order that is better than the current bid or ask enters the option market, the exchange can fill it or post it as the current best bid or best ask. If this is done, the order is considered a *booked order.* The impact to you is that the depth of the market at this price may be pretty small — the order may represent just one or two contracts. Execution quality rules don't apply to such quotes.

Electronic review

There may be other causes of order delays and strange fills. Your broker may have an electronic order review process that delays routing your orders to an exchange. This delay can be several minutes. You may trade actively and never encounter such a delay or experience such a quick review that order routing appears to be seamless. Only a very small fraction of retail orders are reviewed during any given trading day. Check with your broker if it appears to be an issue.

Exiting an existing position

It pays to review the possible order varieties that your broker offers. The order platforms and trading screens available currently may also provide you with a wider variety of approaches to exit an option position. In addition to placing an order for the specific option contract, you can place contingent orders based on the movement of the underlying security. This is extremely helpful in protecting your downside and establishing exits based on technical levels as well as offering another way to manage risk in volatile markets.

Understanding what to expect in actual trading is pretty important. There are times when different types of orders are appropriate, but without a lot of experience using them, you're not sure how to proceed. Your broker should always welcome your call when clarifying exchange rules or proper order entry for their trade platforms.

There are SEC rules in place requiring brokers to provide execution statistics on different orders. The regulation primarily covers market and marketable limit stock orders, but also includes some reporting for options.

Managing risk with single options

There are a couple of different ways to manage risk when you hold a single option position. The first includes using a stop order on the option itself and was discussed earlier. The second involves placing a conditional or contingent order on the underlying stock.

Conditional or *contingent orders* refer to those that rely on movement in the underlying or an index to trigger an option order. A variety of criteria can be established on the underlying or index, including the following:

- Closing price equal to, greater than, or less than a certain value
- Intraday price equal to, greater than, or less than a certain value
- Percentage changes in price
- Quote levels equal to, greater than, or less than a certain value

After setting the criteria for the trigger, you enter the specifics for the option order, which has the standard qualifiers available. A big distinction between a stop order and a contingent order is that a stop order is active on the exchange whereas a contingent order is active on your broker's system. The market doesn't have a view of your contingent order. This is an advantage to you because the less the market knows about your stops and overall strategies, the better off you are.

An advantage to placing stop orders to exit a position versus contingent orders on the underlying stock is that you can better estimate the trade value with the option order.

Still, there is some downside, and in some cases you can do too much risk management. Some of the triggers appear similar to a stop order for the option, but remember the contingent order generates an option order when you have much less of a handle on where the option is trading. You can estimate the expected option value using the price of the underlying and the option Greeks.

The absolute best reason to use contingent orders is they allow you to identify technical (or fundamental) exit points for the stock. Since managing risk is critical, this approach allows you to exit the option when conditions in the underlying have changed. You should look at multiple scenarios, especially when you paper trade and figure out which works out best for you, as well as what may be best tailored to any particular market.

Consider using an option calculator to estimate an option's value when a contingent order is triggered.

Be aware of all active orders with your broker — there is a potential to duplicate them if your platform doesn't have safeguards. Having triggers set above the market and below the market at the same time can be dangerous. The best way to manage this is by using the one cancels other (OCO) order type, which you can discuss with your broker.

Exiting a combination

Combination orders are exited in the same way they are created: either by legging out of the position or by entering a combination order for a credit or debit. When presenting a hedged position to the floor, consider shaving off a little from the debit or adding a bit to the credit. Unless you're very close to expiration for the position, you'll likely have the order executed at the more favorable limit.

Rolling an option position

You may hear people talk about *rolling an option* and wonder what exactly is involved in this process. *Roll* is used to describe an option transaction that involves closing one position and opening a similar one for the same stock. It's common for this process to occur near expiration as protective or income positions are pushed further out in time.

Rolling out involves pushing back expiration for a strategy. When rolling an option, you place a combination order similar to the any other combination. Because the expiration date is so close, you may not be able to get a more favorable execution for the combination.

You end up paying an extra commission to close the original option, which probably would have expired worthless, but you are also gaining some time value for the new option sold.

Instead of rolling the option out in time, you can *roll up* in price to avoid assignment risk or capitalize on atypically high implied volatility for a higher strike option.

A third alternative to rolling out or rolling up is *rolling down* the strike price. Again, you may elect to do this to avoid assignment risk or capitalize on atypically high implied volatility for a lower strike option.

These rolling combinations can also be combined so that you can roll out and up or roll out and down, depending on the price for the underlying, your market outlook for it, and implied volatility conditions.

As with any other type of trading, the best solution to trading options is to take it one step at a time. Get a good handle on a particular strategy before you go on to the next. And above all, if keeping it simple while managing risk suits you, then that's the way to go. If you have too many moving parts in your trading system, you may end up doing a lot of work and going nowhere.

Part III

What Every Trader Needs to Know About Options

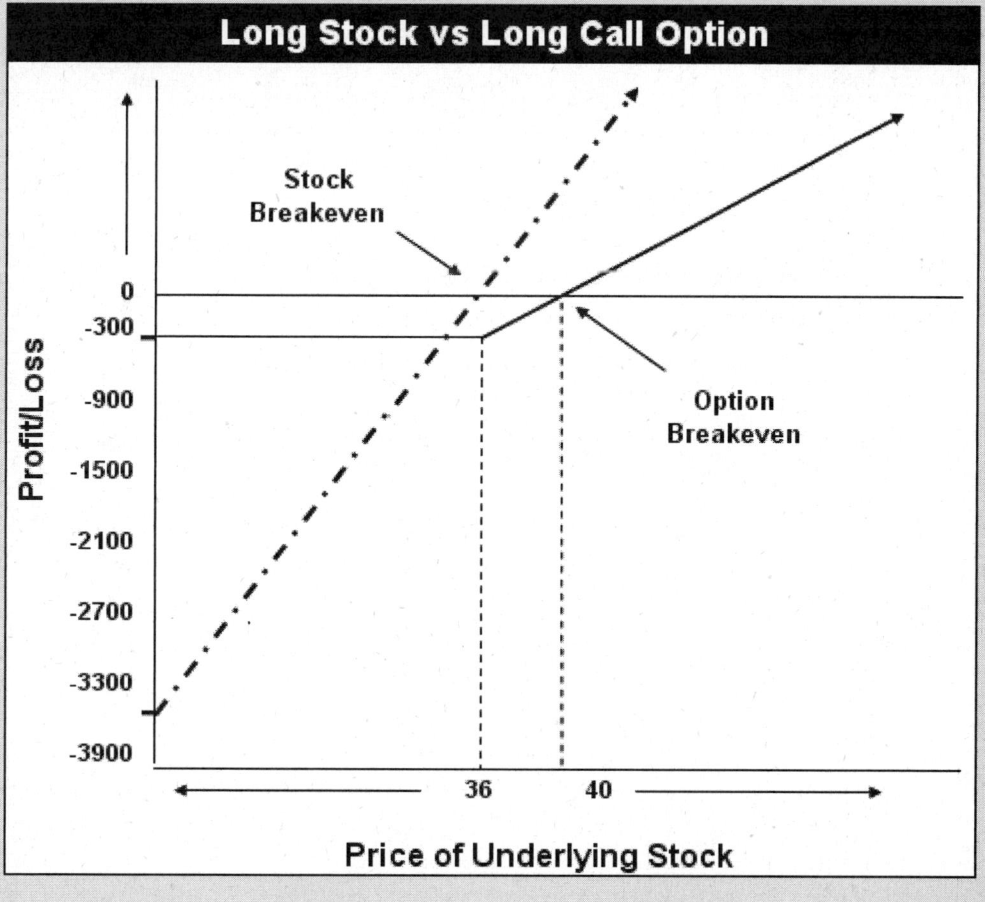

web extras

Check out a free online glossary of options trading terms at `www.dummies.com/extras/tradingoptions`.

In this part . . .

- Understanding option styles and managing risks
- Limiting overall market risk with core strategies
- Implementing existing stock positions, single option positions, and combination option positions
- Reducing portfolio volatility using exchange-traded funds (ETFs)

Chapter 9

Getting to Know Different Option Styles

In This Chapter

- Understanding index and index option details
- Distinguishing option styles
- Exercising option rights and meeting obligations
- Knowing what to do for expiration

Knowledge is indeed power. That's why knowing your risk as a trader means that you really understand the market mechanics for the securities you use, as well as the different ways it can hit you with losses. Options present you with a unique challenge because they are leveraged and they come with an expiration date — you need to know how to handle a security that can be volatile and that eventually "goes away." This chapter focuses on key points about indexes and index options that impact trading. It also addresses exercise style, assignment issues, and other things you need to be wary of going into expiration.

Nailing Down Index Options

Just when you think you're starting to get a handle on things, the options market throws a curve at you. For example, you can group most monthly listed stock options together when applying strategies or managing a position because their basic features match. That's because the last trading date and exercise cutoff time for each are the same for all monthly stock options. Index options, though, are slightly more challenging because those things can vary by contract. Have no fear. Here's a primer on index and index options to help you avoid some unpleasant surprises.

Getting to the nitty-gritty of indexes

An *index* is a tool that combines individual stocks, bonds, or commodities into one value so you can track the health of a particular market as one entity. This helps you target your trading on broad, diversified markets or narrower, focused ones by giving you a general trend as a starting point of analysis.

Taking a peek at popular indexes

You're probably familiar with indexes, by name at least. Here's a refresher that shows you a few of the most popular indexes Wall Street has to offer and what they do:

- **S&P 500 (SPX):** This is the pros' tool for measuring the trend of the U.S. stock market. If you want to get a feel for the health of a diverse group of U.S. large-cap stocks, the S&P 500 Index is the one to do just that. It is used by professional money managers and by individual investors all over the globe to check the pulse of the U.S. stock market. Its companion ETF, SPY, is a popular trading vehicle.
- **The Dow (a.k.a. the Dow Jones Industrial Average):** To gain insight into how 30 select manufacturers in the U.S. stock market are doing, use another widely followed index, the Dow. This index is often used by individuals and the mainstream news media. It can be excellent for trading, via its Diamonds (DIA) ETF, despite its relatively small number of components.
- **Nasdaq-100 Index (NDX):** If you like a faster pace, the Nasdaq-100 Index is made up of the 100 largest nonfinancial companies trading on the Nasdaq exchange. The index is made up primarily of stocks in the technology industry and is most frequently used to measure this sector. It usually swings up and down more widely than the S&P 500 or the Dow. It also has a recognizable ETF trading companion, the QQQ ETF.

REMEMBER

The market capitalization or cap of a company is calculated by multiplying the current stock price by the total number of shares outstanding. Market cap sizes include small, mid, and large.

Shifting to a more specific focus and showcasing variety

If you want to focus on a more specific group of stocks, this list shows you the wide variety of indexes available:

- **PHLX Semiconductor Sector Index (SOX):** If you want to concentrate on just semiconductor stocks rather than all technology stocks, one index you may want to track is the SOX. It's made up of 19 different companies in the semiconductor industry.

- **NYSE Arca Biotech Index (BTK):** Commonly known as *the* Biotech Index, this group of stocks is home to one of Wall Street's most volatile sectors, often an interesting place to trade options.
- **Russell 2000 Growth Index:** This index allows you to narrow your focus on two levels — it tracks stocks that are both small-cap and growth oriented. Expect big moves in both directions because small-cap names take less volume than large-cap names to impact where the stock trades.

TIP

Because an index is made up of a group of stocks, declines in one stock can be offset by increases in another stock. As a result, you'll find that indexes tend to be less volatile than individual stocks. By the same token, if the change in price in one stock becomes "contagious," as can often happen, the index could become as volatile as a single stock. This can be seen in some sectors more often than others. For example, technology and energy stocks often trade "as a block," meaning in similar patterns and trends.

Creating indexes and creating change in stocks

It's important to understand that not all indexes are created equally (well . . . one is). The three ways to construct an index are as follows:

- **Price-weighted:** Favors higher-priced stocks
- **Market cap-weighted:** Favors higher-cap stocks
- **Equal dollar-weighted:** Each stock has same impact

By having a basic handle on the different methods, you gain a much better feel for how changes in one stock translate into changes for the index. The construction names should help. The following examples show what we mean:

- **When a high-priced stock declines in a price-weighted index, it leads to bigger moves down in an index compared to declines in a lower-priced stock.** The Dow is an example of a price-weighted index that is affected more by Boeing (trading near $120) than Pfizer (trading near $30).
- **A market-cap–weighted index such as the S&P 500 is impacted more by higher market capitalization stocks regardless of price.** For example, at the time of this writing, Google (GOOGL) has a market cap of $404 billion. Compare that to Xilinx (XLNX), a specialty semiconductor company. Both are members of the S&P 500. But when Google moves up or down in price, it creates a greater change in the S&P 500 than Xilinx does, which has a market cap of some $11 billion.
- **All the stocks in an equal-dollar–weighted index should have the same impact on the index value.** To keep the index balance, a quarterly adjustment of the stocks is required. This prevents a stock that has seen large gains during the last three months from having too much weight on the index.

The best way to obtain specific construction information for an index is by accessing the website of the company that created the index. You can often bring up a list of component stocks, bonds, or commodities for the index, along with other useful information. For instance, you can access index levels, charts, construction approach, and component lists for Dow Jones indexes when you access `www.djindexes.com`.

So who creates these indexes and why should you care? Different groups construct them, including financial information companies, exchanges, and brokerage firms. By knowing which companies created them, you know how to get the index detail you need for different strategies. Table 9-1 provides sample indexes that include the company that constructs them and how you can use them.

Table 9-1 Sample Index List

Name	*Symbol*	*Company*	*Generally Used For*
S&P 500	SPX	Standard and Poor's	Trading or hedging a diverse U.S. large-cap stock portfolio
S&P Midcap 400	MDY	Standard and Poor's	Trading or hedging a U.S. mid-cap stock portfolio
MSCI EAFE	MSCIEA	Morgan Stanley Capital International	Trading or hedging a diverse global stock portfolio
Footsie-100	FTSE 100	FTSE Group	Trading a narrow international stock group (UK blue chip)
NYSE Arca	BTK	NYSE	Trading focused on a narrow industry stock group (biotechnology)
CRB Index	CRBI	Commodity Research Bureau	Trading or hedging a diverse, commodity portfolio
Goldman Commodity Index	GSCI	Goldman Sachs Group	Trading more narrow commodity group that over-weights energy
CBOE 30-year Yields	TYX	Chicago Board Options Exchange	Trading focused on U.S. 30-year treasury yields

Capitalizing on an index with options

In addition to options with value derived from an individual stock, you can also find many options that are based on index levels. In fact, the S&P 500 (SPX) is one of the most widely traded option series for all stock and index options, so it's very easy to create and exit a position. But because you can't actually own an index, how can you deliver one at expiration if you choose to exercise an index put?

The answer is . . . you can't. Index options don't actually involve the exchange of an asset. Index options are referred to as *cash-settled* transactions because the exercise and assignment process involves the transfer of cash instead of a security. The amount of cash is determined by the intrinsic value of the option. (See Chapter 3 for more details on intrinsic value.)

Determining index option value

Options on an index are very similar to options on a stock. There are calls and puts with different expiration months and strike prices available. The following factors determine the option's value:

- **Its type (call or put):** Calls increase in value as the index increases in price, whereas puts increase in value when the index price falls.
- **The value of the index level relative to the option's strike price:** A call has intrinsic value when the strike price is below the index level, which means that the option is in the money as the index value has moved above the strike price. When the index is trading below the call strike price, the option only has time value. On the other hand, the reverse is true for put options, as a put has intrinsic value when the index is trading below the put strike price.
- **Time to expiration:** Time passed erodes the value of your option. The more time until expiration, the greater the chance that an option will have value at expiration. So you pay more money for options with more time until expiration, regardless of type.
- **Historical volatility:** Past performance affects the price of the option. An index that has made bigger moves in the past will have options that are more expensive than an index that historically moves less, because there is more uncertainty about where it will be at expiration. Index gains or losses can be significant.
- **Volatility expected in the future:** Expectations of degree of future volatility will affect the price as well. The expected future movement affects an option's value in the same way its past movement does — in fact, it's partially based on it. The greater the potential move, the more expensive the option.

Detailing option components

The main components of an index option are basically the same as those for a stock option. (See Chapter 2 for more details.) The main difference is that an index isn't a physical asset. As a result, this affects the exercise or assignment process because settlement is only in terms of cash exchanging hands. Here's a list of index option components similar to stock options:

- **Underlying:** Name of the index the option is based on.
- **Strike price:** Level that determines where the owner has rights and the seller has obligations.
- **Premium:** Total cost of the option based on the current market price and the option multiplier.
- **Multiplier:** Number used to determine the total value of the option premium and the cost of the deliverable package.
- **Exercise/Assignment value:** Amount credited to the option owner and debited from the option owner seller. It is determined by multiplying the strike price by the option multiplier.
- **Settlement value:** Index closing value used to determine intrinsic value.

Moneyness is another term used to describe the option's intrinsic value. It is the amount an index closes above a call option strike price or below a put option strike price. Moneyness is zero for out-of-the-money options at expiration.

Suppose the SPX closes at 1,523 at June expiration, and you own one June 1,520 call. Because a short option holder can't deliver the SPX to you, they satisfy their obligation in cash. You receive a $300 credit in your account, and the short contract holder is debited the same amount. This is how the cash amount is determined:

$$(\text{Index Settlement Value} - \text{Call Strike Price}) \times \text{Multiplier}$$

$$(1{,}523 - 1{,}520) \times 100 = \$300$$

You probably noticed that the cash settlement amount at expiration is similar to the intrinsic value calculation for a stock option. The two types of options do have many similarities, as well as important distinctions. The next section goes over some differences between stock and index options.

Watching Out for Style Risk

This is not about you trading last year's big fashion fad — it's about making sure that you know options have style. An option's *style* primarily refers to the way the contract is exercised, and it also impacts the end of trading for the option. You have to know where to look to find an index option's style and how it affects you.

If you don't know the style for a particular option, you could end up with an unpleasant surprise . . . such as missing an opportunity to sell an index call contract before it takes a tumble on the settlement value day.

The U.S. markets trade two styles for option contracts:

- **American style:** American-style options let you exercise your rights *at any point up to* the exercise cutoff time.
- **European style:** If you own a European-style options, you can only exercise your rights on a designated date.

American-style options

Options that use stock for the deliverable package are American style. Unless stated otherwise, references to American-style stock options describe the general term *option contract* in this book. You can determine an option's style by checking out its product specification sheet, available from the Options Clearing Corporation (OCC) or the different option exchanges. The OCC website (`www.optionsclearing.com`) and exchange websites serve as excellent resources for this information.

American-style stock options have the following characteristics:

- When initiated by the OCC, the option contract trades from that point in time until the last trading day prior to option expiration. Recall that option expiration is the Saturday following the third Friday of the month.
- After purchase, these contracts can be exercised by the holder at any point during the life of the contract. Retail brokers have different requirements for submitting exercise instructions — find out your broker's specific rules. In most cases, you can exercise a long contract at least an hour after the close on the last trading day prior to expiration.

- After assigned, the option seller must fulfill their obligation under the contract by delivering or taking delivery of the option package (usually 100 shares of stock for a stock option).
- The option seller can "buy to close" the option in the market prior to the close on the last day of trading to offset the position and alleviate the obligation.

European-style options

An option that uses an index to derive its value is *often, but not always*, a European-style option. European-style options have a specified exercise date if you are long the contract. So, your choices are limited, because you can't exercise the option prior to that date the way you can with American-style options. Making things a bit more complicated is the fact that not only is there a specified exercise date for an index option, but this date also varies by index — there's not one common index exercise day each month.

Therefore it's extremely important for you to check the product specification sheet prior to trading one of these contracts. Key dates for you to note for European-style index options include the following:

- **Last trading date:** The last date the contract can be traded in the market — it may be two days prior to expiration.
- **Settlement date:** The date (and time) used to determine the index closing value at expiration.
- **Exercise date:** The date in which a long contract holder can exercise their rights under the contract.

Some index options stop trading on a Thursday rather than a Friday, so you need to know the specifics to properly manage your position. The style designation, expiration, and exercise dates, along with other critical trading details, are all included in the option contract specifications available from the OCC or different exchanges that trade the contract.

REMEMBER

The stock option package identifies the deliverable asset(s) for a contract. Although there are securities that track an index, indexes themselves are not physical securities. So, the take-home message is that index options settle in cash rather than a physical asset because a trader can't deliver an index. Most important is that this cash-settlement approach applies to index options regardless of exercise style.

European-style index options have these characteristics:

- When initiated by the OCC, the option contract trades from that point in time until the specified Last Trading Date, which is usually two trading days prior to option expiration. Make sure to check the contract specifications to determine the last trading date for each index option.
- After purchase, these contracts can only be exercised by the holder on the exercise date, which is *usually* the last business day before option expiration. Retail brokers have different requirements for submitting exercise instructions, so you need to contact your broker to get their specific rules — which may be different than stock option exercise.
- When assigned, the index option seller must fulfill their obligation under the contract with a cash settlement. The appropriate amount of money is debited from the account.
- The option seller can "buy to close" the option in the market prior to the exercise date and close of trading for the contract to offset the position and alleviate the obligation.

There are exceptions. Thus, not all index options are European style. The S&P 100 Index (OEX) includes the top 100 stocks in the SPX and is an example of an American-style index option. These contracts can be exercised at any time during the life of the option, which is one reason that they tend to be popular among some traders. The OEX is somewhere in between the Dow Jones Industrial Average and the S&P 500 in its content, but is not as universally known by the public or as quoted in the media.

TIP

Indexes are generally less volatile than stocks, and a diverse index such as the S&P 100 is generally less volatile than a sector-oriented index. That's because a group of stocks in the same industry tends to respond the same way to news, pushing the index in one direction. That won't necessarily happen with a diverse index because some news can be bullish for one industry and bearish for another.

The S&P 500 Index is one of the most widely followed indexes, and options on the index are offered by the Chicago Board Options Exchange (CBOE) as a proprietary product. They are high-volume contracts used by many institutional traders, so they are very liquid. Using this option contract as an example, here are some things to note from the specification available at `www.cboe.com`:

- **Underlying symbol:** SPX.
- **Multiplier:** 100.
- **Premium:** Quote × Multiplier, so 1 point is equal to $100.

- **Expiration date:** Saturday following the third Friday of the expiration month.
- **Exercise style:** European — options generally may be exercised on the last business day before expiration, usually a Friday.
- **Last trading day:** Trading usually stops on the business day (usually a Thursday) prior to the day the exercise-settlement value is calculated.
- **Settlement of option exercise:** The exercise-settlement value (SET) is calculated on the last business day before expiration using the first reported sales price for each component stock from the market where the stock is listed. This day is usually a Friday.
- **Margin:** Check the specification margin rules and then check your broker's rules, which may be more stringent.
- **Trading hours:** 8:30 a.m. to 3:15 p.m. Central Time.

Additional information is available, but key elements are previously listed.

WARNING!

Not all European-style options have the same specifications. One may calculate the settlement value using an opening price, whereas another may use closing values from the previous day. Before trading any index option, first check the specs!

Exercising Your Options American Style

How you exercise an option is much more straightforward than whether or not to exercise, so we cover mechanics first. As a retail trader, you provide exercise instructions to your broker, who then provides these instructions to the OCC. The OCC randomly assigns a broker with accounts holding the same option short, and the broker assigns one of those accounts.

When you own an American-style call or put, you have the right to exercise the contract at any point up until your broker's exercise cutoff time. You exercise the contract by submitting *exercise instructions* to the broker, either by phone or electronically.

WARNING!

Be prepared for the unexpected. This point can't be stressed enough: Do not assume that you have the same exercise cutoff time as your trading partner, a clearing firm, or anyone else. Always check the specific cutoff time and exercise process with your broker. Be sure to leave sufficient time to reach them and provide instructions.

Knowing the nuts and bolts

The best practice before trading any options contract is contacting your broker ahead of time to check their exercise process — you want this information in advance so everything goes smoothly when you actually need to submit instructions. Prior to exercising a stock option contract, be sure to check the following:

- For calls, check that sufficient money is in the account to pay for the stock purchased
- For puts, check that shares are in the account or that you are able (and want to) create a short stock position. This would be prohibited in a retirement account.

Definitely ask any questions you may have during the broker discussion.

TIP

Don't just point and click. There is no substitute for knowing what you're getting into and how it's going to affect your account. That means that even if you can submit exercise instructions electronically, you may want to contact your broker directly the first few times you complete the process.

What you see is what you get

Although clearing and brokerage systems are getting more efficient all the time, you may not immediately see the exercise take place when you submit instructions. Typically you'll see the appropriate transactions in your account by the next trading day.

There is no going back. After you submit exercise instructions to your broker, the action is final. When you exercise an option, the actual option position is reduced by the number of contracts exercised, and a stock buy or sell transaction appears. What that means is that you should be aware of the risks involved and factor them into your decision-making when exercising. For example, if you decide to exercise your call rights to purchase a stock at 10 a.m. on a certain day, and by 2 p.m. that same day the stock drops dramatically due to bad news, you cannot cancel your exercise instructions.

WARNING!

When you exercise a put and do not have the underlying stock in your account, you create a short position. This means a previously limited risk position is now technically an unlimited risk position because a stock can just continue to rise. *Be sure you consider the exercise ramifications before submitting instructions.*

To exercise or not, that is the question

Before you exercise an option, you need to complete a couple of calculations to decide whether it's the best approach. You want to make sure you maximize profits by checking two alternatives:

- Exercising the rights under the contract to buy or sell stock
- Selling the option and then buying or selling the stock in the market

Being ahead of the game is a good idea. So complete both of these calculations when the option contract has time value (premium greater than the intrinsic value). It's a good habit to always complete the checks when first using options. The last thing you want to do is walk away from money on the table . . . or in the market.

REMEMBER

The option-exercise decision is different than the stock-ownership decision. You need to consider the most profitable way to execute your transaction in the market, which is why you want to calculate both alternatives provided in this section.

Here's an example: Suppose you own 100 shares of ABC. You purchased the stock at $23 per share and at the same time purchased one 22.50 put for $0.50. Later the stock is at $27, but news just hit that ABC is under investigation for funny accounting practices. The price plummets to $21 per share, and the 22.50 put immediately moves to $2.50. What should you do?

Assuming you no longer want to own the stock, you need to calculate the net gains or losses for the two alternatives available:

- **Alternative 1: Exercise put**
    - Buy 100 ABC @ $23 = Debit: $2,300
    - Buy 1 ABC 22.50 put @ $0.50 = Debit: $50
    - Exercise Right to Sell @ 22.50 = Credit: $2,250
    - Net Loss = $100
- **Alternative 2: Sell put and sell stock in market**
    - Buy 100 ABC @ $23 = Debit: $2,300
    - Buy 1 ABC 22.50 put @ $0.50 = Debit: $50
    - Sell 100 ABC @ $21 = Credit: $2,100
    - Sell 1 ABC 22.50 put @ $2.50 = Credit: $250
    - Net Gain = $0

In this case, it makes more sense for you to sell both the option and stock in the market. After you add trading costs, the difference narrows, but will still likely favor the second alternative. If you make this part of your trading routine, it will take the guesswork out of your decision-making.

Generally, when an option has more than $0.20 time value remaining, the second alternative will result in a credit that exceeds the extra transaction. This includes commissions and the extra trading costs due to spreads in the market quote.

Exercising Your Options the Euro Way

When trading European-style index options, you need to be even more familiar with the contract specifications. This section covers what you should understand about the index-settlement process, which determines option moneyness at expiration. It is the index settlement value that you use for exercise decision-making.

Stock option moneyness is calculated using the closing value during regular market hours for the stock on the last trading day before expiration. Occasionally, a late print gets posted by the exchanges, which can confuse things a bit, but all stock options use this "last trade" rule.

Tracking index settlement (the SET)

Because stock index values are calculated using a group of stocks, determining option moneyness at expiration is more complicated. Not all stocks have opening and closing trades at the exact same time, so the opening level for an index won't necessarily include the opening price for all components — some prices may include closes from the previous day.

You access the index settlement value to address this timing issue. This index level is calculated using only opening or closing values and is referred to as the *SET.* Check the option specification for more details on how a particular settlement value is determined and the symbol used to access it.

Get the details before you start trading, because exercise instruction procedures for index options can vary by broker and instrument. Even if you provided stock option exercise instructions with your broker in the past, you may find their index exercise process is different. Check with your broker about their exercise process for index options before you need to submit instructions.

Cashing in with exercise

Your window of opportunity to exercise a European-style option is much smaller than with American-style options — *it's usually just a day*. That day is very close to the Saturday of expiration and may or may not coincide with the last trading day for the option.

Because European-style index options are based on something that can't be traded, these options are referred to as *cash-settled*. That means no securities change hands during exercise or assignment — just cold hard cash. The amount of cash for this option is determined by the option moneyness and option multiplier.

You calculate European-style option moneyness using the SET as follows:

Index SET – Option Strike Price = Call Moneyness

Option Strike Price – Index SET = Put Moneyness

So you determine the exercise cash amount this way:

Option Moneyness × Option Multiplier = Cash Settlement Amount

When moneyness falls below zero, an option has no intrinsic value. In this case, no cash would change hands.

Even though there is just one day to exercise cash-settled European-style options, they can be traded any time up to the close on the last day of trading for the contract.

Assuming a SET value of 1523 for SPX and a multiplier of 100, the exercise and assignment amount for expiring call and put options with a 1520 strike price is as follows:

- Call Moneyness: 1523 – 1520 = 3
- Call Exercise Amount: 3 × 100 = $300 credit
- Call Assignment Amount: $300 debit
- Put Moneyness: 1520 – 1523 < 0
- Put Exercise Amount: 0 × 100 = $0 credit
- Put Assignment Amount: $0 debit

Because no asset changes hands during this process, your market risk over the weekend due to good or bad news is nonexistent.

Satisfying Option Obligations

When you sell an option short, you have an obligation, not a right. This makes your decision-making about whether or not you want to be assigned really easy: You have no choice. The only way you can avoid assignment is by purchasing the option back to offset your position. This is the same for both option styles.

Although all stock options are American-style contracts, not all American-style contracts are stock options. There are also American-style index options that settle in cash.

American-style stock options

Assignments usually occur over expiration weekend, but because we're talking about American-style stock options, it could occur anytime after you create the short option position. In either case, you satisfy the assignment through the transfer of shares into or out of your account.

There are a couple of nuances for you to consider regarding assignment, but first consider the following information about basic mechanics. When you are assigned on a stock option, two transactions appear in your account:

- **Assigned:** The short option is removed from your account, and the term Assigned or abbreviation ASG appears.
- **Buy/Sell:** The stock transfer appears the same as a regular stock order.

It's a bit complex, so paying attention to the developments in your account is paramount. The assigned contract(s) is no longer in your account; *however*, you may not have been assigned on all contracts. Be sure to check your positions to see if there are any short contracts remaining. Also, a commission is usually applied to the buy/sell transaction.

You usually get assigned when your short option no longer has time value. Puts generally have a better chance of being assigned early because the person exercising the right will be bringing in money. The risk of your being assigned early on a call jumps significantly when certain corporate actions are pending and the option holder wants to own the stock by the record date. Such actions include the distribution of large cash dividends.

Most short in-the-money (ITM) options get assigned over expiration weekend. Early assignment of puts usually increases when strong market declines drop stock values significantly.

And now for the inevitable nuances.

Short put assignment

Assuming you were assigned on a short put, you are now the proud owner of ABC stock at a cost that is likely higher than the current market.

You need to decide whether or not you want to keep the assigned shares and how the decision to keep them or sell them in the market impacts your account. If you didn't have enough money for the transaction, you can either bring in more cash before stock settlement or you may be able to buy the shares on margin. When you buy shares on margin, you are borrowing money from your broker. This can only be done in certain accounts, and the borrowing terms are determined by the following:

- The cost and margin requirements for the stock
- The cash in your account before the assignment
- Your broker's rules and rates

When buying on margin, your expected returns should exceed the risk-free rate associated with U.S. Treasuries plus the interest rate charged by your broker for using margin. Because the market value of an assigned position is likely below what you paid, you need to consider cutting your losses and selling the position.

Short call assignment

If you were assigned on a short call, things get trickier unless you already owned the stock. Then it simply is sold at the option strike price, which is likely below the current market price.

When you don't own the stock, assignment of the short call results in a short stock position. This exposes you to significant risk because the stock can keep going up. Even if you want to hold the short position, your broker may not have access to shares for lending. If that happens, the stock is bought at whatever price it's trading in the market to close the short position. This can be done with or without your knowledge.

But it can be even more dangerous. The only thing worse than shares bought back without your knowledge is being short the stock without knowing it! Be sure to always monitor your accounts regularly when holding short option or stock positions. Beware of conditions that may trigger assignments, such as deep in-the-money options or news events that significantly impact the value of the underlying.

To create a short position, your broker must go out and borrow the shares. These may or may not be available. As a result, even if you have enough money and want to hold a short position, it may not be a viable alternative.

Expiring uninspiring options

In a perfect world, if you actively manage your account, expiration will come and go without incident. That said, it's likely that there will be a time when you end up holding a position at expiration. Here's what to expect when you are long or short an option going into expiration weekend.

Long option positions

Before you buy an option, you should know how you will close out the position. As the option nears expiration, here is what you need to consider:

- If the option is out-of-the-money (OTM) or roughly at-the-money (ATM) and you don't want to exercise the contract rights, try to sell it when the credit you receive exceeds your commission for the transaction.
- If you want to buy or sell the stock, calculate whether selling the contract or exercising it is more cost effective.

Never assume a slightly OTM or ATM option will expire worthless. It's possible for the stock's last trade to get reported late, resulting in an ITM option. Even if the stock closes exactly at the strike price or is OTM, monitor the news after the close. You may decide to exercise the option if you expect a big change in the company's value over the weekend.

The following sections cover what happens when you hold an ITM option into expiration.

Exercise by exception (auto-exercise)

Currently, when a stock option is ITM by $0.05 or more at expiration, the OCC assumes you did not want an option with value to expire worthless. They exercise it on your behalf over expiration weekend. So even without specific instructions, stock shares are bought or sold for you. This may create a short position in your account without your knowledge.

You can instruct your broker to not allow auto-exercise for specific contracts, but you must do so within their cutoff times. Specific instructions are required for each long option position you hold through expiration. Note that the OCC trigger levels for auto-exercise have declined over the years.

Short option positions

A short stock option obligates you to buy or sell shares of the underlying stock. As a result, you're more reactive at expiration than active. Short options are usually assigned when market conditions are against you. The only way to prevent assignment is to exit that position before the market closes on the last trading day.

TIP

Stock prices can change significantly over the weekend if important news is released. A stock's value will shoot through the roof if the company discovers cures for five major diseases, but can drop like a brick if the company discloses it was just kidding about its profits for the last three years. Monitor news after the close to see if you can benefit from exercising expiring options.

If your short option is OTM, there is a good chance that it will expire worthless. However, traders long the option will monitor conditions after the close. If big news comes out about the company, you still may be assigned over expiration weekend on the OTM option. Table 9-2 summarizes what you should expect heading into expiration weekend.

REMEMBER

Consider your best alternative and plan ahead. Whether you hold a long or short option position, it's best to actively manage the position. This usually means exiting it before the close on the last trading day, but can include providing specific instructions to your broker.

After an option closes even a penny ITM, expect it to be assigned. Currently, if it's ITM by $0.05 or more, auto-execution kicks in for long contract holders. At that point you can forget about dodging the assignment bullet.

Table 9-2 Stock Option Expiration Summary

Option Type	*Typical Action*	*What You Should Consider*
Long: OTM	Expires worthless	If the OTM option has value on the last trading day, don't let it expire worthless when you can close it for a credit greater than the commission. Monitor trading at the close to be sure the option is truly OTM.
Long: ATM	??	Manage an ATM option similar to OTM and ITM options. Either close it for a credit greater than the commission or submit specific exercise instructions. Don't leave the result to chance.
Long: ITM	Auto-exercised when ITM > $0.05	Don't passively manage ITM options through auto-exercise. Either send specific exercise instructions to your broker or exit the position for a credit.

Option Type	*Typical Action*	*What You Should Consider*
Short: OTM	Usually expires worthless	Monitor news and the account after the close. Even when the option closes OTM, anyone can choose to exercise their rights, resulting in an assignment for you. Consider closing the position.
Short: ATM	??	Monitor news and the account after the close. Once the option is ITM by even $0.01, assignment risk increases exponentially. To avoid assignment, close the short position on the last day of trading.
Short: ITM	Assigned	Monitor market news and your account over expiration. Because auto-exercise occurs when an option is ITM > $0.05, you should expect assignment at this level. Close the short position on the last day of trading if you want to avoid assignment.

When you hold a stock position that meets the short option obligation, you'll be less stressed over expiration. But when the assignment creates a new position in your account, you have two choices:

- Exit the position in the market Monday morning.
- Hold the position, if you have sufficient funds.

Your broker may or may not have shares available for a short stock position, so exiting the position could be your only choice.

When trading a European-style option, you must know the option's last trading and exercise days, as well as how the SET is determined.

When you manage risk, it means you manage your positions, long and short. Although you won't typically consider a long option very dangerous, there are times when it can catch you off-guard. A perfect example is when a long put is auto-exercised.

European-style options

European-style options provide you with an advantage over American-style options if you are short the option contract. That's because you don't have to worry about early assignment. You can completely avoid assignment when you buy the option back by a specific date to offset the short position.

Other than covering a short position, you don't have much to decide heading into expiration weekend. If the option is ITM at expiration, your account will be debited the settlement value for the assignment.

There may be a period of time when news affects an index SET, but you are past the last trading day for a European-style option. If you are short OTM SPX puts at the end of trading on Thursday, bad news overnight could result in a strong drop in the morning when the SET is determined. This may result in OTM puts becoming ITM.

Breaking It Down: American-Style Index Options

One of the most popular American-style index options is the S&P 100 Index (OEX) contract. You can exercise your rights anytime you own a long contract or be assigned whenever you hold a short contract. American-style index options settle in cash because an index can't be bought or sold.

Because these contracts can be exercised any time, you have to know how the settlement value is determined prior to expiration. You can find these details in the contract specification.

Using the OEX specification from the CBOE as an example, here's how it works:

- **OEX SET at expiration:** Uses primary market closing prices on the last business day before expiration (usually a Friday).
- **OEX settlement for early exercise:** Uses primary market closing prices for the day the exercise instructions are submitted.

Exercising rights

You need to contact your broker to find out the exercise cutoff time for American-style options because the settlement value for the index option you trade may be determined by closing values. You should consider time value when deciding whether to sell the index option in the market or exercise your contract rights. If you decide to exercise the contract, the amount credited to your account is determined using the option strike price, the index settlement value, and the multiplier, as outlined in the contract specification.

One reason you may decide to exercise your rights even when time value remains in the option is if there is a news event that could significantly impact the index value the next day. Consider the type of rights you own and the likely impact the news will have on index trading levels.

Meeting obligations

The only decision you have as a short contract holder for American-style index options is whether or not to buy back the option to avoid assignment. Because early assignment is possible, you need consider the possibility of this event each day you hold the position, rather than just on the last trading day. If assigned, your obligation is met in a cash amount using the option strike price, the index settlement value, and the multiplier.

Always, *always* check contract specifications prior to trading both European-style and American-style index options. Then plan accordingly, pay close attention to the markets and the news, and stay ahead of the game.

Chapter 10

Protecting Your Portfolio with Options

In This Chapter

- Protecting assets with options
- Hedging a portfolio using options
- Watching out for nonstandard options

The world is a volatile place, and trading activity often reflects both political as well as financial developments. For that reason, adding option strategies to both your investment and trading portfolios helps minimize trading stress. Trading is challenging enough, but when market conditions threaten your long-term holdings, the distraction can be downright destructive. Reducing stress is one key to better decision-making for both aspects of your portfolio.

Options offer protection for both portfolios and trading positions. Because a variety of strategies are available to you, you need to have a plan for implementation. This chapter discusses a few protective strategies and the key factors to consider when putting them into practice.

The last portion of the chapter addresses a unique risk that adjusted options pose to investors and traders alike. *Adjusted* options are those contracts with a non-standard deliverable package due to corporate actions that occurred during the option's life. We cover adjusted options here because they can add risk to even the conservative, protective strategies included in this chapter.

Putting Protection on Long Stock

The focus of this book leans toward shorter-term option trading strategies, but options are definitely well suited for managing risk related to longer-term holdings as well. Applying protective strategies to your existing holdings can turn anxious, sleepless nights into restful ones during market downturns. Because no one knows when these downturns will occur, incorporating protective strategies as a regular consideration in your investment planning could be the difference between meeting your financial goals on time or waiting for the next bull run to get you there.

Combining puts with long stock

Purchasing puts on your existing stock investments provides insurance against significant losses when a major downturn occurs. As with other forms of insurance, it's frustrating to write a check for something you may not need, but it's really nice to have when the time comes. Two strategies that combine long stock with a long put are as follows:

- Married put (stock and put purchased together)
- Protective put (stock and put purchased separately)

The two positions are essentially the same but differ in the timing of purchases. Each consists of one long put for every 100 shares of stock held. There's no need for you to distinguish between the terms. What is important for you is to understand why and how you protect your assets. We use the term *protective put* for the remainder of this chapter.

REMEMBER

A put option gives you the right, but not the obligation, to sell the underlying stock at the contract strike price until the trading day prior to the option's expiration date. You can also sell this right in the market up until this time.

Protection considerations

The expression "A rising tide lifts all boats" is sometimes used to describe the stock market and its tendency for all stocks to rise together during a bullish run. But what goes up eventually comes down, so regardless of the merits of an individual stock, when a bear market hits, it takes no prisoners, and even quality stocks decline.

Trying to anticipate swings in the market is almost impossible, despite a large number of indicators that are considered reliable and that are worth becoming familiar with. But why take chances without considering protecting stocks earmarked for the long term? Suppose you bought stock ABC a few months ago at $34.00 and want to hold it for the long term. You can lock in a sell price for that stock at anytime by purchasing a put. It doesn't matter whether it's your intention to exercise your right or simply offset losses with option gains.

Make options part of all your stock investment decisions. If you have a choice between two different stock investments with equal growth potential and prospects, check to see which has options available. This may make your investment decision easier if one allows you to purchase protection on it while the other doesn't.

Options can buy you time and keep you from making hasty decisions. For example, instead of relying on an all-or-nothing approach that includes selling ABC and trying to buy it back if the market declines, you can protect the position over the short term or long term using puts. Before analyzing specific options, you need to decide whether you will continually protect a position or if you will do so intermittently according to your market outlook.

Choosing your time horizon is important. Suppose you seek temporary protection for ABC (30 to 60 days). When looking at option chains, you'll then need to evaluate options with 60 to 90 days to expiration. This gives you the flexibility to exit the position prior the acceleration of time decay 30 days prior to expiration. The next thing to consider is how much protection you want. Table 10-1 provides partial put option chain data for ABC to help with this decision.

Table 10-1 Put Option Chain Data for ABC on Aug 22nd

Month	*Strike Price*	*Bid*	*Ask*	*OI**
Oct	30.00	0.20	0.25	36,287
	32.50	0.30	0.35	1,965
	35.00	0.60	0.70	24,641
	37.50	1.25	1.45	1,338
Jan	30.00	0.50	0.60	45,795
	32.50	0.75	0.85	156,657
	35.00	1.25	1.35	52,734
	37.50	2.00	2.15	24,225

**OI = Open Interest*

Open interest is the total number of contracts outstanding for a specific option contract. Because option contracts are created by demand, it reflects information from the previous day's trading activity.

One size does not fit all

Since you're concerned with market action in Sep and Oct, it's reasonable to focus on options for Oct and Jan to cover the bearish period. Next you have to identify the losses, if any, that you're willing to accept. You purchased the stock at $34, and it's currently trading at $37.50. Do you want protection ABC at the current price or the level where you purchased it? These are questions you face each time you consider protecting a position.

The more time remaining until expiration, the more uncertainty there is regarding the price of the stock at expiration. An in-the-money (ITM) has more time to become an out-of-the-money (OTM) and vice versa. Option pricing uses past movement in the stock to value different probabilities for future price movement. Use delta as a resource to check the probability the option will be ITM at expiration, given its movement in the past. For more on all the Greeks, see Chapter 3.

Although the protective put is a relatively simple strategy, the number of ways of providing protection is numerous. To help with your analysis, identify your protection time horizon along with the maximum loss you seek prior to viewing option chains. This will aide your decision-making.

Assuming you seek protection above the stock purchase price ($34), you then have limited your analysis to the 35 and 37.50 strike prices. Table 10-2 provides an analysis of the protection provided by select puts if you choose to exercise them.

The Exercise column is calculated by subtracting your purchase price from the option breakeven. From Chapter 4, the breakeven for a put option is:

Put Strike Price – Put Purchase Premium = Put Breakeven

(Put Breakeven – Purchase Price) × 100 = Net Profit/Loss

Table 10-2 Put Short List for ABC on Aug 22nd

Month	*Days to Exp*	*Strike Price*	*Ask*	*Delta*	*Exercise*
Oct	60	35.00	0.35	–0.186	$65
	60	37.50	1.05	–0.460	$245
Jan	150	35.00	1.35	–0.291	($35)
	150	37.50	2.15	–0.440	$135

Unless otherwise stated, the multiplier for a stock option is 100. When working with a combined position that includes 100 shares of stock, be sure to remember to incorporate this value in the formulas.

From this point, the actual option selected for the strategy is definitely a personal decision. You may prefer longer-term protection and include April put options in your review. You may only seek catastrophic coverage, in which case you may add strike prices below 35.00 as well.

To wrap up the example, the 37.50 strike should be selected if you don't want to see a profitable position turn into a loss when exercised. If you're bearish through the entire month of October, the ABC Jan 37.50 put option provides you with protection for the full time period.

There are a variety of things to consider when seeking protection for an existing stock position, including

- Term for the protection (expiration month).
- Level of protection (strike price and option price).

You could also consider the likelihood an option will be ITM at expiration by referencing delta. By making use of options that have a greater chance of being ITM at expiration, you may find you can trade out of the protective position and use the proceeds to help finance a new protective put. The more experience you gain, the more you'll find an approach that suits your style.

You can always sell a protective put before it expires if you feel the markets have stabilized and the intermediate outlook for your stock turns bullish again.

Because no one knows what the next day in the markets will bring, an investor may decide to maintain some level of protection on stock positions regardless of the short-term or intermediate outlook. To minimize expenses, lower strikes may be considered as part of a plan that provides catastrophic coverage — kind of a crash-protection approach.

Accelerated time decay

When trading options for this strategy or others, you need to consider the impact of time decay on the option position. *Theta* is the option Greek that identifies the daily loss of option value associated with the current price of the option.

Using an ABC Oct 37.50 put option with 60 days to expiration, you can obtain theta by accessing an option calculator such as the on located on the OIC website (`www.optionscentral.com`).

The theta value for the option trading at $1.05 is –0.0078. That means if everything stays the same tomorrow, the option quote will lose 0.0078 in value. It may not sound like much, but it can add up.

In addition to the cumulative impact of time decay, this rate of decay accelerates as expiration approaches, particularly within the last 30 days of an option's life.

The impact of time decay accelerates the last 30 days of an option's life. This means extrinsic value will decline more quickly along with the value of the option — assuming all other conditions remain the same.

Always plan ahead. To minimize the impact of time decay within 30 days of expiration, trading strategies that make use of long options should incorporate an exit plan that addresses the issue. It's a good idea to consider exiting a long option position 30 days prior to expiration to avoid accelerating losses to its extrinsic value.

Table 10-3 provides theta values for the ABC Oct 37.50 put for various days to expiration, assuming all other factors remain the same.

Table 10-3 Theta Values for ABC Oct 37.50 Put

Days to Expire	*Ask*	*Theta*
60	0.35	–0.0078
30	0.75	–0.0117
10	0.45	–0.0216
5	0.30	–0.0314

If you think $0.02/day is manageable, consider what this represents in terms of percentages. With ten days to go until expiration, 0.0216 is 4.8% of the contract's value.

The way you go about protecting positions is similar to any other investment decision — it depends on your risk tolerance and personal preferences. Find an approach that suits your style. You can figure this out on paper before you do it too.

Before moving on to the cost of a protective put relative to the stock, the risk graph in Figure 10-1 displays the improved risk-reward profile that results when you add a put to long stock. Losses are now capped.

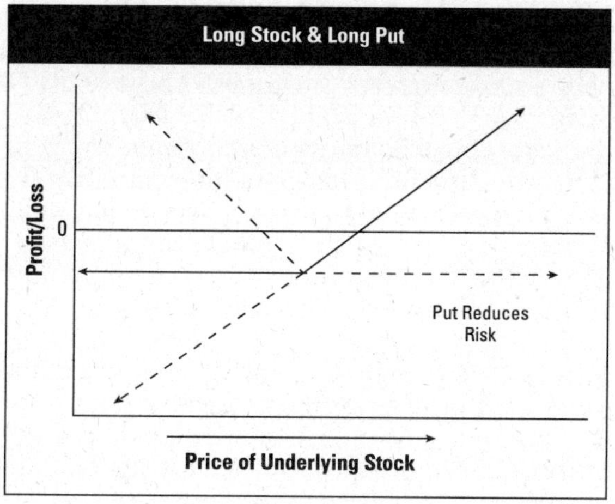

Figure 10-1: Risk graph for a long stock-protective put position.

Image by Optionetics

Weighing protection cost versus time

When you have a specific, reasonably short time horizon to protect a position, selecting the expiration month is pretty straightforward. Once you seek longer-term protection, the analysis requires a bit more effort. Because you expect the security to move upward on a longer-term basis, ATM options should be OTM by expiration and may be minimally effective. You need to weigh the cost of protection against the amount of time the protection is in place.

REMEMBER: The investment process requires you to balance risk and reward. Without risk there is no reward, but it doesn't mean you have to risk it all. Consider protective positions as a means of limiting your losses while letting your profits run.

Long-term protection

In options trading, there is no substitute for doing your homework and thinking things through. Suppose you noted that stock XYZ has consistently realized annual gains of 8%, even during years with a 2% decline along the way. How do you go about protecting such a position? A $2.15 ATM put that provided five months of protection was used in the ABC example. Since ABC was at $37.50, the put premium represents 5.7% of its value. That could cost you a fair amount of your projected return, assuming XYZ and ABC behave similarly.

Balancing the cost of protection versus returns is difficult and requires a game plan. Again, it's not a one-size-fits-all proposition. If you buy puts on a regular basis, you could be sacrificing stock returns and then some. On the other hand, ignoring protection completely could cost you a big chunk of your initial investment.

The short answer to this problem is that you pretty much have to find the balance that is right for you. You may decide to intermittently use puts when bearish periods arise, but if you could time the markets that well, you probably wouldn't need protection. The flipside is that you can factor in how much of a potential reduction to your gains could come from buying puts on a regular basis and adjust your expectations accordingly.

REMEMBER

When purchasing puts to protect your investments, be sure to balance the cost of protection versus net returns for the protective put position.

The goal is to maximize your opportunity for a successful outcome to the trade. So, whereas stocks often require technically based visual cues to execute trades, options require more planning and strategic thinking. By carefully evaluating different options rather than just looking for the cheapest alternative, there is a better chance the option will have some value 30 days prior to expiration. As part of your plan, consider the following:

- The net exercise value and level of protection provided
- The statistical chance the option will be ITM at expiration (delta)
- The cost of protection versus the net impact on returns

Being clear about your strategy goals from the start should definitely help optimize your odds of success.

Cost per day calculations

As a last consideration, when selecting protective puts

- Be careful about buying seemingly cheap puts that don't offer adequate protection and will likely expire worthless.
- Consider the cost of protection over your stock holding period.

Using the 37.50 strike price put for ABC, you can calculate the daily cost of protection for the two options. This is accomplished by dividing the option premium by the number of days to expiration:

- ABC Oct 37.50 put @ $1.05 = $1.05 × 100 = $105
- $105 ÷ 60 days = $1.75 per day
- ABC Jan 37.50 put @ $2.15 = $2.15 × 100 = $215
- $215 ÷ 150 days = $1.43 per day

The ABC Jan 37.50 put translates to a cost of approximately $0.014 per share for the option if held to expiration.

Be careful of letting your emotions run away with you. Do what you can to manage your positions by responding to market conditions, not overreacting to them. No one can completely control emotions when markets race up or come tumbling down. Do your best to manage them by completing your analysis when the markets are closed whenever possible.

Limiting Short Stock Risk with Calls

Long puts provide you with a means of protecting your investments for a specific period of time. Although you probably don't hold any short stock positions in your investment portfolio, you may periodically trade strategies, such as the use of inverse exchange-traded funds (ETFs), that use short stock position that are held overnight. A long call can protect you from losses due to overnight gaps upward.

Protecting a short stock position

In the same way a long put protects a long stock position, a long call protects a short stock position. A call gives you the right, but not the obligation, to buy stock at a specific strike price by the expiration date. You can exercise your call rights to close out a short position if the stock rises quickly.

Because a short stock position is generally held for less time, protective call option selection is much easier. Typically, you can evaluate options with the least amount of time to expiration or those in the following month. Stocks with options will have both months available.

Option months that are closest to expiration are generally referred to as *near month options* and those that expire right after that are referred to as *next month options*.

In addition to paying less for time for the protective call, strike price selection should be easier because there is less of a chance the stock will move far away from the entry price in the relatively short period of time the position is held. Try to use options that match your maximum loss criteria.

Further reducing short stock risk

Selling stocks short is prohibitively risky, especially if you don't have very deep pockets. If you're really committed to reducing short stock risk, why not just consider implementing a long put strategy to capitalize on your bearish view for a particular stock? Suppose you didn't own stock ABC and you are bearish on the stock instead. How does a long put position compare to a short stock position? Assuming ABC is trading at $37.50, Table 10-4 compares a $37.50 put to the stock position, including maximum risk and reward.

Here's what you need to consider:

- **Stock entry cost:** The initial cost for the short stock position is 50% of the current stock price because short selling has a 150% margin requirement. 100% is credited to the account from the stock sale, and the remaining 50% is cash you need to have available for the position.
- **Stock maximum risk:** Because the stock can theoretically rise without limit, the risk to a short seller is also considered to be unlimited. You may try to limit this risk by having an order in place to buy the stock back if it rises past a certain price, but overnight gaps in the stock could result in this maximum risk stop level being exceeded.
- **Option maximum risk:** The maximum risk for a long option position is the premium paid. In this case, that's $105.
- **Option maximum reward:** If you own the right to sell a stock for $37.50 and it is currently trading at $0, the intrinsic value of the option will be $37.50. Theoretically, you can buy the stock in the market for $0 and then exercise your right to sell it for $37.50. The $1.05 you paid for this right must be subtracted from the $37.50 per share gain for the stock transaction to determine the maximum reward for the option position.
- **Option breakeven level:** The breakeven point for the option position is the put strike price minus the option price, or $37.50 – 1.05 = $36.45.

REMEMBER

Puts increase in value when a stock decreases and represent a bearish position. Although they are wasting assets that are negatively impacted by time decay, they have limited risk and limited, but high, reward potential.

Table 10-4 Bearish Positions for ABC on Aug 22nd

Position	*Entry Cost*	*Max Risk*	*Max Reward*
Long 1 Oct 37.50 Put	$105	$105	$3,645
Short 100 Shares ABC	$1,875	unlimited	$1,875

Looking at your risk first, the put position limits the maximum risk to $105. This is equivalent to a $1.05 per share amount that could easily be exceeded with an overnight gap in the stock. From a reward standpoint, you're reducing the maximum gain by the cost of the put ($105), but you have the potential to far exceed the short stock reward when calculating the return on a percentage basis. The bottom line is that buying puts is a less risky bet, when you're bearish, than selling stocks short.

Hedging Your Bets with Options

You can use the following options to protect stock positions:

- A long put with a long stock position
- A long call with a short stock position

The term *hedge* describes a position used to offset losses in a security resulting from adverse market moves. The option can be exercised to close the stock position, or gains in the option can be used to offset losses in the stock. Protecting a position or portfolio with options is a form of hedging. But not all hedges are created equal . . . some are more perfect than others. A *perfect hedge* is a position that includes one security that gains the same value that is lost by a second security. The gain offsets the loss. So, a $1 dollar move down in ABC coincides with a $1 move up in XYZ.

Another important point when you set up a hedge, especially when you're getting started, is to organize your thought process into two sets of equations. First, calculate how much protection your hedge will buy and how that suits your position, whether it's an individual stock position or your entire portfolio. Second, figure out the premium that you will pay. Then you can combine the two steps into your final decision process, which should answer the question: How much am I paying to protect my portfolio with these options?

REMEMBER

The option Greek delta obtained using an option calculator provides the expected change in the option's value given a $1 change in the underlying stock.

Protecting a portfolio . . . partially

You partially hedge a position when you own a security that gains value when the hedged position loses value. Usually, when you combine two securities that tend to move in opposite directions you find it's not always a one-to-one relationship. For example, a $1 gain in one stock may correspond to a $0.75 loss in the paired security. Assuming the relationship between the two continues, combining them provides you with a partially hedged position.

Delta can be used to help construct partially or completely hedged positions.

Hedging stock with stock options

The ABC Oct 35.00 put option has a delta of –0.186. Assuming you own 100 shares of ABC and the Oct 35.00 put, the expected impact to your account with a $1 decline in ABC is calculated as follows:

$$(\text{Change in Underlying}) \times (\text{Delta}) = \text{Change in Option}$$

$$(-1) \times (-0.186) = +0.186$$

When the stock moves down to $36.50, the option should move up to approximately $0.54. The stock position lost $100 and the option position gained about $19. Because the Oct 35.00 put gained value when the stock lost value, it provided a hedge for ABC. However, the option gain was smaller than the stock loss, so it's only a partial hedge for the position. Another way to put it is that this strategy lessened but did not fully cushion your loss. As you will see in upcoming sections, this process is clearly adjustable, and your ability to hedge can be improved.

Listed index options have different characteristics than listed stock options. For instance, an index is not a security, so it's not something you can buy and sell. As a result, index options settle in cash rather than the transfer of a physical asset. See Chapter 9 for details on options characteristics.

Hedging a portfolio with index options

Because listed options are available for both stock and indexes, portfolios can be protected via individual position options or with index options, assuming the portfolio is well correlated to a specific index. In some cases, hedging your portfolio may actually require both an index option for a group of stocks and individual stock options for others that don't correlate well with a given index.

Correlation is a term used to describe the relationship between data sets. In this situation, correlation will help you to figure out how many contracts you will have to pay to protect your position. The values range from –1 to +1 and when applying to stocks provide you with the following information:

- Stocks with returns that move in the same direction, by the same magnitude are said to be perfectly positively correlated (+1).

- Stocks with returns that move in the opposite direction, by the same magnitude said to be perfectly negatively correlated (–1).
- Stocks with returns that do not move consistently in terms of direction and magnitude are considered not correlated (0).

For example, suppose you have a $150,000 portfolio that is well correlated to the OEX, trading at approximately 680. One quick approach to partial hedging uses the portfolio value and index strike price to estimate the hedge. OEX index options are available for different months in five-point strike price increments. When it is trading at 682, a 680 call will have $2 of intrinsic value because option moneyness is the same for index and stock options.

Using a short-term protection approach, Table 10-5 provides potential put candidates for next month options expiring in approximately 60 days. These options may seem pricey, but a five-point move in the index reflects less than 1% of the index value.

Table 10-5 Put Option Chain Data for the OEX

Month	*Strike Price*	*Bid*	*Ask*	*Delta**	*OI*
Mar	665	8.60	9.30	–0.321	1,663
	670	10.00	10.50	–0.361	3,277
	675	11.30	12.10	–0.406	748
	680	13.20	13.90	–0.455	2,883

**Delta using the Ask value*

Here's how to apply our stepwise process and bring it all together. A common multiplier value for an index is also 100, so the total option premium for March 670 put is $1,050 ($10.50 × 100). The option package is valued using the strike price and multiplier, or $67,000 for the March 670 put (670 × 100).

REMEMBER

The option multiplier is the contract value used to determine the net option premium (Option Market Price × Multiplier) and the deliverable value of the option package (Option Strike Price × Multiplier).

Suppose you decide you want to protect the portfolio against market declines greater than two percent. You can estimate the hedge by starting with the current index level (682) and subtracting the decline you're willing to accept to obtain a starting point for strike price selection, as follows:

- 682 – (682 × 0.02) = 13.6
- 682 – 13.6 = 668.4

Both the 665 and 670 strike prices can be considered. Using the 665 put option:

- Protection Provided by 1 Put: 1 × 665 × 100 = $66,500
- Protection Provided by 2 Puts: 2 × 665 × 100 = $133,000
- Portfolio Protected: $133,000 ÷ $150,000 = 88.7%

If the OEX drops below 665, your puts gain intrinsic value at a pace that is equal to the put's delta. The further the OEX declines, the closer the puts get to a 1:1 move with the index. The time remaining until expiration will also affect the actual gains made by the hedge.

At-the-money (ATM) puts and calls have deltas that are approximately 0.50. Once an option moves from ATM to in-the-money (ITM) or out-of the-money (OTM), delta changes in value. The option Greek that provides you with a feel for just how much delta change is *gamma*.

A stock option package generally represents 100 shares of the underlying stock. When using the strike price and multiplier of 100 to value the option package, it's common to think you're paying the strike price for each share of stock. That's okay when applying this to regular stock options, but it's not quite accurate when considering index options or adjusted stock options. In both of these cases, it's best to consider the option package value as simply:

Strike Price × Multiplier

A stock option package is typically 100 shares of stock. When put contract rights are exercised, the stock option owner receives the strike price times the option multiplier — usually 100. The amount the put option holder receives is also called the *option package exercise value.* Other terms you may see for this value include these:

- Option package assignment value
- Option package deliverable value

It depends on what side of the option you're on. All these terms refer to the same thing: the money that is exchanged when the rights of a call or put contract are actually exercised.

Protecting a portfolio . . . completely

Recall from Chapter 3 that delta was given the following ranges:

- Call: From 0 to +1 or 0 to +100
- Put: From 0 to –1 or 0 to –100

To better discuss hedging, it helps to use the alternate range of 0 to +100 and 0 to –100 for delta. That's because it turns out that one share of stock has a delta of 1. So if your strategy is to buy 100 shares of stock, delta is 100. Thus, if you want to hedge 100 shares of stock, your position delta should be as close to 100 as possible.

Using this information and the ABC example, the Oct 35 put with a delta of –0.186 provides a near perfect hedge for 19 shares of ABC stock. That's because when you multiply 100 × (–)0.186, you get (–)18.6, and you basically round up to 19. The next example goes into this in more detail.

TIP

ATM calls generally have deltas that are slightly greater than 0.50, whereas ATM puts are generally slightly less than 0.50. Using 0.50 as an approximation is usually fine for the initial strategy evaluation.

Stock hedge

Starting with a perfect stock hedge using ABC, assume you have allocated approximately $5,000 to a combined position (stock plus put). Because ABC is trading at $37.50, you anticipate owning about 100 shares. Using the ABC option data from Table 10-1, you focus on the Jan 35 strike price option with five months to expiration. The put has a delta of –29.1. Because three puts (see preceding example to figure out how many puts you need to cover the full risk of 100 shares) won't quite hedge 100 shares of stock, you evaluate a potential position using four puts. The delta for four Jan 35 puts is like this:

Position Delta = # of Contracts × Delta = 4 × (–29.1) = –116.4

Given that 1 share of stock has +1 delta, a long position of 100 shares represents +100 deltas. A perfectly hedged position has a combined delta equal to zero, so 116 shares of ABC are required. You calculate the position delta as follows:

- 116 shares × +1 delta per share = +116 Deltas
- 4 puts × –29.1 delta per put = –116.4 Deltas
- Position delta = +116 + (–116.4) = –0.4 Deltas

The cost of the position is the following:

- 116 shares × $37.50 = $4,350
- 4 puts × $1.35 × 100 = $540
- Position cost = $4,350 + 540 = $4,890

This near perfect hedge will not stay intact long, though. Every time ABC moves up or down $1, delta changes approximately by its gamma value. The chapters in Part IV offer ways to profit from this changing situation.

Recall that the delta for an option changes by gamma for each $1 change in the underlying stock. Because of this, options are referred to as a *variable delta* security. The delta for one share of stock, on the other hand, stays constant. One long share of stock will also represent +1 delta, so it is referred to as a *fixed delta* security. Thus, the easy way to remember these relationships is that delta is the middle man between the price of the underlying and the value of gamma. You can expect the value of your option to be affected by the value of delta per $1 change in the underlying. Delta, in turn, will change by the value of gamma, which also responds to the changing price of the underlying.

Portfolio hedge

Hedging a portfolio is a bit more inexact than hedging an individual position, but a perfect portfolio hedge is approached similarly. The greater challenge is due to the fact that not all portfolios are perfectly correlated to an index, causing some strategic problems that can be managed. The bottom line is that the perfect hedge becomes elusive because the option delta changes when the index value changes and there is inexact movement, correlation, between the index and portfolio.

Using a delta approach to protect the $150,000 portfolio will get you closer to a perfect hedge than the strike price estimate. Using an index level of 682, the Mar 690 puts are ITM by 8 points. The market price for these puts is $20.85, which corresponds to a delta of –0.549. Your goal is to get closer to 1:1 protection, so purchasing two Mar 690 puts results in the following:

- 2 × 690 × 100 = $138,000
- 2 × –0.549 = –1.10

In this case, for each 1 point decline in the OEX, the value of the combined puts increases by 1.1. For a short period of time, this results in 1.1 times the protection of a $138,000 portfolio. Multiplying $138,000 by 1.1 yields protection for a portfolio valued at $151,800. Given the variable nature of an option's delta, you'll likely be satisfied with portfolio protection that is a little less exact.

Avoiding Adjusted Option Risk

Adjusted options are those that existed when certain corporate actions took place. As a result of those actions, the contract terms required adjustment to reflect the action. Business activities that can prompt this include the following:

- Stock splits
- Large cash dividend distributions

- Mergers and acquisitions
- Spinoffs

Most dividends do not result in option contract adjustment.

Justifying option adjustments

The two main reasons options are adjusted after different corporate actions are as follows:

- To ensure the existing contracts retain their proper value
- So that the contract reflects the corporate action in its deliverable package

Without adjustments, the stock option market could be even more dangerous. Or maybe *exciting* is the right word, if you're a little morbid and like to live life on the edge. That's not behavior, though, that will lead to sustainable and fairly reproducible gains in investing. Let's put it this way: If options were not adjusted, you could see a scenario where one of your calls could risk losing all of its value after a stock split or one where a put option doubling after a big cash dividend is distributed. The latter could be good if you're on the right side of the trade, but consider the effect on the market if this kind of volatility were happening multiple times during any trading day.

Corporate action 1: Stock splits

Adjustments due to stock splits are the quickest to understand. When a stock you own splits two for one (2:1), you receive one additional share of stock for each share you own on the record date — the date used to identify existing stockholders. On the day you receive the additional share, there is nothing significantly different for the company in terms of its financial statement. To correctly value the stock, its price is divided by 2 in the market on the day of the split.

Option adjustments resulting from a 2:1 split are handled the same way the stock split is handled:

- The number of contracts held is adjusted (similar to shares)
- The price where the owner has rights (strike price) is adjusted

Here's how. A new option contract is created to address this corporate action, and it is provided a new symbol. So, when you own an option with the underlying stock going through a 2:1 split, you'll see two contracts of a new option in your account for each one contract you owned previously.

The important point is that you know that your option symbol will change and that you adjust your analysis and position management based on the change. The problem arises when the option deliverable or multiplier must change to reflect the corporate action, which is the case for a 3:2 split. Adjusting an option after a 3:2 split requires a lot more tweaking to get the valuation right.

WARNING!

When you exercise a put without holding the underlying stock in your account, you create a short position. This is because the put rights allow you to sell the underlying stock at the contract strike price. Selling a stock you don't own reverses the typical order for a stock transaction and creates a short position.

Corporate action 2: Mergers, spinoffs, and dividends

Mergers, acquisitions, spinoffs, and large cash dividends all change the underlying option package when an option contract is adjusted. This happens because the original 100 shares of stock may now represent ownership in

- 100 shares of original stock + shares of acquired stock (merger).
- 100 shares of original stock + shares of new stock (spinoff).
- 100 shares of original stock + cash amount (large cash dividend).
- No original stock + shares of acquiring stock (acquired).

In the last case, the original underlying stock may not exist if the company was acquired by another company. The adjusted options are now based on some ratio of shares in the company that acquired it.

TIP

If you think you found an option deal that seems to good to be true, you may have very well stumbled upon an adjusted option. Traders on the exchanges are very familiar with corporate actions completed by the stocks they trade and know how to value adjustments to them. There's no free money on Wall Street, so don't jump in to these options without fully understanding them.

The way you value these type of contract adjustments is more complex and beyond the scope of this book. It is extremely important to understand your rights, obligations, and position valuations if a contract you own gets adjusted. Contact your broker if this occurs. And never, *never* create a new position using an adjusted option contract you don't completely understand.

TIP

Whenever a combined position (stock plus option) you own is adjusted, be extremely careful about exiting the stock or option position separately. The combined position maintains the proper stock-option ratios initially created, but by selling any portion of the adjusted stock position, you may be creating high risk in the option position. Call your broker to discuss any position changes.

Adjusting from adjustments

It's all well and good that the options markets have a way to address contract valuations and deliverable packages for different corporate actions, but what does that mean for you? Two things:

- When you note any adjusted option in your account, be sure to check the contract specifications so you understand your new rights or obligations, as appropriate.
- More importantly, be aware of adjusted options when establishing new positions so you properly value securities you trade and know your rights and obligations.

Whenever an option quote doesn't seem quite right, be sure you take the time to check the contract details. Call your broker if you don't get what's going on.

Avoid creating new option positions using adjusted options. There's no hidden money in these contracts, just extra effort to understand and value them.

Detecting an adjusted option

The Chicago Board Options Exchange (CBOE) reports on adjusted options and the changes pertaining to them, including any changes in symbols as well as any other pertinent issues related to them including the number of shares per contract and multipliers. You can find daily postings and specific information at `www.cboe.com/tradtool/contracts.aspx`.

Here are some things to check:

- Potential changes in the symbols for the option series.
- The number of shares of stock in the options contract. Contracts related to split stocks may go from pertaining to the standard 100 shares to a different number such as 150 shares.
- Whether the option has changed from one style to another and if and how that may affect your ability to exercise.
- Possible changes in strike prices.

These are primary ways to distinguish adjusted options in the market. As with any security, when something doesn't seem quite right in terms of a quote or volume, be sure to dig deeper so you know why this is the case.

Valuing your split-adjusted options

When an option is adjusted due to a 2:1 split, the new contracts are valued the same way regular options are. Atypical splits, such as a 3:2 split, require a little more of your attention. To value an option after a 3:2 split, do the following:

1. Use the adjusted strike price and multiplier to calculate the package value (JKL 60 call: 60 × 150 = 9,000).
2. Determine the value of the underlying package in the market using current quotes (150 shares JKL × $62 = $9,300).
3. Subtract the package value from the market value to obtain the option's intrinsic value ($9,300 – 9,000 = $300).
4. Assuming an option quote of $3, the extrinsic value is what remains after subtracting the intrinsic value ($3 × 150 = $450, $450 – 300 = $150).

Chapter 11

Increasing Profit Potential and Decreasing Risk

In This Chapter

- Reducing risk with options
- Combining options for trend trades
- Benefiting from strong directional moves

Trading is a conceptually simple event, as prices will eventually rise or fall. That means that you can create a long position to make money when stock prices rise, or you can create a short position to benefit when prices fall. Along the way you may receive or have to pay a dividend here and there, but that's pretty much it on the trading side. Options give you more choices because you can make money from up and down stock movement, while you have the chance to make money in other ways based on changes in prices.

Consider the additional dimensions that you can add to your trading with options. For instance, by establishing a basic option position, you can gain from upward stock movement (call) and downward movement (put). Either way, your initial investment is usually much smaller than a similar stock position, which is a nice benefit if you have a small account or are an active trader. In addition to single option positions, these securities can be combined to further reduce costs. This chapter provides you with ways to trade for less money and less risk.

Leveraging Assets to Reduce Risk

Usually, when you think of leveraging assets, you think of increasing your risk — at least on the stock-trading side. Options are unique because they allow you to leverage your assets while also decreasing the amount of investment at risk. That's a nice combination — less capital at risk, less money spent, and more upside potential in one package. With options, the premium you pay allows you to lock in a price for a stock without putting up 100% of its value. Although there's no guarantee the stock will move in the direction you want, that's the case whether you're trading options or stocks. So why not do it for less?

Determining your total dollars at risk

The take-home message is that options reduce risk because you invest less money. Once you create a position, anything can happen — the stock can skyrocket upwards, drop like brick, or sit around making minimal movements while the rest of the market is active. You just don't know. Nobody knows what's going to happen next, not even the guys on TV and the Internet.

Any stock can drop to zero, so any long stock or call position you own can similarly go to zero. As a result, your initial investment is your maximum potential loss. This is true except in one case: If you buy a stock using margin, you can lose twice as much as your initial investment.

The risk for a long stock position is considered limited, but high. That's because a stock cannot fall below zero. Unfortunately, there's a lot of room for losses between zero and the price of some stocks.

To be sure, there are lots of possibilities between total loss and no losses at all. So, the main takeaway here is that when you invest with less money at the start, you usually have less to lose if things go against you. And yes, there are some caveats. For one, when you trade options, you can't wait around for the move you anticipate to happen or for your investment to rebound because there's a time constraint. And that means that when you trade options, you have to pay much closer attention to the price action and news related to your position than you might have to with some stocks.

Calling risk out when bullish

When you're bullish on a stock, you can

- Create a long stock position.
- Create a long call position.

If the stock goes up, you can profit with either of these positions — the extent you benefit depends on the actual move. The key difference is that your risk is reduced when you purchase a call option because you reduced the total investment.

Figure 11-1 illustrated this, using risk graph overlays for the two positions.

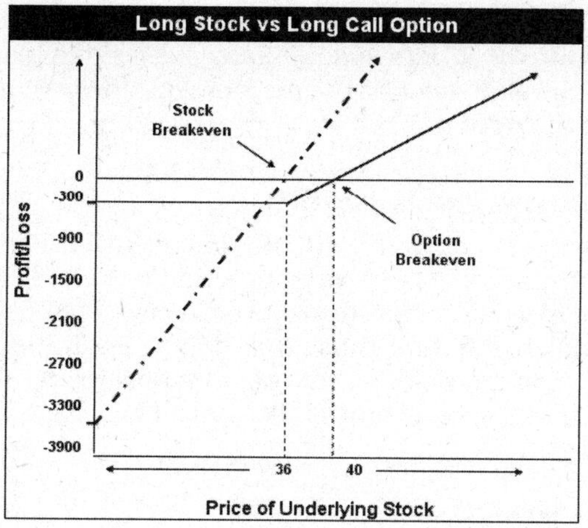

Figure 11-1: Overlay risk graph for XYZ long stock and XYZ call option positions.

Image by Optionetics

Here are the two main things for you to note from the risk graph:

- The significant difference in losses
- Profits accrue faster with the stock position

Because there are a series of tradeoffs in this business, it makes sense to take the slower accrual of gains in an options trade because of the decrease in total risk. It is certainly possible for the stock to remain dormant for months, causing us to exit the position for a loss only to then have it begin a serious upward move. Again, it's a tradeoff we are willing to take.

TIP

A risk graph provides a very efficient way for you to understand the risks, rewards, and breakevens associated with a particular strategy.

When monitoring option values, you'll find that if the stock moves around a little bit over time, the option can gain and lose value as follows:

- Increases or decreases as the stock price increases or decreases
- Increases or decreases as the option's implied volatility increases or decreases
- Decreases as time passes

Price alone doesn't dictate an option's price. The contract's implied volatility (IV) also plays a role in its value, with higher IVs resulting in higher contract values. On a daily basis, time decay plays a smaller role, but the cumulative effect can eat away at the option's value.

Establish long option positions when implied volatility (IV) is relatively low to increase the probability for profits and minimize losses due to decreases in IV. Keep in mind that a relatively low IV environment does not guarantee IV will rise over the life of the option.

Using LEAPS for long-term option positions

A LEAPS contract is a Long-term Equity AnticiPation Security. This isn't a new type of trading instrument; it's just an option that has a long time to expiration — anywhere from nine months to three years. Not all stocks with options have LEAPS available, but for those that do, the expiration month is almost always January. You'll note different root symbols for these options. You can find a complete listing of all stocks that have LEAPS associated with them at `www.cboe.com`.

LEAPS work something like this:

- LEAPS contracts are created in May, June, or July, depending on the option's cycle (see Chapter 3 for more information on option cycles).
- The new contracts expire in January approximately 2 1/2 years from the creation date, so by August 2014 there are options available for both January 2015 and January 2016.
- When new LEAPS are rolled out, the closest January LEAPS (expiring in 2015) becomes a regular option as the Options Clearing Corporation (OCC) revises the symbol to include the regular option root.

LEAPS symbols are similar to regular options symbols. For example, the Google (GOOGL) January 15, 2016 440 call symbol is GOOGL16A15430.0. The symbol is followed by the 16A15 nomenclature signifying the January 2016 expiration. The 430.0 is the strike price. The CBOE website has an excellent set of listings on LEAPS and has easy-to-understand quotes, although they are delayed. They are excellent for paper trading of LEAPS. Your broker or online charting and quote service will also have access to good pricing information on option chains, where you will find LEAPS and regular options.

The more time you have to expiration for an option, the more money you pay. So, it follows that you should expect to pay more for LEAPS contracts. Your risk increases with this increased cost, but the additional time provides you with a greater chance of holding a contract that is in-the-money (ITM) at expiration. LEAPS are

- Available for some stocks and indexes that have regular options.
- An investment alternative, providing you up to 2 1/2–3 years to benefit from your contract rights.

In addition to providing more time for investing strategies, LEAPS provides extended warranties on the asset protection side. Combining a LEAPS put with long stock significantly reduces the cost per day for protection. You do have to balance the reduced cost with your desired level of protection, because ideally the stock will rise over the time as you hold it. If this happens, the put value decreases during this time while the strike price remains the same.

TIP

Stocks that are more volatile generally have a larger number of strike prices available each month because there is a greater chance the stock will reach a strike price that is farther away.

To provide you with some pricing perspective, a partial options chain that features Google Inc. LEAPS (GOOGL) is provided in Table 11-1. It includes both calls and puts. When reviewing the details, assume Google trades at -$597.78 and is exhibiting its normal trading pattern, which fluctuates between periods of quiet trading along with periods of higher volatility.

Table 11-1 Partial Option Chain for Google with LEAPS

Call Contract Name	*Bid*	*Ask*	*Strike Price*	*PutContract Name*	*Bid*	*Ask*
GOOGL\16A15\260.0	337.10	342.00	260.00	GOOGL\16M15\260.0	0.15	1.10
GOOGL\16A15\270.0	327.20	332.00	270.00	GOOGL\16M15\270.0	0.20	1.65
GOOGL\16A15\280.0	317.70	322.50	280.00	GOOGL\16M15\280.0	0.35	1.95
GOOGL\16A15\290.0	308.00	312.90	290.00	GOOGL\16M15\290.0	0.45	2.20

Quotes courtesy of www.cboe.com

TIP

Because options that expire in January could potentially exist for 2 1/2 years, they are the ones that have the highest potential for being adjusted due to different corporate actions. Be especially careful when trading Jan options with quotes that seem "off." Check contract specifications for details on the underlying package.

Putting limits on a moving bear market

When you're bearish on a stock, you can

- Create a short stock position.
- Create a long put position.

If the stock goes down, you can profit with either of these positions. The rewards are limited because a stock can only move down to zero. At the same time, the rewards are potentially high if the stock does become worthless.

Figure 11-2 presents this using risk graph overlays for the two positions.

Here are the two main things for you to note from the risk graph:

- The significant difference in losses, with a short sale being a very bad situation if the stock rises rapidly and in large intervals
- The less-than-significant difference in gains

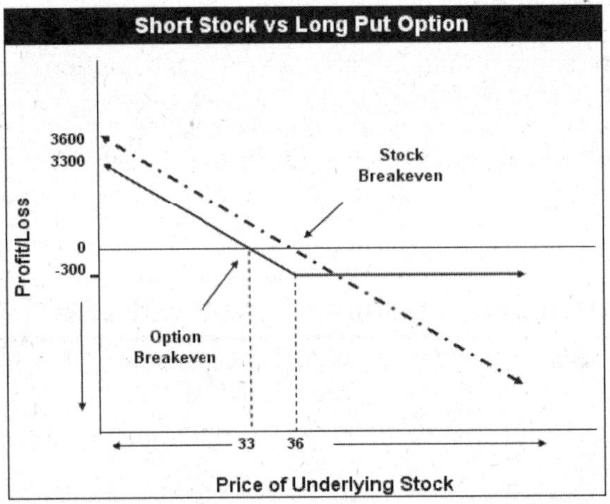

Figure 11-2: Overlay risk graph for XYZ short stock and XYZ put option positions.

Image by Optionetics

Relying on market timing

Trading is difficult, and the more you do it, the more you come to accept that sobering fact. What you eventually conclude is that it's pretty hard to identify the future direction for a stock, let alone how far it will go and by when. But selecting a proper time frame for an option is clearly an important part of trading these securities. That means you have to strike a balance and

- Recognize the role probabilities play in trading stocks and options.
- Be prepared to be "wrong" and limit your losses.
- Pay the right amount of premium for moves that are realistic.

Basic option trading requires you to correctly predict the direction the underlying will move, the magnitude of the move, and the maximum time it will take for the move to occur. All of these things are required for stock trading too — the difference is you can hold on to long stock position for months as it trade sideways. Managing a position this way doesn't mean you're necessarily trading successfully though, because during this period you're basically holding on to dead money that may be put to better use.

TIP

There are times when a stock breaks out of a limited-range, sideways channel, only to return back into the channel. As an investor, you may not do anything, but as a trader, if you've created a directional position based on the breakout, you must exit the position (stock or option) if the stock returns to the channel, since the conditions that justified the trade no longer exist.

Predicting proper direction

In order for you to capitalize on either a stock or single option position, you need to correctly identify the direction of the underlying stock move. Predicting the right direction is a challenge you face regardless of the security you select, so it seems reasonable to favor one that uses less of your capital for at least some of your trading. Only you know the answer to that.

Some general rules of thumb for increasing your probability of success include the following:

- Trading with the trend when using technical tools
- Or (for proficient contrarians) trading against the trend when momentum is weakening and your indicators point to a pending turn
- Trading undervalued stocks that are gaining some positive attention when using fundamental tools
- Limiting your losses in every trade with unbiased exit strategies

Predicting the magnitude of the move

Time risk is the main disadvantage to trading options, but there is another risk that requires discussion. You can be correct about the direction and timing of a stock move and still have the magnitude be too small to make your option position profitable. This happens to all option traders.

How can you minimize these shortfalls? For the most part, it helps to have some tools — technical or fundamental — that provide estimated price projections. It's also important to stay vigilant and to pay attention to what the market is doing and what your position is doing in relation to the market. Your overall trading profitability can be improved by focusing on higher probability trades (higher deltas indicating the move is more likely to occur) over lower-probability, "home run" trades. Allow gains to accumulate over time, and you'll probably be fortunate to get a home run or two along the way.

TIP

Don't get greedy. Consider taking a portion of your profits off the table by exiting part of your total position when the move you anticipated is partially complete.

Option pricing models also help you identify higher probability trades by providing you with

- Expected movement implied by the option price (implied volatility).
- An estimate of the probability the option will be ITM at expiration.

By using these option components in your trade analysis, you can determine whether the option price is relatively expensive or inexpensive given the stock's history, past option pricing, and market conditions. This is shown later in an example.

Predicting the right time

The forced time limits for an option provide newer traders with their first rules-based system when risk is properly managed. This means both of the following:

- The trade represents a reasonable portion of the account.
- The position is exited prior to the acceleration of time decay.

A long option position has a clear, built-in exit rule. Ideally, though, this isn't the only guideline you use to exit a position.

There are no one-size-fits-all criteria for selecting expiration periods, because they can vary by strategy and your trading style. The most straightforward time horizon for option trading is associated with scheduled releases of news or reports that can prompt strong movement by a specific date. These include

- Economic or industry reports such as unemployment figures or semiconductor orders.
- Earnings releases.

Some technical tools also provide estimated time projections, including price patterns or cycles. Identify your time horizons first and then check option chains.

Combining Options to Reduce Risk

In Chapter 4, a put option is combined with long stock to protect it by limiting the position risk. This is also accomplished when a call option is added to a short stock position. In both cases, the position cost increases.

REMEMBER

The breakeven level for a stock is simply the entry price. Because option premiums represent a cost to you above and beyond your strike price contract rights, a breakeven value must be calculated using both the strike price and option price.

When creating positions that are focused on specific market outlooks, you can combine the following:

- Call and/or put options with stocks
- Different call options together
- Different put options together
- Calls and puts together

Adding long puts or calls to stock are the only combined positions discussed so far, but short options can also be used to reduce risk, by

- Further reducing the net cost of the position and/or
- Increasing the potential directions the underlying can trade while still realizing profits.

When a short option is properly combined with the underlying stock or a long option of the same type, it is said to be *covered*. That's because your risk (obligations) under the short contract can be satisfied using the stock or by exercising your rights under the long contract. Without such protection, the short contract is referred to as *naked*. That's kind of a good visual on your exposure and risk of injury in nasty places such as the market.

Trading naked options allows you to receive a credit when you open a position — this credit is equal to the option premium. If all goes well, the option expires out-of the-money (OTM), and you get to keep the credit. Different newsletters promote naked option strategies, and this may seem like a great way to bring in monthly revenue — but seller beware.

Going naked with a call option is the riskiest position you can create, and we strongly advise against such a trade. Rather than creating a limited risk, unlimited reward consistent with good risk management, a naked call is an unlimited risk, limited-reward position.

Unfortunately, what often happens with these strategies is that months of smaller credits get wiped out with losses from just one or two trades that go against you. Although it's not such a bad thought to create a trade for a credit, we just don't like doing it while being completely exposed from a risk standpoint.

Risk can be limited by combining options for credits or debits using covered option positions. The next section introduces spread trades, which are limited-risk, limited-reward combination positions.

Spreading the risk with a debit trade

A *vertical spread* is a position that combines two options, one long and one short option of the same type (calls or puts), having the same expiration month and different strike prices.

It is referred to as *vertical* because that's how the strike prices lineup on when you look at an option chain. It's called a *spread* because it spreads the risk by using two positions based on the same stock. You can create a vertical spread for an initial debit or an initial credit. In each case, the position has limited risk and limited reward. Each option position in a vertical spread is referred to as a *leg*.

The type of vertical spread selected depends on your market outlook. You vary risks and rewards by changing the strike prices used to establish the position. You can create two types of vertical spreads for a debit, one using calls and the other using puts. They are referred to by the outlook for the stock and include the following:

- **Bull call spread:** You create a *bull call spread* by purchasing a call option and simultaneously selling another call option that expires the same month. The short call has a higher strike price. Because the price of that higher strike call is less expensive, you pay a net debit for the trade. The short call ends up reducing the price of the long call, so this spread trade has less risk than buying a long call option alone.
- **Bear put spread:** You create a *bear put spread* by purchasing a put option and simultaneously selling another put option that expires the same month. The short put has a lower strike price. Because the price of that lower strike put is less expensive, you pay a net debit for the trade. The short put ends up reducing the price of the long put, so this spread trade has less risk than buying a long put option alone.

WARNING!

Going naked a put option is a very risky position, even if you're willing to buy the stock at the short put strike price. Short-put assignment generally occurs when the stock is declining or bad news is released. Purchasing a stock in the market or though assignment at a time like this goes against reasonable risk-management principles.

Assessing risk and reward for a call debit spread

Your maximum risk for the bull call spread is the initial debit you paid to create it, similar to a basic long call position. Because the position combines a short call to reduce the long call cost, it also reduces the risk for the position. And because you don't get something for nothing on Wall Street, reducing your risk this way comes at a price in the form of reduced rewards.

If ABC is trading at $37.65 and you are bullish on the stock, you can create a bull call spread by completing the following transaction:

- Buy 1 Jan 35 call @ $4.20 and
- Sell 1 Jan 40 call @ $1.50

The debit for the bull call spread position is $270 ([$4.20 – 1.50] × 100). This is also the maximum risk and occurs when ABC closes at $35 or less at expiration. At this price, both calls will be worthless.

Unlike a basic long call, your maximum reward is limited for a bull call spread because the short obligation prevents you from realizing unlimited rewards. Your maximum reward is the gain you realize from the exercise-assignment transactions minus the initial debit paid for the position $230 [($40 – 35) × 100 – 270.00]. The maximum reward occurs when ABC trades at $40 or higher at expiration.

Your actual gain or loss may be somewhere between the max risk and max reward if ABC closes between 35 and 40. The bull call spread breakeven calculation is similar to the one for a long call. Using the strike price for the long call, you add the difference between the two option prices (the initial debit without the multiplier) to determine your breakeven level. In this example, the breakeven is $37.70 (35 + 2.70).

Figure 11-3 displays the risk graph for the ABC Jan 35–40 bull call spread using Optionetics Platinum, an options analysis software package.

Because a vertical debit spread is a net long position, its value will suffer the same accelerated time decay within 30 days to expiration as a basic long option position. Incorporate a method to exit the spread prior to this time if the position is at risk of losing value this way.

The risk chart identifies the following important areas:

- Max risk of $270 displayed by the lower horizontal line
- Max reward of $230 displayed by the upper horizontal line
- A breakeven stock price of $37.70 displayed by a dark vertical line
- A range from losses to profits displayed by a diagonal line extending from the lower strike price to the higher strike price

Risk, reward, and breakeven calculations for vertical spreads are completed by assuming you're assigned on your short obligation and exercise your long rights.

Assessing risk and reward for a put debit spread

Your maximum risk for the bear put spread is the initial debit you paid to create it, similar to a basic long put position. Because the position combines a short put to reduce the long put cost, it also reduces the risk for the position.

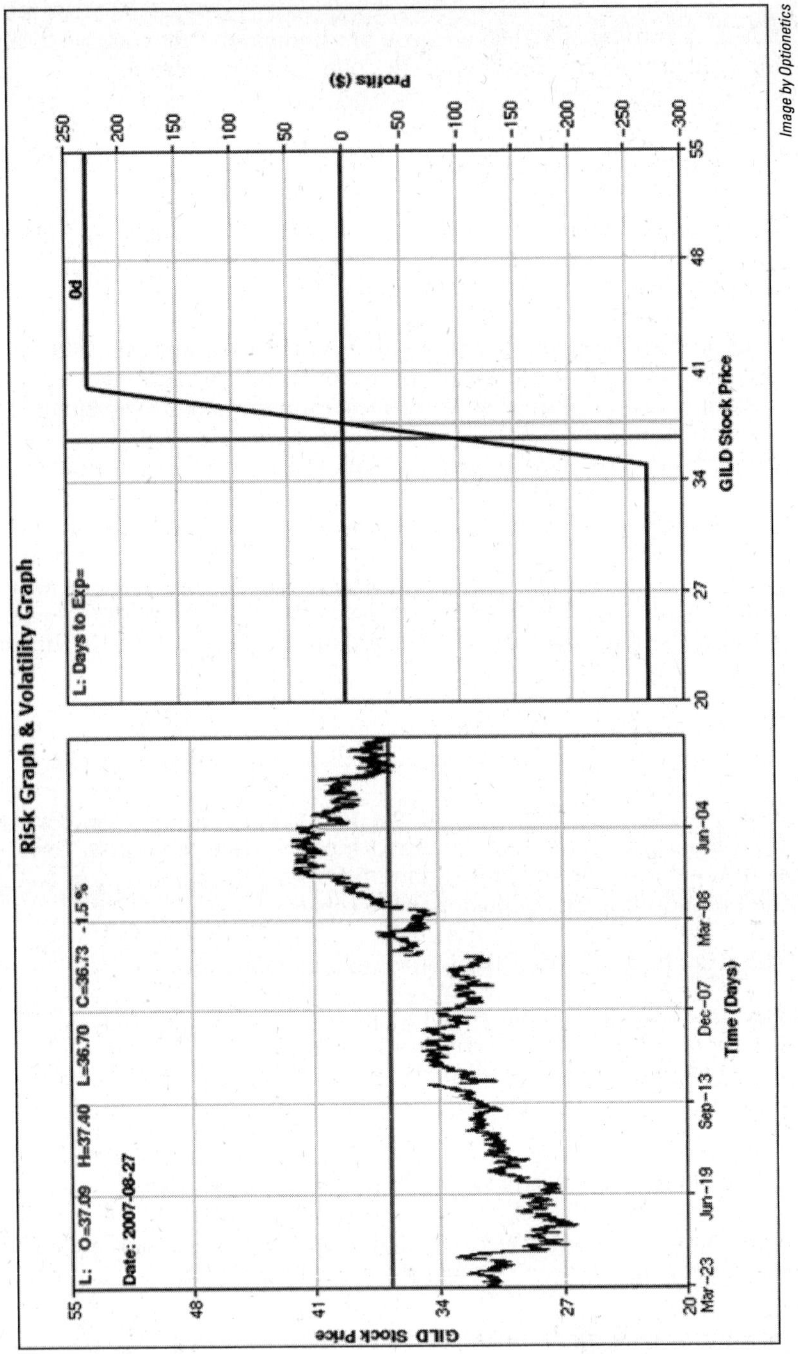

Figure 11-3: Risk graph for ABC Jan 35–40 bull call spread.

If XYZ is trading at $50.85 and you are bearish on the stock, you can create a bear put spread by completing the following transactions:

- Buy 1 Jan 50 put @ $2.75 and
- Sell 1 Jan 45 put @ $1.30

The net debit is also the maximum risk. The risk, reward, and breakeven calculations are *similar* to those for the bull call spread:

- Debit = Max Risk = (2.75 – 1.30) × 100 = $145.00
- Max Reward = [($50 – 45) × 100] – 145.00 = $355.00
- Breakeven = $50 – ($2.75 – 1.30) = 50 – 1.45 = $48.55

The maximum reward occurs when XYZ trades at $45 or lower at expiration.

Figure 11-4 displays the risk graph for the XYZ Jan 45–50 bear put spread using Optionetics Platinum, an options analysis software package.

The risk chart identifies the following important areas:

- Max risk of $145 displayed by the lower horizontal line
- Max reward of $355 displayed by the upper horizontal line
- A breakeven stock price of $48.55 displayed by a dark vertical line
- A range from losses to profits displayed by a diagonal line extending from the higher strike price to the lower strike price

TIP

Consider entering a vertical debit spread when there are at least 60 days to expiration to give the position time to become profitable.

WARNING!

Never exit the long leg of vertical spread without also exiting the short side of the spread — otherwise you are significantly changing your risk profile. This applies even when it appears the short leg will expire worthless.

Summarizing your debit risks and rewards

There are both positives and negatives involved in these strategies. In both vertical debit spreads your risks and rewards are limited. Each spread has less risk than its corresponding basic long option position because you reduce the initial debit by the price of the short option. The decreased risk comes at a cost in the form of significantly reduced rewards for you, because the short option position also caps your profits.

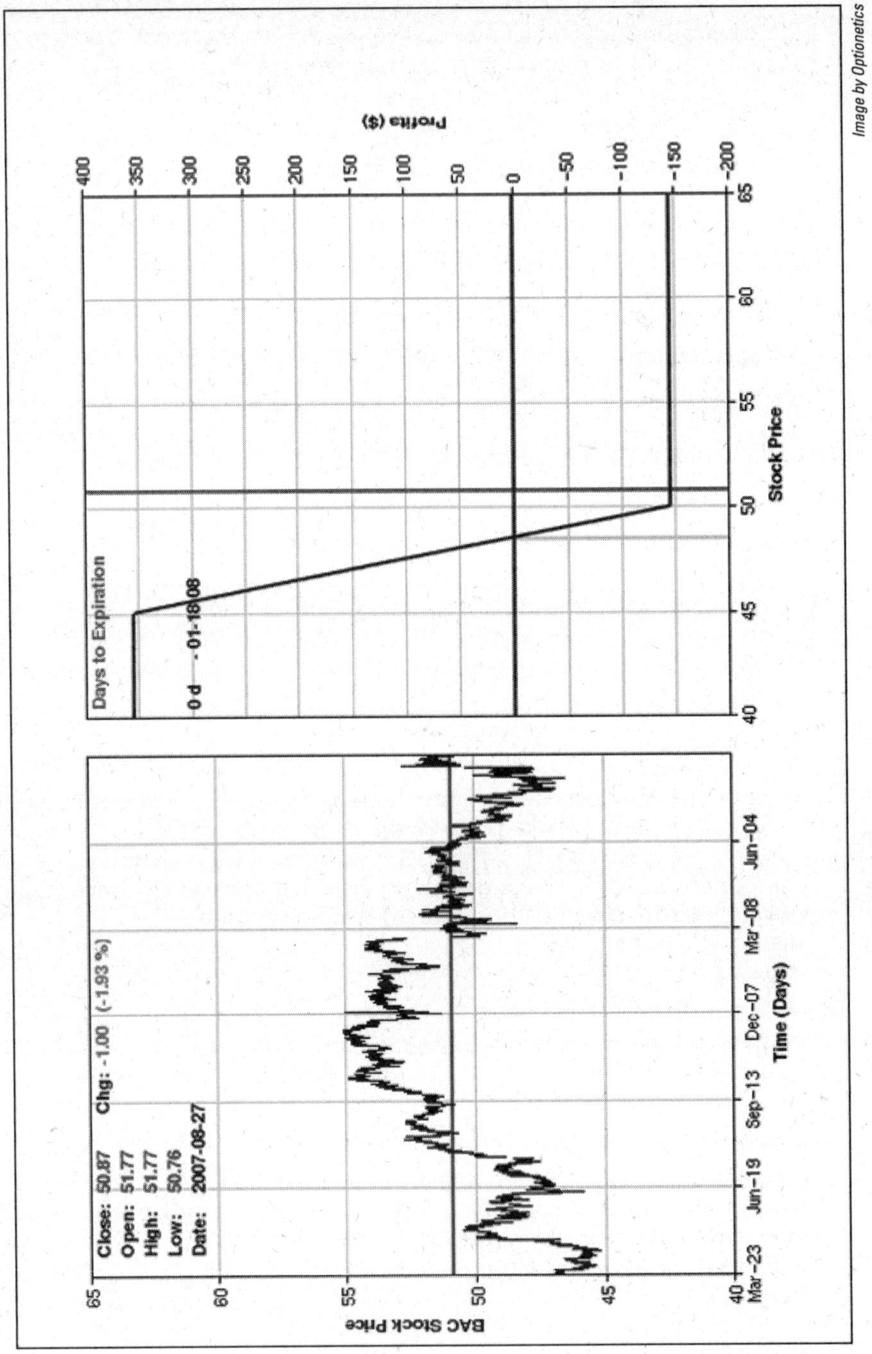

Figure 11-4: Risk graph for XYZ Jan 45–50 bear put spread.

Table 11-2 provides a summary of the risk, reward, and breakevens for a bull call debit spread and bear put debit spread.

Table 11-2 Risk, Reward, and Breakeven for Vertical Debit Spreads

	Bull Call Spread	***Bear Put Spread***
Risk	Initial debit	Initial debit
Reward	[(Higher strike – lower strike) × multiplier] – initial debit	[(Higher strike – lower strike) × multiplier] – initial debit
Breakeven	Long strike price + (long option price – short option price)	Long strike price – (long option price – short option price)

TIP

A trade risk graph provides specific risks, rewards, and breakevens associated with a particular trade.

When you place an order for a new vertical debit spread, consider using a limit amount that is less than the quoted price for the combined position to reduce the impact of slippage. You probably won't be able to execute the trade at the midpoint of the spread, but you likely can get the order filled if you shave a little off the debit amount.

Spread trade floor appeal

Traders on the exchange floors manage their risk by staying hedged in the market. This means that when they make a market for your long call order and end up with a short call position, they will usually buy shares of stock or other long calls to cover this new short position.

When you enter an order for a vertical spread for a debit, the trader can execute your order without having to worry about hedging the position. They basically just create a vertical spread for a credit. It's not that they're trying to trade against you — all they care about is staying hedged.

Vertical spread orders are appealing to floor traders because when they execute the trade, they don't have to do anything else. They're already hedged. That's why you can usually get a vertical spread order executed below the debit quoted in the market.

Spreading the risk with a credit trade

Debit spreads are not the only type of spread trade you can create using calls or puts. You can switch which strike price is purchased and which is sold in the debit spreads to create a credit spread instead. Once again, the spread requires that you buy one option and sell another of the same type expiring the same month. You can create two different vertical credit spreads:

- **Bear call spread:** You create a bear call spread by purchasing a call option and simultaneously selling another call option that expires the same month. The short call has a lower strike price. Because the price of a lower strike call is more expensive, you receive a credit for the trade. The long call ends up covering the short call, so this spread trade has significantly less risk than a naked short call option.
- **Bull put spread:** You create a bull put spread by purchasing a put option and simultaneously selling another put option that expires the same month. The short put has a higher strike price. Because the price of a higher strike put is more expensive, you receive a credit for the trade. The long put ends up covering the short put, so this spread trade has significantly less risk than a naked short put option.

Assessing risk and reward for a call credit spread

Your maximum risk for the bear call spread is limited to the difference between option strike prices minus the credit received when creating the trade. The position uses the long call to limit the short call risk, which by itself is unlimited. Instead of placing an XYZ bear put spread for a debit, you can create an XYZ bear call spread for a credit.

You create the bear call spread by purchasing the higher-strike, less-expensive call option and selling the lower-strike, more-expensive put option:

- Buy 1 Jan 55 call @ $0.95 and
- Sell 1 Jan 50 call @ $3.20

For credit spreads, the net credit is also the maximum reward. The reward, risk, and breakeven calculations for a bear call spread are as follows:

- Credit = Max Reward = (3.20 – 0.95) × 100 = $225.00
- Max Risk = [($55 – 50) × 100] – 225.00 = $275.00
- Breakeven = $50 + ($3.20 – 0.95) = 50 – 2.25 = $52.25

A bear call spread position reduces the risk by capping losses for the short call. Reducing your risk this way means your rewards are reduced. Your maximum reward is the initial credit for the spread. This occurs if XYZ closes below the short call strike price at expiration, resulting in both options expiring worthless.

Figure 11-5 displays the risk graph for the ABC Jan 50–55 bear call spread using Optionetics Platinum, an options analysis software package.

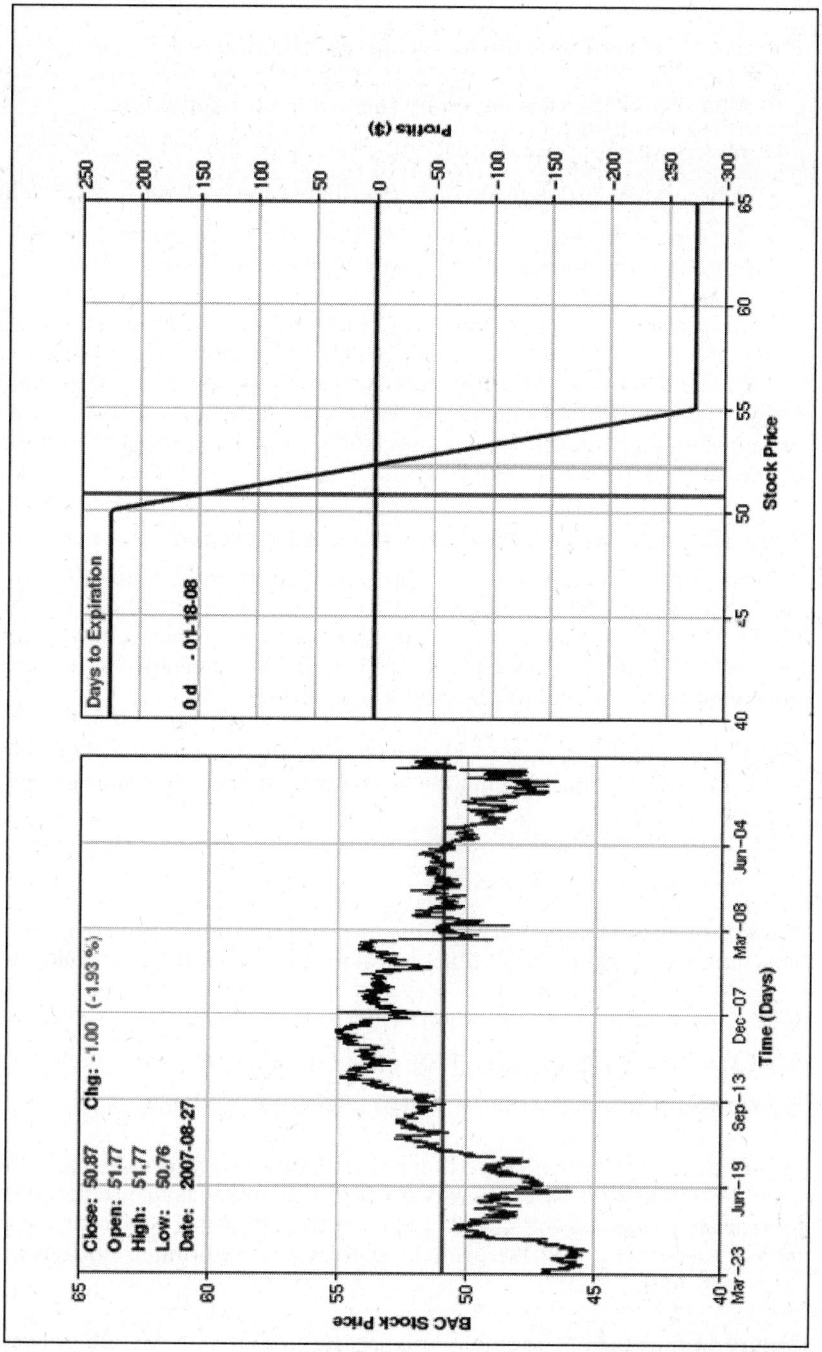

Image by Optionetics

Figure 11-5: Risk graph for XYZ Jan 50–55 bear call spread.

The risk chart identifies the following important areas:

- Max risk of $275 displayed by the lower horizontal line
- Max reward of $225 displayed by the upper horizontal line
- A breakeven stock price of $52.25 displayed by a dark vertical line
- A range from losses to profits displayed by a diagonal line extending from the lower strike price to the higher strike price

WARNING!

Pay attention to the expiration date. If the underlying stock is near the short strike price on the last trading day before expiration, you run the risk of being assigned on the short option over expiration weekend, but may no longer have the ability to exercise your long contract rights. Close a vertical credit spread for a debit on the last trading day before expiration if the price of the underlying is near the short strike price.

Assessing risk and reward for a put credit spread

Your maximum risk for the bull put spread is limited to the difference between option strike prices minus the credit received when creating the trade. The position uses the long put to significantly reduce the short put risk, which is high. Instead of placing an ABC bull call spread for a debit, you can create an ABC bull put spread for a credit.

You create a bull put spread by purchasing the lower-strike, less-expensive put option and selling the higher-strike, more-expensive put option:

- Buy 1 Jan 35 put @ $1.70 and
- Sell 1 Jan 40 put @ $4.10

For credit spreads, the net credit is also the maximum reward. The reward, risk, and breakeven calculations for a bull put spread are as follows:

- Credit = Max Reward = ($4.10 – 1.70) × = $240.00
- Max Risk = [($40 – 35) × 100] – 240.00 = $260.00
- Breakeven = $40 – ($4.10 – 1.70) = 40 – 2.40 = $37.60

A bull put spread position reduces the risk by capping losses for the short put. Reducing your risk this way means your rewards are reduced. Your maximum reward is the initial credit for the spread. This occurs if ABC closes above the short put strike price at expiration, resulting in both options expiring worthless.

Figure 11-6 displays the risk graph for the ABC Jan 35–40 bull put spread using Optionetics Platinum, an options analysis software package.

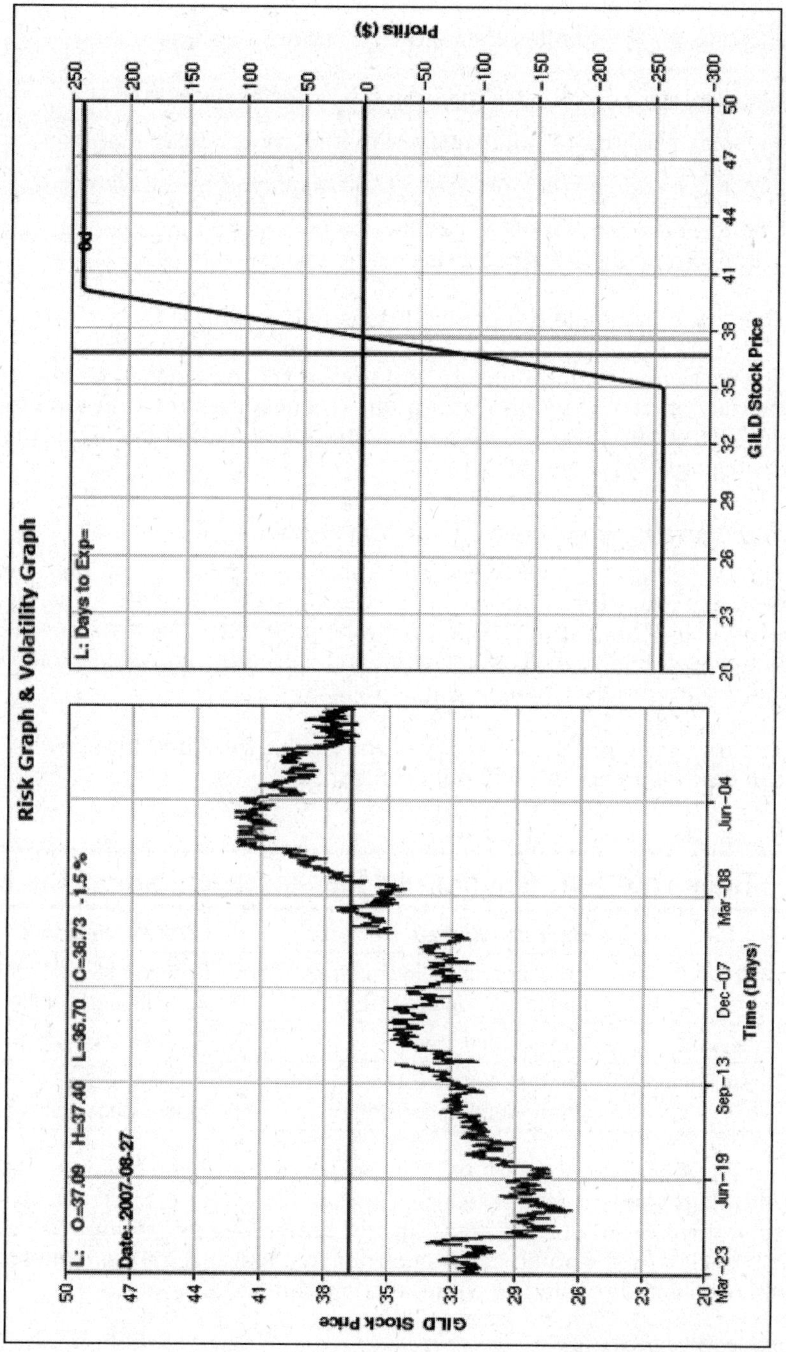

Image by Optionetics

Figure 11-6: Risk graph for ABC Jan 35–40 bull put spread.

The risk chart identifies the following important areas:

- Max risk of $260 displayed by the lower horizontal line
- Max reward of $240 displayed by the upper horizontal line
- A breakeven stock price of $37.60 displayed by a dark vertical line
- A range from losses to profits displayed by a diagonal line extending from the higher strike price to the lower strike price

The cost of slippage is included in this risk graph.

REMEMBER

Always monitor conditions for the stock after the close of trading on the last day of trading before expiration. You never want to allow a limited-risk position to turn into a high- or unlimited-risk position because you failed to manage the trade though the end.

Summarizing your credit risks and rewards

The risk graph for a vertical credit spread is similar to that of the vertical debit spread, with both risk and reward limited. It significantly improves the short call or short put risk graph by capping risks that are either unlimited or limited but high. This is accomplished by creating a position that covers the short option rather than leaving it naked.

Table 11-3 provides a summary of the risk, reward and breakevens for a bear call credit spread and bull put credit spread.

Table 11-3 Risk, Reward, and Breakeven for Vertical Credit Spreads

	Bear Call Spread	***Bull Put Spread***
Risk	[(Higher strike – lower strike) × multiplier] – initial credit	[(Higher strike – lower strike) × multiplier] – initial credit
Reward	Lower initial credit	Lower initial credit
Breakeven	Short strike price + (short option price – long option price)	Short strike price – (short option price – put option price)

WARNING!

Although you can often execute a spread trade at a price more favorable than the current market price, always remember that if your risk parameters signal you should exit a position, just exit it. This can almost always be accomplished by placing a marketable limit order.

Chapter 12

Combination Strategies: Spreads and Other Wild Things

In This Chapter

- Covering options with stock
- Reducing the cost of protection
- Expanding on vertical spreads
- Changing the spread time horizon

Basic option positions reduce risk by reducing your position cost. However, the real power from these securities is unleashed when combining them with stock and other options, adding a new layer of protection and potential profit to your strategies. Starting with option positions covered with stock, in this chapter we analyze the risk and develop a strategy that discounts the cost of put protection for long stock. This strategy is known as a collar.

Covered option strategies with stock are only the beginning. This strategy can be modified to include just options when you vary different components of a vertical spread. By using the same strike price in th-e vertical spread while varying the expiration month for the two options, you create a *calendar spread,* which adds time flexibility to the position. By allowing the strike prices to also change, you create a *diagonal spread* that provides even more flexibility for almost any short-term to long-term outlook.

Combining Options with Stocks

When you protect a short option position with stock or a long option of the same type, it is said to be *covered.* You can sell calls when holding a long stock position to reduce the cost of the position and bring in some incremental income. Similarly, a short put can be sold against short stock to boost the returns. Both positions reduce risk slightly by reducing the stock's cost basis, but neither option protects the position. Fortunately, you can add protection in the form of a collar strategy.

Creating "covered" positions

A *covered position* includes a short option with an obligation that you satisfy with stock or a long option of the same type for the same underlying. Rather than the unlimited or high risk associated with naked options, covered positions significantly reduce your risk. When using the covered position strategy, you sell options against the underlying to bring in additional income and reduce the position risk by changing the cost basis.

Covered calls

When you own stock, you can sell calls against the shares to bring in additional income. Because a credit is brought into your account when you sell the call, you also reduce the risk of the long stock position. But although you gain income, there is a significant downside for you, because you're capping potential gains in your stock position. This will happen if the market price of the stock moves up, rising above the strike price of the call. Then you'll be obligated to sell the stock at the lower strike price.

There is an optimal time to sell calls, so choose wisely when implementing this strategy. If for any reason you need to hold onto a stock position (because of capital gains or similar reasons), do not sell calls against it. Otherwise, the covered call behaves just like a naked call — a position with unlimited risk.

Use long stock with a covered call

- To reduce long stock risk incrementally by the short call credit.
- As an income strategy for a portfolio position.

When implementing a covered call strategy as a shorter-term trade, your preference is to realize gains though assignment. *For that reason, the short call strike price should be above the long stock purchase price.* Always keep in mind that your risk with such a position is still pretty high — just because you have a bullish outlook for the stock doesn't mean it will necessarily go up in the short term (or the long term, for that matter).

It's best to have a long option when the impact of time decay is at a minimum, and it's best to have a short option when time decay accelerates — that is, when there are less than 30 to 45 days to expiration.

Covered puts

When you are short stock, you can sell puts against the position to bring in additional income. Because a credit is brought into your account when you sell the put, you also reduce the cost basis of the short stock position, resulting in slightly reduced risk for the position. The downside is that you're capping potential gains.

But why cap your gains this way? It makes more sense to capitalize on a bearish outlook with a long put or bear put spread.

REMEMBER The short put position is an obligation, not a right. You are at the mercy of the market and circumstances because you can't elect to have the stock put to you to offset the short stock position. The put doesn't serve as protection — you would need to buy a call to change the position risk from unlimited to limited.

So, if you're looking to reduce risk and maximize rewards, it's better to focus more on vertical spreads than on this particular strategy. For that reason, this strategy discussion is limited.

Covering the covered call position

You can use a covered option position as a short-term strategy or to increase income for longer-term holdings. The main thing you need to keep in mind is that short options come with obligations, not rights. The option leg is covered — not the stock, which maintains high risk for the covered call.

Covered call strategy

A short call is a bearish position that is created for a credit. Because time decay works in your favor, you generally establish this position with 30–45 days or less until expiration. There are two reasons you create this position:

- You own the stock and you're long-term bullish on it, but moderately bearish in the short-term, or
- As part of a trading strategy, you're short-term bullish on a stock and seek to boost returns by selling a call and being assigned on the stock.

Even though both of these are slightly different, the risk-reward profile for the combined position is the same. Your risk is high but limited due to the unprotected stock. This risk is slightly reduced by the call credit.

TIP The covered call position makes sense when you have a moderately bullish, short-term outlook for the stock. If you are extremely bullish in the short term, a long call is a better strategy because it allows unlimited gains while the covered call position caps gains.

Your rewards are capped with a long stock–short call position because if the stock rises above the short call strike price by expiration, you will be assigned on the position and forced to sell your shares of stock.

Covered call risk profile

You purchase stock and sell a short call when you have a short-term bullish outlook for the underlying. The short call strike price should be above the stock purchase price so the stock gets called away for a profit. If you remain bullish at expiration, it's ideal for the stock to close just below the strike price so you can sell another call (assuming the original call expires worthless). You can continue to do this if your outlook is bullish and you own the stock.

Your risk associated with a long stock–short call position is similar to a basic long stock position: limited but high. Your maximum reward for the position is capped by the short option. After the stock rises above the short call strike price, you are at risk of assignment. If the strike price is higher than your stock purchase price, you profit when assigned. You calculate risk, reward, and breakeven for a long stock-short call position as follows:

$$\text{Max Risk} = (\text{Stock Purchase Price} \times \#\text{ of shares}) - \text{Call Premium}$$

$$\text{Max Reward} = [(\text{Call Strike Price} - \text{Stock Purchase Price}) \times 100] + \text{Initial Credit}$$

$$\text{Breakeven Level} = \text{Stock Purchase Price} - \text{Call Price}$$

Your breakeven price for the position is the stock purchase price minus the option price when the position is sold. Below this level, losses accrue.

Never allow a short call that is part of a covered position become uncovered by selling the underlying stock. This turns a limited-risk position into an unlimited one. If you want to exit the long stock position, you must buy the call back first or exit both at the same time using a combination order.

Suppose ABC is trading at $37.72, and you're short-term bullish on it. With 30 days to go until expiration, the market for the near-term 40 strike price call is $0.50. This represents a $50 credit, or $50 in your account, when sold. Before entering a trade, you calculate your risk, reward, and breakeven for a position that includes 100 shares of ABC stock and one short call:

$$\text{Max Risk} = (\$37.72 \times 100) - 50 = \$3{,}722$$

$$\text{Max Reward} = [(\$40 - 37.72) \times 100] + 50 = \$228 + 50 = \$278$$

$$\text{Breakeven} = \$37.72 + 0.50 = \$37.22$$

Figure 12-1 displays the risk graph for the ABC covered call strategy. Your breakeven appears as a vertical line drawn where profits = 0 (37.22).

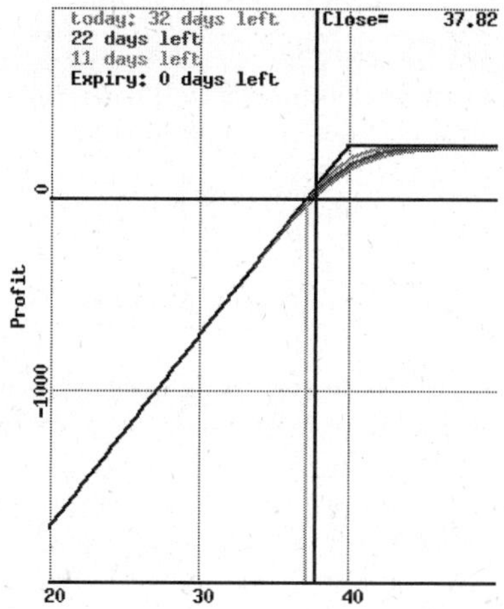

Figure 12-1: Risk graph for long ABC stock with a short call.

Image by Optionetics

The risk graph includes three curved lines displaying the expected value of the position, given ABC's price and the implied volatility of its options. The price of the short option decreases as expiration near.

WARNING!

A short call that is covered by long stock does not protect the long stock. The position risk remains similar to long stock alone.

Reducing protected stock costs

Covering a short call obligation and protecting a long stock position are not the same thing. Although the covered call strategy is considered a relatively conservative approach to investing, it actually leaves you exposed to risk that is very similar to long stock. Another way you can manage stock risk for less money than a protective put strategy (see Chapter 10) is by creating a collar on the stock. You create a collar using the following:

- Long stock
- Protective put on the underlying stock
- Short call on the underlying stock

By selling a call in combination with a protected stock position, you reduce the cost of that protection. Your only obligation is from the short call because the put represents a right. The short call remains covered by the stock.

A short option represents an obligation that is only considered covered if there are no other obligations or requirements for the associated stock or long option.

Defining a collar

You create a collar by purchasing a put and selling a call for a new or existing stock position. It is a limited-risk, limited-reward position that

- Significantly reduces long stock and covered call risk from limited, but high to simply limited.
- Significantly reduces long stock rewards from unlimited to limited.

It's important to keep the differences in these two types of positions straight. A covered call strategy may be considered a short-term trade or income generator, whereas a collared position is considered a protected position. Thus, the collar offers two different risk-management dynamics that together work better if your goal is maximizing your protection. The main goal of the short call is to reduce the cost of protection. This slightly reduces the risk of a protected put position.

Once you sell a call short, you are obligated to sell the underlying stock when assigned. Do not create a collar around a position unless you're willing and able to part with the underlying stock.

Collaring long stock

A collar is a hedged position that has limited risk and limited reward. Your risk is limited to the downside by the put strike price, and your reward is limited to the upside by the call strike price. If the stock goes below the strike price, you don't necessarily need to exercise the put. You can decide to sell the put for a profit instead.

The long put and short call strike prices create a cap on long stock risks and rewards, respectively. The two option positions in combination provide a collar around the stock price.

As a general example, you can use a collar when you have a definite short-term bearish view on a stock position that you prefer to hold in anticipation of longer-term gains. In this instance, you would want to have both the put and call as close to at-the-money (ATM) as possible to minimize both the downside risk and the cost of the protection.

The term *peg* is used to describe the cap a short call creates on long stock appreciation. You may see this applied to the short call position when reviewing account balances.

Profiling collar risks

The risk associated with a collar strategy is significantly less than long stock. The long put caps the risk while increasing the position's cost. This cost is slightly offset by the credit received when selling the call.

Suppose you own 100 shares of ABC at $37.86, and you're bearish on it over the next 1 1/2 months. You want to protect your position, but don't want to spend a lot of money to do it. You decide to create a collar around ABC using next month options, which expire in 45 days.

Before buying a 37.50 strike put option for $1.20 and selling the 40 strike call option at $0.70, you complete the following key calculations:

> Net Debit = (1.20 – 0.70) × 100) = $50
>
> Max Risk = [(Stock Purchase Price – Put Strike Price) × 100)] + Net Debit = [($37.86 – 37.50) × 100] + 50 = $86
>
> Max Reward = [(Call Strike Price – Stock Purchase Price) × 100] – Net Debit = [($40 – 37.86) × 100] – 50 = $164
>
> Breakeven = Stock Purchase Price + Net Debit = $37.86 + 0.50 = $38.36

Your risk for the position is the difference between your stock purchase and the put strike price, plus the net cost of the options. In terms of the maximum reward, after the stock rises above the short call strike price, you are at risk of assignment and will be obligated to sell your shares at the strike. If the strike price is higher than the stock purchase price plus option premiums, you profit when assigned.

Figure 12-2 displays your risk graph for the collar position.

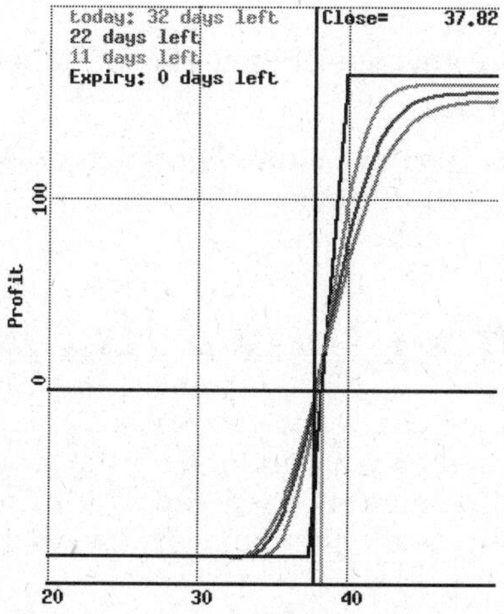

Image by Optionetics

Figure 12-2: Risk graph for a long ABC stock with a collar.

Varying Vertical Spreads

A *vertical spread* is a position that combines a long option and a short option for the same underlying that

- Are the same type (call or put).
- Expire in the same month.
- Have different strike prices.

You can create a vertical spread for a net credit or a net debit, depending on your outlook for the stock and the current level of volatility implied in the options. By changing the strike prices, you can change the risk profile for a given vertical spread.

A calendar or diagonal spread, based on strike price, is long the closer month option and short the further month option and is equivalent to holding a naked position. These are not strategies consistent with good risk management because of the potential for large losses.

It's also possible to create a spread that varies the time until expiration for the two options rather than the strike price. This position is also known as a *calendar spread* and is similar to a vertical spread using the same strike price but different expiration months.

You can also vary both the expiration month and strike prices for the two options. This is a *diagonal spread,* referring to the diagonal line that can be drawn between strike prices on an option chain.

Calendar spreads and diagonal spreads that use a long option for the later month leg of the spread are limited-risk positions.

- Call calendar and diagonal spreads have unlimited reward potential after expiration of the short option.
- Put calendar and diagonal spreads have limited but high reward potential after expiration of the short option.

Changing your vertical spread risk profile

You can change the risk profile for a given vertical spread by changing the strike prices used in it, while maintaining your outlook for the stock. That's one reason you need to explore different vertical spreads. Although a few vertical spreads might satisfy your outlook, there may be one that is best suited to your risk. Calculating the reward-risk ratio for different spreads is one way to obtain an apples-apples comparison for the different alternatives.

You can create vertical spreads for a debit or a credit. To help keep the outlook and credit/debit result clear, consider the outlook for the more expensive option. A short call is bearish and brings a credit into your account. The short call option in a bear call spread is more expensive, so this is a credit spread.

In addition to identifying the vertical spread with the best reward-risk ratio, you may also uncover a volatility skew that makes one particular position stand out. A *volatility skew* is a condition that arises in the option markets where options for the same underlying have implied volatilities (IVs) that are significantly different from the others. This can happen when demand factors impact option prices.

There are two types of volatility skews:

- **Price skew:** Options expiring in the same month have IVs that deviate from normal conditions (such as in-the-money (ITM) options with higher IV than out-of-the-money (OTM) options).
- **Time skew:** Options expiring in different months have IVs that deviate from normal conditions (such as options expiring sooner that have IV that is higher than options expiring later).

You capitalize on volatility skews by selling the option with atypically high IV and/or buying the option with the atypically low IV as part of the strategy.

When uncovering a volatility skew, be sure to check the news for the company to determine if there is a specific reason for the condition.

Spreading time with calendars

To buy yourself time during a period where the market is undecided and your outlook is a bit hazy, you can create a calendar spread by combining a long option and a short option for the same underlying that

- Are the same type (call or put).
- Expire in different months.
- Have the same strike price.

The longer-term option costs more than a shorter-term option with the same strike price, so you create the position for a net debit to your account.

Specifically, you may decide to use a calendar spread in place of a vertical spread if your

- Short-term outlook is neutral to bearish while your long-term outlook is bullish (call calendar spread).
- Short-term outlook is neutral to bullish while your long-term outlook is bearish (put calendar spread).

In both cases, the short-term, short option reduces the cost of the later month long option. The strategy isn't appropriate if you're strongly bearish or bullish because of either of the following:

- The short-term option will be assigned.
- The long-term option will lose too much value.

Your risk is limited when using the long option as the longer-term leg of the spread for both call and put calendar spreads.

TIP: When a debit spread position includes two options that expire in different months, the reward and breakeven levels are estimates based on the price of the underlying and volatility at the earlier expiration for the short option.

Assessing calendar risk and reward

When constructing a call calendar spread, you buy a longer-term call and sell a shorter-term call, both at the same strike price. The longer-term call is more expensive, so the position is generally created for a net debit. This initial debit is your maximum possible risk. Keep in mind that managing this trade is a little different than a vertical spread because you need to consider two time horizons.

Although this is an example of a call calendar spread, a similar breakdown occurs for a put calendar spread position. There are three scenarios to consider at expiration for the short option:

- **Scenario 1:** The stock moved significantly higher than the calendar strike price, and the short call was assigned. In that instance, you need to determine which approach is best:
  - Exercising your long call option to satisfy the short call assignment
  - Buying the shares in the market and selling your long call if time values remain (see Chapter 9)
  - Creating a bull call spread by holding the long call and selling a higher strike call option for the same month

- **Scenario 2:** The stock moved significantly below the calendar strike price, and the short call expired worthless. In that instance, you need to determine which approach is best:
  - Selling your long call option if it still has value
  - Creating another spread with the long call if bullish

  As always, the action in the underlying and your analysis of its price action are crucial. Thus, along with addressing the needs of your current position based on its impact to your strategy and portfolio, also consider your outlook for the stock to determine whether you want to maintain the long call position. If you're bearish, exit the position. This is why it's important to identify a downside exit price for the stock prior to creating a calendar spread. Your decision-making is much easier by being prepared and by having your maximum risk, maximum reward, and breakeven points handy — and thus knowing this value in advance. In fact, if you are well prepared, by expiration you may not have a decision at all if you already exited both legs of the position as part of your trade risk management.

  A *near month option* is one that is the closest to its expiration date. A *next month option* is one that expires in the month that follows the near month option.

- **Scenario 3:** The stock is near the calendar strike price, and the short call expired worthless. In that instance, you need to determine which approach is best:
  - Selling your long call
  - Creating another calendar spread using the existing long call and selling another closer-term option at the same strike price
  - Creating a bull call spread using the existing long call and selling a higher strike call option for the same month

After the short term has expired, you may be left with an unlimited reward (long call) or limited but high reward (long put) position.

Profiling calendar spread risk

Calculating potential rewards and breakeven levels is difficult for calendar spreads with a later-month, long option because of the different expiration months for the two legs. Of course, this doesn't mean you shouldn't try to understand them. The advantage to these strategies is that you can identify a limited, maximum risk for the position.

Options analysis applications can estimate rewards and breakeven levels for calendar spreads using probabilities based on historical and implied volatilities. This data can be extended to risk graphs, which are also available.

Figure 12-3 provides a risk graph, accompanied by a price chart for a call calendar spread.

Profits are now displayed on the x-axis and price for the underlying on the y-axis. This coincides with price levels for the stock chart.

REMEMBER

You must always understand the risks and margin requirements for positions you create. Paper trading helps you better appreciate risk. Contact your broker to be sure you truly understand option margin requirements.

Defining diagonal spreads

Diagonal spreads are vertical spreads with different expiration months. You can vary calendar spread risks and rewards by varying the strike prices used for the options. You create a diagonal spread by combining a long option and a short option for the same underlying that

- Are the same type (call or put).
- Expire in different months.
- Have different strike prices.

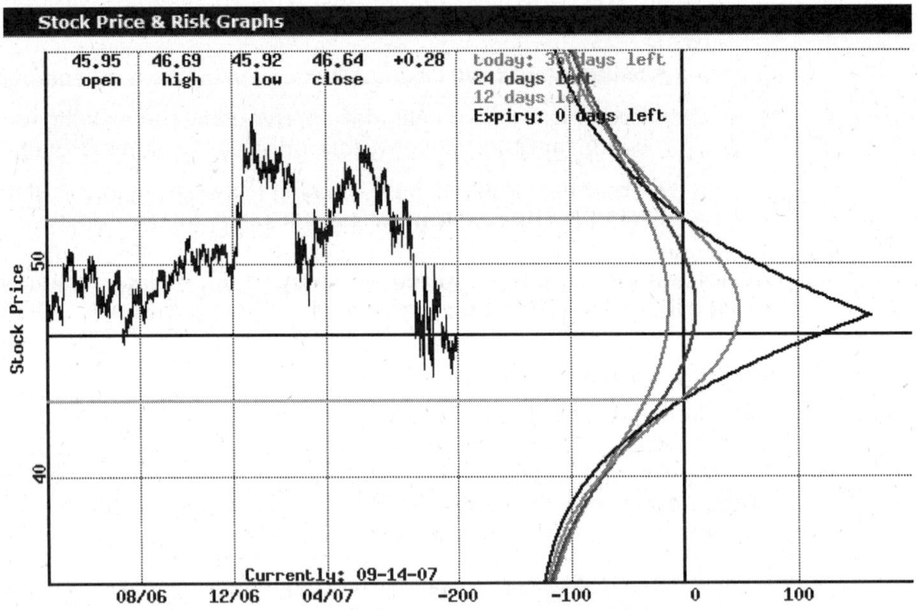

Image by Optionetics

Figure 12-3: Stock chart and theoretical risk graph for a call calendar spread.

The longer-term option may or may not cost more than a shorter-term option — it just depends on the strike prices and expiration months selected for the two. This means that both debit and credit spreads are possible when using a diagonal-spread strategy.

Diagonal spreads have potential built-in strategic variations beyond your initial plan and can morph into different strategies after the short option is exited or expires.

Because so many diagonal-spread combinations are possible, it's more difficult to categorize short-term versus long-term views for the underlying stock. That's not really bad news; it's more of a comment on your flexibility when using these spreads.

You may decide to use a diagonal spread in place of a calendar spread if your

- Short-term outlook is slightly more bullish than neutral and your long-term outlook is bullish (call diagonal spread for a debit).
- Short-term outlook is slightly more bearish and your long-term outlook is bullish (call diagonal spread for a credit).
- Short-term outlook is slightly more bearish than neutral and your long-term outlook is bearish (put diagonal spread for a debit).
- Short-term outlook is slightly more bullish and your long-term outlook is bearish (put diagonal spread for a credit).

These diagonal-spread combinations are provided as a calendar-spread comparison in case you have a dilemma trying to find one that fits your outlook and objectives. The same may hold when considering vertical spreads — a diagonal spread may be more appealing if you feel the long option could benefit from more time or if a volatility time skew exists.

Always think of the downside or what could happen when you exit a position early or your options run their time course. If you exit or allow to expire a long option position that covers a short option, you have a naked option position. Risk ranges from limited but high to unlimited.

You limit your risk when using the long option for the later month leg of the spread for both call and put diagonal spreads. These spreads present the same type of timing problems as calendar spreads when calculating the reward and breakeven values. They should be considered estimates rather than absolutes when using options-analysis applications.

This type of strategy is not without risk. If you are considering a diagonal spread that uses the short option for the later month expiration, think of it as holding a naked position.

Assessing risk and reward for diagonal spreads

Suppose you're moderately bullish on a stock in the short-term and believe that when the market strengthens in a couple of months, it will give a nice boost to the stock. It is currently trading at $46.64. You note there is currently a modest time skew between next month options and those that expire three months later.

You want to purchase a call that is near the money and want to finance the trade with a short call that expires sooner. To reduce the chance of assignment, you decide to use a diagonal spread in place of a calendar spread.

The next month $50 strike price call expires in 35 days and has a bid at $1.80 (IV of 34.6). The 47.50 strike price call expiring three months later has an offer price of $3.10 (IV of 32.4). The risk for the position is the initial debit, which is $130.00. The reward and breakeven are variable.

Figure 12-4 displays the risk graph for the call diagonal spread. If the stock is below $50 at the closer-term expiration and the short call expires worthless, you have a few alternatives available for the remaining long call.

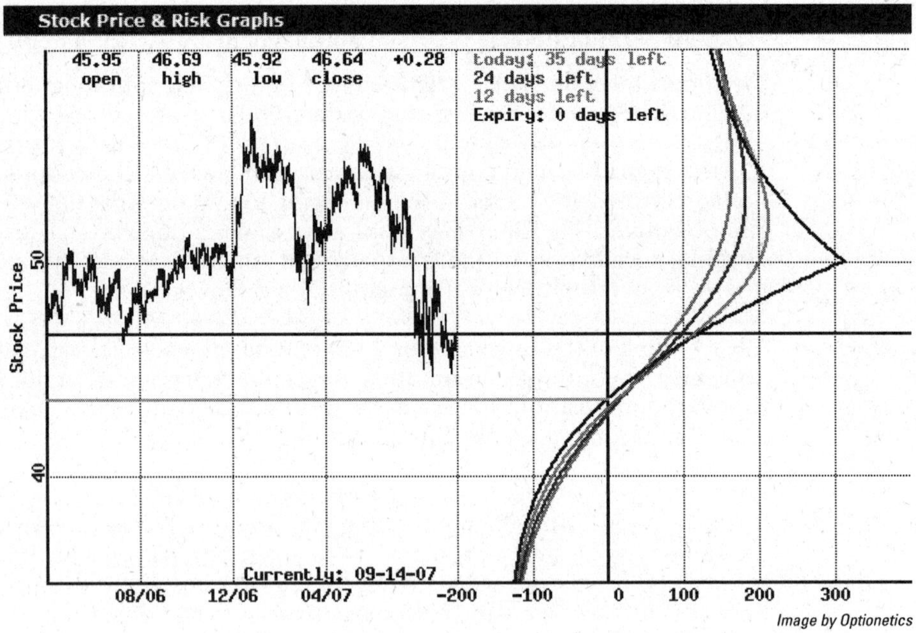

Figure 12-4: Stock chart and theoretical risk graph for a call diagonal spread.

Chapter 13

ETFs, Options, and Other Sneaky Tricks

In This Chapter

- Understanding exchange-traded funds
- Reducing volatility with sectors
- Implementing ETF strategies in your portfolio
- Trading ETFs and ETF options

Exchange-traded funds (ETF) are now a part of the investment scenery and can be extremely useful tools for professionals and individual investors. Much more importantly, ETFs are a great tool for retail traders, enabling you to trade a variety of markets and sectors individually or with options. They are so useful, it's hard to know what we would do without them in the current markets.

ETFs are most useful because they give you access to certain asset classes, such as commodities, and give anyone the ability to implement strategies previously available only to larger investors. ETFs can also reduce volatility, although for options traders, volatility is part of the game and has a place in many strategies. But that place may be best explored after you've taken care of your longer-term financial goals.

Exploring the Exchange-Traded Fund

An exchange-traded fund (ETF) is conceptually similar to a mutual fund, hence the name. To be sure, an ETF is a different animal, but it is still a security that is made up of different component stocks, bonds, and/or commodities and is typically designed to track a specific index or segment of the market. There are ETFs that are more akin to managed portfolios, but the majority of them are still index-inspired vehicles. Thus, a good way to understand them is by comparing them to market indexes. There are many similarities between the two, but one important difference makes ETFs very powerful: You can own an ETF. And that means you expand the option strategies available to you.

Generally speaking, because ETFs track a group of securities, ETF volatility tends to be less than that of its component stocks, bonds, or commodities. That's because a strong decline in one security in the group may be offset by less severe declines or gains in the other components. Option traders don't want to shy away from volatility, but you can benefit from recognizing when using a less volatile instrument is helpful. And you must grasp this concept to understand whether trading options derived from a security that is less volatile makes sense.

ETFs are similar to mutual funds, but trade like a stock. This means you don't have to wait until the end of the day to exit a position.

Comparing ETFs to Indexes

ETFs are similar to indexes in that they both are based on a group of specific, related securities. An *index* is a measurement of the market value for these component stocks, bonds, and/or commodities, whereas an ETF is a security that allows you to own that measurement. Most ETFs actually track a specific index (see Chapter 9 for more on indexes).

One of the best characteristics ETFs and indexes share is they both have options available for trading. Because you can own an ETF, you can create combination positions to include index-like products via the ETF. You'll find this is a really nice strategy addition, given the size of the ETF universe. Navigating through all the available products should be easier with some of the resources identified at the end of this section.

Check with your accountant to fully understand the tax implications of investing and trading ETFs.

Connecting the common ground

Clearly a measure (index) and a security (ETF) are different beasts, but for now consider the similarities. ETFs share the following characteristics with indexes:

- Available for a variety of asset classes, sectors, and regions
- Both impacted by the index construction weighting method
- Offered by a variety of financial service firms

One thing is for sure. If you're looking for a segment of the market to invest or trade, it's likely there's an ETF that will fit the bill for you.

TIP

Weight management for ETFs

ETF managers use weightings similar to the index-weighting method to achieve similar returns.

The weighting method used for index construction determines the impact a component security has on the index value. Although an ETF won't always track an index exactly, the weighting method affects ETF value changes given component changes. Here's what you want to remember about construction methods for stock indexes:

- A market-capitalization weighted index is impacted more by higher-capitalization stocks.
- A price-weighted index is impacted more by higher-priced stocks.
- An equal-weighted index is impacted equally by all component stocks.

Checking out the differences

Before moving on to ways you can access ETFs, here are some differences between ETFs and indexes:

- You can own an ETF but not an index.
- The actual components used to create an index may be different than the component securities in an ETF and can include futures and swap arrangements.
- ETFs can be leveraged or have an inverse relationship with the index it tracks.

There may not be a perfect correlation between an ETF and its accompanying index. That's because ETFs are not comprised of the exact basket of component securities can have moderate daily fluctuations known as *premium* or *discount* trading. Some also possess an additional degree of risk of catastrophic losses if the fund company used more exotic trading instruments (such as swaps) and if not hedged properly.

A *swap* is an option of sorts. It's essentially a contract between two parties with regard to an investment proposition and details the outcome of a trade. When certain previously agreed-upon contractual points are reached, one party must pay the other. Swaps often add significant amounts of leverage to investment transactions. ETFs that use leverage often add that leverage with swaps. What that means is that you might be buying an ETF assuming that you're getting one thing when in fact you're getting another.

REMEMBER

Stock risk is high, but limited to the total amount invested when purchased in a cash account. This option-related risk is leveraged but balanced because the amount of risk capital is smaller.

ETFs and risk

Your risk with an ETF is the same as with stock ownership: limited but high, depending on the price of the ETF and whether it was purchased with cash or on margin. Generally, an index-based ETF will closely mirror the performance of its associated index. However, the performance of some of the managed ETFs — those that are not directly linked to an index but are actually portfolios based on a manager's analysis — is as unpredictable as that of any managed portfolio.

Certain ETFs have gained popularity because of their uniqueness in the market. There is a family of ETFs that offers leveraged, inverse, or both kinds of attributes in the ETF. For instance, QID is the Proshares Ultrashort QQQ, which tracks the inverse value of the Nasdaq 100 Index and multiplies the move by two through the use of leverage. Owning the QID is like being short 200 shares of QQQ. This means you have a second means of creating a limited-risk bearish position for some indexes. Of course, put options top this list of alternatives.

Always know what you're investing in. Many ETFs are passively managed and based upon a specific index such as the S&P 500 Index. Some newer ETFs are actively managed by portfolio managers who select specific securities for investment. Always check the ETF prospectus or tear sheet to determine which index, if any, the ETF tracks.

Pinpointing ETF resources

ETFs trade on major U.S. stock exchanges. Buying and selling these securities is the same as buying and selling stocks — you enter an order via your broker using the same order-entry process. ETF popularity has also given rise to the availability of research and scanning tools for these securities on broker websites.

Avoiding "analysis paralysis" can be tough given the broad range of ETFs available. By identifying your objectives first, you have a better chance of staying on track so you can move forward implementing ETF strategies. When accessing a particular website or other product materials, consider the objective of the site sponsor to be sure all your needs are being met. For instance, the American Stock Exchange (AMEX) benefits when you trade ETFs listed on their exchange, because that's how they make their money.

Table 13-1 provides a brief list of ETF web resources to consider accessing.

Risk can be reduced with ETF option strategies because the initial investment is significantly reduced.

Table 13-1 ETF Resources

Sponsor	*Site*	*Access*
NASDAQ	`www.nasdaq.com/investing/etfs/`	Excellent summary of ETF information and performance analysis
ETF Database	`http://etfdb.com/screener/`	ETF screening tool
Alps Dist	`www.sectorspdr.com`	Listing of family-specific sector ETFs
Barclays	`www.ishares.com`	Listing of widely held Barclays ETF products

Distinguishing ETF and index options

Index options and ETF options both provide you with a way to use option strategies on a group of related securities. The two products differ in three important respects:

- Because ETF options have an underlying security you can own, they lend themselves to combination strategies.
- Index options are cash-settled, whereas ETF options are settled using the underlying instrument.
- Index options are European style or American style, whereas ETF options are only American style.

If you want to avoid assignment on all but the exercise day, then an index option may be your only alternative.

Leverage is a double-edged sword. It can magnify your losses just as it magnifies gains.

Naturally there are similarities as well. Whether using index option or ETF option strategies, be sure to consider the following:

- **Contract liquidity:** Not all options are actively traded. Be sure spreads don't significantly impact your slippage costs.
- **Impact of dividends:** Certain groups of stocks provide higher dividend payouts. Be sure to incorporate dividends in option pricing calculators.
- **Volatility:** Because both represent baskets of securities, they tend to be less volatile then their components. This may not be as much applicable to sector-specific ETFs in some cases.

Checking out strategies and new instruments by paper trading is a good way to get an inexpensive lesson for unexpected risk for either of these securities.

Index and ETF values are both affected by dividends, and as a result, so are the options for them. As soon as dividend announcements are made, these values are priced into calls and puts currently available. Option calculators allow you to incorporate dividend payments that occur during the life of the option.

Identifying ETF option advantages

Because this book focuses on option trading, the number-one advantage of ETF options over index options is the opportunity to access combination strategies. ETF options are more flexible because you can own the underlying security.

ETF option characteristics also make them more straightforward. You won't be worrying about different exercise, expiration, or last trading days for ETF options because they are all American style, just as with stocks. If you have already traded stock options, ETF options are a pretty natural next step for you.

Watch out for expenses. ETFs have expense ratios just like mutual funds. Because so many ETFs are passively managed, they are generally lower than mutual funds fees, but compare ETFs to be sure you're accessing one with reasonable ones. You will find that a growing trend in ETFs is toward managed products, though, because these can levy higher fees.

By using ETFs in your investing, you quickly and inexpensively access a group of securities that can reduce the fluctuations (volatility) in your portfolio. This topic is covered more in the next section, but basically you're able to accomplish a big investing goal: diversification, often at a reduced cost than with a straight stock portfolio. ETF options provide this at an even more significantly reduced cost, reducing your risk.

As with stocks, not all ETFs have options available for trading. For those that do, not all will have Long Term Equity AnticiPation Security (LEAPS) available. LEAPS are long-term option contracts that have expirations ranging from more than 9 months to 2 1/2 or 3 years.

Here are two additional risks ETF options and ETF LEAPS introduce for you:

- Time risks associated with options in general because these securities can expire worthless
- Potential leveraged losses on the downside that can be significantly magnified if you are using options on ETFs that use leverage as part of their investment goals

Consider your choices and whether you are personally okay with increasing the potential percentage loss when you are significantly reducing your initial investment by using options. This is a personal choice, and you must weigh your own risk tolerances and preferences against using such approaches.

You will pay commissions on ETF purchases and sales, which can raise the cost of using these products for investing or trading. Many mutual funds can be bought and sold without a commission (*no load*) if held a minimum period of time.

Accessing combination strategies

ETFs give you access to a larger number of potential strategies than index options or mutual funds. When combining ETFs with ETF options, you have access to an index-based security that you can protect by the use of options, employ in order to reduce overall position cost, or both. Using ETFs, you can incorporate these strategies to manage risk:

- **Protective put position:** Long ETF combined with a long put. Limits the ETF downside risk to the put strike price and slightly increases the cost of the ETF. A high but limited risk is turned into a limited-risk position. Potential rewards remain unlimited above the price of the ETF plus ETF option.
- **Covered call position:** Long ETF combined with a short call. Reduces the cost of the position, moderately reducing risk. As with a stock-based covered call position, this is an income-generating strategy for a short-term bearish outlook on a long-term holding. Potential rewards are capped by the call strike price, so a previously unlimited reward position becomes limited.
- **Collared position:** Long ETF combined with a long put and a short call. Limits the ETF's downside risk to the put strike price and increases the cost of the ETF. This net increase to cost is less than a protective put position because the credit brought in by the call slightly offsets the put cost. As a result, the high but limited risk is turned into a limited-risk position. Potential rewards are capped by the call strike price, so a previously unlimited reward position becomes limited.

Not all ETFs have options available for trading. When researching ETFs for investing or trading, be sure to check whether options trade for the underlying and how liquid the fund and option contracts are.

Reducing Portfolio Volatility with ETFs

Volatility is a measure of security movement and varies by asset. An ETF is less volatile than one of its component stocks. However, if you decide to use longer-term ETF option strategies for investing, you still have to be sure to purchase long options when the volatility conditions are right. If you have access to options analysis software, check relative historical volatility (HV) and implied volatility (IV) levels for the options. If you don't have access to IV charts, you can get a quick view of relative volatility conditions for an ETF using Bollinger bands on a price chart.

Bollinger bands shrink around prices when volatility decreases and expand away from prices when volatility is rising. You can find Bollinger bands with most technical analysis tool packages. You can find free technical analysis tool packages at `www.stockcharts.com` and `www.bigcharts.marketwatch.com`.

In addition to the important role implied volatility has in option pricing, it's not a good idea to ignore historical volatility. Analyzing the relative levels for HV and IV will help an individual select a strategy appropriate for market conditions.

Revisiting volatility

An ETF's *historical volatility* (HV) calculation is just like the one for stock: It uses past price changes over a certain period of time to quantify the range an ETF travels. It allows you to complete an apples-to-apples comparison to

- Different HV time horizons for the ETF.
- The implied volatility of the ETF.
- The HV of another security.

Implied volatility (IV) is the option volatility implied by current market prices. It includes different market participants' expectations for the ETF, along with demand factors for that particular option. IV is a *plug* figure in option pricing models, meaning it's the value needed to correctly price an option after all of the known values such as strike price, ETF price, and so on are considered. *Vega* is the option Greek that measures the expected change in option value for every 1% change in IV.

Getting just a current reading of the IV for an ETF is usually not enough to gain a sense of relative levels unless you are so familiar with the ETF's price movement that you know when the reading is inline with typical values.

By using a chart to compare current IV to previous levels, you gain a much better sense of the general trend and tendencies and whether the values represent high, low, or average readings.

REMEMBER

Trends and volatility are two primary factors impacting market conditions. There are three possible trends for the markets to exhibit: upward, downward, or sideways. In terms of volatility, the markets can be quiet, traveling over a moderate range during a given period, or more explosive, with wider ranges reached over the same period.

Figure 13-1 displays an IV chart for a broad-based stock market index ETF. Different lines are used to identify IV for different expiration periods.

While checking relative IV levels, you should also compare current IV levels to HV. This provides you with a comparison of expectations versus past movement and will alert you to something unusual that may be happening. An "unusual" development may be a trading opportunity or it may be a trading pothole you want to navigate around. Figure 13-2 displays an HV chart for the same broad-based stock market index ETF used in Figure 13-1.

Volatility and risk

Volatility is a measure of risk and reward because the moves a security makes have a direct impact on your returns. The bigger the price swings in an ETF, the bigger the potential risk, because declines can occur rapidly. You may decide to accept this high potential risk because price swings go both ways — gains can accumulate quickly too.

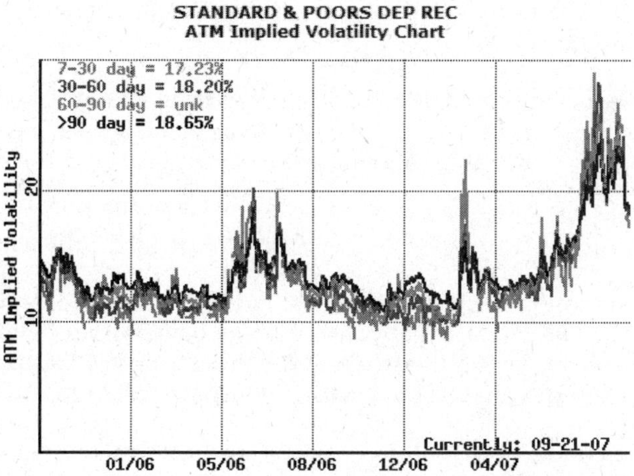

Image by Optionetics

Figure 13-1: Two-year implied volatility chart for SPY.

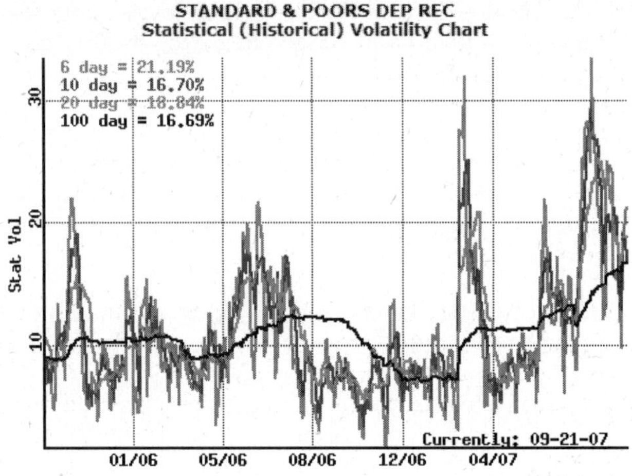

Image by Optionetics

Figure 13-2: Two-year historical volatility chart for SPY.

When buying options, you pay more for those based on an underlying security that is more volatile because its past movement (measured by HV) is a major component in the option's implied volatility (IV). It's really important to understand that IV is part of the time value portion of an option — the portion that decays each day you get close to expiration.

The fact that this risk measure increases an option's cost makes it that much more critical for you to understand both volatility measures (HV and IV). It's not just about increased risk and reward — it's about how much you will be paying for this risk. Do what you can to minimize the cost by purchasing volatility when IV levels are relatively low and selling it when value decay accelerates near expiration.

Don't make false assumptions. HV (also referred to as statistical volatility, or SV) does not predict the future volatility of an asset. It uses past data to quantify movement of the asset and allow for an apples-to-apples comparison to other assets.

Security risk

Risk varies by security type and is inherent in the stock, bond, and commodities markets. Although diversification alleviates some market risk, it doesn't create a risk-free investment. Investors accept market risk to address another financial risk — the risk that savings will not outpace inflation.

You must always understand the risks associated with the securities you choose for investments and trading. If you don't thoroughly understand these risks, you should continue to use securities you do understand.

Generally, higher risk for an individual stock translates to higher volatility, which means rewards can be greater with an investment in an individual stock. Table 13-2 summarizes the relative risk/volatility levels for stocks, sectors, and the market as a whole.

Table 13-2 Relative Risk Levels

	Proxy or Security	*Volatility*
Market	Broad-based index or ETF	Low relative to sectors and stocks
Sector	Sector index or ETF	Generally higher than market but less than individual stock
Stock	Individual stock	Generally high relative to markets or sectors

Investing with ETFs

Although most of the discussions in the book address trading topics, it's hard to focus on trading if things in your investment portfolio aren't in good order. You get inexpensive access to a diversified group of stocks via broad-based index ETFs or a combination of sector ETFs, similar to mutual funds. What ETFs have that mutual funds don't offer is protection via option strategies and the ease of trading at any time during the trading day.

ETF investing opportunities available to option traders include the following:

- Investment in diversified market portfolio via broad-based sector ETFs
- Development of a diversified market portfolio via sector ETFs
- Protective put positions using ETFs
- Collared positions using ETFs
- ETF LEAPS portfolios

Because mutual funds similarly provide an inexpensive way to diversify, the best thing ETFs bring to your investment plan is the opportunity to protect the portfolio with options.

Portfolio management includes the allocation of assets across and within asset classes. This means you seek to diversify holdings by investing in different types of assets (such as stocks, bonds, and commodities) while diversifying within those assets as well.

This section explains one approach to investing using a protective put position for the S&P 500 Index ETF (SPY). Unfortunately, it has to be said that this is just for illustrative purposes — it's not a recommendation, because everyone's situation is different.

Traders managing their investments should complete an investment analysis and trading analysis at separate times because the holding period time horizons are different for each. It's difficult to exit a short-term position on market weakness and not think about similarly exiting your longer-term holdings.

Selecting ETFs for investment (for illustrative purposes only)

Although an ETF may track a major index, it doesn't mean that particular ETF is your best choice. Things to look for when selecting an ETF include the following:

- **How well it tracks the index or benchmark:** The most thorough way to determine how well a passive ETF tracks its benchmark index is to perform a correlation analysis for the returns of the benchmark and the ETF. This requires access to daily closing values for an extended period of time, minimally a year.
- There are websites that allow you to obtain correlation results for either a limited period of time or using a limited number of ETFs. One of the best ways to find current correlation tools information is by completing a web search on "ETF correlation." An example of such a website is `www.ETFreplay.com`, which has both free and subscription options. This website lets you backtest, research, and analyze ETF strategies. It also has an informative blog that gives you insight into ETF-related regulatory, marketing, and performance issues.
- **The liquidity of the ETF:** If you find an ETF that uniquely meets your needs and you're planning on holding it for a longer time, liquidity is less of an issue. If you plan on being more active with the ETF, consider those with volume of one million daily shares as a quick rule of thumb. The problem with illiquid ETFs is twofold. One, you may end up paying more for shares than you should. And two, some ETFs fail, and your investment, although it is not likely to be at risk of total loss, could run into some tax consequences or other issues if the ETF closes down.
- **Whether options are available and option liquidity:** For both ETFs and options, the bid-ask spread can be used as a relative measure of share or contract liquidity. Large spreads indicate less liquid, while small spreads indicate more widely traded issues. Use option chain data to check spreads for the highest open interest contracts to get the best feel of whether the option contracts will meet your needs.

- **The expense ratio for the ETF:** Expense ratio data and the instruments used by the fund to track an index should be available via the research portion of your broker's website, or use prospectus and tear sheet data from the ETF provider or other ETF resources. Generally, illiquid ETFs tend to have higher fees. Whether that's because they are illiquid, or they are illiquid because of the higher expenses, is not as important as the fact that they charge higher fees.
- **What instruments the fund uses to obtain its results:** Some funds may use more exotic derivatives to track its target index. Read the prospectus to determine whether these securities add any additional risk to the ETF. Be aware that ETFs that use leverage, such as those which move at 2X or 3X the underlying index, tend to use swaps. Swaps add a new measure of risk to your portfolio. You should only trade these if you are comfortable with rapid price swings.

WARNING!

Although Wall Street usually pushes a 60% stock and 40% bond asset mix, your asset allocations depend on your individual needs, constraints, and risk tolerance, as well as your outlook on different groups. There is no one-size-fits-all for investing.

Assessing market conditions (illustrative)

Suppose one of your main investment goals is to obtain results that are similar to the S&P 500 Index (SPX). The actual annual returns for the past 30 years for this index suits your risk tolerance and time horizon. Using this as your portfolio benchmark, you want to select an ETF that serves as a good proxy for the index — SPY fits the bill.

Consider the following hypothetical: It's early fall 2007 — you just added $10,000 to an investment account and need to decide how to put the money to work. You are primarily focused on whether you should allocate this money to a broad-based market index now or wait for your next portfolio assessment scheduled in a few weeks.

You plan on evaluating the following to help with your decision-making:

- Weekly chart for SP.Y with volume, a volume indicator, and two moving averages
- Weekly chart for SPY with a momentum indicator and Bollinger bands
- Arm's Index readings for the New York Composite Index (NYA) with an NYA overlay
- Weekly VIX chart with SPX overlay and relative strength comparison

Even though you tend to avoid using market timing techniques for your investment dollars, you're still leery about creating new positions in the fall.

You can't help but think about the quick, strong declines (crashes) that have occurred in the past. Unfortunately, you know nice rallies have developed during this time too. But the news is telling you that life is good, and the market just keeps on going higher, and you really want to put this new money to work.

All you know is what you see at the moment. No one knows what the market will do in the next day, week, month, or year.

Figures 13-3 and 13-4 display the weekly charts referenced for SPY.

What you see is that SPY is well correlated to the SPX and serves as a reasonable proxy to complete market analysis. Rather than analyzing SPX for your market assessment and SPY for position analysis, you decide to use SPY in the market analysis as well. Using the charts you note the following:

- **SPY is in a long-term uptrend:** The 10-week exponential moving average (EMA) is trending upward and is higher than a slightly upward trending 40-week EMA.

  But don't stop there. Check longer-term trends first, because they tend to be stronger.

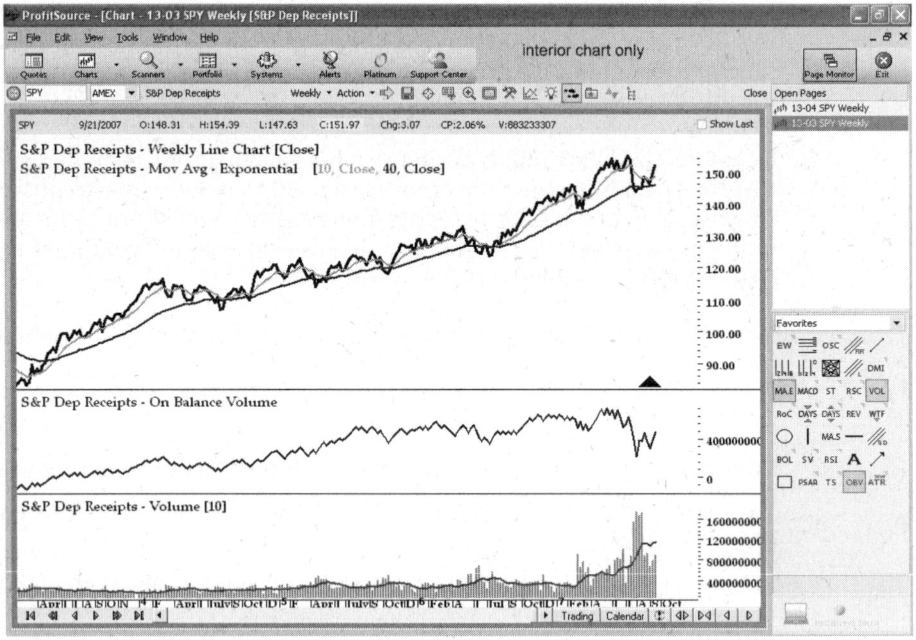

Figure 13-3: Weekly chart for SPY with volume and moving average data.

Image by Optionetics

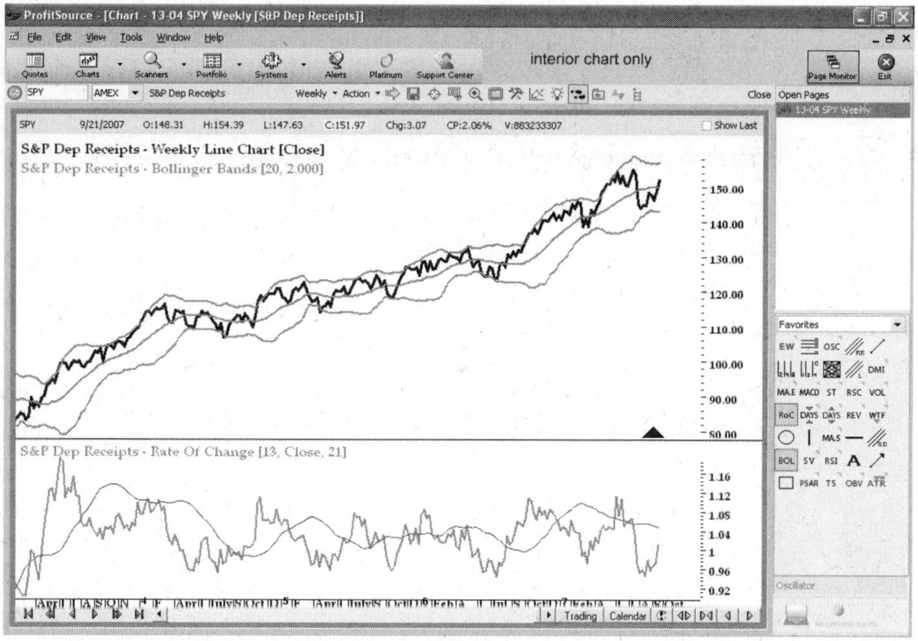

Figure 13-4: Weekly chart for SPY with momentum and Bollinger bands.

Image by Optionetics

- **ETF volume still needs to confirm the move:** Volume is a little bit of a concern because last month's strong decline was accompanied by strong volume, whereas the more recent recovery occurred on lighter volume. In addition, the current on-balance volume (OBV) reading has not yet confirmed the recovery. It's possible it can diverge from here.
- **Momentum is not confirming the move:** Typically, sustainable moves for SPY are accompanied by movement of the 13-week ROC above its 21-period simple moving average (SMA). ROC remains below the SMA, but is not signaling a divergence because it is moving upward.
- **Bollinger bands showing decreased volatility:** Price recently moved above the 20-week SMA as the bands were contracting.

TIP

Technical tools can confirm a price move or may diverge from price actions, providing a warning about the current trend.

This is a difficult bit of analysis. On the one hand, these chart conditions do not provide an overwhelmingly bullish picture. At the same time you can't ignore the long-term trend for the ETF . . . especially because many indicators lag price. This is a good opportunity for an options-aided strategy. You decide to evaluate put options to protect your existing SPY position given the current volatility environment. You continue your market analysis by evaluating the daily Arm's Index (TRIN) chart.

The Arm's Index is a breadth indicator that uses advancing and declining stock data for the New York Composite Index (NYA). (For more detail on applying this tool, see Chapter 5.) The indicator is currently in neutral territory and is strengthening after the recent decline in NYA. This index has a strong positive correlation with SPX and SPY. Recent spikes down on the chart may have signaled a bottom was formed in August.

TECHNICAL STUFF

Many ETFs are actually *unit investment trusts*, which are similar to mutual fund investment companies.

Figure 13-5 displays the weekly charts for the VIX with an SPX overlay and a relative strength comparison line.

The VIX and SPX have a strong negative correlation with spikes down in the VIX coinciding with upward moves in the SPX. The VIX is currently heading downward, indicating a bottom may have formed last month in the SPX.

REMEMBER

The VIX is a measure of implied volatility for SPX options and is also referred to as the "Fear Index."

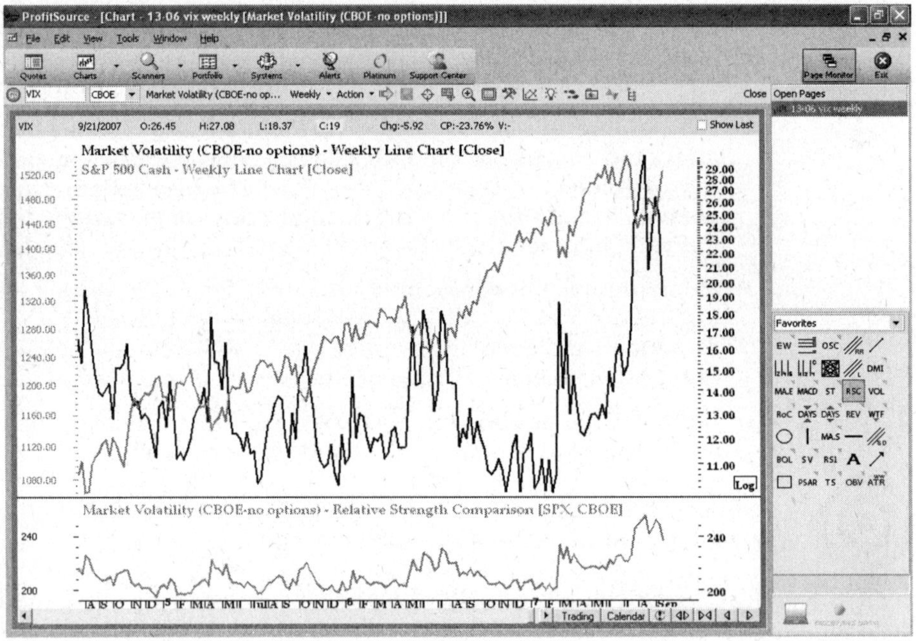

Figure 13-5: Weekly chart for VIX with SPX overlay and relative strength line.

Image by Optionetics

Establishing a position

Here is the bottom line as a trader. Rather than waiting to invest the money because of fear about what may happen, you decide you need to invest the money based on what your technical and sentiment tools are telling you. You are still committed to hedging your risk with the purchase of protective puts.

SPY is trading at $151.97. You purchased 100 shares of SPY in early January at $141.67, which are now valued at $15,197. You consider purchasing an additional 50 shares of SPY for approximately $7,600, providing you can purchase sufficient puts to reasonably hedge all 150 shares.

Because you are buying the options, you consider both November and December expiration months to provide the desired protection while still allowing time to sell the contracts before your 30 days to expiration rule. In either case, you can reevaluate SPY conditions when you sell the puts and roll the contracts out to a later month. You choose not to look beyond December in the event SPY makes a big move upward by mid-November.

After a quick look at the puts for the two months, you note the December options are trading for about $1.00 per contract more than the November contracts. You decide to focus on December options to take you through most of the fall before reaching that 30-day mark. Table 13-3 provides a partial option chain for December SPY puts.

Table 13-3 Partial Option Chain for December SPY Puts

Strike Price	*Bid x Ask*	*Delta*	*Gamma**	*IV*	*OI*
150.00	4.20 × 4.30	–39.00	2.62	19.33	88,278
152.00	4.80 × 5.10	–44.32	2.75	18.94	10,409
153.00	5.20 × 5.50	–47.08	2.82	18.60	17,689
154.00	5.60 × 5.90	–49.96	2.89	18.12	10.275

**The rate of change for gamma is greatest when you move away from the ATM strike price of 152.00.*

Check option delta values when you want to hedge a position.

The tightest bid-ask spread is for the 150.00 strike price puts, reflecting the high open interest and strong market for this put. This should reduce costs on both entry and exit. Although the 153.00 strike price put has a delta near –50, offering a near-perfect hedge, you're considering purchasing four 150.00 strike price puts to reduce slippage costs and gain additional delta protection for slightly less money.

Calculating delta, you obtain the following:

SPY	150 shares × +1 = +150 Delta
154.00 Call	3 × –49.96 = –149.9
150.00 Call	4 × –39.00 = –156.0

Stock delta is +1 per share.

The 150.00 strike price put deltas exceed the SPY position, resulting in a slight directional bias to the downside. Calculating premiums, you obtain this:

154.00 Call	3 × \$5.90 × 100 = \$1,770
150.00 Call	4 × \$4.30 × 100 = \$1,720

Because the position is an investment and has protection beyond the number of shares held, you do not identify an exit for a loss price level. At the 30 days to expiration mark, a new hedge will be implemented.

The stock market actually topped out in late October and early November of 2007. That means that your strategy was well placed because you bought an excellent protection package for your SPY position. By choosing December as your decision point, you also gave yourself enough time to decide your next step.

Tilting Your Portfolio with Sector ETFs

A *portfolio tilt* is an investing approach that attempts to beat a market benchmark by allocating a portion of the funds to an asset that is highly correlated with that benchmark and adding smaller allocations in sectors that are outperforming the benchmark. Alternatively, underperforming sectors can be underweighted.

Both sector index options and ETF options can be used to implement the tilt portion of the portfolio. Using the protected SPY position created in the last section as a base portfolio, sector ETFs are added to tilt the portfolio. Assume there is \$5,000 available for ETF sector allocations.

Adding sector ETFs to a portfolio

The goal of a portfolio tilt is to add a moderate investment in outperforming sectors and/or create a bearish position on underperforming sectors. You can accomplish this using the sector ETFs from a specific family of ETFs and comparing the relative strength for each. This next section outlines one basic approach to selecting outperforming sector ETFs during bullish periods.

Using SPY as the proxy ETF for the benchmark index — the S&P 500 — the sector ETFs in the same family are used for the tilt. The method used to create the tilt is a long-only approach with a very basic moving average market-timing tool to identify bullish periods. Long positions are the only ones considered to minimize risk, and the approach remains out of the market during bearish periods because all of SPDR Sector ETFs have a strong positive correlation with SPY.

Past performance does not guarantee future returns.

Selecting strong sectors

Construct relative strength comparison lines by dividing the price of one security (A) by the price of another (B). A rising line indicates A is outperforming B, whereas a declining line indicates that A is underperforming B. This line does not provide you with information about the trend of A or B — both may be rising or declining. When you plot the result of the A over B price relationship on a graph over time, a relative strength line provides good, unbiased information to compare two securities. A rising relative strength line lets you know that A is the better performer. A falling line tells you that A is the weaker of the two. A rising line is an indication that going long is the best alternative, and a falling line tells you that going short makes sense.

Use the relative strength line along with other indicators such as traditional price charts and technical indicators like On Balance Volume (OBV) and Rate of Change (ROC). Chapters 6 and 7 cover technical indicators.

Make sure that you compare apples to apples when deploying this approach. Using a technology index and utility index and comparing each to a benchmark index, you'll obtain unrelated ratio values because the two sector indexes are trading at unrelated levels. So, in order to compare the performance of technology to utilities, you need to do either of the following:

- Plot a relative strength comparison for these two indexes by using the A over B approach just described
- Calculate the change in value for the sector versus the benchmark

By using changes in the relative ratios instead of the absolute ratio, you have a value that can be compared. This allows you to rank a group of indexes. Another alternative is to simply calculate the change in values for each index over a given period. Again, you can't use index values to rank the sectors, but you can rank the week-over-week percentage change in value (rate of change).

TIP

Put options provide a limited-risk alternative to shorting stock.

Identifying an approach

Using SPY and the nine major Select Sector SPDR ETFs, an investment in an outperforming ETF will be made to tilt an ETF portfolio. The nine ETFs are included in Table 13-4.

Table 13-4 Select Sector SPDR ETF List

Sector	*Symbol*
Materials	XLB
Energy	XLE
Financials	XLF
Industrials	XLI
Technology	XLK
Consumer Staples	XLP
Utilities	XLU
Healthcare	XLV
Consumer Discretionary	XLY

Outperforming sectors are identified during bullish periods as follows:

1. **On a weekly basis, rank the ETFs using three-month returns. The top-ranked ETF is the one with the best returns over a three-month period.**
2. **Invest in the top-ranked ETF.**
3. **Maintain investment in ETF until it drops below the third rank (ranks 4–9) for two consecutive weeks.**
4. **Identify new ETF for investment by repeating steps 1 through 3.**

By requiring a two-week drop in rankings, there are fewer changes to the tilt, keeping costs to a minimum.

TIP

Many technical tools such as moving averages and oscillators can provide you with unbiased rules to follow. See Chapter 6 and 7 for more on technical analysis. *Trading Futures For Dummies* and *Market Timing For Dummies*, both published by John Wiley & Sons, are excellent books that describe the use of technical analysis in active trading.

Tracking bullish and bearish periods

Different sectors outperform the market at different times, but when a strong bear market enters the picture, you'll find few sectors come out unscathed, at least in the short term. To minimize the risk on this basic tilt model, no sector investment is made during bearish periods.

Two other ETF-like securities are currently available for trading. They include the widely held Merrill Lynch HOLDRS and the lesser-traded Exchange-Traded Note (ETN) from iShares.

Once you feel comfortable with the mechanics and risks associated with a tilt approach, consider using a long ETF plus long put combination for top-ranked ETFs during bearish periods or long puts on bottom-ranked ETFs.

Using daily charts for SPY with 50-day and 200-day simple moving averages (SMAs) plotted, bullish periods are identified as those periods when the 50-day SMA is above the 200-day SMA — a bullish crossover. Bearish periods are identified as those periods when the 50-day SMA is below the 200-day SMA — a bearish *crossunder*. So, as the 50-day SMA crosses below the 200-day SMA, a bearish period is identified. In terms of the portfolio tilt, this means the sector ETF position is exited.

The advantage of using SMAs to identify bullish and bearish periods is that it represents an unbiased measure that signal the change. The disadvantage to this method is that there is a reasonably long lag in signals because SMAs use historical prices. It's a trade-off, and its validity is one you have to decide for yourself. If you want to decrease your short-term risk, you can use a shorter pair of moving averages for your crossover indicator. Commonly used pairs include the 15- and 30-day SMAs or the 20-day and 50-day SMAs. It makes sense for you to backtest a few of these pairs and see which one works better. Generally, the fewer the amount of days in the pair, the more frequent your switches will be.

Using the signal to identify bullish and bearish periods, it's assumed that $5,000 is the initial investment in the outperforming ETF as a new bullish period is signaled. The only rebalancing that occurs with the tilt is after the next bearish-bullish cycle takes place.

Measuring results

Using data from 1/3/2000 to 9/21/2007, there were two bullish periods in which the tilt was in place:

- 1/3/2000 to 11/3/2000
- 8/8/2003 to 9/21/2007

Table 13-5 provides some additional statistics for the approach. The SPY columns provide buy and hold comparison returns for the two bullish periods.

Table 13-5 Select Sector SPDR Portfolio Tilt Results

	Period 1	*Period 2*	*SPY 1*	*SPY 2*
Beginning Value	$5,000	$5,000	$5,000	$5,000
End Value	$5,135	$14,080	$4,855	$7,599
# of Trades	4	16	1	1
# Gains	3	11	--	--
# Losses	1	5	--	--
Largest Gain	5.28%	41.65%	--	--
Largest Loss	(4.62%)	(4.39%)	--	--
Consecutive Gains	3	6	--	--
Consecutive Losses	1	2	--	--

The last position entered produced large, atypical gains. Adding mean, median, and standard deviation calculations to those identified in Table 13-4 will help you assess the consistency of results. It's deemed that after removing this last trade, the results are still acceptable. The new largest gain is now 27.09%, and the end of period value, $9,940.

WARNING!

Always complete your own assessment for any system approach you consider implementing to determine suitability.

Selecting the right approach

Investing in the markets requires a reasonable plan that suits your risk tolerances and preferences. From a financial standpoint you may be able to afford a market decline of 10%, but that doesn't mean it suits your long-term goals. Some less-than-scientific ways to identify whether you're risking more than maybe you should is by gauging how you sleep at night or your irritability levels during market declines. These measures do matter and should become part of how you evaluate your trading plan.

Selecting an approach that works for you takes an investment in time. Don't expect to map out your perfect plan the first go-round. By identifying a reasonable approach that manages risk and then testing it, paper trading it, and/or initiating small positions to start, you'll develop a plan that's suitable for you.

Using a sector approach with a portion of your investments has advantages and disadvantages. Considering both is an important part of building your own plan.

Advantages of sector investing with ETFs

The main advantage to sector trading is that it allows you to benefit from gains in outperforming sectors and ideally eke out slightly better returns than a simple buy-and-hold approach using a passive fund. Other advantages to sector investing include the following:

- Produces less volatile result than individual stock positions
- Reduces trading stress by minimizing portfolio decision-making
- Variety of ETF choices makes it a flexible approach

Disadvantages of sector investing with ETFs

The main disadvantage to sector trading is that strong declines in the markets are often widespread — usually all sectors will drop together. This means that you shouldn't count on profits week after week, month after month. Sector investing may only moderately outperform a declining market, if at all. Other disadvantages of sector investing include the following:

- Costs of trading including slippage, taxes and commissions
- Represents risk that is not hedged
- Cost of protection for the core holding may offset or exceed gains from sector approach
- Approaches generally based on past data which cannot be guaranteed in the future
- Requires identifying suitable sector proxies for a group of ETFs
- It is not a substitute for effective risk management unless you use options as part of your strategy

Part IV

Advanced Strategies for Options Traders

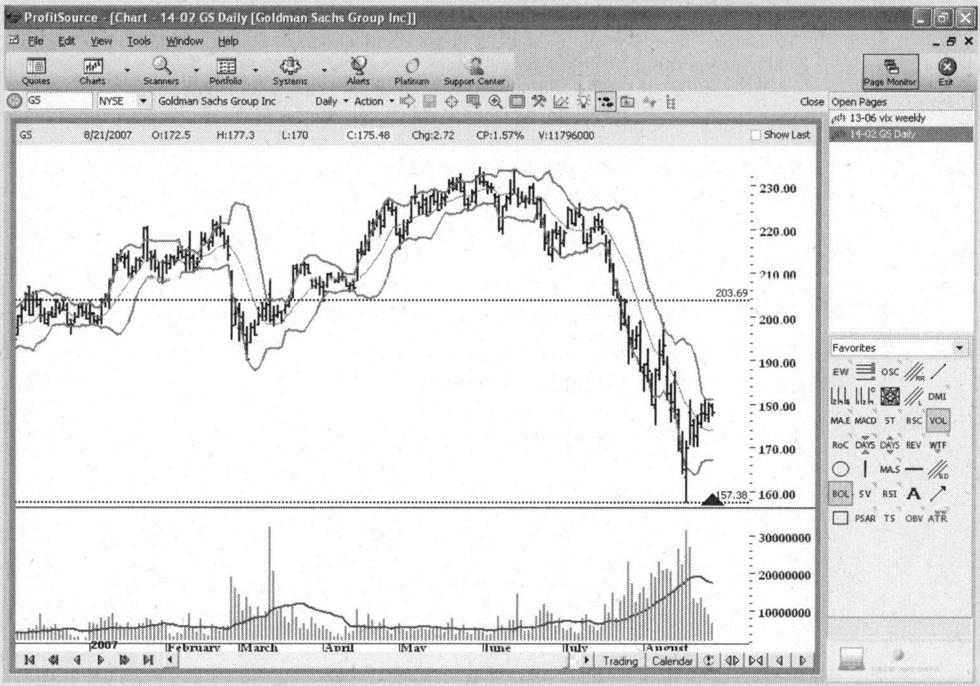

web extras

See the online article about options strategies when volatility is driving you nuts at www.dummies.com/extras/tradingoptions.

In this part . . .

- Benefitting from large moves in stock price, regardless of direction
- Creating a perfectly hedged position that has minimal risk from moves in the underlying
- Profiting while maintaining a neutral market view through position adjustments
- Getting a grip on changing volatility

Chapter 14

Making Money without Worrying About the Market's Direction

In This Chapter

- Gaining with up or down moves
- Identifying neutral approaches
- Monitoring the Greeks
- Adjusting trades

Only one thing is for sure when trading: On any given day the market can move three ways — up, down, or sideways. If knowing exactly what's next is your trading goal, you should find a way to shift your thinking. Managing your risk is the first and foremost rule of trading.

The strategies covered so far have only scratched the surface of option benefits. It's a pretty deep scratch, because a lot of the methods described in this book will significantly decrease risk. But they're still only on the surface. This chapter introduces a trading approach unique to options: profiting without a directional outlook for the underlying stock. By incorporating delta and gamma analysis into your approach, you can apply strategies that make money whether the market goes up or down. Part of this strategy includes adjusting trades so you can take some profits off the table while gearing up for the next directional movement, no matter which way it goes.

Limiting Directional Risk

How would you like to anticipate a big move, be wrong about the expected direction of the move, and still profit? Rather than *direction*, the two strategies discussed in this section rely on *increasing volatility*. Anticipating this type of activity is more straightforward than anticipating direction because volatility changes often occur when scheduled reports and other news items are released.

TIP

It's generally easier to anticipate a change in volatility for a stock than a change in price.

Here are two basic strategies that allow you to profit under such conditions:

- A straddle
- A strangle

Both of these positions combine a long call and a long put. The strategy works best when the stock moves enough to have the call or put realize gains that cover the cost of both options with some profits to spare.

Capitalizing on a big move

A *straddle* is a combination position you create by purchasing both a call and put for the same underlying stock. You use the strategy when you expect a big move to occur in the stock, but you're not sure of the direction. You construct a straddle using the following:

- A long call and long put
- The same expiration month
- The same strike price

The reason the basic form of this strategy requires a large directional move is because all the profits are expected to result from one leg of the position while the other leg expires close to worthless. The reality is that there are a few different ways the straddle position can realize profits.

Straddling opportunities

In terms of finding straddle opportunities, there are a few different times you can anticipate big moves:

- When observing sideways trending consolidation patterns on a price chart, you'll find it's not uncommon for price to break away from the pattern and make a big move.
- Prior to scheduled events such as earnings reports and company announcements get released.
- Prior to scheduled events such as economic reports. The biggest swings generally occur when the news is counter to the market's expectations.

The advantage of a straddle is that it doesn't matter which way the price moves, as long as it moves. Using straddles helps you trade with the odds because rather than betting on one direction, there are two possible directions for the stock to move.

TIP

For a straddle to be profitable, the stock doesn't actually have to move above or below the position breakevens. There are times when a smaller move is profitable because the out-of-money (OTM) option will probably not decrease as quickly as the in-the-money (ITM) option increases. The implied volatility (IV) for both options usually increases as well.

Straddling the markets

There are three different scenarios for the underlying stock that can make a straddle profitable:

- When the move results in an increase in the value of the call or the put by an amount that exceeds the cost of both options
- When a smaller move increases the ITM option faster than the OTM option decreases
- When the move allows you to sell one option for a profit and then changes direction, allowing you to sell the other option for a modest gain or loss

You want to purchase a straddle when IV is relatively low and expected to increase. As always, time is a factor. Thus, because there are two long options in the position, you also need to factor in enough time for the stock to react without giving up too much value to time decay.

Size (of the move) matters with a straddle. Because a straddle is comprised of two long options, your maximum risk is the net debit you paid to enter the position. The stock can move up or down for you to gain — it just has do so with some magnitude. There are two directions the stock can move and still realize profits, so there are two breakeven points associated with the position.

For you to profit from a downward move, the stock must go lower than the strike price minus the net option cost. Below this level, your gains are limited but high. For you to profit from an upward move, the stock must go higher than the strike price plus the net option cost. Above this level, your gains are unlimited.

Figure 14-1 displays a generic view of the straddle risk graph which is drawn by overlaying a long call risk graph (thicker line with dotted line) on a long put risk graph (thinner line with dashed line).

TIP

It's ideal to purchase a long straddle when IV is relatively low and to sell it when IV is relatively high.

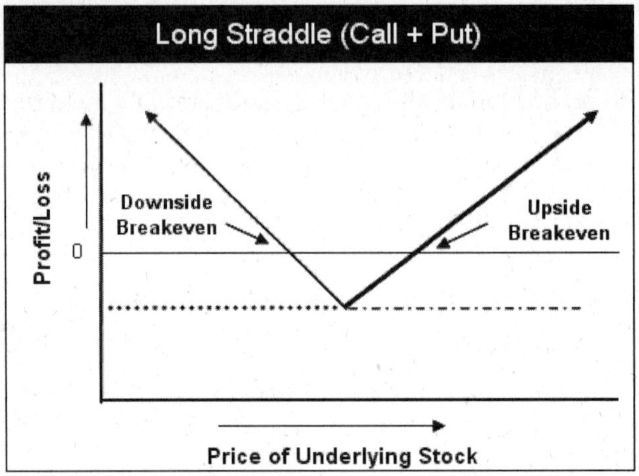

Figure 14-1: Straddle risk chart (long call + long put).

Image by Optionetics

Benefiting from a big move

REMEMBER

Whenever Wall Street worries, market volatility rises.

Here is an example trade. Monitoring an investment bank stock you like to trade options on (symbol GS), you notice that it's pretty quiet a few days ahead of a holiday weekend. The stock recently took a slide after some hedge fund headlines, but typically it performs well. The company's earnings announcement is due two days after the Fed meeting. After noting low relative IV levels, you decide to take a look at a straddle, anticipating increased volatility as the news comes out in the very near future.

Figure 14-2 displays a daily bar chart of GS with volume, Bollinger bands, and two horizontal lines. The lines denote an upper area of resistance and a lower extreme level reached a couple of weeks earlier.

The dotted lines represent potential moves for the stock.

REMEMBER

Time is a very big deal with straddles because time decay accelerates in the last 30 to 45 days for a long option. This means a straddle is impacted twice as much because the position includes two long options. When purchasing a straddle, be sure to leave enough time for the event to occur and still be outside the window for accelerated time decay.

Figure 14-3 displays the six-month IV chart for at-the-money (ATM) options.

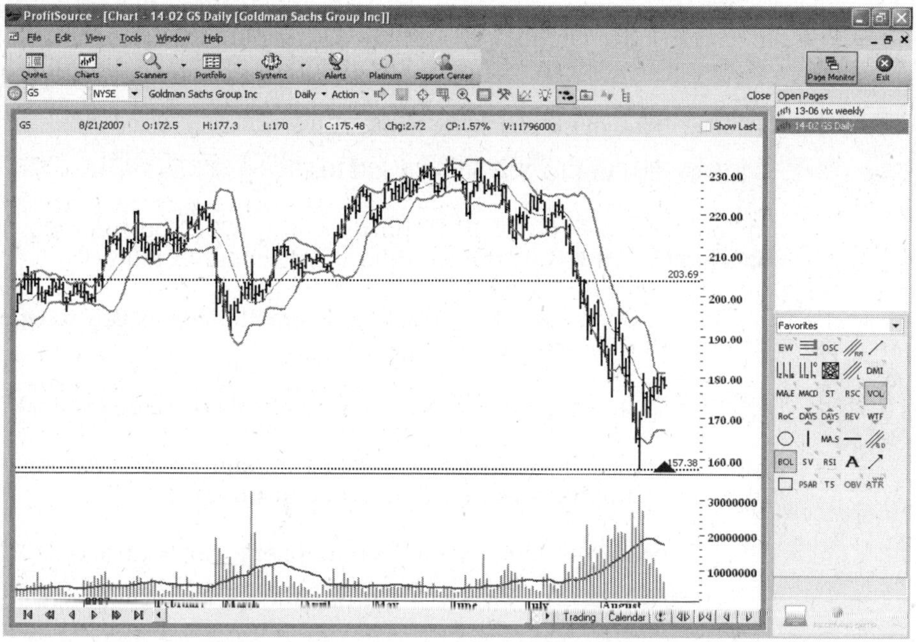

Figure 14-2: Daily bar chart for GS with volume and Bollinger bands.

Image by Optionetics

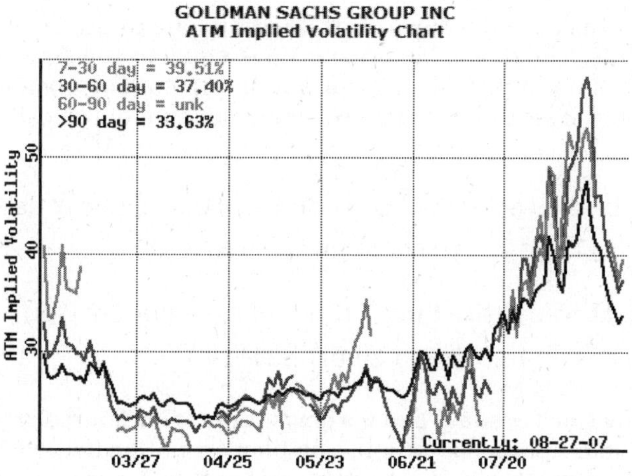

Figure 14-3: Six-month IV chart for ATM GS options.

Image by Optionetics

The two news events you expect to cause volatility will both pass about 30 days prior to October expiration. Because the stock closed at $178, you check the Oct 180 strike price calls and puts, obtaining the following:

> Oct 180 Call Bid: $9.20 by Ask: $9.50
>
> Oct 180 Put Bid: $10.50 by Ask: $10.80

The quotes reflect IV levels of approximately 37%. You enter a trade by placing a limit order to buy the straddle at a discount as follows:

> Buy to Open 2 GS Oct 180 calls and simultaneously Buy to Open 2 GS Oct 180 puts, for a net debit of $20.10

Volatility in the market and individual stocks tends to be cyclical.

Your risk for the position is the initial debit (sum of the two long options times the multiplier and the number of contracts).

$$[(\text{Price of Put} + \text{Price of Call}) \times \text{multiplier} \times \#\text{ of contracts}] = \text{Max Risk}$$

$$[(\$9.40 + 10.70) \times 100 \times 2] = \$20.10 \times 100 \times 2 = \$4{,}020$$

Your potential reward for the position is limited but high to the downside (long puts), and unlimited to the upside (long calls).

There are two breakeven levels for this position, one to the downside and one to the upside. The downside breakeven is equal to the straddle strike price minus the sum of the call and put option prices. The upside breakeven is equal to the straddle strike price plus the sum of the call and put option prices:

$$\text{Downside Breakeven: Strike Price} - (\text{Price of Put} + \text{Price of Call})$$

$$\$180 - (\$9.40 + 10.70) = \$180 - 20.10 = \$159.90$$

$$\text{Upside Breakeven: Strike Price} + (\text{Price of Put} + \text{Price of Call})$$

$$\$180 + (\$9.40 + 10.70) = \$180 + 20.10 = \$200.10$$

The Fed meeting (on Tuesday) and earnings report (on Thursday) occur the week of September option expiration. You plan on exiting half the ITM leg if price makes a move that is 80% to the target region. On the day earnings are released, you plan on closing out the remaining options. This is one full month before expiration.

If you purchase an even number of contracts for straddle positions, you have an opportunity to do some profit-taking while allowing greater gains for the portion of the trade left in place.

Reviewing the straddle risk profile

Your risk with a long straddle is limited to the initial debit paid because the position combines a long call and a long put. A strong move up or down in the underlying will result profits.

Figure 14-4 displays the straddle risk graph with an adjoining price chart.

This risk graph includes three curved lines that estimate the position value given various days to expiration. The curved line closest to the straight lines (expiration) uses 18 days to expiration — note how large the gap is between this curve and the value at expiration. This is the time decay factor.

Using the target areas identified in the daily bar chart for GS, you plan on exiting half of the ITM leg if the stock moves up to 198.50 (80%) or down to 161.50 (80%). On the day of the Fed meeting, the stock closed at 200.50, and one call was exited at a price of $22.80 (IV = 40%). Two days later when earnings were released, the remaining call and two puts were sold for $30.10 and $0.70, respectively. The net gain for the position follows:

$$[(\$22.80 + 30.10 + 0.70 + 0.70) \times 100] - 4{,}020 = \$5{,}430 - 4{,}020 = \$1{,}410$$

Figure 14-4: Risk graph for GS straddle with price chart.

Image by Optionetics

The purpose of options trading is to manage risk. By leaving the long put part of the position in place until you decide to close the position, you are leaving yourself in a protected position should the call options gains reverse and you decide to wait some before closing out the position. The key is to make sure that the gains on the winning side of the straddle are big enough for the trade to remain profitable in the wake of the losing side decreasing in price.

Reducing straddle risk and reward

A *strangle* is very similar to a straddle, but reduces the risk and generally the reward for the position. You accomplish this by purchasing a call and a put with different strike prices that are OTM and expire the same month.

Because OTM options are less expensive, the initial debit is smaller, and you have less money at risk. Reducing your risk is not without some cost, though. It usually means giving up something, and that something is usually gains. The move generally needs to be larger for a strangle because both options begin OTM.

A strangle requires a bigger move than a straddle because there is a spread between the strike prices.

Defining a strangle

A strangle is created by purchasing a call and a put:

- For the same underlying stock
- Using the same expiration month and
- Different strike prices that are both usually OTM

The ideal scenario is for a move in the underlying to be sufficient to sell one leg of the strangle while covering the costs (and then some) for both legs. When this happens, it's not uncommon for the remaining OTM option to expire worthless or with little value. It just depends on conditions.

A strangle is a straddle that reduces potential risk by reducing the cost of the position.

Using the straddle setup, you decide you want to risk less on the position by placing a strangle instead of a straddle. You still believe the move can be large enough to yield profits. With the stock closing at $178, you check the Oct 185 strike price call and the 170 strike price put, obtaining the following:

Oct 185 Call Bid: $6.90 by Ask: $7.20 (IV = 36)

Oct 170 Put Bid: $6.50 by Ask: $6.70 (IV = 40)

You enter the trade by placing a limit order to buy the strangle at a discount as follows:

> Buy to Open 2 GS Oct 185 calls and simultaneously Buy to Open 2 GS Oct 170 puts, for a net debit of $13.90

The short strangle is an extremely risky position because it combines a limited but high risk if the stock moves down (short put) and an unlimited risk if the stock moves up (short call).

Your risk for the position is the initial debit — the sum of the two long options times the multiplier and the number of contracts:

> [(Price of Put + Price of Call) × multiplier × # of contracts] = Max Risk
>
> [($7.20 + 6.70) × 100 × 2] = $13.90 × 100 × 2 = $2,780

Your potential reward for the position is limited but high to the downside (long puts) and unlimited to the upside (long calls).

There are two breakeven levels for this position. The downside breakeven is equal to the put strike price minus the sum of the call and put option prices. The upside breakeven is equal to the call strike price plus the sum of the call and put option prices.

> Downside Breakeven: Put Strike Price – (Price of Put + Price of Call)
>
> $170 – ($7.20 + 6.70) = $170 – 13.90 = $156.10
>
> Upside Breakeven: Call Strike Price + (Price of Put + Price of Call)
>
> $185 + ($7.20 + 6.70) = $185 + 13.90 = $198.90

The exit for the GS strangle is similar to that of the strangle, which includes an exit of all option positions by the close on earnings day.

The term *leg* is used to describe the different securities in a combined position.

Reviewing the strangle risk profile

By separating the strike prices and using two OTM options, there is a range of prices in which both options expire worthless, resulting in the maximum loss. Rather than a V-shaped bottom, the strangle risk graph has a flat loss region that moves upward toward profits, similar to a straddle.

Figure 14-5 displays the risk graph for the GS 185call–170put strangle with an adjoining price chart.

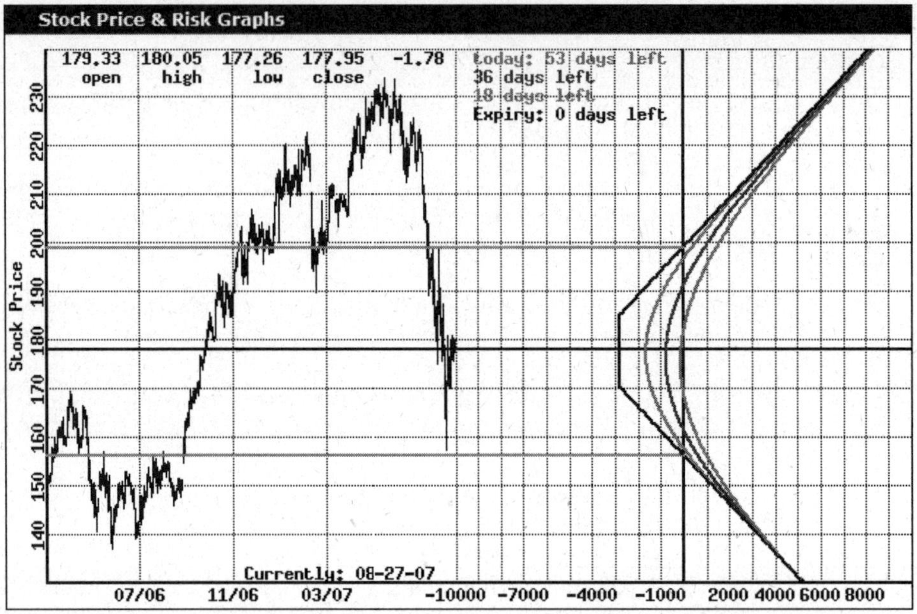

Figure 14-5: Risk graph for GS strangle with price chart.

Image by Optionetics

Exiting the position on the same day as the straddle yields the following:

$$[(\$18.80 + 25.5 + 0.30 + 0.30) \times 100] - 2{,}780 = \$4{,}490 - 2{,}780 = \$1{,}710$$

REMEMBER

Always have an exit strategy before you exit a position. Including specific price levels where you exit for a loss and exit for a profit is a great risk management tool to use whenever possible.

Neutral View versus Neutral Position

The term *neutral* can have two meanings in the market, and it's important to clarify them here. You may hear of an analyst having a *neutral view* on a stock, suggesting it is neither a buy nor sell and that it will likely move with the market. The other use refers to a *neutral strategy,* which is one that can benefit from a move upward or downward — in this case, there is no directional bias, only a method designed to let you profit in either case.

Options help you implement neutral strategies. Straddles and strangles are examples of such strategies, but there's more to these positions than meets the eye. Optimizing a neutral trade means looking once again at delta.

Hedging a position means you invest in securities that go up in value when the original security goes down.

Defining a neutral approach

A *neutral approach* is a combination of stock and options or just options that limit directional bias, especially in a particularly uncertain market, or in a situation in which the market will respond by rallying or falling but there is no way to predict the direction. As a result, trading with a neutral approach allows you to realize gains whether the market goes up or down because you've covered all your bases and you have a plan which will let you respond to the situation as it develops. When market moves are accompanied by increased volatility, neutral strategies can really benefit.

You successfully implement long delta neutral strategies by focusing on delta and gamma during low IV periods. Using these measures allows market conditions to dictate the positions you establish rather than trying to force a particular strategy or view on the market.

But don't get too comfortable. It's important to note that delta neutral trading isn't the "holy grail" for option approaches. You still need to consider the position's risk profile to see whether the trade has a reasonable reward:risk ratio and is one that fits your risk tolerance and financial situation. Stocks that are trading sideways can continue to do so for extended periods, so there are no guarantees that the position will yield profits.

Delta neutral trading does not guarantee profits or give you an excuse to be sloppy. You still must evaluate potential risks and rewards for a position and identify reasonable positions sizes and exits to minimize losses.

Identifying neutral positions

Neutral approaches were introduced with hedged positions in Chapter 10. Using puts for the underlying stock, you protect a position because a move down in the stock price results in a move up in the put's price. When this movement is one to one — that is, the put goes up $1 for every $1 decline in the stock — the stock is said to be *perfectly hedged.* This occurs when the put is deep ITM and has a delta of –1.0. The combined position behaves neutrally to price changes.

The relationship between stock and put movement can vary depending on the put(s) used for the strategy. When the movement between the two is less than one to one, the position is referred to as a *partial hedge*. This occurs when the cumulative delta for the put position is less than –1.0 in absolute terms.

A problem you encounter when using options to hedge a stock is that delta changes as the price of the underlying changes. So, what may initially be a perfect hedge can turn into a partial hedge. The expected change in delta is measured using gamma and varies, depending on the moneyness of the option.

The stock-put position is not the only one available to you for hedging purposes. By combining other stock and options, or just options, you can achieve perfectly and partially hedged positions that are neutral.

Delta neutral trading is more geared toward longer time frames (on the higher end of 30 to 90 days). This gives the position time to yield profits.

Calculating delta for combination positions

Stock has a +1 delta per share, whereas option deltas vary. You calculate the position delta by adding the deltas for all the individual legs.

Suppose you held a protective put position with two puts and 100 shares of long stock. If each put has a delta of –45 (net –90), you calculate the delta for the combined position as follows:

$$(\text{Shares of Stock} \times \text{Stock Delta}) + (\text{Contracts} \times \text{Option Delta})$$

Together, the puts move up $0.90 for every $1 decline in the stock. This is a partial hedge with a minor loss in the position when the stock goes down. Your position gains modestly when the stock goes up. As a result, it is has a slight directional bias to the upside.

Delta values can be used to identify the directional bias for a position. Combined delta values that are less than 0 have a downward directional bias, whereas those with deltas greater than 100 have an upward bias. The bias indicates the direction for the underlying to move for the position to realize gains.

Trading with Delta

Delta is the Greek value that tells you the expected change in an option for every dollar change in the underlying stock. You can access delta values using an options calculator based on one of a variety of different option pricing models. Options trading systems also provide Greek data for you. This is important from the standpoint of understanding that each pricing model has assumptions you need to keep in mind.

You can gain an intuitive sense about delta values by considering an ATM call option. Suppose ABC is trading at $50. It's expected that a 50 strike price call option will have a delta of 50, so if ABC goes to $51 the call option will increase by $0.50. Why 50? One model assumption is that a stock has a 50% chance of going up and a 50% chance of going down. So the call option has a 50% chancing of being ITM.

A problem arises once the stock actually moves up and the option price changes. Using an options calculator, again you'll find delta has gone up. Trading neutrally with this moving target presents a challenge. Fortunately, the change in delta is not some random amount. By looking at an option's gamma, you'll have some idea of the expected move in delta.

REMEMBER

Gamma is like the delta for delta. It represents the expected change in delta for each $1 change in the price of the underlying stock.

Monitoring two key Greeks

Trading neutral strategies means monitoring the position delta and gamma, along with the stock and option price movement. And in case you've forgotten, the foremost objective of options trading is managing your risk. Delta and gamma values are accessible via an options calculator (see Chapter 3 for more on their impact on option prices). Options-analysis software may also provide you with a graphical view of both of these values.

Understanding changes in delta

Delta is primarily affected by the option strike price relative to the price of the underlying, but there are other factors as well. Both volatility and the time remaining until expiration impact delta values.

- As volatility increases, all option deltas move towards 0.50 (+0.50 for calls and –0.50 for puts).
- As time to expiration decreases, all options deltas move towards 0.

These trends often describe general shifts for delta. A 10% increase in volatility does not cause a call option with a +0.80 delta to jump to +0.50.

Assessing gamma changes on delta

Understanding changes in delta also means understanding the option Greek gamma. Gamma is greatest for ATM options and then decreases once the option becomes more ITM or OTM. As a result, you'll find the biggest moves in delta occur for your ATM options.

TIP

Gamma is greatest for ATM options, so delta changes the most when holding an ATM option.

Like delta, gamma is a moving target, but on a smaller scale. Here are some general characteristics you should note about gamma:

- Gamma is always positive.
- Gamma is highest for ATM options.
- Gamma increases as you approach expiration.

Because gamma is always positive, when the price of a stock goes up $1, a call's delta increases by gamma. The put delta also increases, but this translates to a reduction in the magnitude of the put's delta because a put delta is negative.

Creating a delta neutral straddle

As mentioned, creating a straddle allows you to realize gains whether a stock moves strongly up or down. Sometimes it's not even necessary for the move to be that big — the stock just has to keep moving. You establish a straddle position by purchasing a long call and a long put, with the same expiration month and strike price. That strike is either at or near the money, so paying attention to gamma and delta when initiating a neutral position is important.

The changing nature of both option pricing factors also makes it necessary to monitor delta and gamma throughout the position's life and adjust the position as prices change. And because change in prices can happen fairly swiftly, it pays to stay on top of the position and to have some contingent plans in place. A once-neutral position can become directionally biased within one day's trading. In terms of a straddle, that's not terrible news, because half the position will then be profitable. The bottom line is that returning to delta neutrality may mean adding to the position or taking profits off the table.

WARNING!

Be thorough in your pre-trade analysis and planning. When purchasing at- or near-the-money straddles, you are predominantly purchasing time value. You must manage your risk by minimizing the effect of accelerating time decay on such a position by closing it at least 30 days prior to expiration.

Checking delta status

Going back to the GS straddle example earlier in this chapter, the initial position delta is obtained using the options calculator from Optionetics Platinum or another similar premium trading system that offers high-end technical analysis and option tools:

GS Oct 180 call trading at $9.40: (Call delta = +51.191)

GS Oct 180 put trading at $10.70: (Put delta = –48.688)

Position Delta: [(2 × +51.191) + (2 × -48.688)] = +102.382 – 97.376 = +5.006

Thus this position was similar to one that was long five shares of stock.

What about a few days into the position — is there directional bias? It actually didn't take long at all for bias to be introduced. The next trading day GS dropped seven points, decreasing the magnitude of the call deltas and increasing the magnitude of the put deltas. Within a week, the bias was positive once again.

TIP

An increase in the volatility of the underlying causes all option deltas, positive and negative, to move *toward* 50. This increased volatility increases uncertainty as well as the potential for a deeper ITM option to expire OTM. Delta decreases towards 50. However, this increased uncertainty also increases the chance that an OTM option will expire ITM, increasing delta towards 50.

Table 14-1 displays stock and option prices, delta and gamma values, and the position delta on different days over the 24-calendar-day life of the straddle. The table assumes all options were held for the 24 days. T is day 1, whereas T+16 signifies day 16 of the trade. Note how the individual delta values adjust to the price of the underlying stock and how the changes in these Greeks affect the overall position delta.

Table 14-1 Position Delta

	T	*T+1*	*T+8*	*T+16*	*T+24*
GS Price	177.95	170.95	178.98	188.47	207.55
Call Price	9.40	6.80	11.10	14.9	30.10
Delta	+51.191	+40.762	+52.976	+67.179	+86.906
Gamma	1.613	1.539	1.425	1.459	0.741
Put Price	10.70	15.20	11.10	5.4	0.70
Delta	–48.688	–58.667	–47.061	–32.363	–7.106
Gamma	1.569	1.485	1.439	1.509	0.637
Position Delta	+5.006	–35.810	+11.830	+69.632	+159.600

Maintaining a delta-neutral position

The method of using primary support and resistance areas as places where you make position adjustments, such as addressing the position's delta, is reasonable and offers you some targets, but there are no guarantees that price will reach these key chart points. That could be a problem with a straddle. Applying this technical analysis tool primarily for risk (and profit-taking) is good for identifying extreme points.

TIP

Stock deltas are considered fixed — 1 long share of stock always represents +1 stock. Option deltas, on the other hand, are variable, covering a range of values determined primarily by the option's moneyness.

With the benefit of hindsight, wouldn't it have been nice to return the straddle towards delta neutrality by going long on another call on T+1 (position delta from –35.810 to 4.952)? What if two calls were exited on T+16 when the position only had about one week remaining (position delta from +136.81 to 2.453)?

So, to what extent do you need hindsight to act on T+1 and T+16? To make this example accessible, random trading days along the way were picked and examined with the goal of finding the easiest way to return the position to delta neutrality. In real time, with real money, timing issues certainly come into play when thinking about adding to or reducing a position, but hopefully this quick example provides incentive to incorporate delta-neutral trading into your overall approach to the markets.

Reviewing changes to the risk profile

Are you wondering how adding a call to the position impacted the risk profile of the trade? First, the dollars at risk are the total debit for the position, which now includes an additional call. Assuming the call was purchased at $7.00, the net position risk was $4,720. The directional bias with this addition was reduced most of the days that were tracked.

TIP

When adding to or reducing a position, it helps to review the current risk graph to most easily see the impact the change has on the strategy.

The original call was exited on T+22 at the more favorable price of $22.80. As a result, both approaches to the trade yielded a gain of $1,410, but the delta-neutral approach relied less on potentially subjective price targets and had less directional risk.

Figure 14-6 provides an updated risk graph for the adjusted straddle position on the T+1 date. In this case, the risk area decreased slightly because the straddle acted as it was supposed to — increased volatility resulted in the put value increasing at a faster rate than the call decreased. When the third call was purchased, there were already profits in the position, reducing the impact of the additional debit.

TIP

The stock prices that occur between straddle strike prices identify the range for maximum risk. At these prices, both options expire worthless.

The "risk area" refers to the distance between the two trade breakevens. In the straight straddle, the breakevens were 159.90 and 200.10 (40.20), whereas the adjusted straddle breakevens were 156.40 and 195.73 (39.33).

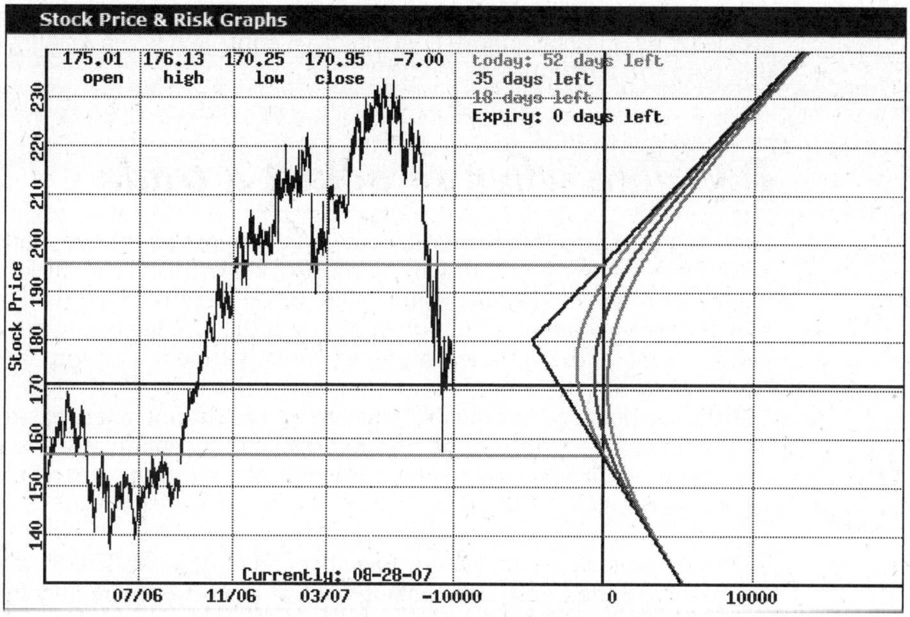

Figure 14-6: Risk graph for adjusted GS straddle.

Image by Optionetics

Understanding Trade Adjustments

Adjusting a trade is something you do to maintain delta neutrality — not something to avoid taking losses when a position has gone against you. In the GS straddle example, an addition was made to a leg that had declined in value, but the position as a whole increased in value. The straddle was basically working as it should, with the ITM leg increasing at a faster rate than the OTM leg was decreasing. An increase in volatility also helped.

REMEMBER

Adjusting is not the same as *avoiding*. If a position has gone against you and is not acting properly, you should exit it and take your losses.

The purpose of adjusting trade is to keep the positional bias to a minimum. You accomplish this by maintaining delta neutrality — but not at all costs. At some point, you may need to simply exit the position. Factors that impact your decisions include the following:

- Time to expiration and whether the adjustment buys or sells time value
- Relative IV levels
- Trading costs

A quick comment on the last item: Straddle positions can be hedged with stock, which may be a more cost-effective approach when making adjustments to the position.

Deciding when to adjust a trade

Focusing on a straddle position, trade adjustments should be made once the position becomes overly reliant on the stock moving in one direction. That's when one leg really begins losing value. If you've purchased the straddle in a high IV environment and IV declines, then the ITM leg is not gaining at a faster rate than the OTM leg, and it's probably time to cut your losses.

Different aspects of trading are referred to as "art, not science." Although you can specifically identify some trading rules and mechanical steps, other parts of trading require experienced assessment of conditions and a best guess of how to proceed.

So far, comments about "when" have been kind of fuzzy. Unfortunately, it's the nature of the beast, and looking back at a position, you may find a more optimal adjustment time or method. The following should help you more successfully implement delta-neutral strategies:

- Experience with the specific strategy — in this case, straddles
- Understanding the cyclic nature of IV for a specific stock
- Analyzing how a stock behaves after different events

Some traders make adjustments every trading day to start out as close to delta neutral as possible. Others may use specific delta values above or below zero to trigger adjustments. It just depends on style.

It's reasonable to consider a set time schedule for adjustments or to base adjustments around different event dates. Just be sure you understand the implications of the position delta you hold and how it may deviate from a delta-neutral approach.

You can make money in the markets in a variety of ways. Find approaches that suit your temperament, time, and style.

Deciding how to adjust a trade

Straddles can be adjusted in the following ways:

- Purchasing more calls (+delta) or puts (–delta)
- Selling calls (–delta) or puts (+delta)

- Buying stock (+delta)
- Selling stock (–delta)

Deciding which approach is best depends on your cost of trading (commission and slippage) and how many contracts you use to create positions. Even though you hold rights with the two option types, you may decide shorting stock is not a way you want to reduce delta. This means the fourth alternative is only possible if you hold a position that is long stock.

Another factor for you to consider is how much time remains to expiration. You may be at a point when it's best for you to do some profit-taking by closing out one or more positions if the 30-day to expiration mark is coming.

If there is plenty of time to expiration and IV is relatively low, you can purchase more of the original strike price options or improve delta neutrality by selecting options with strike prices that best adjust the position to a net delta of zero.

Chapter 15

Letting Volatility Lead You to Trading Opportunities

In This Chapter

- Monitoring option volatility for prospects
- Trading implied volatility price skews
- Identifying the best strategies for current conditions

Although stock prices exhibit some cyclical properties, the cyclic nature of volatility is much more reliable for certain stocks. Even the market as a whole can display such tendencies, as seen by the CBOE Volatility Index (VIX), a measure of implied volatility of S & P 500 index options (see Chapter 5). And although stock traders hate volatility, options traders know how to make the most of it. This is especially true when it cycles and has a certain predictability to it, as it sometimes does. Thus, regularly monitoring volatility and using specific strategies to capitalize on relative changes in volatility levels, you can increase the odds of making profitable trades.

Ratio spreads and backspreads are strategies that also benefit from volatility changes. Incorporating delta-neutral concepts can then help improve strategy success. As your experience builds, you'll develop more skill implementing approaches that are well suited to existing market conditions.

Analyzing Implied Volatility Levels

Implied volatility (IV) is impacted by some of the following factors:

- Past price movement (historical volatility, or HV)
- Time until expiration

- Expected future movement given scheduled events before expiration
- Demand factors for the specific option

IV determines the time value for an option. The greater the value of the listed factors, the greater the option's extrinsic value. Because they all vary, it's really important to buy and sell options under proper IV conditions.

It's all relative but not overly scientific

You don't have to be an Einstein to use volatility to your advantage. There are two types of volatility to consider when analyzing an options trade:

- HV for the underlying security
- IV for the option

Because you're paying for IV, focusing on this measure is pretty critical. But that doesn't mean you can ignore historical volatility — far from it. HV gives you a starting point, allowing you to take the first step in determining whether IV is reasonable. So, when gauging an option's IV level, you need to look at both types of volatility.

REMEMBER

An option's intrinsic value is its "moneyness" factor. For a call option, *intrinsic value* is the stock price above the call strike price, and for a put option, it is the stock price below the put strike price. Intrinsic value is set to zero for any options that are out of the money.

Evaluating past movement

Here is where things get relative. HV provides you with information about past stock movement. HV can be calculated using any number of trading days, but the measure itself gives you information about annual movement. The data is extrapolated, which means what happens during the shorter term is extended to a one-year period using statistical techniques.

HV periods include 6-day, 10-day, 20-day, and 100-day periods. But you have to take some key components into consideration when analyzing this key metric. That's because the movement that occurs during any period measured varies, depending on what's happening in the markets and for the security at that time. So, although an annualized measure that is created using 10 trading days can suggest much more volatility than one using 100 trading days, much really depends on events taking place over the 10 and 100 trading days during which the measurement took place. For example, if it's summertime, especially in the dog days of August, and Wall Street is vacationing in the Hamptons, the ten-day measure may understate volatility.

The best way for you to get a good feel for past volatility in a stock is by viewing HV charts. Charts quickly provide you with a visual on HV conditions and can filter out the relativity, or the "when" factor of the whole dynamic.

Extrinsic value is the time value component of an option price. It's what is left over after intrinsic value is determined.

Figure 15-1 displays a 12-month HV chart for Akamai Technologies, Inc. (AKAM), a computer services company. The chart includes 6-day, 10-day, 20-day, and 100-day HV measures and is courtesy of Optionetics Platinum.

One year typically consists of 252 trading days.

When analyzing HV charts, it helps to consider each period charted individually and then compare it to other periods. In this chart, you can see that the six-day measure (69.90%) reflects increased volatility during the last few days. The 10-day (53.99%) and 20-day (52.32%) measures include this recent volatility, along with quieter trading days, which bring down their respective values.

It appears these "quieter" periods may be less typical for the stock, given a 100-day HV at 61.90%. This 100-day measure is telling you that if the stock moves similarly to the last 100 trading days in the next 252 trading days, its volatility for that period will be 61.90%.

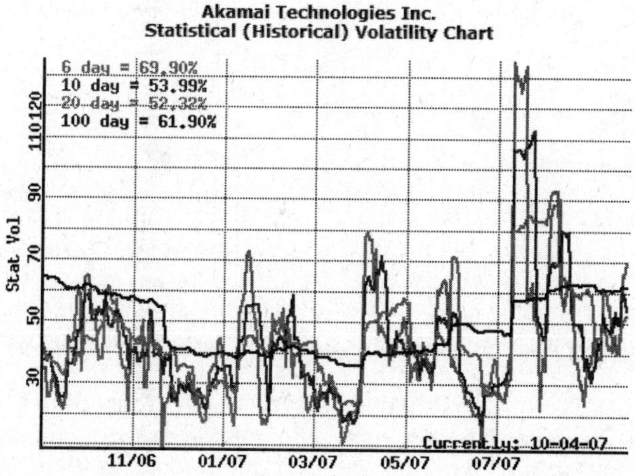

Image by Optionetics

Figure 15-1: Twelve-month historical volatility chart for AKAM.

Note the different spikes in volatility, which has recently reached two-year highs. Expect options for this stock to have IV levels that incorporate these HV spikes in its value.

What may be typical HV levels for one security may be high for another. Viewing a stock's HV chart gives you the quickest feel for recent volatility for a stock and, more importantly, for how this movement relates to what's happened in the past. You can also confirm a stock's general volatility by looking at a price chart. The general tendencies for price swings will enhance the information in the HV chart.

Viewing implied volatility

IV levels change over time, similarly to HV levels. When using an options calculator to determine the current IV for a particular option, you'll want to take the next step of viewing an IV chart that displays at-the-money (ATM) IV values to determine whether conditions do the following:

- Reflect reasonable levels given past IV values
- Are relatively low, making the option cheap
- Are relatively high, making the option expensive

Things may not be what they seem at first glance. A cheap option in terms of relative IV levels can remain cheap through the life of the option. Try to dig deeper into this measure to determine what's driving relative IV levels.

Before viewing the 12-month ATM IV for AKAM, look at the price chart to gain insight on what was happening to the stock during the most recent 12 months. Figure 15-2 displays the price chart for AKAM. Generally, price charts are also available with volatility charts when accessing an options analysis package.

Option type refers to call or put.

So, here's the relativity thing again. Looking at the chart, you can see AKAM experienced two significant drops right before and after March 2007 — that's approximately 10% in a few days, which is pretty significant price action. After asking and answering, "Why did this happen?" don't forget to double-check news stories for that time period. Look into management changes, earnings misses, losses of customers, or mismanagement-related news. Also consider any external events, such as general market news and events.

A look at the S&P 500 during the March 2007 period showed that the market was starting to stumble. The first price gap coincided with a market decline that occurred in late February on concerns that a stock market bubble was bursting in China. Price recovered a bit and then gapped down in late July,

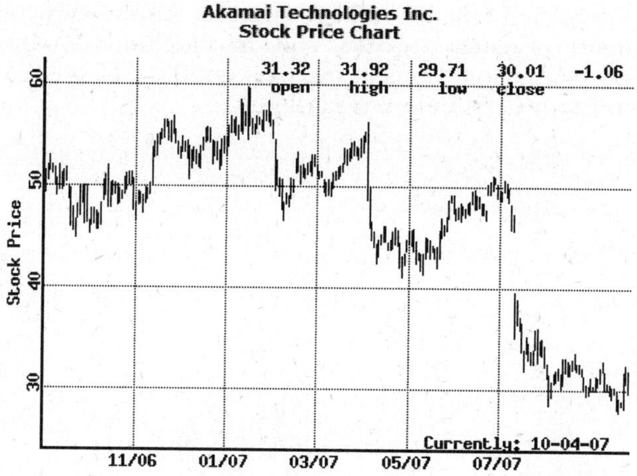

Image by Optionetics

Figure 15-2: Twelve-month daily price chart for AKAM.

possibly in sympathy with a declining U.S. market dealing with sub-prime mortgage problems. It's also important to note that the market recovered after the spring swoon, while shares of AKAM continued to lag, highlighting the fact that the type of strategy that may suit shares of AKAM may differ from those that work for stocks more in tune with the market. More detective work was clearly required.

When an ATM IV figure reflects a range of days, the value is a composite of call and put IV values expiring in that time period.

Was AKAM just a victim of a turbulent market or was something else going on? After checking headlines for AKAM, the following was noted:

- In late February, AKAM hosted a conference call and raised 2007 earnings expectations. No other significant news was found during the search, so it appears AKAM fell with the market.
- In mid-March, news of significant insider selling during a six-month period made the headlines — this could potentially have amplified AKAM's losses as other technology stocks were also dropping.
- In late July, AKAM had an earnings report that disappointed investors and analysts, even though they were in line with expectations.

An option position that is delta neutral — meaning one where the value remains unchanged with small movements in the underlying stock — when created will become directionally biased as the price of the underlying changes and/or IV levels change. See Chapter 14 for more on delta-neutral option strategies.

Figure 15-3 displays the 12-month ATM IV chart for AKAM with corresponding HV peaks identified using asterisks. The chart includes composite IVs for both option types with expirations in 7 to 30 days, 30 to 60 days, and greater than 90 days, courtesy of Optionetics Platinum.

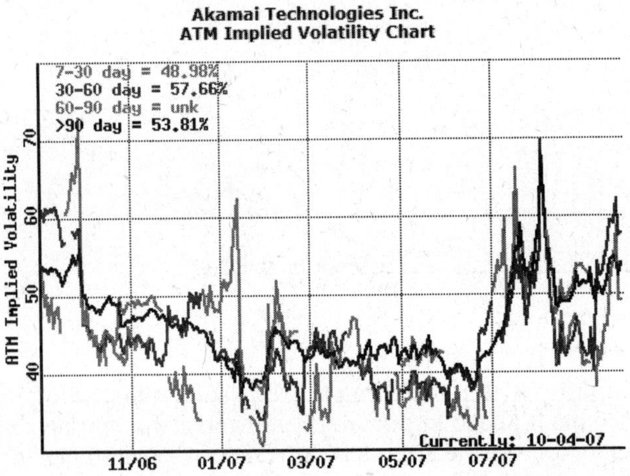

Image by Optionetics

Figure 15-3: Twelve-month ATM IV chart for AKAM.

Spikes in the IV correspond pretty well with spikes in HV for AKAM, with HV spikes appearing slightly more extreme. If you compare the two y-axis volatility scales, you can see that the range for HV is greater.

REMEMBER

HV is one component that impacts IV values.

Suppose you were considering a long option expiring in 30 to 60 days with an IV of 57.9%. You note the following from the two volatility charts:

- The current composite IV value for options expiring in 30 to 60 days is 57.7%, so the option you're analyzing is very slightly above the average.
- Recent HV for the stock was approximately 54.0% (10-day) and 52.3% (20-day), so the IV in your option is above short-term movement.
- Longer-term HV for the stock 53.8%, so the IV in your option is about 8% greater than longer-term movement.
- The current IV levels for options expiring in 30 to 60 just recently spiked to 60%, up from 40% 2 1/2 weeks ago.
- Although there have been times when IV remained at high levels, it seems IV returned towards longer-term IV (>90 day) values more often.

A current relatively low IV value can remain low.

After comparing current IV levels to past levels, as well as the current and past HV levels, does this appear to be an optimal time to purchase the option? Although you can't predict IV, its cyclic nature seems to favor selling the option rather than buying it. Because this may not be consistent with your directional outlook for the stock, you can consider the following:

- Monitoring the stock and option to see what happens to price and IV during the next few days
- Evaluating combination positions that are consistent with your outlook while allowing you to be a net seller of elevated IV
- Buying the option and hoping that when you wake up tomorrow IV has increased again or the stock has moved your way

Of course, that last approach is not really one associated with disciplined trading and is not recommended. It was placed there to make sure that you're paying attention. That said, it's something we've all experienced once or twice or more times than we might admit along the way in our careers. Anytime the word *hope* gets strongly associated with a position, alarm signals should go off in your head that it's a trade you need to avoid (or seriously consider exiting). Hope is eternal, but losses are not. They stop when you've lost everything.

The *margin requirement* is the amount needed to establish a position, whereas *maintenance requirements* are those needed to hold the position in the account.

Recognizing potential changes to volatility

When viewing IV charts, you may notice seasonal tendencies. The most common reason for such periodic changes to volatility levels is the release of a quarterly earnings report.

Figure 15-4 displays a two-year IV chart for Cisco Systems, Inc. (CSCO). It provides a great example of seasonal tendencies for volatility.

Short options that are either naked or covered by another option generally have margin and maintenance requirements.

A two-year chart is provided to show how consistent the increase in IV was for CSCO during the highlighted period, particularly for the shorter-term options. The eight spikes in the chart coincide with earnings announcements for the company. This seasonality has persisted for years.

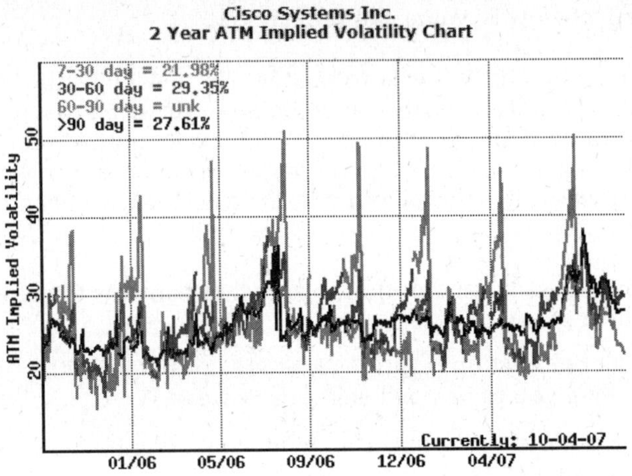

Image by Optionetics

Figure 15-4: Two-year implied volatility chart for CSCO.

You may find that you trade certain stocks and options more frequently than others. By becoming familiar with IV charts and potential seasonality in this pricing component, you can better tailor strategies that meet current market conditions for the underlying and also anticipate future conditions. Although there are no guarantees that IV will continue to exhibit a specific seasonal pattern, such an approach is consistent with putting the odds in your favor. If nothing else, you want to be aware that these conditions exist. Equally important is noting when things change and figuring out why.

TIP

An *IV smile* is the term used to describe the typical IV pattern for equity and index options, with IV levels lowest for the ATM strike price options and increasing moderately as you move away from this central area.

When options are skewed

The Black-Scholes Option Pricing Model is the Nobel Prize-winning model created to price European-style options and serves as the basis for many other pricing models that followed. A significant model assumption is that IV is constant across strike prices and expiration months. The reality is IV can vary across both, sometimes significantly. It's important to understand this so you can select the strategies and options that are the best given current conditions.

Skew is the term used to describe option IV levels that vary from normal conditions. The two types of skews include the following:

- **Price skew:** Condition where certain options have atypically high IV compared to others expiring in the same month. The skew will often follow a pattern.
- **Time skew:** Condition where options expiring in later months have atypically high IV compared to those expiring earlier.

Skews can exist when demand for specific contracts increases price. Calendar and diagonal spreads are optimal when the right time skew exists (see Chapter 12 for more on this). In this section, strategies that have the most success when a price skew exists are discussed. There are two types of price skews:

- **Forward price skew:** Condition where higher strike price options of the same type have higher IV compared to those expiring in the same month
- **Reverse price skew:** Condition where lower strike price options of the same type have higher IV compared to those expiring in the same month

When trading option spreads, skews help increase the odds of profitability when you sell the relatively high IV options and buy the normal or relatively low IV options. Chapter 12 provides a volatility skew example focusing on price impact.

REMEMBER

A forward price volatility skew exists when higher strike options have greater IV than lower strike options.

Identifying volatility skews

A *skew chart* is a visual display of option IV versus strike price for each type of option by month. Figure 15-5 displays typical IV conditions with ATM options having the lowest IV, increasing moderately as you move away from this strike price. Note the smile that results when a curved line is drawn through the data points.

REMEMBER

A reverse price volatility skew exists when lower strike options have greater IV than higher strike options.

Figure 15-6 displays a forward price skew and a reverse price skew. These skews can remain in place for extended periods of time and do not necessarily revert to the typical skew pattern. However, changing conditions can improve profits when using strategies that sell relatively high IV options and buy relatively low options.

TIP

Options-analysis applications can save you a great deal of time searching for optimal market conditions for a specific strategy.

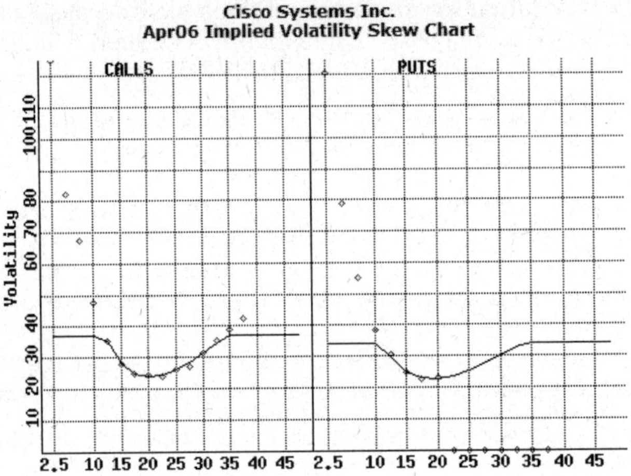

Image by Optionetics

Figure 15-5: Typical IV skew for CSCO.

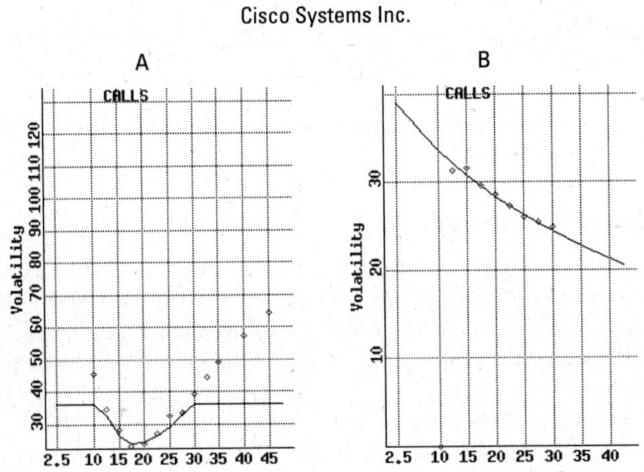

Image by Optionetics

Figure 15-6: Forward price skew (left) and reverse price skew (right) for CSCO.

In addition to viewing a skew chart, you can locate volatility skews by using an options-analysis application that scans the market for them. Figure 15-7 displays an output table for a basic IV scan seeking price skews. Positive values in the skew results reflects a price skew for the option pair listed.

Taking advantage of skews

Trading opportunities emerge when a large IV skew exists, allowing you to create combination positions for a smaller debit or a larger credit than when normal conditions are in place. Skews can persist for the life of the option in any expiration month, so there are no guarantees IV levels will return to normal.

Click the option prices to get the Risk Graph.
Open Risk Graph in: ◯ this window ◉ new window New window size: 718x924

Rank Close	Stock News	Strategy	Strike	Expire	Price (bid/ask)	Volume	Open Interest	Diff (Days)	Days to Expiration	IV (%)	Skew (%)	Ext Ratio
1 156.33	SPY news	Call Spread	Sell 155.00 Buy 163.00	Nov 2007 Nov 2007	4.35 0.65	998 66	39214 12823	0	35 35	18 14	30.74	4.65
2 156.33	SPY news	Call Spread	Sell 155.00 Buy 162.00	Nov 2007 Nov 2007	4.35 0.90	998 853	39214 15176	0	35 35	18 14	26.93	3.36
3 156.33	SPY news	Call Spread	Sell 155.00 Buy 161.00	Nov 2007 Nov 2007	4.35 1.22	998 2531	39214 9896	0	35 35	18 15	22.54	2.48
4 156.33	SPY news	Call Spread	Sell 155.00 Buy 160.00	Nov 2007 Nov 2007	4.35 1.59	998 1604	39214 42720	0	35 35	18 15	18.79	1.90
5 141.12	DIA news	Call Spread	Sell 140.00 Buy 146.00	Nov 2007 Nov 2007	3.35 0.65	1008 641	3506 3875	0	35 35	15 12	17.74	3.43
6 141.12	DIA news	Call Spread	Sell 140.00 Buy 142.00	Oct 2007 Oct 2007	1.77 0.58	4109 1470	14362 7435	0	7 7	14 12	16.20	1.12
7 165.90	MDY news	Call Spread	Sell 165.00 Buy 175.00	Nov 2007 Nov 2007	4.60 0.75	1 0	1107 148	0	35 35	19 17	14.43	4.93
8 156.33	SPY news	Call Spread	Sell 155.00 Buy 159.00	Nov 2007 Nov 2007	4.35 2.04	998 3475	39214 14101	0	35 35	18 16	14.38	1.48
9 141.12	DIA news	Call Spread	Sell 140.00 Buy 145.00	Nov 2007 Nov 2007	3.35 0.94	1008 610	3506 5665	0	35 35	15 13	13.83	2.37
10 165.90	MDY news	Call Spread	Sell 165.00 Buy 174.00	Nov 2007 Nov 2007	4.60 0.95	1 0	1107 117	0	35 35	19 17	13.01	3.89
11 97.22	HIG news	Call Spread	Sell 95.00 Buy 105.00	Nov 2007 Nov 2007	4.50 0.60	20 152	261 226	0	35 35	27 24	12.23	3.80
12 156.33	SPY news	Call Spread	Sell 155.00 Buy 158.00	Oct 2007 Oct 2007	2.17 0.59	11902 10020	58968 78933	0	7 7	16 14	11.79	1.42
13 101.09	PRU news	Call Spread	Sell 100.00 Buy 110.00	Nov 2007 Nov 2007	4.50 0.80	42 151	6041 1449	0	35 35	30 27	11.16	4.26
14 165.90	MDY news	Call Spread	Sell 165.00 Buy 173.00	Nov 2007 Nov 2007	4.60 1.20	1 0	1107 324	0	35 35	19 17	11.02	3.08

Image by Optionetics

Figure 15-7: Skew scan output table.

If you are going to use this analysis to develop strategies and positions, be prepared to act quickly. That's because the ideal IV skew scenario is when the atypical IV results from temporary contract demand — the demand may simply reflect institutional hedging for a large stock position. In this instance, the skew is likely temporary, allowing you to capitalize as conditions return to normal.

REMEMBER

Make sure you match your strategies to existing market conditions.

Understanding Ratio Spreads

Ratio spreads are similar to vertical spreads, but with an uneven number of long and short contracts. They are generally created for a net credit by selling more contracts than you buy. Unlike limited-risk vertical spreads, the extra short contract(s) in a ratio spread create risk that is either unlimited (call ratio spread) or limited, but high (put ratio spread). Given the high-to-unlimited risk for a ratio spread, you must know and execute your exit point for a loss prior to establishing a ratio spread. In this case, more than in most, trade management is key to risk management.

As part of the risk-reward trade-off, the maximum gain possible when creating a call ratio spread can actually exceed the initial credit you receive when establishing the position. Ratio backspreads, covered in the next section, are limited risk alternative to ratio spreads.

Ratio spreads have an uneven amount of short and long options of the same type, with the number of short options exceeding the number of long options. As a result, the position incorporates naked options and has either unlimited risk (call ratio spreads) or limited but high risk (put ratio spread).

Reviewing ratio spread risk profiles

As you might expect by now, there are two types of ratio spreads you can create — one for each option type. So ratio spreads include

- Call ratio spreads.
- Put ratio spreads.

A review of these spreads follows, along with risk profiles and basic guidelines to consider when employing them.

A ratio spread has limited reward with risk that is either high or unlimited. Risk graphs provide a great, quick view of your potential risk and rewards with a strategy. Combine them with price charts to get the maximum information about future potential price movements and to optimize strategies.

A call ratio spread has the following characteristics:

- Includes a long option plus a greater number of short options expiring the same month, with the short options having a higher strike price
- Is used when your market outlook is bearish or moderately bullish for the underlying
- Should be implemented for an initial credit
- Generally uses a 1:2 or 2:3 ratio for long to short call options
- Is best when a forward price skew exists for IV because the higher strike price options are being sold
- Is an unlimited-risk position with high margins required due to one or more uncovered short calls

The net credit for the position is the credit received from selling the short, higher-strike call minus the debit required to purchase the long, lower-strike call. Although IV may be high for the short options when the position is initiated, maximum profits are achieved when the stock moves to the short option strike price at expiration.

Suppose XYZ is trading at $115.70 and you were evaluating this call ratio spread, which expires in approximately 43 days:

> Buy 1 XYZ 110.00 Call @ $7.70 and simultaneously Sell 2 XYZ 115.00 Calls @ $4.20 each

Delta values may be measured on a scale from –100 to +100 or –10 or +1.0, both of which are acceptable.

Because a call ratio spread includes an unprotected short call, it's critical for you to identify and execute an exit criteria before you establish the position to minimize your risk if the stock moves upward.

The combined position brings in a credit of $70 and has a bearish directional bias (delta of –38). It has unlimited risk, but limited reward. You calculate the potential reward by breaking the position into a vertical debit spread (110–115) plus one short call (115), as follows:

> Spread: [(115 – 100) – (7.70 – 4.20)] × 100 = $150
>
> Short Call: (4.20 – 100) = $420
>
> Call Ratio Spread: $150 + 420 = $570

See Chapter 11 for details on calculating vertical spread risks, rewards, and breakeven levels. Losses accumulate after XYZ moves above the upside breakeven, which you calculate as follows:

> Breakeven: Higher call strike + [(Difference in strikes × # of short calls) ÷ (# of short calls – # of long calls)] – net option prices*
>
> Breakeven: 115.00 + (5 × 2) ÷ (2 – 1) + 0.70 = 115.00 + 5.00 + 0.70 = 120.70
>
> * *This is a negative value if there is a credit.*

The worst-case scenario for the position is when XYZ moves upward above $120.70. Although your losses are capped for one of the short calls, they will accumulate as prices rise due to the remaining naked short call in the position.

The best-case scenario for the position is when XYZ closes at $115 on expiration, allowing you to keep the credit for the short calls while maximizing the value of the long call.

An option's intrinsic value is the value associated with the option's moneyness, whereas the extrinsic value is the portion associated with time.

Figure 15-8 displays the risk graph for the XYZ call ratio spread.

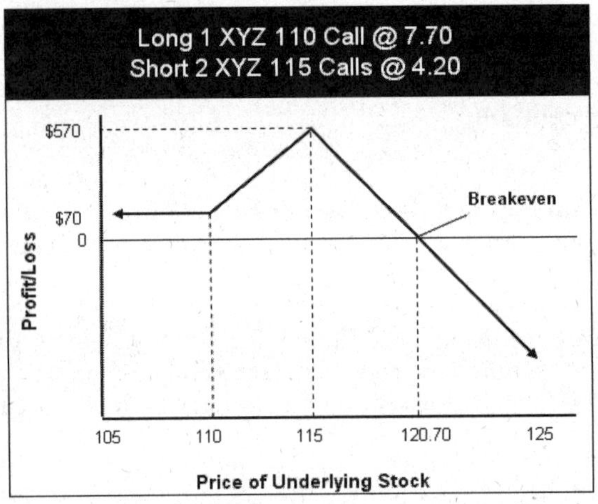

Figure 15-8: Risk graph for 110–115 call ratio spread.

Image by Optionetics

Implementing this call ratio spread strategy provides you with a reasonably sized price range for profits given the time until expiration. The fact that profits can increase beyond the initial credit is also nice. Regardless, the thing that should really catch your attention is that downward sloping arrow displaying unlimited losses as prices rise. Clearly this is not a strategy that you would want to implement as your first foray into real-time options trading. It is, however, worth working on as a paper trade exercise until you feel comfortable with it.

Always contact your broker to obtain their specific margin and maintenance requirements for option combination positions.

A *put ratio spread* has the following characteristics:

- Includes a long option plus a greater number of short options expiring the same month, with the short options having a lower strike price
- Is used when your market outlook is bullish or moderately bearish for the underlying

- Should be implemented for an initial credit
- Generally uses a 1:2 or 2:3 ratio for long to short put options
- Is best when a reverse price skew exists for IV because the lower strike price options are being sold
- Is an unlimited risk position with high margins required due to one or more uncovered short puts

The net credit for the position is the credit received from selling the short, lower-strike puts minus the debit required to purchase the long, lower-strike put. Although IV may be high for the short options when the position is initiated, maximum profits are achieved when the stock moves to the short option strike price at expiration.

WARNING!

Because a put ratio spread includes an unprotected put option, it's critical for you to identify and execute an exit criteria before you establish the position to minimize your risk if the stock moves downward.

REMEMBER

Always ask yourself, before you pull the trigger on a trade, "What if I'm wrong on my outlook?" Know your risk.

Calculations for risk, reward, and breakevens for this position are similar to the call ratio spread, with some minor adjustments. A put ratio spread is a limited but high risk, as displayed by the risk graph in Figure 15-9.

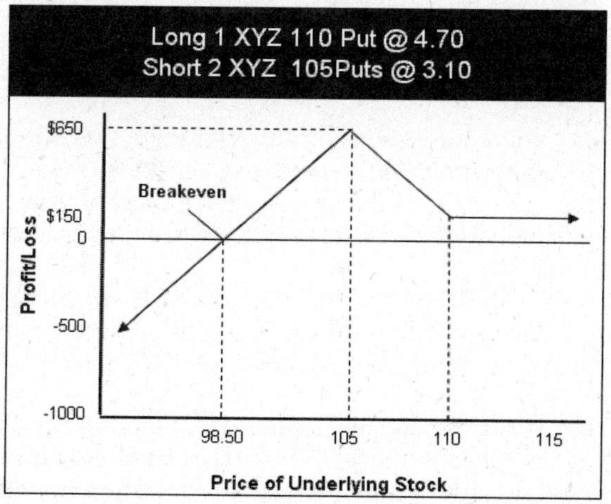

Figure 15-9: Risk graph for 110–105 put ratio spread.

Image by Optionetics

TIP

Ratio spreads generally rely on moderate movement once established.

The reward for the put ratio spread reaches the maximum when the stock trades at the lower strike price heading into expiration. Even though the stock can trade anywhere above the lower strike price to realize profits, the fact remains that a significant risk is taken for limited reward potential.

Identifying best conditions for ratio spreads

Because you are selling IV on a net basis when using a ratio spread, optimal market conditions for either strategy occur when IV is relatively high for the options being sold. This means the following:

- Capitalizing on a forward price skew when creating a call ratio spread
- Capitalizing on a reverse price skew when creating a put ratio spread

Elevated IV often accompanies elevated price volatility. However, both types of ratio spreads realize maximum reward when the stock settles down and its movement is limited to the short option strike price. Additional conditions to seek for ratio spreads include the following:

- **Call ratio spread:** When implementing this strategy, you should also have a neutral to moderately bearish outlook on the stock because these conditions yield profits or limited risk. A strong bullish move for the underlying is extremely detrimental to the position, with unlimited losses possible.
- **Put ratio spread:** When implementing this strategy, you should also have a neutral to moderately bullish outlook on the stock because these conditions yield profits or limited risk. A strong bearish move for the underlying is extremely detrimental to the position, with limited but high losses possible.

TIP

When short options have very little time value remaining (say, less than $0.20), your chance of assignment goes up significantly.

Look for things to calm down before implementing this strategy. The range of profitability for a ratio spread is dictated by both the long and short option strike prices, but generally tends to be narrow when implemented for a credit. As a result, the best conditions to implement a ratio spread occur when there has been recent volatility in price of the underlying and that volatility is expected to subside.

Deciding your strategy

When deciding on which strategy to use, you need to consider both current market conditions and your future outlook for those conditions. Here are two areas to consider for option trading:

- **Directional bias:** Bullish, bearish, or sideways (neutral)
- **Volatility bias:** Implied volatility and stock volatility

You can identify the current directional and volatility bias with price and volatility charts. Because volatility displays stronger seasonal tendencies and is often driven by scheduled reports, you can generally identify a more reliable IV outlook for the future price.

The bottom line is that you don't want to swim upstream. Instead, use strategies that are consistent with current market conditions and that can benefit if your outlook plays out. With this in mind, now is a good time to identify strategies that may be used in place of the unlimited-risk call ratio spread or the limited-but-high risk put ratio spread.

TIP: Always protect your assets and look to manager risk before deciding on your next trade. When evaluating high- or unlimited-risk strategies, ask yourself whether there are other strategies that can capitalize on the same market conditions.

Considering other bearish alternatives

A call ratio spread is best employed under forward volatility skew conditions (higher strike price options have higher IV) when you have a neutral to moderately bearish directional outlook for the stock.

Other strategies discussed that can also profit under such circumstances include the following:

- Limited-risk, bearish call credit spread
- Limited-risk, bearish put debit spread
- Limited-but-high risk covered call position
- Limited-risk collar position

Although it generally takes more capital to initiate a combination position that includes stock (covered call or collar), keep in mind that a short option position has margin requirements that can increase the costs associated with a trade. Rather than an unlimited-risk call ratio spread, it makes sense for you to consider alternate strategies that can reduce risk.

TIP

List the conditions that are optimal for each strategy you use in your trading.

Looking to gain with other bullish options

A put ratio spread is best employed under reverse volatility skew conditions (lower strike price options have higher IV) when you have a neutral to moderately bullish directional outlook for the stock.

Other strategies discussed that can also profit under such circumstances include the following:

- Limited-risk, bullish put credit spread
- Limited-risk, bullish call debit spread
- Limited-but-high risk covered put position

Again, although it takes more capital to initiate a combination position that includes stock (covered put), margin requirements for a put ratio spread must also be considered as part of the overall costs for the trade. Rather than a limited-but-high risk put ratio spread, it makes sense to consider other, less risky strategies.

The next section identifies two strategies that take advantage of price skews when your directional outlook is stronger: ratio backspreads.

TIP

Exchange-traded funds (ETFs) can also be used in place of stocks for ratio spreads and ratio backspreads, by using puts or calls — just be sure to check IV characteristics of the specific ETF.

Using Ratio Backspreads

Ratio backspreads are similar to ratio spreads because there are an uneven amount of long and short options of the same type. However, this strategy has limited risk because you buy more option contracts than you sell. Ratio backspreads are useful strategies because the risk is limited, whereas reward is potentially unlimited. Add to this the fact that you can create these positions for a credit, which puts money in your pocket at the start of the trade, and that's always a good place to start.

This section covers two types of ratio backspreads (call and put), along with risk profiles and optimal conditions for their use.

REMEMBER

Ratio backspreads have an uneven number of short and long options, with the number of long options exceeding the number of short options. As a result, the position is like a vertical spread plus additional long option(s).

Defining ratio backspreads

You can create ratio backspreads using calls or puts, for either a debit or a credit. Creating credit spreads makes a bit more sense because gains can actually be greater than the amount of the credit. This section provides some detail on the two types of backspreads.

A *call ratio backspread* has the following characteristics:

- Includes a short option plus a greater number of long options expiring the same month, with the long options having a higher strike price
- Should be established when a reverse price skew exists for IV because the lower strike price options are being sold
- Is used when your market outlook is *strongly bullish*
- Realizes the largest losses when the underlying closes at the long call strike price at expiration
- *Is most profitable when an explosive upward move occurs* (increasing intrinsic and extrinsic long call value)
- Is best when implemented for an initial credit, which allows the position to yield profits when the underlying declines modestly
- *Is a limited-risk position with unlimited reward potential*

REMEMBER

Ratio backspreads have risk that is limited, whereas reward is potentially unlimited (call ratio backspread) or limited but high (put ratio backspread).

A *put ratio backspread* has the following characteristics:

- Includes a short option plus a greater number of long options expiring the same month, with the long options having a lower strike price
- Should be established when a forward price skew exists for IV because the higher strike price options are being sold
- Is used when your market outlook is strongly bearish
- Realizes the largest losses when the underlying closes at the long put strike price at expiration
- Is most profitable when a strong bearish move occurs (increasing intrinsic and extrinsic long call value)
- Is best when implemented for an initial credit, which allows the position to yield profits when the underlying rises modestly

- Realizes the largest losses when the underlying closes at the long put strike price at expiration
- Is a limited-risk position with limited but high reward potential

Both positions can be established for a credit or debit. When paying a debit to enter the position, try to get as close to $0 as possible. In either case, it's best to maintain a short to long ratio multiple of 1:2 or 2:3 for these positions.

The most important thing to keep straight when entering a ratio backspread is the fact that there are more long option contracts than short option contracts. This results in a position with short options that are covered.

Profiling call ratio backspread risk

When properly implementing a call ratio backspread, you're taking advantage of a reverse price skew in volatility to improve trade odds and offset long call costs. This is accomplished when you sell a lesser number of high IV calls.

Your losses are greatest with a call ratio backspread when a moderately bullish move occurs and the underlying stock closes at the long call strike price at expiration. At this level, the long calls expire worthless, whereas the short calls realize their maximum loss.

You may have more success finding ratio backspreads for a credit when you focus on stocks trading between $25 and $75 per share.

The trade does best when an explosive move upward occurs, increasing the long call moneyness and IV. Because long calls have unlimited profit potential, a call ratio backspread also has unlimited profit potential.

Here is the initial credit for a call ratio backspread:

> [(# of Short Calls × Short Call Price) – (# of Long Calls × Long Call Price)] × 100

The combination may result in a net debit rather than credit.

Your maximum risk occurs when the underlying expires at the long call strike price and is calculated as follows:

> [(Number of Short Calls × Difference in Strike Prices) × 100] – Initial Credit (or + Initial Debit)

Your maximum reward is unlimited above the position breakeven level.

There are two breakevens for this position when it is established for a credit. The upside breakeven is calculated as follows:

> Higher Strike Price + [(Difference in Strikes × # of Short Calls) ÷ (# of Long Calls – # of Short Calls)] + net option prices*
>
> ** This is a negative value if there is a credit.*

There is no downside breakeven if the trade is established for a debit. In the event the position is created for a credit, downside breakeven is calculated as follows:

> Lower Strike Price + (Net Option Prices* ÷ # of Short Calls)
>
> ** This is a negative value if there is a credit.*

Margin requirements are dictated by your brokerage company and should be factored into your risk assessment and financial situation.

Call ratio backspread example

While completing a volatility scan, you find a reverse skew for options on a consumer discretionary company that are expiring in 67 days. The longer-term chart looks bullish, but because you're approaching a traditionally bearish period for the market, you decide to evaluate a slightly out-of-the-money (OTM) call ratio backspread. Assume ABC is trading at $69.90 when you note the reverse price skew. You analyze the following trade:

> Buy 3 ABC 75.00 Calls @ $0.60 and simultaneously Sell 2 ABC 70.00 Calls @ $2.45

The net credit for the position is $310, [(2 × 2.45) – (3 × 0.60)] × 100. The best move for the stock is one that is strongly bullish, but if the stock follows the market downward, the position will still be profitable.

TIP: Using a delta-neutral approach to ratio backspread positions may increase your strategy success.

Figure 15-10 displays the skew chart for the ABC options expiring in 67 days.

REMEMBER: Identify your risk, reward, and breakevens when you evaluate a potential trade.

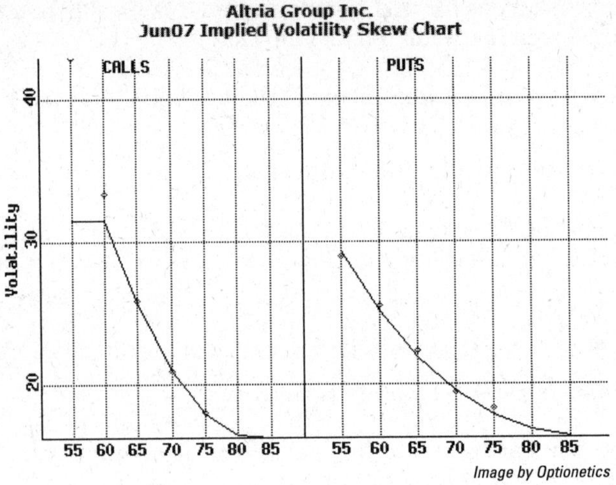

Figure 15-10: Reverse skew chart for potential call backspread trade.

Calculating other important trade values, you obtain the following:

- **Maximum risk:** Your maximum risk occurs when the underlying expires at the long call strike price, or 75:

  [(Number of Short Calls × Difference in Strike Prices) × 100] – Initial Credit (or + Initial Debit)

  [(2 × 5) × 100] – $310 = $690

- **Maximum reward:** Unlimited above the position breakeven level.

- **Upside breakeven:** There are two breakevens for this position because it is established for a credit:

  Higher Strike Price + [(Difference in Strikes × # of Short Calls) ÷ (# of Long Calls – # of Short Calls)] + Net Option Prices*

  75 + [(5 × 2) ÷ (3 – 2)] – 3.10 = 81.90

  * *This is a negative value if there is a credit.*

- **Downside breakeven:**

  Lower Strike Price + (Net Credit / # of Short Calls)

  70 + 3.10 = 73.10

TIP

The initial credit and debit amounts usually refer to the total amount received as a credit or paid as a debit. When calculating breakeven values, the calculation refers to the option prices themselves, without the option contract multiplier.

Figure 15-11 displays the risk graph for the ABC call ratio backspread.

TIP

Risk management is an important aspect of all trades — including those with limited risk. Have an exit plan that includes purchasing the short leg of a ratio backspread when you want to avoid assignment.

So, how did things work out? From the time the position was established until the last trading day before expiration, this stock barely moved — it closed at $70.65. The short options were $0.65 in-the-money (ITM) and were bought back at $0.65 ($130) to avoid weekend assignment. These conditions are far from optimal for the strategy, but you ended up making $180 [$310 – $130]. That really is not too bad.

Sometimes it's exciting to see a textbook example of a trade, but in this case it was actually better to see a trade where conditions weren't optimal and things didn't really go as expected and you still have gains. That's pretty powerful stuff, not being right and still making money. (See the end of this chapter for hints on creating call ratio backspreads with the best chances of success.)

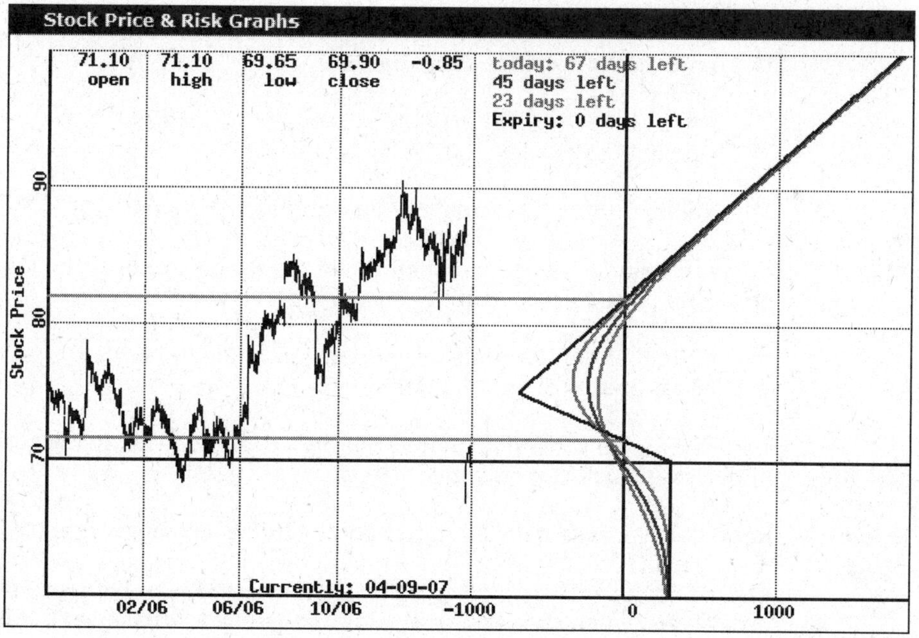

Figure 15-11: Risk graph for the 70–75 call ratio backspread.

Image by Optionetics

Profiling put ratio backspread risk

When evaluating a put ratio backspread, you want to look for a forward price skew on the IV so that the higher strike price put — those being sold — have the higher IV. You then buy a larger number of lower strike prices, lower IV puts, ideally for a credit.

Your losses are greatest with a put ratio backspread when a moderately bearish move occurs and the underlying stock closes at the long put strike price at expiration. At this level, the long puts expire worthless, whereas the short puts realize their maximum loss.

Say exactly what you mean when placing your orders. If placing a ratio backspread order with a broker, keep the order as simple as possible by specifying both the long and short options along with the number of contracts for each. Avoid a lot of terminology shortcuts that could result in placing the wrong type of ratio spread.

The trade does best when an explosive move downward occurs, increasing the long-put moneyness and IV. Because long puts have limited but high profit potential, a put ratio backspread also has limited but high profit potential.

The initial credit for a put ratio backspread is:

> [(# of Short Puts × Short Put Price) – (# of Long Puts × Long Put Price)] × 100

The combination may result in a net debit rather than credit.

Your maximum risk occurs when the underlying expires at the long put strike price and is calculated as follows:

> [(Number of Short Puts × Difference in Strike Prices) × 100] – Initial Credit (or + Initial Debit)

Your maximum reward is limited but high to the downside because the underlying stock can only fall to zero.

Ratio backspreads have an upper and lower breakeven value.

There is no upside breakeven if the trade is established for a debit and two breakevens when created for a credit. The upside breakeven is calculated as follows:

> Higher Strike Price + (Net Option Prices* ÷ # of Short Puts)
>
> ** This is a negative value if there is a credit.*

In the event the position is created for a credit, downside breakeven is calculated as follows:

> Lower Strike Price – [(Difference in Strikes × # of Short Puts) ÷ (# of Long Puts – # of Short Puts)] – Net Option Prices*
>
> * *This is a negative value if there is a credit.*

Margin requirements are dictated by your brokerage company — be sure to contact them for specifics *before placing any trades!*

This time when scanning IV, you find a minor forward price skew for a stock with a pending news that could be bearish. The stock is that of a company that is in the brokerage business and is trading at $73.85. There's a moderate skew between the 75 and 65 strike price puts. Because the stock is volatile, you look at a shorter-term ratio put backspread in case the stock takes off higher instead. You consider the following trade:

> Buy 2 XYZ 65.00 Puts @ $2.75 and sell 1 Put XYZ 75.00 Puts @ $7.20 each

The combined position brings in a credit of $170, [(1 × 7.20) – (2 × 2.75)] × 100.

When you find volatility skews, identify the strategies you can implement to take advantage of the skew.

Your maximum risk occurs when the stock expires at 65. This maximum risk is as follows:

> [(Number of Short Puts × Difference in Strike Prices) × 100] – Initial Credit (or + Initial Debit)
>
> [(1 × 10) × 100] – $170 = $830

Your maximum reward occurs if the stock goes to zero. You can calculate this maximum reward by breaking the position into a put credit spread and a long put, and assuming the stock goes to zero:

> Spread: [(7.20 – 2.75) – [(75 – 65)] × 100 = ($555)
>
> Put: [(65 – 0) – 2.75] × 100 = $6,225
>
> Put Gain – Spread Loss = $6,225 – 555 = $5,670

There are two breakevens when created for a credit. The upside breakeven is calculated as follows:

> Higher Strike Price + (Net Option Prices* ÷ # of Short Puts)
>
> 75 – (1.70/1) = 73.30
>
> * *This is a negative value if there is a credit.*

The downside breakeven is calculated as follows:

> Lower Strike Price – [(Difference in Strikes × # of Short Puts) ÷ (# of Long Puts – # of Short Puts)] – Net Option Prices*
>
> 65 – [(10 × 1) ÷ (2 – 1)] + 1.70 = 56.70
>
> * *This is a negative value if there is a credit.*

REMEMBER

Always consider the margin requirements necessary to implement a trade.

Because the stock is already trading above the upside breakeven and the reward to risk is reasonable, you establish the position. You'll allow the trade to expire if the stock continues upward and exit one month prior expiration if a move down has occurred.

Figure 15-12 displays the risk graph for the XYZ put ratio backspread.

TIP

Don't beat yourself up. Instead, be prepared for when things don't go right. Recognize that all trades don't play out in textbook fashion — manage your risk so you can build experience that allows you to most effectively manage different trades.

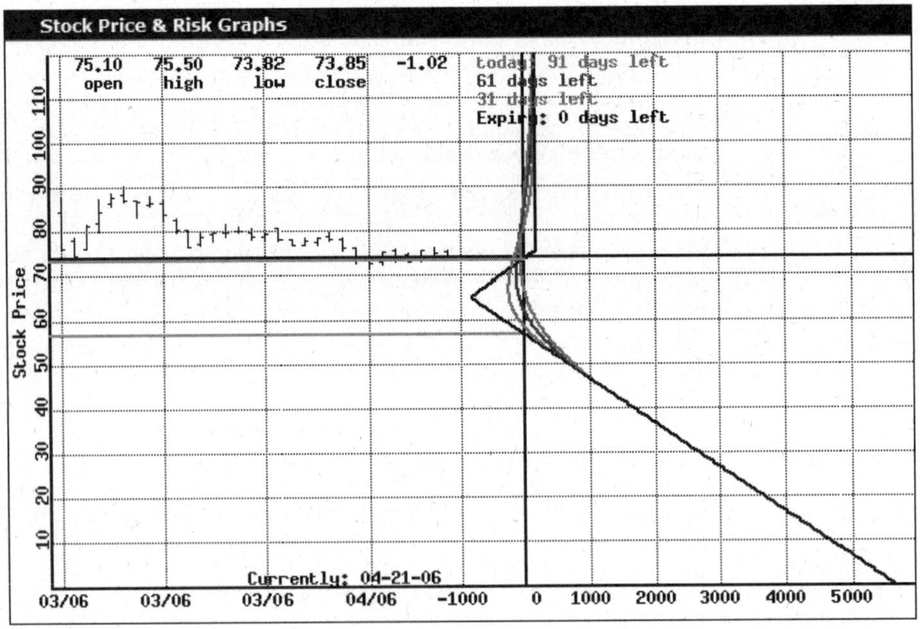

Figure 15-12: Risk graph for the 75–65 put ratio backspread.

Image by Optionetics

The stock was near a peak when the trade was put in place. About three weeks before your exit date, the stock reaches a low and bounces back. On your planned exit date, the stock has reached the low again and is moving upward. It's possible a double-bottom has formed. Regardless, this is your planned exit date.

The stock was trading at $55.08 when you exited the put ratio backspread. Both options were in-the-money, the short options were bought back at $20.20 ($2,020), and the long options sold for $10.70 ($2,140), for an additional profit of $120. The position gain was $290 because it was initially established for a credit.

It can be difficult to find ratio backspreads for a credit, but by understanding the IV conditions that are optimal for these types of trades, you have a much better chance of locating credits. If you do establish the position for a debit, try to keep that debit as low as possible.

WARNING!

The trickiest option to manage at expiration is a barely out-of-the-money short option leg that is covered by another expiring option. If the short option is ATM or even slightly OTM while your long option is OTM, you could have the short option assigned after the long option has expired. Always manage your risk by actively managing the assignment possible as much as possible.

Spotting best conditions for ratio backspreads

Both ratio spreads and ratio backspreads rely on volatility price skews for best results. Although backspreads are clearly the preferred strategy — you have unlimited to high rewards for the ratio backspread versus unlimited to high risk for the ratio spread — your outlook for the underlying stock ultimately determines which strategy is reasonable.

REMEMBER

Price skews provide ratio backspread opportunities, whereas time skews provide calendar spread opportunities.

Putting a call ratio backspread to work

A call ratio backspread combines a lower-strike, short call with a greater number of higher-strike, long calls that expire in the same month. The risk for the position is limited, whereas the potential gain is unlimited.

When seeking a call ratio backspread position, look for the following market conditions:

- A reverse price skew in IV so the lower strike short calls have a greater IV than the higher strike long calls
- Bullish conditions for the underlying stock, with the potential for an explosive move upward (such as what can happen upon the release of a very favorable report)
- A potential increase in IV for both options

When noting the preceding conditions are in place, here are some additional tips to help you successfully implement a call ratio backspread:

- Even though the trade can be created for a credit, losses occur when there is limited movement in the stock. To avoid getting hurt badly, be disciplined and prepare for the worst. Identify a maximum loss amount for the combined position and exit the position if it is reached, no matter what.
- Keep the ratios you use to multiples of 1:2 or 2:3 at most. Calculate net delta to determine which ratio best minimizes directional bias for the position.
- Seek an initial credit. If you create the trade for a debit, keep that debit as low as possible.
- Give yourself time. Use options with 90 days to expiration when possible to allow time to for the stock to continue an upward move.
- Focus on stocks valued between $25 and 75 per share because they are likely to have options which are liquid and are easier to trade.
- Always think about how you will pay yourself. Consider exiting an equal number of long and short calls when the position has 50% profit above the upper breakeven. This allows for profit-taking while leaving one or more long calls in place for additional profits.
- Always leave the back door open. Exit the position with 30 days to expiration when time decay negatively impacts the long calls — be particularly diligent when the stock is trading between the two call strike prices, the price area that represents the area of maximum risk.
- Avoid getting assigned. Never hold an ITM, ATM, or slightly OTM short option into expiration weekend. Manage your assignment risk by buying the short option back to cover the position.

Patience pays off. Successfully implementing a call ratio backspread strategy takes a little time to find the proper market conditions and identify options that work best. This means it's perfectly suited to paper trading — in other words, for honing your skills. You'll find the time you invest can be well worth it.

Always work out the kinks of any strategy before risking it in real time. Paper trading is a great way to gain experience with different strategy dynamics.

Making the most of put ratio backspreads

A put ratio backspread combines a higher-strike, short put with a greater number of lower-strike, long puts that expire in the same month. The risk for the position is limited, whereas the potential gain is limited but high.

When seeking a put ratio backspread position, look for the following market conditions:

- A forward price skew in IV so the higher-strike short puts have a greater IV than the lower-strike long puts — generally low IV conditions will help.
- Bearish conditions for the underlying stock, with the potential for an explosive move downward (as can happen upon the release of an unfavorable report).
- A potential increase in IV for both options.

Expect the unexpected. Never assume a short OTM option will expire worthless. Always monitor conditions through expiration weekend to confirm you have not been assigned on a short option.

When noting the preceding conditions are in place, here are some additional tips to help you successfully implement a put ratio backspread:

- Even though the trade can be created for a credit, losses occur when there is limited movement in the stock. Identify a maximum loss amount for the combined position and exit the position if it is reached.
- Keep the ratios you use to multiples of 1:2 or 2:3 at most. Calculate net delta to determine which ratio best minimizes directional bias for the position.
- Seek an initial credit. If you create the trade for a debit, keep that debit as low as possible.
- Use options with 90 days to expiration when possible to allow time for the stock to continue an upward move.
- Paper trade the strategy to hone your trade selection skills and understand how changes in the underlying impact the position value throughout its life.
- Consider exiting an equal number of long and short puts when the position has 50% profit below the lower breakeven. This allows for profit-taking while leaving one or more long puts in place for additional profits.

- Exit the position with 30 days to expiration when time decay negatively impacts the long puts — be particularly diligent when the stock is trading between the two put strike prices, the price area that represents the area of maximum risk.
- Never hold an ITM, ATM, or slightly OTM short option into expiration weekend. Manage your assignment risk by buying the short option back to cover the position.

Again, successfully implementing a put ratio backspread strategy takes time and practice. If it didn't require an effort, everyone would be doing it.

Chapter 16

Trading Profitably When Markets Move Sideways

In This Chapter

- Boosting current returns
- Trading sideways markets
- Understanding spread impact

The headlines always capture those periods when the markets move up or down. But the fact is that major averages, sectors, and individual securities all display varying degrees of trending (up or down) and trendless (sideways) conditions. As a straight stock or ETF trader, these trendless market periods are difficult to handle, especially if you use the markets as part of your overall income.

Option strategies are unique because they allow you to realize profits when markets move sideways. By using options, you can reap additional rewards on existing positions or trade the markets with limited risk. Long butterflies and condors are two such strategies introduced here. And although these strategies are complex, they are ideal for sideways markets because they can produce income or moderate gains as you manage the position, while limiting risk. Thus, there are two question to be answered as a trader during sideways markets: Am I willing to take limited chances, in most cases, to make limited rewards, which may be better than what I get just for waiting? Or is my best strategy to just sit and wait for the market to decide on a direction and then use trend-geared strategies? If you answer yes to the first question, then these strategies are for you. If you answer yes to the second question, I recommend that you read this chapter anyway, because it may change your mind or give you something you can use in your overall trading strategies anyway.

Winning Positions in Sideways Markets

You have two dilemmas when the markets move sideways:

- Dealing with stagnant returns on existing positions
- Finding gains with new positions

You may find yourself getting restless when sideways movement persists, wondering whether you should close out current positions and when things will get moving again (and in which direction). The truth is that even though the market spends time in this sideways mode, you can still trade options profitably by using the right options strategies. To be sure, a sideways market is a specific situation, but because it is an optionable trend, from a trading standpoint it is just another challenge, albeit one that requires a special set of trading techniques. With this in mind, let's look first at position management when the market settles into a sideways-trading range.

Managing existing positions

You already know that long calls allow you to realize gains from bullish moves, whereas long puts allow you to realize gains from bearish moves. What many don't realize is that when the markets are moving sideways, you can realize gains by combining positions. Hopefully, by now you're comfortable with combination positions, because there are so many different ones available to you. As a starting point, you can add options to existing stock or exchange-traded funds (ETFs) to boost returns when the markets seem to be directionless. Perhaps the key point to consider is that these strategies are meant to have the best chance of success in sideways markets. Thus, part of your management strategy should be to look for potential changes from sideways trends to up or down trends and to manage the position accordingly.

REMEMBER: As a general rule of thumb for initiating new positions, you want to sell premium when implied volatility (IV) is relatively high and buy it when it is relatively low.

Sideways gains: XYZ case study and comparison to real-life historical example using Dell

This example features the imaginary XYZ Technology company initially and is then further documented by a historical example using shares of Dell, during its publicly traded period. Suppose it's late 2012 and you purchase XYZ Technology for $24.00 because technology names are finally strengthening. This came after a long decline in this sector, and you felt XYZ was a leader in its field. You identify $22.00 as your stop-loss exit point, which represents a decline of 8.3%.

After a move upward in price, XYZ has stalled a bit. You re-evaluate some of the technical indicators you prefer under such conditions and decide the longer-term outlook for XYZ remains bullish. Rather than having the asset just sit there, you evaluate a covered call strategy to increase your returns.

In March 2013, XYZ is trading at $26.50, about 10% higher than where you purchased it. You note that historical volatility (HV) and implied volatility (IV) are relatively low for the stock compared to the last 12 months, so you monitor conditions to see if IV strengthens at all. You also note that the next quarterly earnings report for XYZ is due in mid-May.

Leg is the term used to describe each individual security in a combined position.

Selling a call against a long stock position doesn't protect it — it moderately reduces risk by reducing your net costs.

Because you'd prefer to keep the shares of XYZ, you rule out the two in-the-money (ITM) calls with a strike price of 25.00. You also note that the May earnings report is due one day prior to May expiration and decide to wait until you are closer to that time to capture an IV boost for options expiring in May. Instead of May options, you focus on the Apr 27.50 and 30.00 strike price calls expiring April 19.

After capturing the sideways price movement by drawing a linear regression channel from the share purchase date to the current date, you extend the channel lines to the right to monitor price changes. (See Chapter 6 for more information on price movements and projections using this technical tool.)

Selling the Apr 30.00 will barely break even after commission, so you sell the Apr 27.50 call for $0.70. You note there is a 39% chance the shares will be called using pricing model assumptions (delta = 39.1). You also note the upward directional bias for the position has been reduced from +100 to +60.9.

Volume levels may provide hints about the direction of a breakout from a consolidation pattern, as well as its chance of success. Volume should increase with the breakout. Adding a moving average line to volume data helps with this approach.

XYZ traded in a range from $27.13 to 27.70 on the Friday before expiration, closing at $27.34. You retained the shares. After April expiration, you note the following:

- Your indicators remain long-term bullish for XYZ, while the short-term view remains flat.
- IV levels are relatively low and they will likely increase as you get closer to the quarterly earnings report.

- Because the earnings report is so close to expiration, you'll sell a May call when IV increases and roll that option to June after earnings are released. This assumes XYZ remains within its sideways channel and you remain long-term bullish on the stock.

Use this tool if you are a visual investor or to verify your IV analysis. Bollinger bands are bands constructed above and below a simple moving average, using a standard deviation calculation. As a result, the expansion and contraction of the bands coincide with expanding and contracting volatility. See Chapter 6 for more on Bollinger bands. If you're really interested, check out *Market Timing For Dummies* (John Wiley & Sons, 2008), where Bollinger bands are used extensively as a trading tool to pinpoint periods of potential changes in the trend.

XYZ moves down to its lower Bollinger band near the end of April, but remains well within its sideways channel. It then moves back to its 20-day simple moving average (SMA) with an increase in IV a couple of days later. Once again it is trading near $26.50, and you evaluate May 27.50 and 30.00 strike calls.

Even if you can realize additional gains by selling calls against an existing stock position, it doesn't mean you should necessarily hold onto that position. Consider both your shorter-term and longer-term outlook for the security before you decide whether to offset position cost by selling calls against it.

The cost basis for XYZ is now $23.30, because the covered calls that were sold for $0.70 expired worthless. Although IV increased for the Apr 27.50 call, time decay had a greater impact on the option premiums. You decide to sell the May 27.50 strike call for $0.55.

Do not sell calls against a position you are not willing to part with. Although a stock can seem to spend lengthy periods of time moving sideways, it can explode upward at any time.

Four days after the call is sold, XYZ declines rapidly through the lower regression channel line, but remains above your stop-loss exit price. The stock once again rebounds, but you do note there are wider Bollinger bands and longer daily price bars, indicating conditions are getting more volatile.

Expectations are bullish on the day earnings are set to be released (after the close), and XYZ moves up to $27.85. The report is good, and the stock opens up an additional $0.42, with movement remaining within the channel lines. You roll out the May call to June and also roll it up from 27.50 to 30.00 to minimize the risk of being called out of a longer-term bullish position.

The IV for the May 27.50 call sky-rocketed with one day remaining to expiration, resulting in a $0.30 loss for the Apr 27.50 call. The position cost basis rises to $23.60. The June options do not realize the same magnitude spike in IV. You tell yourself to remember that for next time. As a result of selling the June call, your cost basis declines to $22.90.

Conditions deteriorate, and XYZ closes at 23.98 on the Friday of expiration weekend in June. You allow the Jun 30.00 strike price call option to expire worthless and decide to reevaluate the stock position over the weekend. The short-term trend is downward, and on a longer-term basis it appears a more bearish picture has emerged. You elect to sell the stock at the open on Monday, rather than protecting the position with a collar (long put, short call).

Figure 16-1 displays the daily bar chart for Dell, Inc., an example of a trade that closely matches the theoretical XYZ trade example just described. The chart features a regression channel based on nearly five months of trading. The vertical lines denote stock entry and exit days, as well as short call transaction days. Volume data with a 20-day moving average and the directional movement indicator (see sidebar) are also included.

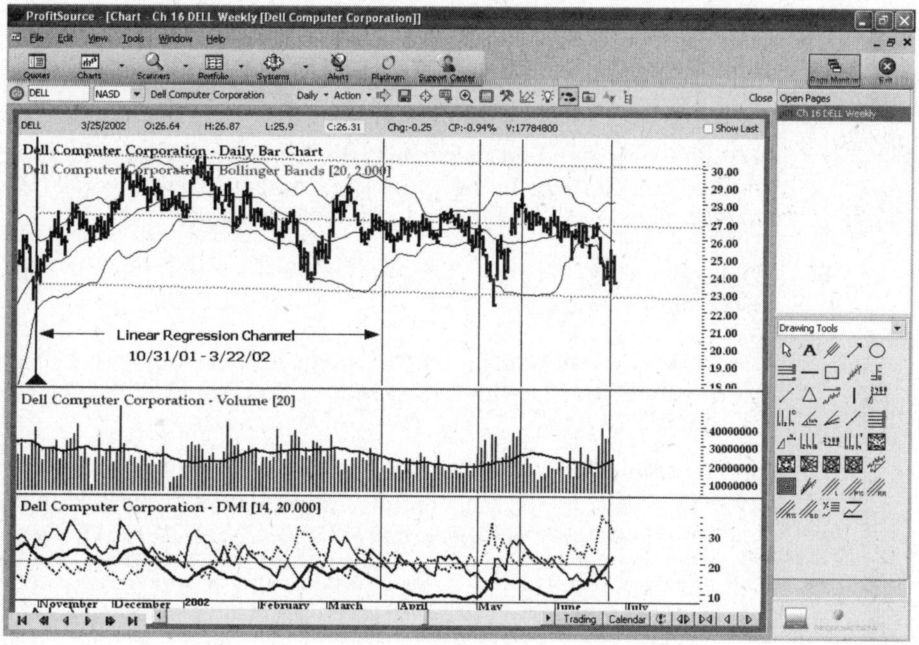

Figure 16-1: Daily price chart for Dell with regression channel.

Image by Optionetics

XYZ was sold for $23.68, for a net gain of $0.78 per share, when the short call positions are included. These results do not include commissions, which would have added approximately $0.60 for an active trader (option and stock commissions). Although this is certainly significant, compare this to a net loss inclusive of stock commissions (approximately $0.52 per share) if the stock was held by itself until this time. These values translate to a 0.8% gain for the covered call approach versus a 2.2% buy-and-hold loss.

When a stock is consolidating, and its volatility decreases, IV for the stock's options will likely also decrease. This creates an environment that's not ideal for covered call strategies because premiums are decreasing. Regardless, the strategy can still be profitably implemented.

Strategy comments

Assuming for illustrative purposes that XYZ mirrored the action in Dell as the chart shows, it would have had one more daily close below the lower regression channel line, and a few closes above the upper regression channel later in its trading history, before finally breaking out above the sideways consolidation pattern in May 2003. The price remained within the channel range all but a handful of days for 18 months.

Referring to the Dell chart in Figure 16-1, the covered call strategy could have been continued for profits throughout this period. Had the stock been called away during the May breakout, it could have been purchased again later that month when Dell returned to test the upper channel line, which now serves as support.

Do not place a standing stop-loss order for the underlying stock used in a covered call strategy. In the event the stop is triggered, you'll be left holding a short, naked call — which is an unlimited-risk position.

While reviewing this case study, hopefully you noted the following important points:

- The short call is an income strategy. It does not protect the stock position; it will typically just reduce the cost basis, which moderately decreases risk.
- You still need to manage your risk by identifying a stop-loss exit level, even if that means buying back a short call option to exit the stock.
- HV and IV both generally decrease when a stock is in a trading range.
- Earnings reports and other company and economic-related news can significantly impact IV, even when price is basically moving sideways.
- You should consider your longer-term view for the long stock position because there is potential for limited but high losses with such a strategy (short call).
- As an alternative approach, you can purchase a long-term put while the calls are sold each month to protect the downside.
- Short calls that close ITM may be rolled out a month and up a strike price for a modest gain when the stock moves upward.

- Commissions can significantly impact trade results.
- Other trading costs such as tax consequences need to be considered when implementing this or any trading strategy.
- Trading rules based on stop-loss exits and regression-channel breaks help implement a strategy successfully while managing risk.
- Paper trading provides you with issues that can arise when implementing a new strategy, such as the price impact of IV versus time.
- When a breakout away from a longer-term consolidation occurs, it's common for the stock to return to test the pattern.

Don't necessarily abandon a strategy without keeping it on your radar screen for a while. If you exit or get called out of a position while implementing a covered call strategy during a consolidation, a move back to the same trading pattern by the underlying may provide you with another opportunity to establish a new directional position in the stock.

REMEMBER

A Long-term Equity AnticiPation Securities (LEAPS) contract is a long-term option available for certain underlying indexes, ETFs, and stocks. LEAPS contracts generally have more than 9 months to 2 1/2 years to expiration and become regular options after that time decreases.

When selling calls on a long stock or ETF position, you increase the number of ways the stock can move while still allowing for gains. You also limit your potential gains if an explosive upside move occurs. That's simply a strategy trade-off you need to weigh when considering different trade approaches.

Option strategies for sideways moves

The covered call strategy is just one that can yield gains during sideways trading periods. As mentioned in the preceding section, you may elect to protect the stock position with a longer-term put option and then sell calls each month until a breakout occurs or the long-put expiration month nears.

In addition to stock and option combination positions, you can extend the same concept to just option combination positions using a LEAPS contract in place of the stock leg. This approach typically reduces risk by reducing the overall cost of the position, especially the commission costs.

REMEMBER

Set your priorities straight. Managing risk comes before bringing in income. If your analysis suggests that prolonged sideways movement for a security you hold may set up a more bearish outlook for the stock, either exit the position or protect it with puts.

Things to consider with option combinations

One advantage options generally have over the individual stocks and ETFs that serve as the underlying for the options is that they generally require less of an investment. The end result is that you have less money at risk. The trade-off is that the entire asset can expire worthless. And so it goes for you on the trading side — there are a series of things to consider for every asset type you decide to use. That is why managing your risk should be your first priority. The only security considered to be risk-free is a U.S. Treasury Bill.

TIP

When a stock moves sideways for a period of time, it is said to be in a *consolidation* phase. The longer the consolidation, the greater the chance for a strong directional move away from this consolidation. The direction of the potential move is often the only open question.

Rather than a portfolio of individual stocks or ETFs, you may hold LEAPS contracts for different sectors or stocks. A covered call strategy can also be implemented using the LEAPS option as the sideways moving asset from which your income is boosted. You need to consider a few things if you go this route:

- Using a LEAPS contract as an underlying will subject you to margin requirements because the position technically represents a spread, not a pure covered call position.
- Spread strategies require a different option approval level from your broker — you may or may not be able to access these strategies depending on the account type (for example, IRAs).
- Because LEAPS are also subject to the same pricing factors as a regular option contract, IV conditions that are good for selling calls are not necessarily optimal for buying LEAPS. The strategy may work best on an existing position.
- The double-edged sword of IV may result in conditions where you're better off selling your LEAPS contract, which may have declined less than the underlying asset itself.

In addition to a LEAPS strategy, additional income may be generated from a calendar strategy using simply an existing long call. In this case, shorter-term calls are sold against a long call for the same underlying. Risk is moderately reduced by reducing your net investment in the position, and the same considerations apply as those listed for a LEAPS short-call approach.

REMEMBER

The option term *roll out* refers to the process where an existing option position is closed with an offsetting transaction, and a new similar position is created for a later expiration month.

Strategy shortlist

A few strategies covered in this book can either provide gains during sideways markets, moderately reduce risk, or do both, including the following:

- Long stock — covered call (limited-but-high risk position)
- Call credit spread (slightly out-of-the-money, or OTM)
- Put credit spread (slightly OTM)
- Call calendar
- Put calendar
- Call ratio spread (unlimited risk position)
- Put ratio spread (limited-but-high risk position)

Next up, two limited-risk strategies specifically designed to benefit from sideways market action: the butterfly and the condor.

Understanding Butterfly Positions

A *butterfly* is a strategy specifically designed to gain when a stock or ETF is trading sideways. Some characteristics of the strategy include the following:

- Limited risk and limited reward
- Can be created using calls or puts
- Combines two vertical spreads
- Is shorter term in nature
- Is generally created for a debit
- Maximizes gains when the underlying security remains within a trading range dictated by the option strike prices

A variation on the basic butterfly is the *iron butterfly*, which combines calls and puts. This position is generally created for a credit with time decay working in its favor.

TECHNICAL STUFF

A sideways moving market can also be referred to as *trendless* or *directionless*. An older terminology credited to veteran technical analyst Stan Weinstein called a sideways market a Stage 1 Market, with Stage 2 being a rising market, Stage 3 being a topping market, and Stage 4 being a declining market.

Defining the long butterfly

As with most of the strategies in this book, the butterfly comes in two varieties:

- Long call butterfly
- Long put butterfly

Both of these strategies combine a vertical credit spread and a vertical debit spread to capitalize on sideways moves in the markets. The strategy name (butterfly) comes from the three options used to create the position, as follows:

- **Body:** Two short options of the same type
- **Wing 1:** One long lower strike price option
- **Wing 2:** One long higher strike price option

Generally, the short option strike prices are at-the-money (ATM) or near the money, with profits maximized when the underlying closes at expiration at the short option strike price.

TIP

Always consider more than one strategy as possibly being suitable to current market conditions. You may decide that an alternate strategy does a better job of reducing your risk.

Call butterfly

A long call butterfly combines a bull call spread and bear call spread, using the same strike price for the short leg of each. It is a limited-risk, limited-reward position that is profitable during range-bound trading for the underlying stock or ETF.

The butterfly is constructed by creating two spreads:

- A bull call spread with a short option strike price that is near the money or ATM
- A bear call spread with the same short option strike price as the bull call spread

The maximum risk for the position is the initial debit, which is determined by subtracting the bear call spread credit from the bull call spread debit. (See Chapter 11 for more information on vertical spreads.)

TIP

The best way to think about risks and rewards for a butterfly is to remember that it combines two vertical spreads.

The long call butterfly strike prices compare to the spread strikes as follows:

- The lower strike price long call in the bull call spread is the lowest strike price call in the butterfly position and serves as the first wing.
- The two short options represent the next higher strike price and represent the body.
- The last call is the highest strike price in the group and comes from the long call in the bear call spread position.

Because the short options are approximately ATM, profits are maximized with the strategy when the stock moves very little and closes at the short option strike price on the last trading day before expiration. At this level, three of the four options expire worthless. The lower-priced long call will be ITM by an amount equal to the butterfly spread.

As price moves away from the short option strike price, profits diminish to the position breakeven levels where they are equal to zero. Beyond these price levels, the initial debit is the maximum risk.

REMEMBER

Because a butterfly combines three different options, you must consider trading costs when evaluating a specific position.

Suppose it's late July and you feel the market has finally settled into vacation doldrums after some initial summer volatility. You note the Average Directional Index (ADX) is declining below 20, and the 20-day and 30-day simple moving averages (SMAs) are relatively flat. ADX is a measure of the strength of a trend, not the trend's direction. In Figure 16-2, it is a warning sign that the uptrend is losing some strength.

The Diamonds ETF (DIA), which is based on the Dow Jones Industrials, is trading at $106.48, and you evaluate a few long call butterfly alternatives with August 106 calls serving as the strike price for the short options (body).

Figure 16-2 displays the daily price chart for DIA with the ADX and SMAs.

REMEMBER

Because butterflies combine vertical spreads, there are margin requirements for the position.

Different DIA butterfly spreads are discussed in the next section, so for now, assume the Aug 103-106-109 call butterfly spread was established. This trade shorthand translates to the following:

- Long 1 Aug 103 Call @ $4.00
- Short 2 Aug 106 Calls @ $1.45
- Long 1 Aug 109 Call @ $0.30

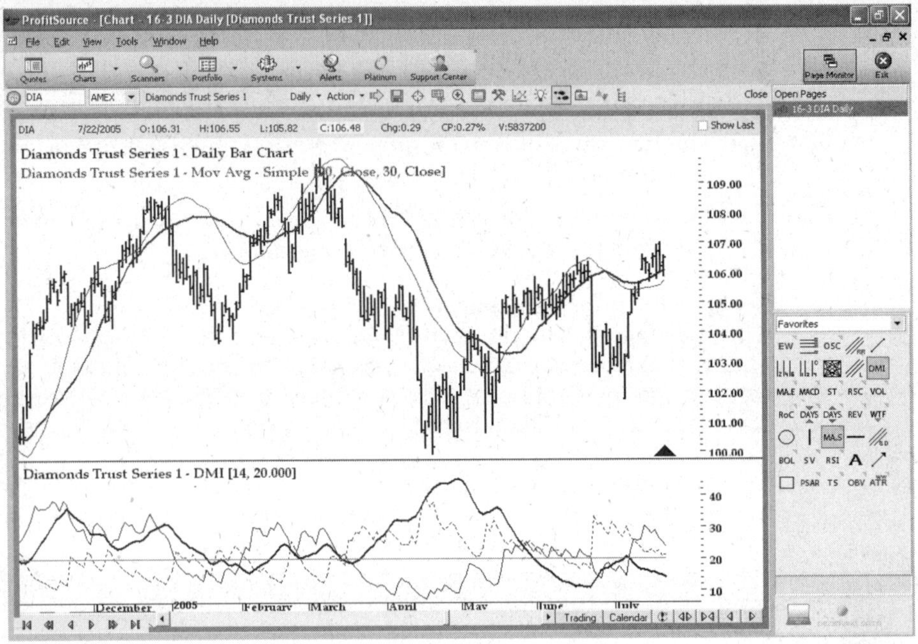

Figure 16-2: Daily price chart for DIA.

Image by Optionetics

Calculating the net debit for these options, you obtain the following:

> [(Wing 1 Option Price + Wing 2 Option Price) – (2 × Body Option Price)] × 100
>
> [(4.00 + 0.30) – (2 × 1.45)] × 100 = $140

To remember which options are long and short in the butterfly strategy, imagine a butterfly with a short body and long wings.

Figure 16-3 displays the risk chart for this butterfly position.

When maximum risk is identified for a position with short options, it's assumed that assignment risk will be managed properly by 1) meeting any assignment obligations with existing shares or exercising a long call, or 2) closing out any short options that could be potentially assigned over expiration weekend.

As always, you need to know the risk, reward, and breakevens for the position:

- **Maximum risk:** The initial debit of $140 is the maximum risk for the DIA Aug 103-106-109 call butterfly position.

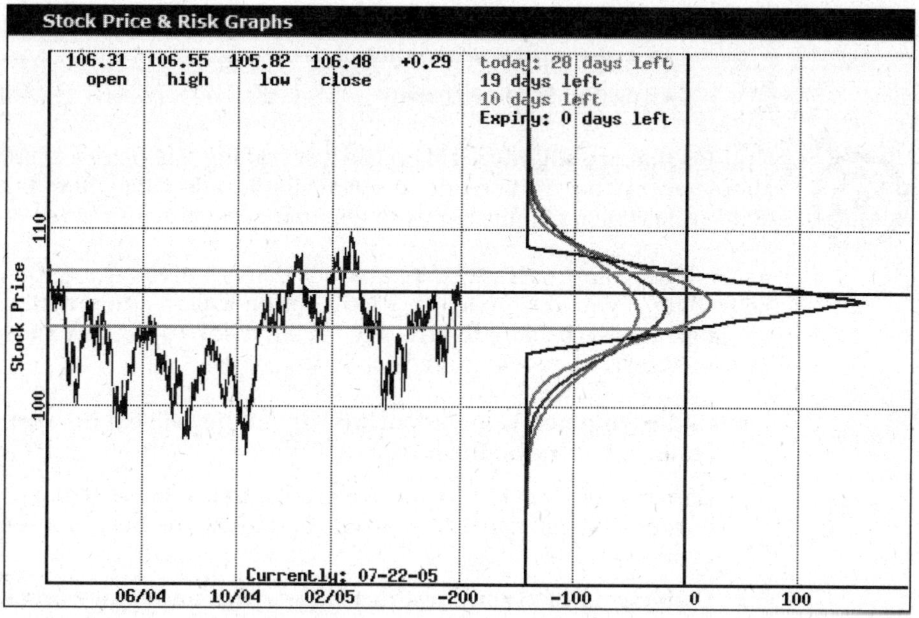

Figure 16-3: Risk chart for DIA Aug 103-106-109 call butterfly.

Image by Optionetics

- **Maximum reward:** There are a couple of ways to calculate the maximum reward for the position. You can either calculate each spread separately (as shown) or use a single butterfly formula (put butterfly example).
- **Bull call spread:**
  - [(Difference Between Strikes) – (Long Option Price – Short Option Price)] × 100
  - [(106 – 103) – (4.00 – 1.45)] × 100] = (3 – 2.55)] × 100] = $45.00
- **Bear call spread:** Initial credit
  - ($1.45 – 0.30) × 100 = $115
- **Call butterfly:**
  - Bull call spread maximum reward + Bear call spread maximum reward
  - $45 + $115 = $160
- **Upper breakeven:**
  - Highest strike price – initial debit
  - 109.00 – 1.40 = $107.60

- **Lower breakeven:**
  - Lowest strike price + initial debit
  - 103.00 + 1.40 = $104.40

Options that are slightly OTM on the last trading day before expiration will almost always have some offer price available, allowing you to buy it back at $0.05 or less plus commissions, to eliminate assignment risk.

As expiration approaches, there are four distinct areas where the stock could be trading. If you elect to sell any long option legs to either realize gains or minimize losses, be sure to also buy back the corresponding short option. The four areas to consider are as follows:

- **Underlying below lowest strike:** All options will expire worthless, realizing the maximum loss.
- **Underlying from the lower breakeven to the short strike price:** Close out the bull call spread for profits and allow the bear call spread to expire worthless.
- **Underlying between the short strike price and upper breakeven:** Close out the bull call spread plus the additional short call for profits.
- **Underlying above highest strike price:** Close out both spreads and realize maximum loss.

If assigned a short option early on, use the corresponding long option or evaluate costs to buy shares in the market to meet the short obligation (see the section "To exercise or not, that is the question" in Chapter 9).

Don't allow long options to expire worthless while you still have short option assignment risk. Properly manage a butterfly position into expiration weekend by focusing on potential risk.

In the DIA example provided, the ETF was trading at 105.73 into the close on the Friday before expiration. The bull call spread was closed out for $255 by completing the following transactions:

> Buy to Close 1 Aug 106 call @ $0.05 and simultaneously Sell to Close 1 Aug 103 call @ $2.60

Both options making up the bear call spread expired worthless. Because the initial debit was $140, the position gain was $115 ($255 – 140).

If you have a slightly bullish to neutral outlook, you can purchase a call butterfly using an OTM instead of ATM body.

Put butterfly

A long put butterfly combines a bull put spread and bear put spread, using the same strike price for the short leg of each spread. It is a limited-risk, limited-reward position that is profitable during range-bound trading for the underlying stock or ETF.

The butterfly is constructed by creating two spreads:

- A bull put spread with a short option strike price that is near the money or ATM
- A bear put spread with the same short option strike price as the bull put spread

The maximum risk for the position is the initial debit, which is determined by subtracting the bull put spread credit from the bear put spread debit. (See Chapter 11 for more information on vertical spreads.)

Calculate the net delta for the butterfly to identify the directional bias for the position.

Because both positions focus on range-bound markets, what would have happened if a put butterfly was used in place of a call butterfly for the DIA example? Before checking out an Aug 103-106-109 put butterfly for DIA, consider a few questions first — keep in mind that DIA was trading at $106.48 when the position was initiated and closed at $105.73 going into expiration:

- Would you expect the put butterfly spread to be higher or lower than the call butterfly spread, assuming the same strike prices were used?
- Using your first answer, would the range of profitability for the put butterfly be more or less than the call butterfly?
- Would you expect the gains for the put butterfly to be higher or lower?

Long put butterfly

Here is a likely scenario. It's late July . . . vacation doldrums . . . market's flat. DIA is trading at $106.48, and you're evaluating a long put butterfly spread with August 106 puts serving as the short option strike price (body). Assuming you purchase the Aug 103-106-109 put butterfly spread, the following position is created:

- Long 1 Aug 109 Put @ $2.85
- Short 2 Aug 106 Puts @ $0.85
- Long 1 Aug 103 Put @ $0.30

WARNING!

Look for liquid options to avoid additional trading costs in the form of *slippage*, which is the difference between the bid-ask spread. These costs can be significant given the number of legs used to create butterflies.

Calculating the net debit for these options, you obtain the following:

[(Wing 1 Option Price + Wing 2 Option Price) – (2 × Body Option Price)] × 100

[(2.85 + 0.30) – (2 × 0.85)] × 100 = $145

Figure 16-5 displays the risk chart for this butterfly position.

If you flip back quickly to Figure 16-3, you can hardly tell the difference between the two butterflies. Calculating the risk, reward, and breakevens for the position, you have the following:

- **Maximum risk:** The initial debit of $145 is the maximum risk for the DIA Aug 103-106-109 put butterfly position.
- **Maximum reward:** The maximum reward for a long butterfly position is a single spread value minus the initial debit.

  [(Difference Between Bull Put Spread Strikes × 100)] – (Initial Debit)

  [(106 – 103) × 100] – $145 = $155

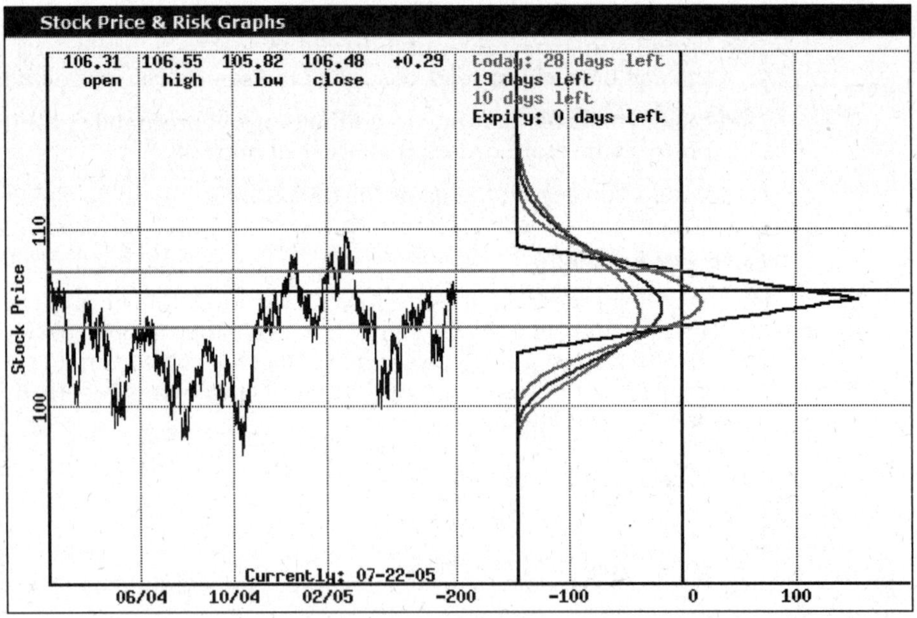

Image by Optionetics

Figure 16-4: Risk chart for DIA Aug 103-106-109 put butterfly.

- **Upper breakeven:** Highest strike price – initial debit

  109.00 – 1.45 = $107.55

- **Lower breakeven:** Lowest strike price + initial debit

  103.00 + 1.45 = $104.45

  The breakeven range is the same, but has shifted upward $0.05, reflecting the additional debit required to create the spread.

Many ETFs have dollar strike price increments, giving you a great deal of flexibility when selecting butterfly options. By varying the long and short option strike prices, you vary your risk profile.

Approaching expiration, you have four distinct areas where the stock could be trading. If you elect to sell any long option legs to either realize gains or minimize losses, be sure to also buy back the corresponding short option. Here are your positions and options:

- **Underlying below lowest strike:** Close out both spreads and realize maximum loss.
- **Underlying between lower breakeven and short strike price:** Close out the bull put spread plus the additional short put for profits.
- **Underlying at short strike price to upper breakevens:** Close out the bull put spread for profits and allow the bear put spread to expire worthless.
- **Underlying above highest strike price:** All options will expire worthless, realizing the maximum loss.

Because vertical spreads create a naturally hedged position for the floor trader, they are desired orders. Try to execute the order below the market price by shaving a little bit off the debit-limit amount for your order.

With DIA trading at 105.73 into the close on the Friday before expiration, the bear put spread was closed out for $295 by completing the following transactions:

> Buy to Close Aug 2 106 puts @ $0.35 and simultaneously Sell to Close Aug 103 put @ $3.30

The long option for the bull put spread expired worthless. Because the initial debit was $145, the position gain was $150 ($295 – 145). This higher return should be expected, given the moderately bearish move for the ETF.

Be prepared for potential setbacks and give yourself time when executing these trades. Combination orders may take additional time to execute, so keep this in mind if you want to cancel and replace the limit amount for the trade — the market may have moved by the time the order is updated.

In this example, the short options were approximately ATM, so profits are maximized when the stock closes at the short option strike price on the last trading day before expiration. At this level, three of the four options expire worthless. The higher-priced long put will be ITM by an amount equal to the butterfly spread.

As price moves away from the short option strike price, profits diminish to the position breakeven levels where they are equal to zero. Beyond these price levels, the initial debit is the maximum risk.

Digging deeper into butterfly risk

When selecting a butterfly spread, you need to make some trade-offs in terms of risk and reward, along with the range of profitability for the position and its directional bias. This applies to both call and put long butterflies. In general, the following hold true:

- Using an OTM option for the body increases directional bias
- Increasing the spread distance increases the range of profitability
- Increasing the spread distance decreases the reward-risk ratio

TIP

If you have a slightly bearish-to-neutral outlook, you can purchase a put butterfly using an OTM instead of ATM body.

Paper trading helps you see how these trade-offs impact your trade success without having money on the line during your learning curve. Paper trading is especially useful in implementing these more complex strategies.

Narrow wings — smaller risk

When you decrease the spread distance for long butterflies, you also decrease the risk. This is true for vertical spreads as well. By using the DIA long call butterfly spread example and narrowing the spread, Table 16-1 provides the position impact.

In this table, the initial debit is the Butterfly Risk, and the Breakeven Range is the difference in breakevens divided by the short option strike price of 106.

TIP

Calculate the range of profitability for a butterfly by obtaining the difference in breakevens and dividing it by the security's price to get a quick feel of whether the range is reasonable given past movement in the underlying security.

Table 16-1 Narrowing the Spread for Aug DIA Butterflies

Butterfly Strikes	Butterfly Risk	Max Reward	Reward-Risk	Breakeven Range	Butterfly Delta
105-106-107	30	70	2.33	1.3%	–3.7
104-106-108	75	125	1.67	2.4%	–10.1
103-106-109	140	160	1.14	3.0%	–16.6

Here are a few observations you should make as you decrease the butterfly spread distance:

- The risk decreases and the reward-risk increases
- The breakeven range decreases
- The directional bias generally becomes more neutral

Both art and science are involved in this. Most importantly, you need to properly manage your risk, but also be realistic about the range in which the underlying will travel.

Wider wings — bigger risk

When trading a sideways market, you may be tempted to push the envelope and maximize potential gains from a position. The downside is that if you increase the spread distance for long butterflies, you also increase the position risk. Once again using the DIA call example as a starting point, Table 16-2 provides similar data to Table 16-1, creating wider spreads for the butterfly.

Table 16-2 Widening the Spread for Aug DIA Butterflies

Butterfly Strikes	Butterfly Risk	Max Reward	Reward-Risk	Breakeven Range	Butterfly Delta
103-106-109	140	160	1.14	3.0%	-16.6
102-106-110	215	185	0.86	3.5%	-20.7
101-106-111	305	195	0.64	3.7%	-25.3

Here are a few observations you should make as you increase the spread distance:

- The risk increases and the reward-risk decreases.
- The breakeven range increases.
- The directional bias generally becomes more bearish for a call butterfly and bullish for a put butterfly.

In the case of the long call butterfly, as the bearish directional bias increases, the following happens:

- The position realizes increased losses for bullish moves in the underlying, to a point (the upper breakeven).
- The position realizes increased gains for bearish moves in the underlying, to a point (the lower breakeven).

If you're trading different underlying securities, explore different-sized spreads to get a feel for what's suitable for the security and your risk preferences. Fortunately, the limited-risk nature of the strategy provides you with the time needed to build your butterfly skills.

REMEMBER

Always check the news when you see big drops or advances in a company stock. You need to beware of adjusted options resulting from a potential corporate action. It's also just as important to know significant news impacting the underlying for options you trade. Pay special attention to where the news is most likely to have a short- or longer-term impact on the shares.

Creating an iron butterfly

The long iron butterfly is a twist on call-and-put butterflies that allows you to create the position for a credit. You do this by using a bear call spread and a bull put spread, both for a credit. The position remains one that has limited risk and limited reward. It also relies on sideways movement to maximize gains. In the category of "you don't get something for nothing," these spreads require additional margin because both vertical spreads are credit positions.

The call-and-put butterfly

The iron butterfly combines two vertical credit spreads to capitalize on sideways movement in a stock as follows:

- A bear call spread with a short option strike price that is near the money or ATM

- A bull put spread with a short option strike price that is near or ATM and the same strike price as the short call

Brokers may base iron butterfly margin requirements on a short straddle–long strangle combination instead of two vertical credit spreads. Check with your broker for their specific requirements before creating a position.

The vertical-spread differences are the same for the two credit spreads; the maximum risk for the position is the difference in strike prices for one vertical spread minus the initial credit. The long iron butterfly has strike prices that line up like this:

- The lowest strike price is a long put.
- The next lowest strike price is a short put.
- The same strike price is used for a short call.
- The highest strike price is a long call.

When creating the iron butterfly, you use the same strike price for the short option. The initial credit you receive when establishing the position is your maximum reward.

Iron butterfly risk

Using an iron butterfly with a wider spread reduces the reward-risk ratio for this position. This next example uses a stock that typically moves more quietly (100-day HV 12%), with slightly low IV levels relative to the last 12 months.

Corporate actions can lead to adjustments to existing option contracts. Be sure to check the specs for the options you use, especially when the prices seem off. Stock splits and dividends are the most common corporate actions that can affect your options.

Long iron butterfly example

It's mid-June, and after a big drop in the stock three months ago, MO has returned to a more typical trading range. It turns out it had a spinoff that changed the company's valuation (see Chapter 10 for information about adjustments to existing options due to corporate actions). MO is trading around $70, and after deciding the spinoff shouldn't impact the stock going forward, you evaluate the following iron butterfly:

- Long 1 Jul 60 Put @ $0.05
- Short 1 Jul 70 Put @ $1.20

- Short 1 Jul 70 Call @ $1.30
- Long 1 Jul 80 Call @ $0.05

So now, instead of a $3 spread on index-based stock trading around $106, you've increased the spread to $10 on a $70 stock.

An iron butterfly combines four different options — remember to consider your trading costs, including any applicable margin, before entering a position.

Calculating the net credit for these options, you obtain the following credit, which is your maximum reward:

Bear Call Spread Credit + Bull Put Spread Credit

[(1.30 – 0.05) + (1.20 – 0.05)] × 100 = $240

Because both spreads are the same distance, the maximum risk is the difference between the two strike prices minus the initial credit:

[(Difference in Strike Prices × 100)] – Initial Credit

[(80 – 70) – $240] = $760

Figure 16-5 displays the risk chart for the MO iron butterfly position.

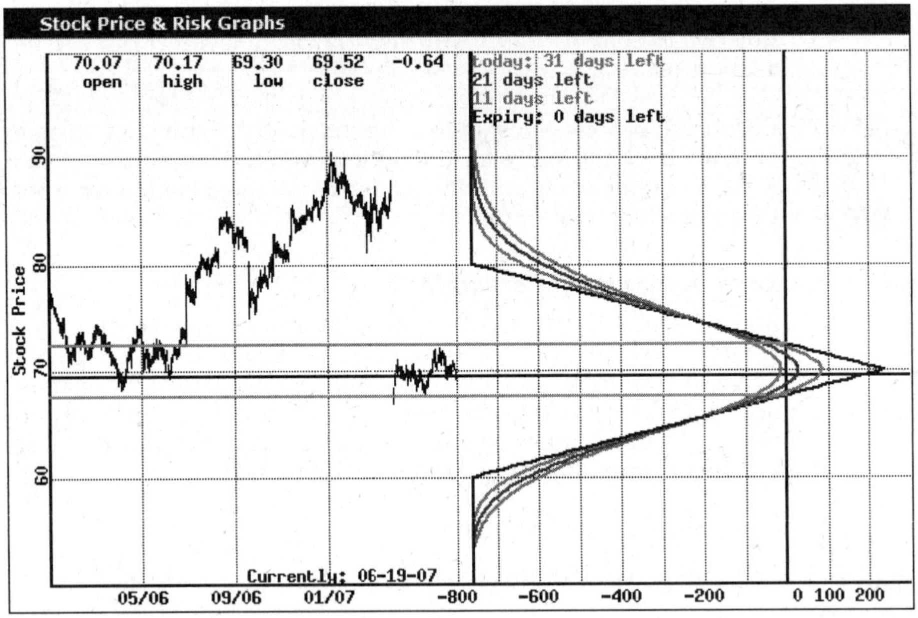

Figure 16-5: Risk chart for MO Jul 60-70-80 iron butterfly.

Image by Optionetics

The breakeven calculation is centered on the short option strike price:

- **Upper breakeven:**
  - Short call strike price + initial credit
  - 70.00 + 2.40 = $72.40
- **Lower breakeven:**
  - Short put strike price – initial credit
  - 70.00 – 2.40 = $67.60

WARNING!

Spreads can be tricky. Always manage your assignment risk into expiration weekend. Don't assume a short option will expire worthless when the underlying is trading near the short option strike price.

As expiration approaches, there are four distinct areas where the stock could be trading. If you elect to sell any long option legs to either realize gains or minimize losses, be sure to also buy back the corresponding short option. Here are your options:

- **Underlying below the long put strike:** Both put options are ITM, and the maximum risk for the bull put spread is realized. The maximum reward is realized for the bear call spread.
- **Underlying from the lower breakeven to the short strike price:** Partial profits are realized for the bull put spread. The maximum reward is realized for the bear call spread.
- **Underlying from the short strike price to the upper breakeven:** Partial profits are realized for the bear call spread. The maximum reward is realized for the bull put spread.
- **Underlying above the call strike price:** Both call options are ITM, and the maximum risk for the bear call spread is realized. The maximum reward is realized for the bull put spread.

If assigned early on a short option, use the corresponding long option or evaluate costs to buy shares in the market to meet the short obligation (see Chapter 9).

In the MO example provided, the stock was trading at 69.80 into the close on the Friday before expiration. The short put position was bought back for $20, and the remaining options expired worthless. Because the initial credit was $240, the net gain was $220 (240 – 20).

TIP

The impact of dividends already declared are priced into the value of existing call and put options if they expire after the dividend is issued. It is new dividend declarations that can affect the value of options you hold.

Understanding Condor Positions

The *condor* relates to a butterfly in the same way that a strangle relates to a straddle — it splits the center strike price (see Chapter 14). The condor then combines two vertical spreads for the same type of option (call or put) using four different strike prices. Condors do the following:

- Increase the range of profitability versus a similar butterfly
- Decrease the maximum reward versus a similar butterfly

Condors are limited-risk, limited-reward positions that rely on sideways trading action in the underlying to maximize profits.

Evaluate limited-risk positions before high- to unlimited-risk positions so you can make a strategy comparison prior to establishing a new position.

Defining a condor spread

There are actually three types of long condors available to you for trading:

- Long call condor
- Long put condor
- Long iron condor

The iron condor combines a bear call credit spread and a bull put credit spread, with the short option legs at least one strike price apart.

Single type condors

Long call condors and long put condors allow for more movement in the underlying stock during the life of the trade than a similar call or put butterfly position. The trade-off is that you have a better chance of making a profit, but that profit will be smaller.

HV does not predict future prices, and IV may incorporate factors beyond HV. Regardless, using past HV and IV data provides you with valuable information when evaluating strategies because it frames the potential for future movements and allows you to make better educated guesses about potential positions.

Suppose a stock is trading at $134.45. You can create the following positions expiring in 31 days that include 10-point vertical spreads:

- A call or put butterfly using a short strike price of $135 (125-135-145)
- A call or put condor using $130 and $140 strike prices for the short options (120-130-140-150)

When evaluating strategies, you need to decide whether the higher probability gain using a condor is worth the additional risk. In this particular example, your risk is almost three times your potential reward. Your risk using a butterfly is less than your potential reward, but the stock can only travel in a range of 8%, versus 11% for the condors.

Similar strategies will provide different advantages and disadvantages in terms of risk, reward, and breakeven, depending on a variety of factors. Be sure to evaluate a few alternatives.

The actual comparison between different strategy statistics is impacted by the specific underlying stock, option strike prices, and spreads used. The choice between risk-reward-versus-profitability-range alternatives will not always be so clear. If the stock was trading at a midpoint between two strike prices, all the statistics for both strategies would be closer. The main point to keep in mind is that when you're selecting a trade that seeks to capitalize on sideways movement, explore different strategies and spread alternatives.

Iron butterflies and iron condors combine call and put vertical spreads rather than combining vertical spreads for just calls or just puts.

Iron condors

Throwing an iron condor into the mix for the butterfly-condor comparison, a similar table can be created using an iron butterfly versus an iron condor. Using a stock trading at $134.45, the following positions expire in 31 days:

- An iron butterfly using a short strike price of $135 (125-135-145)
- An iron condor using $130 and $140 strike prices for the short options (120-130-140-150)

Again, the iron condor increases the profitability range, but sacrifices potential gains while taking on additional risk. Both positions combine two vertical credit spreads (call plus put), so the margin requirement can be significant.

Always contact your broker prior to implementing new strategies to determine the margin requirement calculations and approval levels for the strategy. Condor and butterfly strategies are not for beginners. They are strategies you can work on with paper trades as you progress with your options trading.

Recognizing condor risks

As you gain experience and work through these strategies on paper, you will recognize their possibilities and their limitations. What is clear is that these positions can be managed depending on changes in the market, the underlying, and how each part of the trade evolves and responds to market conditions.

Thus, butterflies and condors are not all or nothing positions — you can close out either or both spreads for the position to reduce the maximum risk level if you choose to do so. Just remember that after creating a limited-risk position, you want to keep it that way. Don't remove legs that will expose you to unlimited risk.

Condor risk profiles

As expiration approaches, there are four distinct areas where the stock could be trading relative to the condor strike prices. If you elect to sell any long option legs to either realize gains or minimize losses, be sure to also buy back the corresponding short option.

If assigned early on a short option, use the corresponding long option or evaluate costs to buy shares in the market to meet the short obligation (see Chapter 9).

REMEMBER

Even if you don't have access to an options-analysis software package, understand the risk graph for strategies you're evaluating.

Iron condor risk profile

The original example used in this chapter was for an ETF trading at 106.48 with $1 strike price increments. Using the same trade setup, an iron condor can be created with slightly OTM short options to explore the iron condor risk profile.

Creating a $3 spread iron condor for DIA trading at $106.48, you have the following:

- Long 1 Aug 103 Put @ $0.30
- Short 1 Aug 106 Put @ $0.85
- Short 1 Aug 107 Call @ $0.85
- Long 1 Aug 110 Put @ $0.15

The maximum reward is the initial credit, and the maximum risk is one spread difference minus this credit. Calculating these values, you have the following:

- **Maximum reward:**
  - $[(0.85 - 0.15) + (0.85 - 0.30)] \times 100 = \$125$

- **Maximum risk:**
  - (3 × 100) – $125 = $175

It's easy to forget that options are essentially derivatives of the underlying. So, after calculating breakeven levels, ask yourself whether the stock will realistically trade in the area(s) of profitability during the life of the trade.

Calculating the breakevens using short option strike prices and initial credit:

- **Lower breakeven:**
  - Short Put Strike Price – Initial Credit = 106 – 1.25 = 104.75
- **Upper breakeven:**
  - Short Call Strike Price + Initial Credit = 107 + 1.25 = 108.25

Figure 16-6 displays the risk chart for the DIA iron condor position.

By increasing the bear call spread by one point and combining puts and calls to create the position, the maximum risk was increased $35 (25%), the maximum reward reduced by $35 (22%), and the breakeven ranged increased 0.30 (9%). This reflects a pretty good improvement when you can better split the price of the underlying between the two short options.

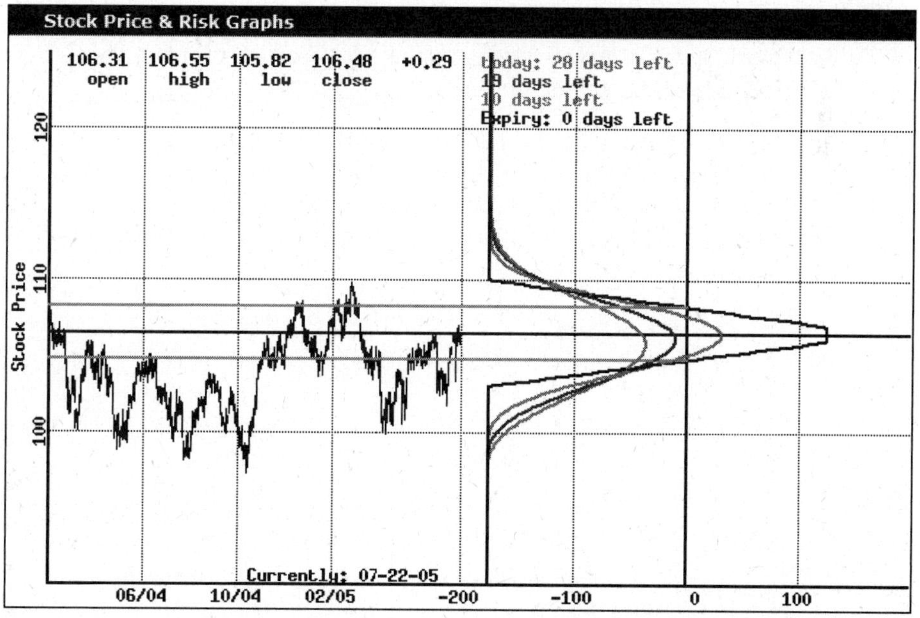

Figure 16-6: Risk chart for DIA Jul 103-106-107-110 iron condor.

Image by Optionetics

REMEMBER

Work it out before your risk real money. Paper trading really makes a difference because it allows you to understand strategy mechanics without risking capital.

Because the underlying closed at 105.73 going into expiration weekend, the short 106 put would have been bought back at $0.35 for a net position profit of $90, versus $115 for the long call butterfly and $150 for the long put butterfly. The condor's sweet spot was a closing value between $106 and 107.

Part V

The Part of Tens

Get an extra Part of Tens chapter at `http://www.dummies.com/extras/tradingoptions`.

In this part . . .

- Ten great strategies for option traders
- Ten things to do and not do as an option trader

Chapter 17

Ten Top Option Strategies

In This Chapter

- Developing an option strategy list
- Trading with a focus on risk

Trading is part art, part science, part adaptability to markets, and part experience. Sometimes you have to rely on your gut, although it's best if your gut has had experience in telling you what to do and has a good record of calling it right when you need it to.

But let's not get into a Zen detour here. You can check out *Meditation For Dummies* (2012) and *Stress Management For Dummies* (2013), both published by John Wiley & Sons, if you like. This book is still about developing specific rules and steps to follow as part of a process that gets you up and running on a path toward skillful trading. It is also equally about implementing these rules and steps with a focus on managing risk that gives you the time needed to develop your craft — and gives your gut something to work with.

A great first step on the science side is creating a strategy list. A strategy list allows you to methodically approach a new type of trade so that you gain the most knowledge and experience possible.

To get you started, this chapter outlines ten great option strategies. The common thread here is that they have limited risk and are alternatives for you to consider. The unlimited-risk or limited-but-high risk strategies they could potentially replace are provided with the strategy summary.

Each top ten strategy includes the following:

- Strategy name and components
- Risks and rewards
- Optimal market conditions (trends, volatility)
- Advantages and disadvantages

- Basic risk profiles
- Additional information by strategy

Some option strategies require margin. Ask your broker for details before you put any trading technique to work.

By all means, consider adding notes to these to make them your own. The more you study each individual strategy, the faster you will find the ones that work best for you.

Timing is essential. Each strategy listed has a reference regarding the optimal timing of deployment. Make it a habit to study the market and look for specific conditions that are best suited for each strategy.

Married Put

A *married put* combines long stock with a long put for protection. The position is created by purchasing the stock and put at the same time, but the key is creating put protection and managing the risk of stock ownership. Buying a put for existing stock or rolling out an option to a later expiration month remains true to that strategy goal. Long out-of-the-money (OTM) options should be sold 30–45 days before expiration. Table 17-1 gives you some ideas on strategy, and Figure 17-1 shows you a married put risk profile.

Table 17-1 Married Put Summary

Strategy	***Outcome***
Components	Long Stock + Long Put
Risk/Reward	Limited risk, unlimited reward
Replaces	Long stock with limited but high risk
Max Risk	[(Stock Price + Put Price) – Put Strike Price] × 100
Max Reward	Unlimited
Breakeven	Stock Price + Put Price
Conditions	Bullish, low IV
Margin	Not typically required — check with broker
Advantages	Changes limited but high risk to limited risk
Disadvantages	Increases cost of position by option premium

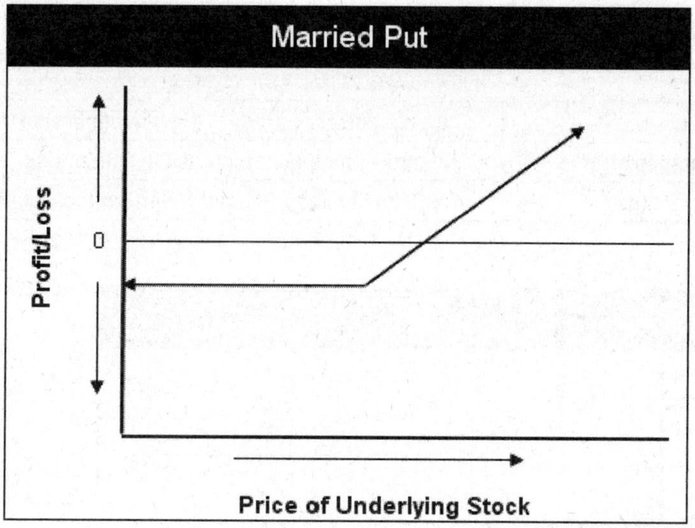

Image by Optionetics

Figure 17-1: Married put risk profile.

Collar

A *collar* combines long stock with long put protection and a short call that reduces the cost of protection. The call premium is a credit that offsets, at least partially, the cost of the put. Timing this strategy's execution is a worthy goal. An optimal scenario occurs when you can buy the stock and long put during low volatility conditions, allowing you to buy longer-term protection. Calls are sold as volatility increases, and there are 30–45 days to expiration, so that time decay accelerates short call gains. Check out the summary in Table 17-2 and the profile in Figure 17-2.

Table 17-2 Collar Summary

Strategy	*Outcome*
Components	Long Stock + Long Put + Short Call
Risk/Reward	Limited risk, limited reward
Replaces	Long stock with limited but high risk
Max Risk	[Stock Price + (Option Debit) – Put Strike Price] × 100
Max Reward	[(Call Strike Price – Stock Price) + (Option Debit)] × 100
Breakeven	Stock Price + (Option Debit)
Conditions	Bullish, low IV that increases

(Continued)

Table 17-2 *(Continued)*

Strategy	*Outcome*
Margin	Not typically required — check with broker
Advantages	Changes limited but high risk to limited risk
Disadvantages	Replaces unlimited reward with limited reward

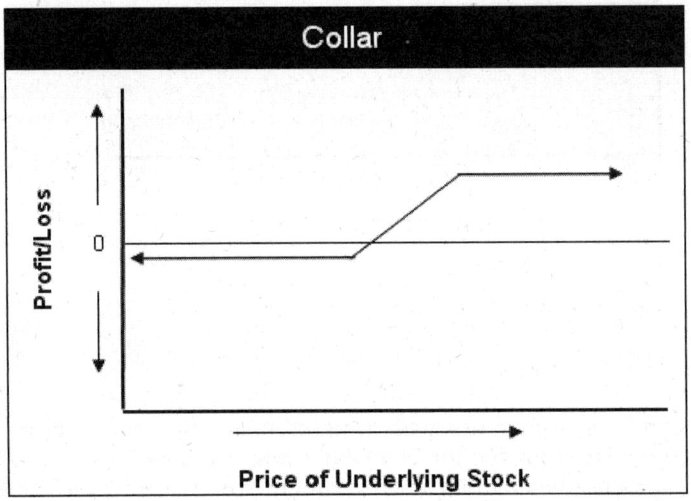

Figure 17-2: Collar risk profile.

Image by Optionetics

Long Put Trader

A *long put* is a limited-risk, bearish position that gains when the underlying declines. This is a much better bet than an unlimited-risk, short stock position that requires more capital to establish. The bearish move must occur by option expiration, and out-of-the-money (OTM) puts should be exited 30–45 days prior to expiration. See Table 17-3 for a summary of strategies and Figure 17-3 for an example of the profile.

Table 17-3 Long Put Summary

Strategy	*Outcome*
Components	Long put
Risk/Reward	Limited risk, limited but high reward
Replaces	Short stock with unlimited risk

Strategy	*Outcome*
Max Risk	Put Premium: (Put Price × 100)
Max Reward	(Put Strike Price – Put Price) × 100
Breakeven	Put Strike Price – Put Price
Conditions	Bearish, low IV that increases
Margin	Not required
Advantages	Changes unlimited risk to limited risk
Disadvantages	Time constraints for move to occur due to expiration

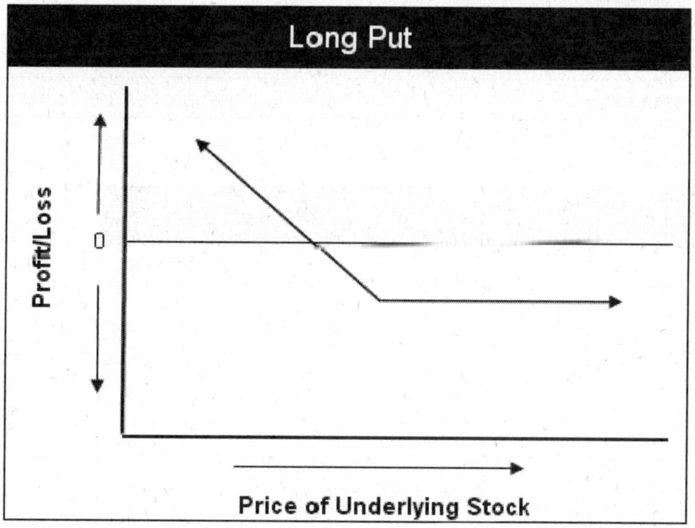

Figure 17-3: Long put risk profile.

Image by Optionetics

LEAPS Call Investor

A Long-term Equity AnticiPation Security (LEAPS) call option reduces the cost and risk associated with a long stock position. The position is best established when implied volatility (IV) is relatively low. One drawback is that the LEAPS owner doesn't participate in dividend distributions, which reduce the stock value. At the same time, the amount risked in the position will be less than owning the stock outright. See Table 17-4 for a summary of investment strategies and Figure 17-4 for an example of the profile.

Table 17-4	LEAPS Call Investor Summary
Strategy	***Outcome***
Components	Long call with expiration greater than nine months
Risk/Reward	Limited risk, unlimited reward
Replaces	Long stock with limited but high risk
Max Risk	Call Premium: (Call Price × 100)
Max Reward	Unlimited
Breakeven	Strike Price – LEAPS Price
Conditions	Bullish, low IV that increases
Margin	Not required
Advantages	Changes limited but high risk to limited risk
Disadvantages	Pay for time value that erodes and misses dividends

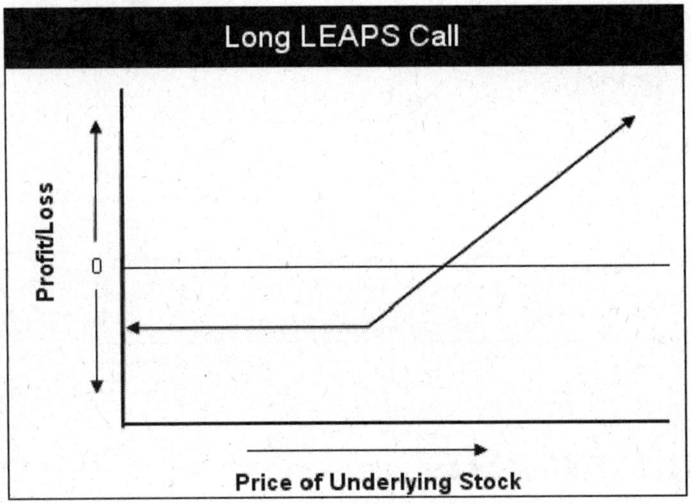

Figure 17-4: LEAPS call risk profile.

Image by Optionetics

Diagonal Spread

A *diagonal spread* combines a short near-month option with a long later-month option of the same type. When the strike prices are the same, it is referred to as a *calendar spread.* A near-term neutral view allows you to sell the short option to offset the long option costs. A call diagonal is described here, but a put diagonal works equally well when you're bearish longer term. See Table 17-5 for a summary of investment strategies and Figure 17-5 for an example of the profile.

Table 17-5 Call Diagonal Spread Summary

Strategy	*Outcome*
Components	Long Lower Strike Call + Short, near month call
Risk/Reward	Limited risk, potential unlimited reward*
Replaces	Long call
Max Risk	(Long Call Price – Short Call Price) × 100
Max Reward	* Unlimited when short call expires worthless
Breakeven	Detailed
Conditions	Neutral with IV time skew, then trending
Margin	Required
Advantages	Reduces cost of long option
Disadvantages	A fast, bullish move results in limited reward

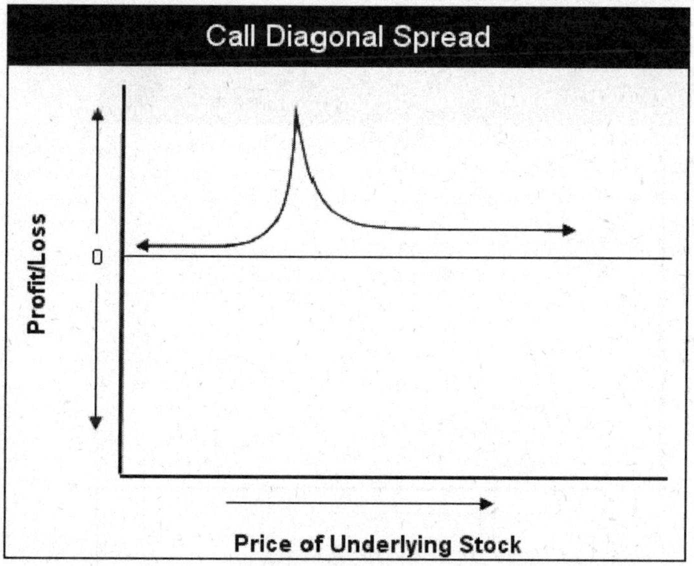

Figure 17-5: Call diagonal spread risk profile.

Image by Optionetics

Bear Call Credit Spread

A *bear call spread* combines a short, lower strike price call and a long, higher strike price call expiring the same month. It creates a credit and replaces a short call with unlimited risk. Again, timing is important in the deployment of this strategy. It's best applied when IV is high and there are fewer than 30 days to expiration. See Table 17-6 for a summary of investment strategies and Figure 17-6 for an example of the profile.

Table 17-6	Bear Call Credit Spread Summary
Strategy	***Outcome***
Components	Short Lower Strike Price Call + Long Higher Strike Price Call (same month)
Risk/Reward	Limited risk, limited reward
Replaces	Short option
Max Risk	(Difference between Strike Prices – Initial Credit) × 100
Max Reward	Initial Credit
Breakeven	Short Strike Price + Net Credit
Conditions	Bearish, high IV
Margin	Required
Advantages	Reduces risk from unlimited to limited
Disadvantages	Reduces reward from limited-but-high to limited

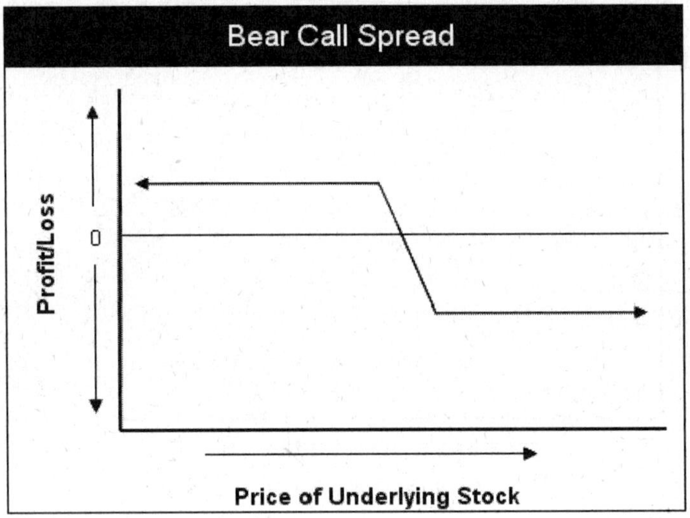

Image by Optionetics

Figure 17-6: Bear call credit spread risk profile.

Straddle

A *straddle* combines a long call with a long put using the same strike price and expiration. It's created when volatility is low and expected to increase and gains when prices moves strongly up or down. This is a useful strategy to set up before an important announcement such as an earnings or key economic report release. It may be useful with an underlying stock in the former scenario and with an ETF in the latter. Because there are two long options, exit the position with 30–45 days to expiration to avoid time decay. See Table 17-7 for a summary of investment strategies and Figure 17-7 for an example of the profile.

Table 17-7 Straddle Summary

Strategy	*Outcome*
Components	Long Call + Long Put (same strike price, month)
Risk/Reward	Limited risk, high to unlimited reward
Replaces	Single option with directional bias (call or put)
Max Risk	Net Debit: (Call Price + Put Price) × 100
Max Reward	Up: Unlimited, Down: (Strike Price – Net Debit) × 100
Breakeven1	Strike Price + Net Option Prices
Breakeven2	Strike Price – Net Options Prices
Conditions	Neutral, low IV with strong moves expected in both
Margin	Not required
Advantages	Reduces directional risk of single option position
Disadvantages	Increases cost of single option position

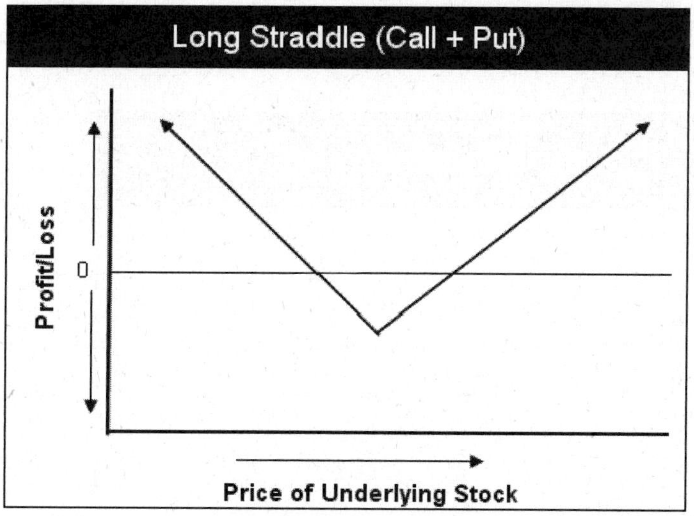

Image by Optionetics

Figure 17-7: Straddle risk profile.

Call Ratio Backspread

A *call ratio backspread* combines long higher strike price calls with a lesser number of short lower strike calls expiring the same month. It's best implemented for a credit and is a limited-risk, potentially unlimited reward position that is most profitable when a strong bullish move occurs.
See Table 17-8 for a summary of investment strategies and Figure 17-8 for an example of the profile.

Table 17-8 Call Ratio Backspread Summary

Strategy	*Outcome*
Components	Long Calls + Less Lower Strike Short Calls (same month)
Risk/Reward	Limited risk, potential unlimited reward
Replaces	Bear call credit spread
Max Risk	Limited: Detailed, see Chapter 15
Max Reward	Up: Unlimited, Down: Initial Credit
Breakevens	Detailed, see strategy discussion in Chapter 15
Conditions	Bullish, IV skew with strong increase in price and IV
Margin	Required
Advantages	Changes limited reward to unlimited reward
Disadvantages	Initial credit less, complex calculations

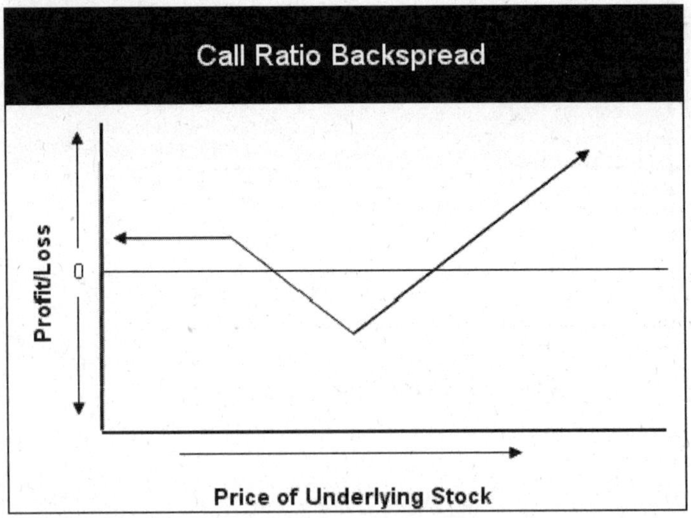

Figure 17-8: Call ratio backspread risk profile.

Image by Optionetics

Put Ratio Backspread

A *put ratio backspread* combines long lower strike price puts with a lesser number of short higher strike puts expiring the same month. It's best implemented for a credit and is a limited risk — limited, but a potentially high-reward position. It is most profitable when a strong bearish move occurs. See Table 17-9 for a summary of investment strategies and Figure 17-9 for an example of the profile.

Table 17-9 Put Ratio Backspread Summary

Strategy	*Outcome*
Components	Long Puts + Less Higher Strike Short Puts (same month)
Risk/Reward	Limited risk, limited but potentially high reward
Replaces	Bull put credit spread
Max Risk	Limited: Detailed, see Chapter 15
Max Reward	Up: Initial Credit, Down: (Long Strike Price + Initial Credit) × 100
Breakevens	Detailed, see strategy discussion in Chapter 15
Conditions	Bearish, IV skew with strong decline and increased IV
Margin	Required
Advantages	Changes limited reward to limited-but-high reward
Disadvantages	Initial credit less, complex calculations

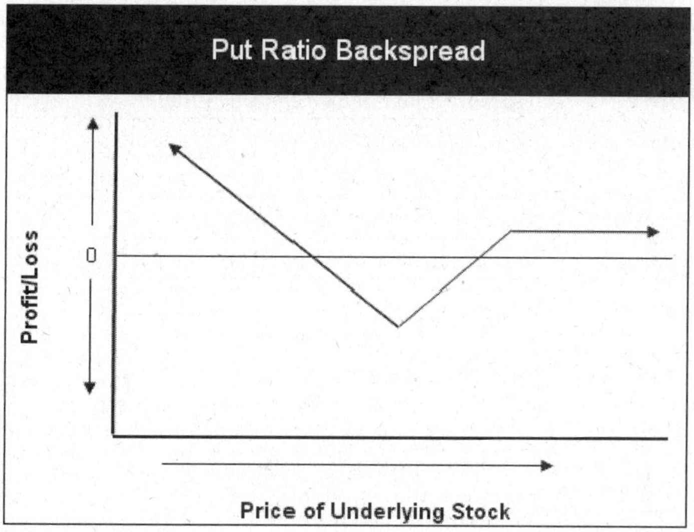

Figure 17-9: Put ratio backspread risk profile.

Image by Optionetics

Long Put Butterfly

A *long put butterfly* combines a bull put spread and a bear put spread expiring the same month for a debit. The two short puts have the same strike price and make up the body. The two long puts have different strike prices (above and below the body) and make up the wings. Time decay helps the trade. See Table 17-10 for a summary of investment strategies and Figure 17-10 for an example of the profile.

TIP

Consider organizing these strategies in categories that allow you to combine key shared characteristics. One way to do it would be to list all the strategies that require margin versus those that don't. This would let you ease your risk tolerance and financial situation over time from one type of strategy to another.

REMEMBER

Paper trading is the best way to avoid major problems with any trading strategy.

Table 17-10 Long Put Butterfly Summary

Strategy	***Outcome***
Components	Bear Put Spread + Bull Put Spread (same month)
Risk/Reward	Limited risk, limited reward
Replaces	Short straddle
Max Risk	Net Debit: [(Lowest Strike Put Price + Highest Strike Put Price) – (2 × Middle Strike Put Price)] × 100
Max Reward	[(Highest Strike Price – Middle Strike Price) × 100] – Net Debit
Breakeven 1	Highest Strike Price – Net Debit Price
Breakeven 2	Lowest Strike Price + Net Debit Price
Conditions	Sideways to moderately bearish, IV skew
Margin	Required
Advantages	Changes unlimited risk to limited risk
Disadvantages	Trading costs associated with three positions

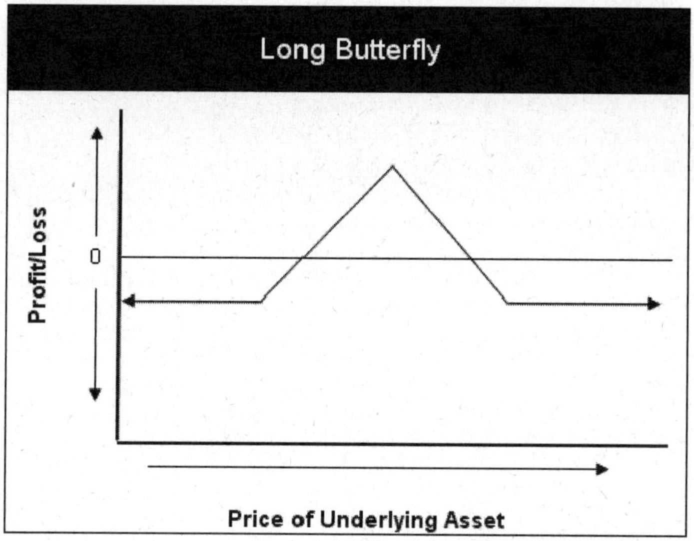

Figure 17-10: Long put butterfly risk profile.

Image by Optionetics

Chapter 18

Ten Do's and Don'ts in Options Trading

In This Chapter

- Understanding what makes a trader successful
- Creating your success

Trading is all about preparation with a hefty dose of obsessive compulsive attention to detail, and the understanding that things could go against you, which is why risk management is your first objective. The markets don't care who you are or what you stand for. All they know is that you've got money that they want to take from you. To become a trader, you must understand that so deeply that it becomes part of your DNA, or you will lose a lot of money in a hurry. That's why developing as a trader begins with using a formula-type trading plan as part of your approach to the markets along with being familiar with different strategies. Skillfully applying your trading plan as a seasoned pro requires practice, patience, and experience. It's a journey that, ideally, you must welcome, hone, and implement as part of your life.

Hopefully, in this book you'll find plenty of rules, steps, and concrete methods to take away with you. This book is meant to provide you with some important trading nuances . . . things that can't quite be mechanically applied. This chapter focuses on those.

Do Focus on Managing Risk

Managing risk is the name of the game and your number one priority. The less money that you can manage to lose, the better off you will be. In fact, when people ask you about your trading and what you do, tell them you're a risk manager. Become one with it. How's that for nuance? It could make you popular at dinner parties too — or not.

By just exploring option strategies, you are actively addressing other financial risks in your life. These include inflation risk, income risk, and even market risk associated with buy-and-hold investing. The study of options trading — because it is all about risk management, attention to detail, and planning your exit before you make a decision to trade in real time is likely to subconsciously rewire the way your brain look at the markets, and perhaps life.

When your trading is built on risk management, you train yourself to

- Thoroughly understand the risks and rewards associated with the markets you trade.
- Learn and test strategies before putting money on the line.
- Create a plan that identifies trade sizes entry and exit approaches and maximum loss allowed.
- Identify how the plan will be implemented to honor your risk parameters.
- Understand how to establish positions and manage a trade, including communication with your broker regarding any margin requirements for complex options strategies.
- Have a plan for taking profits.
- Ask yourself, "What if I'm wrong?"

Other, more general risk considerations include diversifying sectors and strategies traded. You may properly allocate trade sizes, but if you enter five trending trades using the same strategy on stocks in the same sector, well then, you've kind of gone against that trade-sizing rule. That's the nuance. By extending these guidelines on a portfolio basis, you're acting more as an effective risk manager.

Don't Avoid Losses

There is an old adage in trading: *Keep your losses small and let your winners roll.* What that means is that one way or another, you will have losses in your trading. It's not a beginner's trait; it's simply a cost of doing business. As a matter of fact, taking small losses is a skill that's developed by experienced traders. Try to get to that level sooner than later.

Avoiding losses is a sure way to make them bigger. You can follow your rules and see positive results with a series of small gains and losses, only to have the slate wiped clean (and then some) with one big loss. It's a discouraging setback, and one that will happen no matter what you do, because you don't control the markets.

The key is to change the way you think about trading. By shifting your view of what constitutes a successful trade from one that is profitable to one that follows your rules, you're on your way to true success. To be sure, this is so counterintuitive that it will be difficult. In fact, you can tell yourself to do this, but most often you only become a true believer with experience. As this happens, you become more committed to a rules-based approach, and that's when the shift occurs.

Do Trade with Discipline

Trading with discipline means following your rules on each and every trade. Not some of the time, or most of the time, but every time. Will you have a perfect record on the discipline front? Probably not . . . somewhere along the way, your human emotions will get the better of you. It *will* happen. But don't worry. It takes time. If you lack discipline early on, and you're fortunate enough to remain in the trading game, you may be in more trouble than you realize. The fact is, your luck will eventually run out. It's best to work at it so that your discipline will continually improve. Otherwise, it's just a matter of time before your luck will run out, and so will your money.

Unfortunately, those experiencing initial success may delay an appreciation and commitment to disciplined trading. Early success can give you a false feeling of *being right,* which is not what trading is about.

Characteristics of trading with discipline on each trade include the following:

- Allocating a reasonable amount of money to a trade
- Identifying a maximum risk for the trade
- Identifying entry and exit signals
- Executing an order when your plan requires it

Those are the checklist items, but trading with discipline goes beyond this. Doing your homework, reviewing your trades, assessing your plan . . . a comprehensive list would take the rest of this chapter. The bottom line is that the process involves learning what you have to do to trade successfully, mapping out how you'll do it, and then putting it into practice.

Don't Expect to Remove Your Emotions

Some traders assume that trading successfully means completely conquering your greed and fear emotions. Forget it. When that day comes, it means you won't have any emotions at all . . . definitely not a good thing. Eliminating emotions when trading is not a reasonable goal; however, *managing* them is.

Things that can elevate emotions include the following:

- Trading using a discretionary approach
- Making trading decisions when the markets are open
- Using an underlying stock or sector that "owes" you on a trade due to previous losses

Here are ways to address these specific items:

- Focus on more systematic approaches.
- Identify an after-hours time for trade review and management.
- Step away from a specific stock or sector, even if you typically trade with it successfully.

TIP

Take a deep breath once in a while. Buy yourself some time if things aren't going as you'd like. There are even times when stepping away from trading for a period of time is the best way to adjust your attitude and approaches.

Monitoring your emotions is the first step to managing them. Consider adding a note to your trade-management sheets to track your emotions. Also note your emotions during off-market hours . . . if you wake up cranky or even worse, can't get to sleep at night, your emotions are managing you.

Do Have a Plan

Many Wall Street sayings have been around for awhile simply because they remain true, year after year. Other adages do as well, including one that fits perfectly here: "When you fail to plan, you plan to fail."

Creating a base plan should definitely be considered a process rather than a one-time event. Think *draft* and start by writing an outline. Completing it with an easily edited word-processing document or spreadsheet may be great, but if you feel you're at the computer too much, a plain old piece of paper and pen is fine. The old-fashioned approach allows you to jot notes along the way without procrastinating because your computer is off. The bottom line is to create something and put it in writing.

When working on your first trading plan, set a timeframe for completion and revisit it about three months later. This gives you a chance to kick the wheels, identifying what seems to be working and not working. It also highlights what elements may be missing. Anticipate a second review about six months later and then get on a regular schedule that makes sense.

In addition to primary risk-management elements, start incorporating items such as general rules (for example, buying low implied volatility (IV) options and selling high IV options when feasible) and the steps you'll be taking to accomplish this (such as reviewing historical and implied volatility charts and checking IV levels with an options calculator).

Identifying other aspects of your trading job helps too (such as analyzing market conditions for long-term investments separately from short-term trading). And again, identify how you'll be accomplishing this (for example, monthly Saturday analysis for investments, weekly Sunday analysis for trades).

Because both the markets and your personal situation change over time, expect your trading plan to change as well. Better yet, plan on it.

Do Be Patient

Because so much emphasis is placed on managing risk and creating a plan, you may feel a lot of pressure to create the "right" plan. Try to understand that there's almost always more at stake when there is no plan as opposed to a plan that needs some work.

Part of the trading plan process includes making adjustments to your rules. That's definitely something you do outside of market hours. Making adjustments as the result of assessing strategy performance works toward improving your overall trading plan. It may mean increasing trade allocations or your stop-loss percentages or trading fewer strategies at one time.

Your plan may be too aggressive or too conservative, but at least it serves as a base for making adjustments. Will your second draft be better? Probably, but changing market conditions could impact the effectiveness of your adjustments. It's okay; at some point you will have traded under a variety of conditions and will have learned techniques to capitalize on them. It's called experience, and it takes time.

Patience is not just for trading plans. Sometimes the best thing a trader can do is nothing . . . waiting for the trade or waiting to take profits are useful skills that can have a big impact on trading profitability.

Don't Suffer from Analysis Paralysis

If you like playing around with numbers, the economy and financial markets provide you with an endless supply of them. You could probably go years seeking out relationships between different measures, trying to obtain market timing signals. Then you can backtest and forward test every existing indicator to see which ones give you the optimal trading signals. The truth is that sometimes they will work and sometimes they won't. That's because even though the data may be sound, the market is, by nature, predictably unpredictable.

Going live will change everything. Just like singers can nail the notes at sound check but sometimes miss during a real performance, paper trading it the whole time won't necessarily get you any closer to successfully trading. At some point, you need to experience the markets, where you, the human trader, will respond differently in a live trade.

As mentioned, part of trading successfully means managing your emotions, not removing them. There's another side to that, because you also bring great emotions and traits to the trading table. Confidence becomes so important when the market picture begins to get hazy — it's what keeps you following your reasonably tested rules.

There is a point of balance. Because the market with all its data can provide some interesting diversions, it can also keep you from the task at hand. After all your learning, reviewing, testing, practicing, and analyzing are done for a strategy, taking it live provides experience that solidifies your understanding of it all. If it's your first time trading options, use limited-risk strategies and proper trade sizes to gain that experience. And if all goes well, you'll also make some money along the way.

Do Take Responsibility for Your Results

It's all on you. In his book *Trader Vic: Methods of a Wall Street Master* (Wiley, 1993), veteran trader Vic Sperandeo talks about how he lost a lot of money one day on a trade because his wife called him to tell him about how her hair dryer was malfunctioning. He admits he should have told her to call him back later. Instead, he listened to her sympathetically, but lost his shirt on the trade. Maybe he should have closed out the trade or had a rule in place that he wasn't going to answer the phone while actively trading. At the end of the day, it was his fault, not hers, that he lost money. Never, ever, ever shift any responsibility for your trading results on anyone or anything but you. Why put your success in someone else's hands? It makes it too elusive.

In your trading career, different situations or problems will certainly arise that impact trade profitability. If there's a problem with executions, consider how you're placing the orders and discuss it with your broker. If problems persist, remedy it by shifting a portion of your assets to another broker and measure those results.

When you don't have sufficient time for your standard analysis due to work constraints, personal commitments, or whatever, shift to strategies that you *do* have time to do the right way. If there is still insufficient time, stepping away from trading is your only responsible choice. Don't worry. The markets will still be there chugging away when you're able to get to them. And when you do, you will have preserved some assets for trading.

By always acknowledging the fact that you are responsible for your own results, you seek out solutions faster and take control. You don't have to wait for someone else to take action or for some event to occur. Accepting responsibility early in the game helps you assert much greater command over your learning curve and accelerates successful trading.

Don't Stop Learning

No single strategy or analytic technique works every single time. If there was a sure fire strategy that did, everyone would be using it. The changing nature of the markets make it almost impossible to avoid this fact. Because external events such as wars, pandemics, economic conditions, and bullish and bearish phases for the market and international markets never repeat themselves exactly, there's always the opportunity to learn.

There are a variety of analytical approaches to trading, each with techniques and tools for you to explore. Add to the mix new products, such as ETFs and Bitcoin, which are periodically introduced, and you have your work cut out for you.

There may seem to be a conflicting message here. The goal is not to confuse but to compartmentalize and get you organized. When you are starting out, it's important to master one or two strategies at a time before moving on. However, as you gain experience, add a manageable number of new strategies to consider and explore. Market conditions will simply dictate it.

It's helpful to have a game plan regarding continued education . . . especially if you want to stay on good terms with your friends, family, and work colleagues. You need balance in your life. Here are some quick thoughts to help you when creating your continued education plan:

- When mastering strategies, you'll find topics you want to understand better. Address those in a focused manner through self-study (including books, audiobooks, and periodicals).
- Move on to additional analysis forms and strategies through more formal education if needed (live courses online and/or offline, or self-study.
- Start the year with general topic goals (for example, *learn two strategies and more on technical analysis*), along with more specific goals (such as *find strategies benefiting in sideways trending markets, better understand intermarket analysis*).

Most traders naturally continue learning because they gravitate toward books, articles, news programs, and conversations that deal with the markets. This is a perfect lead-in to our closing piece of advice that will be critical to your success in trading.

Do Love the Game

Successful traders love what they do. They love reading about trading, learning new strategies, and hearing the adventures of other traders. You learn and improve by participating in as many aspects of your craft as possible. Believe it.

Primary drivers for successful traders include really enjoying the challenge of understanding the markets, applying the right approach, and being disciplined. For them, it's not about getting even or making money. That's partially because you have to love something that requires such intense work — not necessarily long hours, but certainly focused ones. Simply making money, as a singular driver, will eventually lead to large losses for most traders.

Any old hand on Wall Street or any other professional venue will tell you: Be passionate about your chosen field and embrace its challenges. Trading is no different. You should have a healthy excitement about this lifelong pursuit you've chosen.

Index

• *Number* •

• *A* •

• *B* •

• D •

• E •

• F •

• G •

• H •

• P •

• Q •

• R •

• S •

• T •

• U •

• V •

• W •

• X •

• Y •

• Z •

About the Authors

Dr. Joe Duarte is a professional writer, market analyst, and investor. Dr. Duarte is a former Registered Investment Advisor and president of River Willow Capital Management. He has written articles for Marketwatch.com and has been quoted in the major media, including *Barron's* and *The Wall Street Journal*. He has appeared on numerous radio programs and has been a guest on CNBC, where he was one of the original CNBC Market Mavens. He is author of nine books, including *Trading Futures For Dummies, Market Timing For Dummies, Futures and Options For Dummies,* and *The Everything Investing in Your 20s and 30s Book*. He is a board-certified anesthesiologist. You can visit his website at www.joe-duarte.com.

Optionetics has provided investment education services and trading tools to more than 250,000 people from more than 50 countries since 1993. Every day, Optionetics helps traders navigate the markets and chart paths to financial security. In fact, it not only stands by its pledge to provide the highest quality investment education possible, it guarantees it. Its high-profit, low-stress strategies are based on dozens of trading techniques perfected by the late master trader George Fontanills, founder of Optionetics. Visit www.optionetics.com for more information.

Dedication

To George Fontanills, the author of the first edition. RIP.

Author's Acknowledgments

Thanks to the Wiley team, especially Stacy Kennedy and Corbin Collins. Stacy: Thanks for thinking of me. Corbin: Thank you for being patient. And to Tim Ord, who made sure this text was accurate.

Very special thanks to Grace Freedson, the best agent in the world.

As always, thanks to my family for putting up with me as I slouched over the keyboard and drank too much caffeine.

And finally, thanks to the readers, without whom there would be no need for books.

Publisher's Acknowledgments

Acquisitions Editor: Stacy Kennedy

Editor: Corbin Collins

Technical Editor: Tim Ord

Project Coordinator: Erin Zeltner

Cover Image: ©iStock.com/rsiel